Racing the Storm

Racing the Storm

Racial Implications and Lessons Learned from Hurricane Katrina

Edited by Hillary Potter

LEXINGTON BOOKS

A division of
ROWMAN & LITTLEFIELD PUBLISHERS, INC.
Lanham • Boulder • New York • Toronto • Plymouth, UK

LEXINGTON BOOKS

A division of Rowman & Littlefield Publishers, Inc.
A wholly owned subsidary of The Rowman & Littlefield Publishing Group, Inc.
4501 Forbes Boulevard, Suite 200
Lanham, MD 20706

Estover Road
Plymouth PL6 7PY
United Kingdom

British Library Cataloguing in Publication Information Available

Library of Congress Cataloging-in-Publication Data

Racing the storm : racial implications and lessons learned from Hurricane Katrina /
edited by Hillary Potter.
    p. cm.
  Includes bibliographical references.
  ISBN-13: 978-0-7391-1973-0 (cloth : alk. paper)
  ISBN-10: 0-7391-1973-7 (cloth : alk. paper)
  ISBN-13: 978-0-7391-1974-7 (pbk. : alk. paper)
  ISBN-10: 0-7391-1974-5 (pbk. : alk. paper)
1. Hurricane Katrina, 2005. 2. Disaster relief—Louisiana—New Orleans. 3. United
States—Race relations. I. Potter, Hillary, 1969–
 HV636 2005 .N4 R33 2007
 976.3'35064—dc22   2007015412

To the victims of Hurricane Katrina—may those who survived the wrath of the storm and continue to contend with the disadvantages of social life never be forgotten.

Contents

Introduction

Hillary Potter

On August 29, 2005, we began to witness more than the natural impact of a ghastly storm. The devastating effects of Hurricane Katrina revealed to the nation and the world that the United States continues to suffer from considerable racial and class inequities, regardless of the proclamations by many that every citizen has the opportunity to live the "American dream." Soon after Katrina battered and flooded communities along the Gulf Coast, the media images of the aftermath sparked political, intellectual, and public debates about government responsibilities and social interactions. Although the hurricane is now "history," the racial (and class) implications that were uncovered by Katrina continue to be of grave concern. The social aspects surrounding the disaster afford scholars the opportunity to utilize a highly publicized incident to enlighten others about the ongoing issues of racial classification and identity in the United States. *Racing the Storm: Racial Implications and Lessons Learned from Hurricane Katrina* serves as an important outlet for this vital topic.

Racing the Storm is a compilation of mostly original works. The overarching focus is on what we can learn from the aftermath of Katrina and how we can use this knowledge to improve (a) government and social responses to racially and economically disadvantaged individuals, (b) perceptions and media representations of people of color, and (c) interactions across race groups. Chapters include theoretical, observational, and policy analyses. The authors expressively describe how social and political outcomes of Katrina and the media portrayals in the aftermath reveal the state of race relations in the United States. *Racing the Storm* serves to invalidate the allegorical tales expounded via various channels and to uncover the unadulterated experiences of those affected and implicated because of race by imparting the voices of Katrina survivors and analyses of official action to assist New Orleanians. An assortment of chapters also highlights the perceptions among those living outside the affected areas and the U.S. government's prioritization of domestic and international (e.g., war in Iraq) interventions.

Though this book is primarily of a sociological scope—that is, the study of society, social institutions, and social relations—the contributors include scholars from other fields, thus lending it an interdisciplinary perspective. Aside from sociology, contributors also represent the fields of psychology, criminology, political science, economics, and journalism. This book is significant in that it not only specifically addresses issues of race relations as they were implicated in Hurricane Katrina, but how we can move beyond the event and work toward highlighting the continuing significance of race. It emphasizes ways in which we can continue to make efforts to alleviate racial inequality using Katrina as a case study. This composition serves as not only an academic resource to augment scholarly discourse and research on race relations, but as a community, political, and policy-reform resource, as well.

Hurricane Katrina directly affected a large area of the U.S. Gulf Coast, including portions of Alabama, Florida, Louisiana, and Mississippi. However, the concerns of racial identity, race relations, and racial implications related to the storm were heavily influenced by the images fed to the general public of the ravage of New Orleans and its immediate surrounding areas. Accordingly, much of what is reported in this book focuses on New Orleans and its residents. This is not to deny or ignore that many others were just as gravely affected by the storm. Nor does it serve to disavow that the storm detrimentally impacted Whites and economically advantaged individuals. But the consequences of Katrina on New Orleans and its largely African American population (many of whom are economically *dis*advantaged) provide us with a harrowing exploration into the prolonged implications of racial status in the United States.

The chapters offered in this book are empirical and/or conceptual in nature. A broad array of presentation is provided, with chapters using qualitative and quantitative methods of analysis, policy analysis, and theoretical application. Though each of the chapters epitomizes the common theme of the book, each contribution has been grouped into three parts: (1) perception and typecasting; (2) culture and community; and (3) citizenship, politics, and government priorities.

Part One establishes the racial implications of Hurricane Katrina by demonstrating perceptions—often stereotypically based—of the evacuees and a country of onlookers. Much of the perceptions of those witnessing the tragedy unfold were based on that which was portrayed in television and print news media. Angela P. Cole, Terri Adams-Fuller, O. Jackson Cole, Arie Kruglanski, and Angela Glymph launch the readings with their chapter "Making Sense of a Hurricane: Social Identity and Attribution Explanations of Race-Related Differences in Katrina Disaster Response." Cole and her colleagues report on survey data that reveal racial identity variations in the way individuals perceived the events surrounding Katrina. They utilize social psychology theories of social identity and attribution to describe the race-based interpretations of and reactions to the storm. In the following chapter, "The Color(s) of Crisis: How Race, Rumor, and Collective Memory Shape the Legacy of Katrina," Michelle Miles and Duke W. Austin demonstrate the role of rumor and the effects of shared experiences on race-based issues of Katrina. Through their analysis of in-depth interviews and news media reports on the disaster, Miles and Austin reveal the damaging role of the information communicated alongside the racialized collective memories of individuals.

The remaining two chapters of the book's first section specifically consider the issue of crime, criminality, and racialized perceptions of crime. In "Reframing Crime in a Disaster: Perception, Reality, and Criminalization of Survival Tactics among African Americans in the Aftermath of Katrina," I present an analysis of in-depth interviews conducted with Katrina evacuees residing in a temporary shelter. I examine the racial biases and stereotypes surrounding the evacuees' survival tactics (such as looting) and government agents' methods in aiding the evacuees in the aftermath. The conclusions of my chapter, along with the selections by Cole et al. and Miles and Austin, are synergized in the section's concluding chapter by Meera Adya, Monica K. Miller, Julie A. Singer, Rebecca M. Thomas, and Joshua B. Padilla. Adya and colleagues write in "Cultural Differences in Perceptions of the Government and the Legal System: Hurricane Katrina Highlights What Has Been There All Along" that Katrina is basically a conduit for drawing attention to race biases and the U.S. government and criminal justice system.

Part Two highlights the importance of and challenges for race-based culture and community in recovery efforts. Factors indicative of Latina/o and African American cultures and communal orientation are considered here. These elements include a more expansive history of the racial make-up and ethos of New Orleans, the history and meaning of music in New Orleans, and the importance of religion and faith for African Americans. Nicole Trujillo-Pagán dispels the narrow media-spawned images of Latinas/os in the aftermath of Katrina in the chapter "From 'Gateway to the Americas' to the

'Chocolate City': The Racialization of Latinos in New Orleans." She supplies an assessment of interviews with Latina/o residents of New Orleans and a content analysis of print news articles concerning Latinas/os in post-Katrina New Orleans to demonstrate the presuppositions and realities of the presence and contributions of Latinas/os in the New Orleans area. In short, Trujillo-Pagán demystifies the inferences that Latinas/os only arrived to New Orleans as undocumented immigrants from Mexico and Central America, or migrants from other service and labor industries within the United States, in the Katrina recovery phase of New Orleans.

Susan C. Pearce provides a cultural sociology perspective on the effect of Katrina on New Orleans in "Saxophones, Trumpets, and Hurricanes: The Cultural Restructuring of New Orleans." She draws on the jazz music culture of the city to demonstrate the relationship between culture and the social structure. This chapter outlines the value of social movements and factors important for reconstructing the city and benefits for doing so. Susan M. Sterett and Jennifer A. Reich round out the section with "Prayer and Social Welfare in the Wake of Katrina: Race and Volunteerism in Disaster Response," where they scrutinize the cultural significance of volunteer groups in a disaster. Sterett and Reich discuss the challenges of meeting the needs of disaster evacuees relocated to areas far from home, particularly when these areas are composed of strikingly distinct cultures and races.

Finally, Part Three addresses the inequities of race and class stratification in the United States and how the inequities are judged within the schema of government priorities in the United States and abroad. In the first chapter of this section, Allison M. Cotton uses Robert K. Merton's theory of deviance and modes of adaptation to develop a "typology of citizenship." In "Stipulations: A Typology of Citizenship in the United States after Katrina," Cotton argues that U.S. citizenship is more than simply being born in or officially recognized by the United States. The events surrounding Katrina demonstrate support for disparate levels of U.S. citizenship and the corresponding assistance afforded citizens based on this typology. Following Cotton's composition, Rachael A. Woldoff and Brian J. Gerber expand on the concept of blameworthiness and government responsibility as related to race-based conceptions in "Protect or Neglect? Social Structure, Decision Making, and the Risk of Living in African American Places in New Orleans." Public policy that has situated certain individuals—such as people of color and the poor—in deficient neighborhoods and residences positions them to be disadvantageously affected when a natural disaster strikes. Woldoff and Gerber contend that such public policy includes the historically intentional exploits of the U.S. government that have continued to impinge on African Americans in particular.

Part Three concludes with three contributions that consider the role and priorities of the U.S. government in dealing with the aftermath of Katrina, as compared to the management of the "war on terrorism" and the Persian Gulf wars (both the 1991 and the 2003 incursions). Accordingly, these chapters link two gulfs (Persian and Mexican) and two disasters (the September 11, 2001, terrorist attacks and Hurricane Katrina). Related to the matter addressed in Woldoff and Gerber's chapter, Tom Reifer considers the residential (mis)fortune of poor people of color in "Blown Away: U.S. Militarism and Hurricane Katrina." However, Reifer expands on the residential life-chances by considering the shift in funding away from U.S. urban locales and their disaster planning to military spending and anticipated terrorist threats by non-U.S. citizens. Reifer argues that this trend continues to be apparent in the resources allocated to the reconstruction of areas damaged by Katrina. Ganesh K. Trichur continues the conversation of misplaced national government priorities and funding in his chapter, "Spectacular Privatizations: Perceptions and Lessons from Privatization of Warfare and the Privatization of Disaster." Trichur examines the similarities between Baghdad and New Orleans in relation to the current Gulf War and Hurricane Katrina, respectively. He concludes with a series of concerns and suggestions for the reconstruction of New Orleans, while considering the broader implication of social justice for disadvantaged individuals and groups within the United States. Everette B. Penn concludes the selection of readings with "Running Faster Next Time: Blacks and Homeland Security." Penn discusses the role of the U.S. Department of Homeland Security and what should be expected from the agency in the form of domestic assistance to U.S. citizens. Further, he argues the need for African Americans to take greater responsibility for themselves, particularly since reliance on government entities has not proven especially effective.

Racing the Storm exposes the stories and implications of the vexing experiences of poor people of color in New Orleans. It shows how these residents were unable to *race* from the storm. Their circumstances and social status location and the many inadequacies of the local, state, and federal governments (directly and indirectly related to hurricane preparedness) entrapped them both figuratively and literally. As follows, we are able to conduct research and provide scholarly theorizing in *racing* the storm—that is, necessarily attributing racial implications—because the condition of the situation was already in place for us to do so. Specifically, certain members within U.S. society, particularly those with power and privilege, have maintained a social order that is racially unjust. The stage was set, and Hurricane Katrina provided a performance that allowed the nation and the world to see who the players were and that each role had not been afforded an equal part in this tragic production of social reality.

Part One

PERCEPTION AND TYPECASTING

Chapter One

Making Sense of a Hurricane

Social Identity and Attribution Explanations of Race-Related Differences in Katrina Disaster Response

Angela P. Cole

Terri Adams-Fuller

O. Jackson Cole

Arie Kruglanski

Angela Glymph

The United States has never experienced a natural disaster the magnitude of Hurricane Katrina and its aftermath, a catastrophic disaster of epic proportions. Although people of all racial and economic backgrounds were impacted by the storm, media reports documented disproportionate loss of life and devastation among Blacks and the poor.[1] These population segments were both hardest hit and least likely to have adequate evacuation resources. Also, news reports of the devastation identified slow emergency responsiveness, communication failures, and poor emergency preparedness as the underlying causes of the disproportionate impacts.[2]

This event and its aftermath of suffering presented the nation with a unique set of challenges, bringing the intersection of race and class to the forefront of public discourse. Specifically, there is need to better understand racial differences in evaluations of responses to the disaster. This chapter explores the feasibility of using social identity and attribution theory approaches as explanations of race differences in evaluations. Consideration of the role of the media necessarily occurs because citizens throughout the nation were eyewitnesses to the unfolding disaster as a consequence of weeks of continuous media coverage.

BRIEF REVIEW OF WHAT HAPPENED IN NEW ORLEANS

Although Hurricane Katrina impacted nearly the entire Gulf Coast region of the country, most media accounts of devastation focused on New Orleans. Within hours of Katrina's landfall, New Orleans experienced what local politicians and the public long had feared—levee system breaches. Combining with the hurricane's onslaught, the levee breaches caused unprecedented flooding, water levels climbed to eighteen feet in certain areas, and 80 percent of the city eventually flooded to some degree.[3] Consequently, New Orleans and its residents confronted two major disasters as city and state officials scrambled to get residents to safety, and federal officials and the Red Cross remained for a time notably absent.

City and state officials encouraged voluntary evacuation prior to the disaster, and tens of thousands of the city's residents joined endless lines of vehicles seeking to leave. However, not until approximately twenty-four hours before Katrina's landfall did New Orleans Mayor Ray Nagin order mandatory evacuation.[4] Nonetheless, numerous residents stayed and thus thousands were trapped in their homes, medical facilities, nursing facilities, and designated shelters, and on bridges and overpasses. There are myriad reasons residents remained or sought refuge in the city's emergency shelters.[5]

The New Orleans Superdome was designated as a last resort refuge for citizens with special needs, those without the means to evacuate, and others. Within forty-eight hours of the hurricane's landfall, approximately 20,000 residents essentially were trapped in the Superdome.[6] Overcrowding prompted officials to open the Convention Center as an additional shelter. Prominent were news media reports of deteriorating conditions in the Superdome, the result of overcrowding, compounded by inadequate food, running water, lighting, and air conditioning, and the dome's partial failure, which in combination created horrifying sanitation problems.[7] Also, there were reports of extreme heat, violent crime (occurrences later found exaggerated), deaths, suicides, and declining health conditions.[8] Although media reports covered a variety of issues associated with the storm's aftermath and the levee breeches, most constant were the images of citizens—primarily Blacks, children, the infirm, the poor—suffering and seemingly abandoned, especially by their federal government. This raw, unfiltered, concentrated media coverage made it undeniably obvious to viewers that the disaster's most immediate and negative impact fell disproportionately on these vulnerable population segments.

The stark images of desperate Americans, overwhelmingly Black and predominantly impoverished persons, stranded in this major city made perceptions of race and class highly salient to onlookers of the unfolding tragedy. In addition, polls immediately after the disaster documented the divergent reactions and perceptions of Black and White Americans to Katrina's aftermath, including attitudes regarding governmental responsiveness and sensitivity, and the behavioral appropriateness of the stranded victims, New Orleans residents.[9] Also, there were race differences in ratings of the degree of responsibility and fault attributable to different levels of government (local, state, federal). Although there was no consensus concerning fault and responsibility for the disproportionate deaths and devastation among Blacks and the poor,[10] the continued broadcast of these images reinforced the conclusion that this tragedy should not have happened in the United States. Images of residents stranded in polluted water, without food and drinking water, and dying on the streets, are associated with developing countries, not the world's most powerful and technologically advanced nation.

Initially, many assumed that residents who stayed behind had remained by choice (e.g., prior hurricane veterans). As time passed and media coverage progressed, especially real-time, wall-to-wall cable TV accounts, a more nuanced understanding emerged of why people remained, especially as victims told their personal stories (e.g., people were infirm, had no transportation, resources, or place to relocate). Despite this growing perception and recognition, we believe a gulf remains in the perceptions of Black and White Americans, which social psychology would suggest is attributable to onlookers' deeply engrained preconceptions and pre-existing beliefs about the behaviors, motives, and dispositions of the groups left behind.

This chapter systematically examines the efficacy of social identity and attribution theory explanations for race differences in evaluations of (a) governmental handling of the crisis, (b) liability for New Orleans's rebuilding costs, and (c) authorities' ability to secure the homeland from future disasters. We will analyze survey data measuring observers' judgments of the Hurricane Katrina calamity to examine the influence of racial identity on these evaluations. Only a few existing studies examine the intersection between group identity, attributions, and judgments in response to an actual natural disaster, and thus this study provides additional critical information to advance understanding of the confluence of these variables.

THEORETICAL FRAMEWORK

Social Identity Theory

Social identity theory provides one possible framework for understanding race differences in interpretations of and reactions to the Katrina disaster. Because this disaster was characterized by intense conflict between the victims and the government, onlookers' judgments should be biased in favor of the groups they identified with most. Research in the social identity tradition shows (a) when the parties we judge are in conflict, our judgments are biased in favor of the party we identify with most strongly and (b) this process is heavily impacted by our associations, thus our group identities. The group identity concept commonly is used to explain inter-group politics, but is rooted in the social identity concept, which refers to the self-assignment of individuals to particular groups (i.e., gender, ethnicity, social class). Social identity theory grew out of collaborative efforts by Henri Tajfel and John Turner aimed in part at distinguishing between individual traits and those derived from group membership.[11] According to these theorists, individuals' self-concepts consist of multiple group identities, which inform them about who they are as individuals and group members.

Group identity influences significantly with whom individuals identify and how they perceive the surrounding world.[12] When people become aware of the existence of a group, they evaluate whether they belong to it, a practice labeled *social categorization*. Groups you perceive yourself as belonging to are labeled *in-groups* and groups you perceive yourself as not belonging to are labeled *out-groups*. In-group members are rated more positively than out-group members along important self-relevant dimensions, in the service of self-esteem maintenance. This tendency to rate in-group members more positively is labeled *in-group favoritism, social discrimination*, or *inter-group discrimination*.

In-group favoritism or inter-group discrimination is influenced by the group's history. The collective history of group experiences can impact how group members perceive, judge, and respond to everyday life situations and crisis events. Hence, one's perceptions and attitudes toward current events are considered rooted both in the historical experiences of the individual and the collective conscious experience of one's group identity.

In sum, a social identity theory analysis of racial differences in perceptions of and reactions to the Katrina disaster suggests that the heightened salience of onlookers' racial identities was a consequence of the constant broadcast both of images of one racial group suffering disproportionately and media commentaries on the race and victimization relationship. Consequently, onlookers' judgments about the Katrina disaster would be significantly impacted by group identification, with judgments breaking down along racial lines, explainable primarily from in-group favoritism. Evidence consistent with social identity explanations for group differences would assume the following form: race differences in opinions about government officials' and Katrina victims' behaviors during the crisis should be mediated completely by measures of group identification, with non-group-identity factors of little consequence in shaping these opinions.

Attribution Theory

Attribution theory provides an alternative framework for understanding race differences in perceptions of the Katrina disaster. This conception's relevance for understanding observers' judgments about the Hurricane Katrina crisis stems from its utility for explaining how observers interpret chains of events and ultimately make attributions. Attribution approaches maintain that judgment is a natural human response.[13] Because of the enhanced connectivity across space and time and access to information and current events that communications and information technology enable, stimuli constantly bombard us that we must decipher, differentiate, categorize, label, and judge. The around-the-clock media coverage of the Katrina disaster inundated the public with images and messages about the ongoing saga and its enormity, and embedded these public events in the minds of Americans and prompted judgments of the unfolding events.

From its inception, attribution research focused primarily on how, and under what conditions, individuals use available behavioral, situational, and dispositional cues to draw inferences about others and themselves.[14] These inferences, in turn, are posited to guide behavior and behavioral intentions.[15] Early attribution theorists argued we use a combination of situational (physical/social circumstances) and dispositional (personal characteristics) factors to explain behavior.[16] Harold Kelley argued that we use a very rational process in determining whether behavior results from a person's disposition or the situation.[17] However, one of the most replicated and perplexing findings in early studies was that individuals make attribution errors; they discount situational effects and overestimate the effect of personal characteristics, even when situational pressures are obvious and overwhelming. Its prevalence prompted Lee Ross to label this phenomenon *the fundamental attribution error*.[18] A self-serving, in-group-serving bias characterizes this error tendency.[19] Namely, individuals attribute their own and in-group members' negative behaviors to environmental responses, but assign responsibility for dissimilar others' negative behaviors to individual or group characteristics. For positive behaviors, this pattern is reversed; they are attributed to personal characteristics for the self and similar others, but to situations for out-group members.

For early attribution theorists, errors resulted from a combination of informational deficits, low self-awareness, and in-group bias.[20] Later theorists, however, conceptualized attributions as involving cognitive stages, progressing from perception, to interpretation, to inference, and posited that errors arise automatically, subconsciously, not necessarily because of bias. Yaacov Trope's hierarchical theory of dispositional attribution describes the process as follows: first, observations are interpreted; next, translated into relevant categories; and finally inferences are drawn based on these categorizations.[21] Moreover, individuals use context cues and prior personal experiences to comprehend difficult-to-categorize behaviors (e.g., responses subject to multiple interpretations). Stated differently, interpretation of ambiguous events is influenced by personal experiences and attitudes, even without awareness. Therefore, in the Katrina situation, race differences in judgments about the government's disaster performance may not reflect bias. Instead, differences in judgments may result because racial groups differentially interpreted and remembered events observed, coincident with their varying personal experiences with racism, classism, and discrimination. An attribution theory explanation would hold if considering memories of and causal attributions for events reduced or eliminated completely race differences in judgments.

Later attribution research has highlighted additional important factors—namely, fault and responsibility attributions—as liability judgment determinants in conflict situations where negligence or deliberate harm are at issue.[22] This work's relevance to understanding race differences in opinions about payment responsibility for rebuilding New Orleans is apparent. We hypothesize, therefore, an important intervening role for fault and responsibility attributions in explaining the relationship between liability judgments for the Katrina disaster and race.

METHOD

Research Participants

The study sample consisted of 239 student participants from two northeastern universities in the same metropolitan area. One institution was a private urban historically Black institution (HBI); the other a suburban, public university with a predominantly White student body (PWI, predominantly White institution). Concerning institution type, 77 percent of the participants attended the HBI and 23 percent the PWI, which had a more racially/ethnically diverse student population than the HBI, but was majority White.

Table 1.1 displays the six racial/ethnic categories of this study's participants. Slightly more than three-quarters (76.1 percent) identified themselves as either Black or Black-Multiracial, while approximately one-sixth (15.5 percent), the next largest grouping, identified themselves as White. Displayed also in Table 1.1 is the race/ethnicity distribution of participants at the universities. At the HBI, nearly 96 percent identified themselves as Black or Black-Multiracial, almost 2 percent as either Asian or Latino, less than 1 percent as White, and just over 2 percent as Other. At the PWI, 13 percent of the participants identified themselves as Black, almost 19 percent as either Asian or Latino, 66.7 percent as White and

Table 1.1. Distribution of Race/Ethnicity in the Total Study Sample and by Institution

Category	Criteria for Inclusion in the Category	% of sample (N = 239)	Historically Black Institution % of sample	Predominantly White Institution % of sample
African American/Black	Self-identified as Black &/or African American	71.1%	89.1%	13.0%
African American/Black-Multiracial	Self-identified as Black &/or African American and at least one other ethnic group	5.0%	6.6%	0.0%
Asian/Asian American	Self-identified as Asian &/or Asian American	4.2%	1.1%	14.8%
Caucasian/White	Self-identified as Caucasian, European, &/or White American	15.5%	0.5%	66.7%
Latino/Hispanic	Self-identified as Latino &/or Hispanic	1.3%	0.5%	3.7%
Other	Self-identified as "other"	2.1%	2.2%	1.9%
Missing values		0.8%		

Table 1.2. Age, Gender, and Income in Study Sample

Variable	Descriptive Statistics	Number of Respondents
Age	Mean = 20.8 years	213
Females	78%	185
Males	22%	52
Income—Personal	Median = $5,000	154
Income—Parents	Median = $75,000	155

slightly less than 2 percent as Other. Hence, HBI participants were almost exclusively Black, while fully two-thirds of PWI participants were White.

Age, gende,r and income data for the total sample are in Table 1.2. Also, politically, 65 percent of the sample identified themselves as Democrats, 3.8 percent as Republicans, and 6.7 percent as Independents; the remainder was unaffiliated or non-responsive.

It is reasonable to expect respondents' judgments were influenced by the extent the hurricane personally affected them. Thus, responses to several demographic variables were used to generate a new categorical variable that indexed Katrina's "personal relevance" to participants. The distribution of levels of personal relevance is presented in Table 1.3.

Survey Instrument Questionnaire Administration

Participants completed a multipart questionnaire that contained demographic measures and other scales to assess race-related differences in opinions about (a) the government's handling of the Katrina crisis (*dissatisfaction judgments*), (b) who should bear the cost to rebuild New Orleans (*liability judgments*), and (c) authorities' ability to secure the homeland from future natural or man-made disasters (*confidence judgments*). Other measures were posited to mediate the race-related differences in opinions: (a) recollections of events surrounding Hurricane Katrina (*memory*); (b) exposure levels to media coverage on the Katrina disaster (*media coverage*); (c) two types of group identification (with Katrina victims and government officials); and (d) three types of attributions (fault, causality, responsibility) about the events that occurred. (Questions comprising these scales and measures appear in Appendix 1.1.)

Students received credit in social science courses for voluntarily participating in this study and could withdraw without jeopardy. Participants responded anonymously to the survey instrument, which they were informed assessed their "experiences with, perceptions of, and reactions to the aftermath of Hurricane Katrina," and could be completed in approximately one hour. Also, they were told the study's broader impact was for researchers to learn how to intervene better in disaster and national security risk situations.

Table 1.3.   Levels of Personal Relevance in Study Sample

Category	Criteria for Inclusion in the Category	% of Sample (N = 239)
(0): Lowest	Neither the participant nor his/her close family &/or friends have any hurricane experience	37.2%
(1) Intermediate	Participant has close relatives and/or friends who have experienced hurricane(s) other than Katrina, but no personal hurricane experience	13.8%
(2) Intermediate	Participant has previous personal hurricane experience, but no other connection to Katrina	15.5%
(3) Intermediate	Participant has close relatives and/or friends who are Katrina victims	27.6%
(4) Highest	Participant is a Katrina victim—participants who self-designated as Katrina victims, or were permanent residents of or residing in the Gulf Coast FEMA Disaster Area when Katrina made landfall	5.4%
Missing Values		0.4%

DEMA = Federal Emergency Management Agency.

Method Note: Rationale for Using
Institution-Type as a Proxy for Race

Our goal was to understand race effects on individuals' judgments regarding the government's handling of and liability for Katrina and its aftermath, and their future disaster management competency. Due to the small sample sizes of Whites at the HBI and Blacks at the PWI, the effects of participants' race and institution type could not be disentangled in our data. Therefore, our approach when reporting participant institution effects in this study is to interpret "institution-type" differences as reflecting race differences.

This approach was supported by results obtained when we examined participant race effects on this study's scales. We first ran one-way analyses of variance (ANOVAs) on each dependent variable with institution type as a predictor. Then these one-way ANOVAs were rerun, replacing institution type with the race/ethnicity categorical variable described in Table 1.1 as the predictor. Next, we dichotomized this race/ethnicity variable, placing Black or Black-Multiracial participants in one category, labeled "Black," and assigned remaining participants to the "Other Ethnicity" category. When this new dichotomous variable was included as the predictor in the one-way ANOVA sets, in the main, occurrence of a significant institution effect coincided with a significant race effect.[23] Moreover, the race effects we obtained were consistent with the Pew Research Center findings obtained immediately after Katrina's landfall.[24]

RESULTS

Our first goal was to verify that study participants' views about events surrounding the Katrina disaster differed along racial lines. Our second goal was to assess the extent to which group differences resulted from in-group favoritism and out-group derogation, consistent with social identity theory predictions. Therefore, we tested for evidence of group identity mediation using nested sets of regression models. Our final goal was to pit social identity and attribution theory explanations against each other, using a backward elimination regression approach. This approach allowed us to identify the set of predictors that best accounted for group differences in New Orleans disaster opinions, and to determine whether that set consisted exclusively of either social identity or attribution theory predictors, or some combination from both theories.

Race-Related Differences

On the basis of widespread reports of racial differences in reactions to and perceptions of the Katrina aftermath, we expected to find differences in opinions concerning the government's handling of the crisis (dissatisfaction judgments), and who should pay the cost of rebuilding New Orleans (liability judgments), plus differences in beliefs about authorities' ability to secure the homeland in future natural or manmade disasters (confidence judgments).

Dissatisfaction Judgments

We assessed participants' dissatisfaction with (a) the time it took federal authorities to respond to the crisis (the president, director, and U.S. Federal Government), (b) how long it took local authorities to respond to the crisis (including both New Orleans Mayor Nagin and Louisiana Governor Blanco), and (c) governmental response, at all levels, to the crisis. Data presented in Appendix 1.2 show, on average, participants were very dissatisfied with federal response time (mean = 5.38, on a 6-point scale[25]), somewhat satisfied with the mayor's and governor's response time (mean = 2.70), and very dissatisfied with the overall government response (mean = 4.91). Also, HBI and PWI students differed significantly on these three dissatisfaction judgments (Table 1.4). Specifically, HBI students, relative to PWI students, were more dissatisfied with federal response time, more critical of the timing of the mayor's and governor's responses, and more dissatisfied with the overall government response.

Liability Judgments

We measured agreement with (a) the idea that the federal government should be more liable than city residents for New Orleans's rebuilding costs and assessed (b) liability ratings of local governments (the City of New Orleans and Louisiana State) for the rebuilding costs. On average, the sample attributed more liability to the federal government than to New Orleans residents (67.47 percent and 6.4 percent, respectively) and felt that local governments should pay 23.7 percent of the rebuilding costs (see Appendix 1.2). Table 1.4 shows that HBI students, compared with PWI students, assigned significantly higher liability to the federal government relative to residents[26]; however, the two groups did not differ in the liability amount they assigned to local governments.

Confidence Judgments

We measured participants' confidence in authorities' (police, military, homeland security personnel, the federal government) ability to secure the homeland from future natural and manmade disasters. On average, participants were not very confident (mean = 2.23, see Appendix 1.2), and as shown in Table 1.4, there was an institution-type effect on confidence judgments. Namely, HBI students had significantly less confidence in authorities' future readiness.

Table 1.4. Institution-Type Mean Differences in Reactions to Hurricane Katrina's Aftermath

Measures	Historically Black Institution	Predominantly White Institution	Mean Difference
Dissatisfaction with federal government's response timing	5.53 (0.06)	4.86 (0.14)	0.67***
Dissatisfaction with local government's response timing	2.79 (0.07)	2.40 (0.11)	0.39**
Dissatisfaction with government's overall response	5.05 (0.07)	4.43 (0.16)	0.62***
Liability assigned to federal government relative to New Orleans residents	0.83 (0.01)	0.73 (0.02)	0.10***
Liability assigned to local government	23.37% (1.83%)	24.54% (2.75%)	−1.17%
Confidence in authorities' ability to respond to future disasters	2.12 (0.07)	2.60 (0.14)	−0.48**

Standard errors in parentheses.
** $p < .01$.
*** $p < .001$.

Social Identity Effects on Race-Related Differences

To determine if evidence existed that favored a social identity explanation for the race-related differences in the dissatisfaction, liability, and confidence judgments just described, we first determined whether there were significant institution-type effects on identification with either Katrina victims or the government, at all levels. Second, we tested for evidence of group identity mediation.

Race-Related Differences in Group Identification

Ignoring all other factors, our study's participants identified significantly more with Hurricane Katrina victims than with government officials at any level (see Appendix 1.2). Furthermore, HBI and PWI students differed significantly in identification with the victims, with HBI students identifying both relatively more with Katrina victims and less with government officials (Table 1.5).

Mediating Effects of Group Identification on Group Differences

We performed a series of nested regression analyses (Table 1.6) to determine whether differences in dissatisfaction, liability, and confidence resulted from corresponding differences in group identification. In all but one case, group identification either partially or fully mediated the difference between HBI and PWI students' judgments.[27]

First, group identification *fully* mediated race-related differences in (a) dissatisfaction with local government officials' response timing and (b) confidence in authorities' future disaster management ability. Stated differently, including our two identification indexes eliminated the highly significant differences between HBI and PWI students' levels of dissatisfaction with local government response time and confidence in authorities. However, for both judgments, only the effect of identification with the government was significant, and identification with Katrina victims related marginally to dissatisfaction and confidence.

Second, group identification *partially* mediated race-related differences in (a) dissatisfaction with the government's overall handling of the disaster and (b) relative liability assigned to the federal government. Specifically, our two identification indexes together significantly reduced, but did not completely eliminate, HBI–PWI differences in government response dissatisfaction and relative federal government liability. Identification with both victims and government officials significantly predicted government response dissatisfaction, but only identification with Katrina victims significantly predicted liability.

Table 1.5. Institution-Type Mean Differences in Responses to Group Identification, Media Exposure, Memory, and Attribution Measures

Measures	Historically Black Instituion	Prdominantly White Institution	Mean Difference
Group Identification Measures			
Identification with government officials	2.93 (0.05)	3.39 (0.09)	0.46***
Identification with Katrina victims	4.81 (0.06)	4.50 (0.08)	0.31*
Media Exposure Measure			
Exposure to media coverage (hours per day)	6.19 (0.46)	3.30 (0.51)	2.89**
Memory Measures			
Recollections of percentages of Black and poor pre-Katrina evacuees	14.10 (0.80)	18.30 (1.71)	4.20*
Recollections of percentages of White, wealthy, and middle-class pre-Katrina evacuees	71.60 (1.58)	68.68 (2.85)	2.92
Recollections of the timing of the mandatory evacuation order (days prior to landfall)	4.16 (1.06)	3.30 (0.67)	0.86
Recollections of the arrival of federal assistance (days after landfall)	7.05 (0.68)	7.11 (1.22)	0.06
Fault Attribution Measures			
Fault attributions about federal government	4.01 (0.12)	3.39 (0.16)	0.62*
Fault attributions about post-Katrina evacuees	3.28 (0.11)	3.52 (0.21)	0.24

Causal Attribution Measures

Measure			
Positive dispositional attributions about post-Katrina evacuees	2.87 (0.10)	2.93 (0.14)	−0.06
Negative dispositional attributions about post-Katrina evacuees	1.88 (0.07)	2.22 (0.13)	−0.34*
Positive situational attributions about post-Katrina evacuees	4.63 (0.07)	4.68 (0.10)	−0.05
Negative situational attributions about post-Katrina evacuees	3.10 (0.10)	2.94 (0.15)	0.16
Negative dispositional attributions about federal government officials	4.91 (0.08)	3.70 (0.15)	1.21**
Attributions that federal response failures were due to the disaster's unprecedented nature	2.25 (0.07)	3.31 (0.11)	−1.06***
Attributions that federal response failures were due to homeland security challenges	2.67 (.10)	3.44 (0.15)	−0.77**

Responsibility Attribution Measures

Measure			
Percentage of responsibility assigned to local government	30.39 (2.13)	24.26 (2.75)	6.13
Percentage of responsibility assigned to federal government	66.00 (1.93)	54.50 (2.84)	11.50***
Percentage of responsibility assigned to New Orleans residents	12.41 (1.36)	17.50 (2.52)	−5.09
Responsibility assigned to federal government relative to New Orleans residents	0.77 (0.01)	0.69 (0.02)	0.08**

Standard errors in parentheses.
* $p < .05$.
** $p < .01$.
*** $p < .001$.

Table 1.6. Mediating Effects of Group Identification on Group Differences in Dissatisfaction, Liability, and Confidence

	β	t	R^2	F
Dissatisfaction with Local Government's Response Timing				
Model 1			3.5%**	7.85**
Institution type	0.19	2.80***		
Model 2			18.5%***	16.11***
Institution type	0.06	0.94		
Identification with government officials	−0.38	−5.82***		
Identification with Katrina victims	0.11	1.76†		
Dissatisfaction with Federal Government's Response Timing				
Model 1			11.20%***	27.02***
Institution type	−0.34	5.20***		
Model 2			20.6%***	18.36***
Institution type	0.24	3.75***		
Identification with government officials	−0.17	−2.69**		
Identification with Katrina victims	0.25	.96***		
Dissatisfaction with Government's Overall Response				
Model 1			6.7%***	15.39***
Institution type	0.26	3.92***		
Model 2			11.5%***	9.22***
Institution type	0.19	2.76**		
Identification with government officials	−0.16	−2.36*		
Identification with Katrina victims	0.15	2.23*		

Liability Assigned to Federal Government Relative to New Orleans Residents

Model 1				
Institution type	0.24	3.46**	5.8%**	11.94**
Model 2				
Institution type	0.18	2.49*	12.6%***	9.28***
Identification with government officials	−0.05	−0.76		
Identification with Katrina victims	0.26	3.77***		

Confidence in Authorities' Ability to Respond to Future Disasters

Model 1				
Institution type	−0.22	−3.24**	4.7%**	10.49**
Model 2				
Institution type	−0.11	−1.68†	13.2%***	10.74***
Identification with government officials	0.27	3.94***		
Identification with Katrina victims	−0.12	−1.90†		

† $p < .10$, marginally significant.
* $p < .05$.
** $p < .01$.
*** $p < .001$.

Finally, group identification did not mediate the observed HBI–PWI difference in dissatisfaction with federal government response timing. Instead, all three variables—participant institution, identification with government officials, and identification with Katrina victims—explained a significant proportion of the variance in this dissatisfaction judgment.

Race-Related Effects on Attribution Variables

Before performing backward elimination regression analyses to identify the best set of predictors for dissatisfaction, liability, and confidence, we examined the effects of institution-type on those variables attribution theory would identify as potential race-difference mediators. Social identity theory would predict significant race-related differences in attribution-related variables.

Memory and Media Exposure

Data in Appendix 1.2 show that participants spent an average of 5.51 hours daily following media coverage of the hurricane disaster (television, radio, and print media). Also, they recalled higher proportions of White, middle-class, and wealthy New Orleans residents, almost 71 percent, leaving before Katrina made landfall, in contrast to only 15 percent of Black and poor New Orleans residents evacuating. In addition, their recollections were Mayor Nagin issued the mandatory evacuation order 3.96 days before Katrina's landfall (actually issued one day before landfall) and federal assistance arrived in New Orleans 7.06 days after landfall (it is difficult to pinpoint precisely when federal assistance was actually sent[28]).

A few noteworthy group differences in the time participants spent following Katrina news coverage and their memories of events were found (Table 1.5). Compared to PWI students, HBI students spent significantly more hours per day following Katrina news coverage; also, they recalled that significantly smaller proportions of Black and poor New Orleans residents evacuated before the storm hit. HBI and PWI students' memories of the proportions of White, wealthy, and middle-class pre-Katrina evacuees were the same. Also, institution type did not influence participants' recollections of the mandatory evacuation order timing or the arrival of federal assistance to New Orleans.

Fault Attributions

Data in Appendix 1.2 show participants were significantly more likely to believe that the federal government's response to Katrina was intentional, than to believe the responses of New Orleans stranded residents were intentional. They agreed slightly (mean = 3.86) that the federal government responded deliberately to the hurricane disaster in the manner that it did and disagreed slightly (mean = 3.31) that stranded residents deliberately stayed behind. There were no significant institution-type differences in fault attributions for New Orleans residents who failed to evacuate before Katrina's landfall. However, HBI students were significantly more likely than PWI students to believe the government acted intentionally (Table 1.5).

Causal Attributions

Data in Appendix 1.2 show that in making inferences about stranded New Orleans residents' failure to evacuate before the storm's landfall, participants tended to (a) disagree moderately with negative dispositional attributions, (b) disagree slightly with positive dispositional attributions, (c) agree slightly with negative situational attributions, and (d) agree moderately with positive situational attributions. With only one exception, institution type did not influence these causal attribution ratings. Although both student groups strongly opposed characterizing stranded residents as lazy, uneducated, and opportunistic (i.e., negative dispositional attributions), HBI students were significantly more opposed to these characterizations (Table 1.5).

In making inferences about federal government officials' failure to respond quickly and effectively to the disaster, participants tended to (a) agree moderately that insensitivity, race, and class influenced government officials' decisions (negative dispositional attributions); (b) disagree moderately that the government's disaster response was attributable to the unprecedented nature of the natural disaster; and (c) disagree slightly that the government's poor disaster response was attributable to homeland security challenges (see Appendix 1.2). Relative to PWI students, HBI students were both significantly more likely to endorse negative dispositional attributions about federal government officials and less likely to attribute the federal response to homeland security concerns or the natural disaster's magnitude (Table 1.5).

Responsibility Attributions

We measured agreement with the idea that the federal government, rather than New Orleans residents, was primarily responsible for the negative outcomes following Katrina and obtained ratings of local governments' responsibility for the disastrous outcomes. Participants attributed more responsibility to the federal government than to New Orleans residents (63.3 percent versus 13.6 percent) and assigned 28.94 percent of the responsibility for the disaster to local governments (see Appendix 1.2). In addition, compared to PWI students, HBI students attributed to the federal government

a significantly higher level of relative responsibility for the disaster[29];
however, there were no institution-type effects on local government responsibility judgments (Table 1.5).

Comparing Social Identity and Attribution Explanations

A final interest was in identifying the sets of predictors that best accounted
for group differences in dissatisfaction, liability, and confidence judgments.
Thus, we examined the effects of institution type, group identification, memory, media exposure, and attributions of fault, cause, and responsibility on
judgments of dissatisfaction, liability, and confidence.

Explaining Dissatisfaction Judgments

Slow federal response dissatisfaction. The most efficient explanatory model
for dissatisfaction with timing of the federal response included memory and
attributions of fault, cause, and responsibility (Table 1.7). In particular, participants most critical of the federal government's slow response were also
(a) most likely to remember that a larger proportion of White, wealthy, and
middle-class residents evacuated before landfall; (b) least likely to attribute stranded residents' behaviors to laziness, low education, and opportunism;
(c) most likely to believe insensitivity, race, and class influenced government
officials' decisions; (d) least likely to attribute government response failures
to homeland security challenges; and (e) most likely to attribute a higher portion of responsibility for the disastrous events to the federal government than
victims. Unexpectedly, federal government fault attributions were negatively
related to dissatisfaction with federal response timing.

Slow local government response dissatisfaction. The best predictor set for
dissatisfaction with timing of local government officials' responses included
group identification and causal, fault, and responsibility attributions (Table 1.8).
Specifically, the least critical participants of the mayor's and governor's slow
responses were (a) most likely to identify with government officials, (b) most
likely to believe stranded residents stayed by choice, (c) most willing to attribute the federal government's response failures to homeland security challenges,
and (d) least likely to attribute high responsibility to the local governments.

Overall government response dissatisfaction. Causal attributions concerning the events related to Katrina and its aftermath provided the best explanation of participants' dissatisfaction with the government's handling of the
hurricane and the ensuing situation (Table 1.9).[30] Specifically, the most dissatisfied participants were (a) most likely to attribute stranded residents' behavior to their bravery, optimism, resilience, and pride; (b) most likely to believe insensitivity, race, and class influenced government officials'

Table 1.7. Predictors of Dissatisfaction with Federal Government's Response Timing

Predictors	β	t	Fit Index
Recollections of percentages of White, wealthy, and middle-class pre-Katrina evacuees	0.17	2.44*	
Fault attributions about federal government	−0.17	−2.50*	
Negative dispositional attributions about post-Katrina evacuees	−0.31	−4.50***	
Negative dispositional attributions about federal government officials	0.28	3.70***	
Attributions that federal response failures were due to the disaster's unprecedented nature	−0.14	−1.75†	
Attributions that federal response failures were due to homeland security challenges	−0.15	−2.11*	
Responsibility assigned to federal government relative to New Orleans residents	0.18	2.53*	
R^2			52.60%***
F			18.84***

† $p < .10$, marginally significant.
* $p < 05$.
*** $p < .001$.

Table 1.8. Predictors of Dissatisfaction with Local Government's Response Timing

Predictors	β	t	Fit Index
Identification with government officials	−3.86***		
Fault attributions about post-Katrina evacuees	−0.16	−2.07*	
Attributions that federal response failures were due to homeland security challenges	−0.26	−3.50**	
Responsibility assigned to local government	0.22	2.80**	
R^2			30.8%***
F			13.55***

* $p < 05$.
** $p < .01$.
*** $p < .001$.

Table 1.9. Predictors of Dissatisfaction with Government's Overall Response

Predictors	β	t	Fit Index
Identification with Katrina victims	1.71†		
Positive dispositional attributions about post-Katrina evacuees	−0.18	−2.28*	
Negative dispositional attributions about federal government officials	0.31	3.72***	
Attributions that federal response failures were due to homeland security challenges	−0.19	−2.36*	
R^2			22.2%***
F			8.69***

† $p < .10$, marginally significant.
* $p < 05$.
*** $p < .001$.

decisions; and (c) least likely to attribute government response failures to homeland security challenges.

Explaining Liability Judgments

Federal government and Katrina victim liability. The most efficient explanatory model for the amount of liability assigned to the federal government, relative to Katrina victims, included memory, causal attributions, and responsibility attributions (Table 1.10). Specifically, assignment of the highest level of liability to the federal government occurred among participants who (a) recalled the earliest issuance of the mandatory evacuation order, (b) were least likely to attribute response failures to the disaster's unprecedented nature, and

Table 1.10. Predictors of Liability Assigned to Federal Government Relative to New Orleans Residents

Predictors	β	t	Fit Index
Recollections of the timing of the mandatory evacuation order	0.22	3.02**	
Attributions that federal response failures were due to the disaster's unprecedented nature		−0.28	−3.59***
Responsibility assigned to federal government relative to New Orleans residents	0.48	6.15***	
R^2			40.6%***
F			26.22***

*** $p < .001$.

(c) attributed the highest portion of responsibility for the disaster to the federal government.

Local government liability. Judgments about the percentage that should be paid by the local governments of New Orleans' rebuilding costs were best explained by group identification, memory, fault, causal, and responsibility attributions (Table 1.11). Specifically, liability judgments were highest among participants who (a) identified most with Katrina victims; (b) recalled the mandatory evacuation having been ordered latest; (c) attributed more fault to the federal government; (d) were least likely to believe stranded residents stayed behind because they were infirm, lacked transportation, or a place to relocate; (e) were most likely to believe stranded residents stayed behind because of property seizure or emergency shelter inconvenience concerns; (f) least likely to believe insensitivity, race, and class influenced government officials' decisions; and (g) attributed more responsibility for the disaster to local governments.

Explaining Confidence Judgments

Judgments of confidence in authorities' ability to effectively manage future disasters were best explained by memory and attributions (Table 1.12).[31] Confidence was negatively related to attributions that victims were brave, optimistic, resilient, and proud and were positively related to (a) Katrina victim fault attributions, (b) attributions assessing Katrina victims as lazy, uneducated opportunists, (c) attributions that government response failures resulted

Table 1.11. Predictors of Liability Assigned to Local Government

Predictors	β	t	Fit Index
Identification with Katrina victims	0.17	2.53*	
Recollections of the timing of the mandatory evacuation order	−0.23	−3.49**	
Fault attributions about federal government	0.14	2.07*	
Positive situational attributions about post-Katrina evacuees	−0.22	−3.40**	
Negative situational attributions about post-Katrina evacuees	0.17	2.58*	
Negative dispositional attributions about of federal government officials	−0.24	−3.44**	
Responsibility assigned to the local government	0.65	10.15***	
R^2			55.30%***
F			20.36***

* $p < 05$.
** $p < .01$.
*** $p < .001$.

Table 1.12. Predictors of Confidence in Authorities' Ability to Respond to Future Disasters

Predictors	β	t	Fit Index
Recollections of percentages of White, wealthy, and middle-class pre-Katrina evacuees	−0.13	−1.75†	
Fault attributions about post-Katrina evacuees	0.20	2.62*	
Positive dispositional attributions about post-Katrina evacuees	−0.18	−2.16*	
Negative dispositional attributions about post-Katrina evacuees	0.34	4.13***	
Attributions that federal response failures were due to the disaster's unprecedented nature	0.38	4.86***	
Responsibility assigned to the local government	0.17	2.36*	
R^2			41.40%***
F			13.87***

† $p < .10$, marginally significant.
* $p < .05$.
*** $p < .001$.

from the disaster's unprecedented nature, and (d) attributions of local government responsibility.

Personal Relevance Findings

Using a one-way ANOVA procedure, we assessed the extent to which Hurricane Katrina's personal relevance to participants influenced their levels of identification with the victims and the government. We found that personal relevance differences affected the level of identification with Katrina victims ($p < .004$). Participants with no personal hurricane experience (mean = 4.61, $se = .08$) identified significantly less ($p < .006$) with Katrina victims than did students who were themselves Katrina victims (mean = 5.48, $se = .05$). Also, students with personal hurricane experience, but no connection to Katrina, identified less with Katrina victims than did students who were Katrina victims ($p < .03$). These findings were not surprising, but consistent with social identity theory predictions. Unexpectedly, however, personal relevance had no effect ($p > .38$) on participants' identification with government officials.

Finally, we examined whether personal relevance significantly affected dissatisfaction, liability, and confidence judgments, after controlling for the best predictor variable sets obtained for each of these judgments, using an analysis of covariance approach. Only in the case of local government liability did personal relevance contribute significant explanatory power to a best predictor set ($p < .02$).

CONCLUSION

Our primary interest was in elucidating the basis for race-related differences in reactions to Hurricane Katrina. We found significant differences between HBI and PWI participants, similar to race differences documented in national surveys and news reports contemporaneous with the disaster. Compared to PWI students, HBI students were more dissatisfied with the response times of federal and local government authorities, and the government disaster response at all levels; assigned a higher proportion of liability to the federal government (relative to New Orleans residents) for New Orleans's rebuilding costs; and were less confident in the ability of police, military, and homeland security personnel to respond to future disasters. Somewhat unexpectedly, the significant race-related differences were consistently small and reflected variation in evaluation magnitude rather than in evaluation direction. Overall, participants were highly critical of the federal government, very sympathetic with Katrina victims, and somewhat sympathetic with local authorities.

After establishing that race-related differences in judgments of dissatisfaction, liability, and confidence existed, we determined whether social identity or attribution theory best explained these group differences. Social identity and attribution theory together accounted best for group differences, but attribution variables tended to be the most important determinants of these judgments. Causal attributions were among the most significant predictors of the six dissatisfaction, liability, and confidence judgments studied; responsibility attributions were among the most significant predictors in five of these judgments, fault attributions in four, and memory among the most significant for three.

In contrast, social identity variables influenced dissatisfaction, liability, and confidence judgments, but these effects were primarily indirect rather than direct. Group identification and institution type influenced memories of and attributions about events; memories and attributions, in turn, tended to account best for dissatisfaction, liability, and confidence judgments. Also, only with local government officials as the referent (the group whose behavior we assumed participants assessed with least certainty) did identification directly affect dissatisfaction and liability judgments.[32]

In sum, our findings suggest: (a) consistent with hierarchical attribution theories, onlookers' judgments about the Katrina disaster progressed through a series of stages, from observation to interpretation to inference to decision; and (b) consistent with social identity theory, onlookers' judgments were influenced by in-group bias, but primarily in early judgmental stages, which are known to be influenced most often without individual awareness or control.

This last finding of biasing effects arising automatically and uncon-
sciously is reminiscent of classic studies of prejudice and social judgment by
Gordon Allport; Albert Hastorf and Hadley Cantril; and Robert Vallone, Lee
Ross, and Mark Lepper.[33] These studies found that individuals remembered
and interpreted events differently, depending on their racial, political, and institutional backgrounds, which reflects in-group favoritism. Similarly, our
findings suggest Katrina onlookers were probably not purposefully discrimi-
nating in their responses to the disaster. This conveys a hopeful message, suggesting progress in race relations.

There is also a sad note, however. Historically, different racial groups' experiences with discrimination in this country have varied. These divergent experiences, in turn, color judgments differently, through their influence on
memories, interpretations, and inferences about events, and not necessarily at
the level of individual awareness or control. Moving forward, this suggests
authorities must consciously consider the impact of past experiences of
racism and discrimination, even benign neglect, on interpretations of current
events and, most important, their potential effect on race relations, as they develop their disaster plans and responses. Culturally sensitive and careful handling of future disasters will provide positive input to the nation's collective
memory surrounding these events.

Given that onlookers' attributions about authorities were important determinants of reactions to the disaster, it is reasonable to assume they also will
influence individuals' responsiveness to future disaster warnings. Specifically, if onlookers attribute their in-groups' negative outcomes to government
insensitivity and discrimination, then diminished responsiveness, cooperation
with authorities, and compliance with orders, plus increased confusion,
should occur in reactions to future warnings. For example, Katrina evacuees
and many local and regional non-profit organizations criticized the American
Red Cross for culturally insensitive, ill-prepared handling of relief efforts,
which created massive confusion.[34] To counteract such negative perceptions,
officials need to implement more culturally sensitive practices. Recognition
of this principle was demonstrated by Lt. General Russel Honore, director of
the National Guard's relief efforts, who upon arriving, ordered military troops
and police officers to lower their weapons and show sensitivity toward the
stranded victims; thereafter, the victims responded more positively toward
authorities.[35] Thus, Honore's intervention dramatically affected victims'
morale and cooperativeness.

Onlookers' low confidence in authorities' future disaster management ability is another important finding with practical implications. Disaster management literature suggests that diminished confidence in authorities will ham-
per first responders' efforts in future disasters because public cooperation and

compliance are reduced.[36] To rebuild trust and confidence, government agencies and relief organizations should identify key community leaders to serve as liaisons between communities and authorities—thereby reducing skepticism about the federal government's ability to handle and manage future disasters and recovery efforts. The Red Cross recently recruited more racial and ethnic minority staff and volunteers, responding to criticism of insensitivity toward Blacks during relief efforts, in order to bolster confidence and cooperativeness of racial and ethnic minorities.

Increased inter-group conflict, decreased civic participation, and even protest and civic unrest may arise when individuals perceive that authorities are deliberately negligent and discriminatory against their in-groups. Greater meaningful interaction among racial groups could dispel negative out-group preconceptions and reduce inter-group conflict, increasing the likelihood that people will judge on the basis of knowledge, rather than stereotypes and prejudices. The implication that increased interaction reduces prejudice derives from studies like Muzafer Sherif et al.'s classic "Robbers Cave Experiment" that showed increased inter-group interaction dramatically reduced conflict.[37]

Another strategy authorities might employ to ameliorate negative feelings resulting from catastrophes comes from social justice research, which suggests: (a) treatment of citizens by authorities during disasters communicates important information to them about their regard as valued, respected society members; and (b) when citizens perceive authorities as trustworthy public servants who treat people fairly, increased pride and commitment to society result.[38] Thus, respectfulness and impartiality when interacting with citizens of all racial backgrounds should be stressed to all disaster responders. Moreover, fairness is necessary when distributing recovery aid and adopting measures to minimize negative outcomes for victims, regardless of race and socioeconomic status.

Frederick Douglass's observation concerning the many negative outcomes of injustice on society, made over 120 years ago, applies aptly to Katrina's aftermath: "Where justice is denied, where poverty is enforced, where ignorance prevails, and where any one class is made to feel that society is an organized conspiracy to oppress, rob, and degrade them, neither persons nor property will be safe."[39] When authorities' actions or inactions—whether intentional or unintentional—in disasters result in overwhelmingly negative outcomes for segments of society, societal unrest is probable. When future disasters occur—human-made or natural, predicted or unpredicted—our government must never again be perceived as having abandoned any large segment of citizens, especially along race or class lines. Otherwise, inter-group relations will deteriorate, threatening our nation's stability. Our findings highlight the need for additional research that expands and amplifies understanding of the complex manner in which perception shapes attributions, and how these in turn influence decisions and behavior in the face of disaster. The result will be informed authorities, with more knowledge about intervening in disasters that place populations or our nation's security at risk.

NOTES

1. Lynne Duke, "Block that Metaphor: What We Mean When We Call New Orleans Third World," *Washington Post*, October 9, 2005, B1.

2. Wil Haygood and Ann S. Tyson, "'Was as if All of Us Were Already Pronounced Dead': Convention Center Left a Five-Day Legacy of Chaos and Violence," *Washington Post*, September 15, 2005, A1.

3. Ray Nagin, "Testimony before the Senate Committee on Homeland Security and Governmental Affairs" (February 2006).

4. Gordon Russell, "Nagin Orders First-Ever Mandatory Evacuation of New Orleans," *Times-Picayune*, August 28, 2005.

5. Douglas Brinkley, *The Great Deluge: Hurricane Katrina, New Orleans, and the Mississippi Gulf Coast* (New York: HarperCollins, 2006).

6. Bill Walsh, "FEMA's Dome Airlift Plan Never Got Off the Ground, Concept Not Viable, National Guard Says," *Times-Picayune*, December 9, 2005, 4.

7. Scott Gold, "Refugees Forced to Endure Appalling Conditions," *Irish Times*, September 2, 2005, 10.

8. Gold, *Irish Times*, 2005.
Genevieve Roberts, "Hurricane Katrina: The Suicide of a Policeman Who Could Not Endure His City's Fate," *Independent*, September 7, 2005, 22.

9. Pew Research Center, "Huge Racial Divide over Katrina and Its Consequences: Two-in-Three Critical of Bush's Relief Efforts," September 8, 2005, <http://peoplepress.org/reports/display.php3?ReportID=255> (September 8, 2005).

10. Lynne Duke and Teresa Wiltz, "A Nation's Castaways; Katrina Blew In, and Tossed Up Reminders of a Tattered Racial Legacy," *Washington Post*, September 5, 2005, D1. Haygood and Tyson, *Washington Post*, 2005.

11. Henri Tajfel and John Turner, "The Social Identity Theory and Intergroup Behavior," in *Psychology of Intergroup Relations*, ed. Stephen Worchel (Chicago: New-Hall, 1986), 7–24.

12. Michael Hogg and Graham Vaughan, *Social Psychology* (New York: Prentice Hall, 2002).
Jeff Greenberg, Sheldon Solomon, and Tom Pyszczynski, "Terror Management Theory of Self-Esteem and Cultural Worldviews: Empirical Assessments and Conceptual Refinements," in *Advances in Experimental Social Psychology Volume 29,* ed. Mark Zanna (San Diego, CA: Academic Press, 1997), 61–139.

13. Emory Griffin, *A First Look at Communication Theory, 2nd Edition* (Boston: McGraw-Hill College, 1994).

14. Fritz Heider, *The Psychology of Interpersonal Relations* (New York: Wiley, 1958).

15. Heider, 1958.

16. Heider, 1958.

17. Harold Kelley, "The Processes of Causal Attribution," *American Psychologist* 28, no. 2 (February 1973): 107–28.

18. Lee Ross, "The Intuitive Psychologist and His Shortcomings: Distortions in the Attribution Process," in *Advances in Experimental Social Psychology Volume 10*, ed. Leonard Berkowitz (New York: Academic Press, 1977), 173–200.

19. Dale T. Miller and Michael Ross, "Self-Serving Biases in the Attribution of Causality: Fact or Fiction?" *Psychological Bulletin* 82, no. 2 (March 1975): 213–25.

20. Allan Fenigstein and Charles Carver, "Self-Focusing Effects of Heartbeat Feedback," *Journal of Personality and Social Psychology* 36, no. 11 (November 1978):1241–50.

David Wilder, "Cognitive Factors Affecting the Success of Intergroup Contact," in *Psychology of Intergroup Relations*, ed. Stephen Worchel (Chicago: New-Hall, 1986), 49–66.

21. Yaacov Trope, "Identification and Inferential Processes in Dispositional Attribution," *Psychological Review* 93, no. 3 (July 1986): 239–57.

22. Ewart A. C. Thomas and Mary Parpal, "Liability as a Function of Plaintiff and Defendant Fault," *Journal of Personality and Social Psychology* 53, no. 5 (November 1987): 843–57.

23. In particular, we found significant Black-White differences in (a) identification with government officials, (b) causal attributions about the government's ill handling of the disaster, (c) judgments about the proportion of New Orleans' rebuilding costs that should be paid by the federal government, (d) dissatisfaction with the timeliness of the federal response, and (e) dissatisfaction with the governmental response, at all levels, to Katrina and its aftermath. In addition, we found significant Black-other ethnicity differences in (a) media exposure, (b) recollection of which residents evacuated before the hurricane's landfall, (c) identification with government officials, (d) identification with Katrina victims, (e) perceptions of federal government fault, (f) perceptions of Katrina victims' fault, (g) causal attributions for the inadequate federal government response, (h) attributions about the federal government's level of responsibility for the disaster, (i) judgments of the federal government's and Katrina victims' relative liability for rebuilding New Orleans, (j) dissatisfaction with the timeliness of the federal response, (k) dissatisfaction with the timeliness of local officials' responses, and (l) dissatisfaction with the governmental response, at all levels, to Katrina and its aftermath.

24. Pew Research Center, 2005.

25. Responses were measured on 6-point scales throughout the remainder of the Results, unless otherwise noted.

26. This relative liability measure was derived by subtracting the percentage of New Orleans's rebuilding costs participants assigned to Katrina victims from the percentage of the costs they assigned to federal government, then rescaling the obtained differences on a 0-to-1 scale. Therefore, numbers greater than .5 indicate higher federal government liability, numbers less than .5 indicate higher Katrina victim liability, and .5 indicates equal liability assigned to the two groups.

27. There were no race-related differences (HBI–PWI, Black-White, or Black-Other Ethnicity) in the amount of liability assigned to the New Orleans and Louisiana governments. Consequently, mediational analyses for this variable were not included.

28. For example, the National Guard arrived soon after the winds subsided, FEMA officials were given two days to arrive in New Orleans, and buses arrived to evacuate the Superdome and Convention Center on Friday. We suspect participants' memories of the arrival of assistance reflect the time that elapsed before buses arrived to evacuate emergency shelters.

29. We computed relative responsibility in the same way that we computed relative liability (cf. Endnote 26).

30. Note, in Table 1.9, the most efficient explanatory model for overall dissatisfaction with the government response also included identification with Katrina victims. Because this index was marginally significant, its effects are not discussed further.

31. Participants' memories of the numbers of White, wealthy, and middle-class pre-Katrina evacuees were negatively related to their confidence judgments. However, this effect was only marginally significant and consequently is not discussed further.

32. Participants were assumed to hold greater uncertainty about local government officials' behaviors because (1) city and state officials were the focus of less media attention than Katrina victims and the federal government, especially FEMA; (2) participants' responsibility attributions for local officials increased as their exposure to Katrina media coverage increased; and (3) factor analyses revealed participants did not differentiate city and state officials in their judgments.

33. Albert Hastorf and Hadley Cantril, "They Saw a Game: A Case Study," *Journal of Abnormal and Social Psychology* 49 (1954): 129–34.

Gordon Allport, *The Nature of Prejudice* (Oxford, England: Addison-Wesley, 1954).

Robert Vallone, Lee Ross, and Mark Lepper, "The Hostile Media Phenomenon: Biased Perception and Perceptions of Media Bias in Coverage of the Beirut Massacre," *Journal of Personality and Social Psychology* 49, no. 3 (September 1985): 577–85.

34. Jacqueline Salmon, "Counterparts Excoriate Red Cross Katrina Effort," *Washington Post*, April 5, 2006, A14.

35. "Lt. Gen. Honore a 'John Wayne Dude,'" September 3, 2005, <http://www.cnn.com/2005/US/09/02honore.profile/index.html>. (September 3, 2005).

36. Terri M. Adams-Fuller, Angela P. Cole, Billie L. Saddler, and Tarra Jackson, "A Critical Analysis of the Impact of the Homeland Security Advisory System on Local Law Enforcement and the Public," *Criminal Justice Studies* (In Press, 2007).

37. Muzafer Sherif, O.J. Harvey, B. Jack White, William Hood, and Carolyn Sherif, *Intergroup Conflict and Cooperation: The Robbers Cave Experiment* (Norman, OK: Institute of Group Relations, 1961).

38. E. Allen Lind and Tom R. Tyler, *The Social Psychology of Procedural Justice.* (New York: Plenum, 1988).

Angela P. Cole and Ewart A. C. Thomas, "Group Differences in Fairness Perceptions and Decision Making in Voting Rights Cases," *Law and Human Behavior*, 30 (2006): 543–60.

39. Frederick Douglass, "The Nation's Problem," 1889 <http://teachingamericanhistory.org/library/index.asp?document=494> (September 15, 2006).

Chapter Two

The Color(s) of Crisis

How Race, Rumor, and Collective Memory Shape the Legacy of Katrina

Michelle Miles[1]
Duke W. Austin

We black folk, our history and our present being, are a mirror of all the manifold experiences of America. What we want, what we represent, what we endure is what America is. If we black folk perish, America will perish. If America has forgotten her past, then let her look into the mirror of our consciousness and she will see the living past living in the present, for our memories go back, through our black folk of today, through the recollections of our black parents, and through the tales of slavery told by our black grandparents, to the time when none of us, black or white, lived in this fertile land.

—Richard Wright, *12 Million Black Voices*

By the time Hurricane Katrina crashed ashore on August 29, 2005, *part* of the story had already been written; certain facts were already known: the levee system built to help protect the New Orleans area was inadequate and had been largely neglected for years, thousands of people were either stranded in the path of the storm or had chosen to attempt to ride it out, the Gulf Coast comprises perhaps the poorest region in the United States, meaning many residents would be hard-pressed to relocate and later, to recover, National Guard troop levels in the area were lessened by the demands of the war in Iraq . . . the list goes on. What was known as the first of the punishing winds and rain made landfall was that this was going to be a devastating storm.[2] What was not known was how everyone—from first responders, to survivors, to journalists, to government officials—would respond.

In the time since Katrina hit, discussions have focused on the storm as a physical *event*, with wind speeds and flood levels documented, casualties estimated, and economic costs still being debated. The authors of this chapter propose that perhaps the "story of Katrina," also rests in its *stories*. That is to say, that to understand how Katrina was experienced by many who lived through the storm, we must investigate the stories—particularly the *rumors*—that evolved and influenced people's actions.

Hurricane Katrina sparked countless unsubstantiated stories, many promulgated by the mass media and most telling for their racialized aspects. The authors traveled to the Gulf Coast after Katrina (and Hurricane Rita[3]) and spent weeks collecting numerous media accounts and conducting dozens of interviews with evacuees, aid workers, government officials, and survivors who were stuck in the storm. Almost every interviewee cited rumors they had heard, and in most cases, (a) the rumor influenced decision-making and (b) race played a part in how the rumor was received. During and after Katrina, Blacks and Whites[4] experienced two different realities in large part due to their differing negotiation of rumor—and the mass media played to and exploited this.

METHOD

The authors spent just over three weeks in the Gulf Coast region following Hurricanes Katrina and Rita, spread over two separate research trips. The first began one month after Katrina had hit and lasted eleven days. We returned to the New Orleans area roughly six months after Katrina had hit and spent another eleven days in the area. In the interim, we continued to collect media accounts of the initial crisis as well as coverage detailing the experiences of evacuees.

During the first trip, we spent two days at a National Guard base where evacuees from both hurricanes were being housed. From there, we traveled south, conducting research in four Louisiana cities and towns. We spent six days in New Orleans, where we visited every major neighborhood. At each of these destinations, we spent as much time as possible becoming acquainted with the surroundings and local concerns, collecting and recording Katrina-related media accounts, and gathering interviews.

We conducted our second research trip in March 2006 and spent the entire eleven days in New Orleans. Again, we spent time in every major neighborhood of the city, observing what had changed, speaking with local leaders, monitoring media coverage, and gathering interviews.

In total, we conducted fifty-three in-depth, formal interviews with evacuees and survivors, National Guard soldiers, Red Cross volunteers, and Federal Emergency Management Agency (FEMA) workers. Formal interviews lasted from 30 to 90 minutes, and we took every effort to find a location for the interviews that was comfortable for both the interviewee and the interviewer. In addition, we have made every effort to ensure the anonymity of the respondents when recording and analyzing their interviews. We digitally recorded the interviews except when, on rare occasions, our digital equipment was not functioning.

In addition, we conducted twenty informal interviews with members of the same populations. Informal interviews differed from formal interviews in that the respondents in the informal interviews were unwilling or unable (due to job restrictions) to sign the consent form or have their words recorded. Nevertheless, those who gave informal interviews were very willing to answer questions and share their experiences. Information gathered through informal interviews provides background information for this work, but has not been directly quoted.

While it was impossible to contact persons who were not visibly present at the sites we visited, every attempt was made to select respondents from a wide range of demographic backgrounds. We completed this task by visiting a variety of shelters, relief centers, and affected neighborhoods and actively approaching persons who appeared to be from demographics that had yet to be represented in the study. Therefore, we collected a purposive stratified sample from a wide range of available respondents in order to prevent a simple confirmation of existing ideas about the racial world.

Respondents were grouped into two categories. The first category consists of evacuees and survivors, and the second consists of rescue, relief, and reconstruction workers. Since the primary research questions deal with race, equal numbers of Black and White respondents were selected. An attempt was made to select an equal number of males and females, although males from the evacuee/survivor category outnumber females almost two to one. In sum, 29 Blacks were interviewed (11 females, 18 males), 39 Whites (18 females, 21 males), 4 male Latinos, and 1 male who identified as multi-racial (White-Hispanic-Asian). Of these, 58 were evacuees and survivors of the hurricanes and 15 were rescue, relief, or reconstruction workers.

While recognizing our role as social actors in the reification of race as a social category, we used our own racial identities as tools in the gathering of data. One member of our research team is a Black female and the other is a White male. Often in ethnographic research, respondents show reticence to speak across racial lines, especially when discussing the topic of race. Consequently, we matched the race of the respondent with that of the researcher whenever possible. This proved especially useful for the purposes of this research since interviewees often "othered" members of a different race when narrating their experiences. For example, respondents spoke freely about "them" (members of the other race) when speaking with someone of their own race. Given the entrenchment of race as a social category, we feel that the benefits gained from racial matching outweigh the cost associated with their individual reification of race.

FINDINGS

Race Relations, Collective Memory, and Rumor

TV news and talk radio airwaves were filled in the days following Katrina's initial blow with citizens across the United States expressing shock and outrage at what they saw happening along the Gulf Coast, especially in New Orleans. They could not believe that so many of their fellow citizens were in such peril. However, many of these commentators were *White*. Many Blacks, on the other hand, expressed outrage, but not shock. Why the dissonance? Because despite the shared values of many U.S. citizens across racial lines and regardless of the successes of the Civil Rights Movement, cultural narratives continue to be greatly informed by race.[5] These narratives are based not only on a sense of contemporary shared experience, but more important, perhaps, on the collective memory of a group over generations. Blacks did not convey the same sort of shock as many Whites over the perceived neglect of poor Blacks after Katrina because the historic and systemic disenfranchisement of Blacks in this country is a pertinent, permanent, and *living* part of their collective memory. As a forty-three-year-old Black man told us in an interview: "Business as usual for this country. When is the last time America lifted a finger to do right by a Black man? We were worth more when we were slaves."

White observers, on the other hand, may not have been as quick to connect the disproportionate poverty among New Orleans Blacks and sluggish governmental response after the storm, for instance, to a pattern of treatment from White authority that has included the institution of slavery and the Jim Crow era. According to scholars such as Michael Eric Dyson, the collective memory for many Whites in the United States does not emphasize the oppression and exploitation of Blacks. Dyson cryptically suggests that "USA" actually stands for "United States of *Amnesia*" when it comes to analyzing contemporary conditions for both the urban poor and the suburban rich.[6] Because an ahistorical approach melds best with the myth of meritocracy, White collective memory births cultural narratives that support today's status quo as normative. Thus, when something like the first O.J. Simpson verdict is read, the Rodney King rebellions break out, *or* Hurricane Katrina occurs, otherwise like-minded and similarly situated Whites and Blacks often have very different perspectives.

Perhaps where this peculiar dichotomy is best illustrated in day-to-day life (and exaggerated in highly charged circumstances such as a deadly hurricane) is in the negotiation of rumor. Rumors, understood as unsubstantiated stories, have long been a part of U.S. culture, and have long served as commentary on U.S. race relations. As far back as 1775, rumors persisted that Lord Dunmore, then governor of Virginia, was secretly enticing Blacks to murder their slave owners in order to help the British win the Revolutionary War.[7] Rumors served a pivotal role in bringing about the Civil War, as allegations of a "Slavocracy" helped unify the North[8] and allegations that Abolitionists ultimately sought the annihilation of the South unified the Confederacy.[9] And certainly rumors catalyzed and/or fueled many of the prominent "race riots" of the twentieth century, including in Chicago in 1919, in Harlem and Los Angeles in 1943,[10] and in Watts in 1965.[11]

Rumors are often propagated along the lines of long-standing, cultural narratives (i.e., that "Blacks are inherently violent" or that "Whites want to 'keep Blacks down' at all costs") that remain viable, if not as visible, as in years past. Though integration in public schools was introduced over fifty years ago and the workplaces across the country have undoubtedly become more racially diverse, statistics suggest U.S. neighborhoods and public schools are slightly *more* segregated than thirty-five years ago.[12] With limited direct experiences with large numbers of people from a different racial group, rumors (and media representations, which will be addressed shortly) often serve to fill in the gaps of "knowledge" one group has about another. Gary Alan Fine and Patricia A. Turner[13] suggest that

> even seemingly innocuous legends reveal much about how people cope with bothersome and distressing aspects of their day-to-day life. Rumors and legends address those aspects of life about which we receive mixed or ambiguous messages. Given that matters relevant to race remain charged and divisive in many corridors of U.S. society, it is not surprising that rumors and legends that reflect racial misunderstanding and mistrust frequently circulate.

So rumors, even in relatively calm times, have a tendency to further, rather than challenge, race-based prejudice and racial mistrust.

Complicating this already complex dynamic is the evolving nature and pervasiveness of the U.S. mass media. If, as James Carey[14] suggests, communication is "a symbolic process whereby reality is produced, maintained, repaired and transformed," what are we to make of the "realities" conveyed through our venues of mass communication in regards to race and rumor? Several commentators, including but not limited to, Michael Eric Dyson,[15] bell hooks,[16] Donald Bogle,[17] Herman Gray,[18] and Vincent Rocchio[19] have analyzed and argued the ways in which Hollywood movies and primetime TV programs have negatively portrayed Blacks and what this cultural imagery has meant in terms of racism, race relations,[20] and public policy.[21]

Robert Entmann and Andrew Rojecki found the negative stereotyping carried over to *news* programming as well. In *The Black Image in the White Mind*, Entmann and Rojecki[22] summarize:

> The news presents a face of Black disruption, of criminal victimizing and victimization, that compares unfavorably with Whites. Such depictions may increase Whites' fear of entering Black neighborhoods, as it reduces their sympathy for Blacks—who are in fact far more afflicted by violence and crime than most Whites. In our Indianapolis interviews, only those who had prolonged personal contact with Blacks in arenas beyond the workplace failed to make comments that touched on the deep-seated fears and anxieties attached to Blacks as a social category. Ambivalent Whites spontaneously associated Blacks with poverty and welfare cheating, even where their lived experiences taught otherwise. The respondents expressed parallel frustration with Black leaders perceived as opportunistic and whining (Jesse Jackson), extremist (Louis Farrakhan), or corrupt (Marion Barry)—neglecting the many White politicians who match those descriptions. As suggested by our own audience research and that of others, such thinking finds nourishment, if not its origin, in images and implicit comparisons constructed in the news.

The Entmann and Rojecki study suggests that an acknowledged authority— the nightly news—reifies White cultural narratives defining Blacks, as a group, as generally criminal and needy.

While such portrayals in entertainment and "factual" media productions may not be new, the changing character of mass mediated journalism might be. With the advent of 24-hour cable news programming came increased competition for advertising dollars and an evolution in the mindsets of programming directors from viewing news as a service of their stations to viewing news as a profit-making proposition. With that has come an emphasis on a different type of "news"—that of *speculative journalism*.[23] As news programming has become more popular and pervasive, the accepted standard of evidence before going to air (and also to print) has decreased. Subsequently, much of what is reported is actually guesswork or speculative. Take any of a number of high-profile crime cases of recent years as an example. Entire shows have been built around the premise that *guessing* what will happen at the next arraignment or press conference will sell as *infotainment*. Guesses as to the number of dead after a catastrophe now scroll across the TV screen on the CNN crawl, ostensibly as "news." Speculation now ranks as part of the journalist's craft. Couple this development with the ever-increasing saturation of mass media in daily life and an established pattern of "othering" if not demonizing Blacks,[24] and the conditions are rife for the mass dissemination of racially tinged rumor—as was the case during and *after* Katrina.

Marauding Gangs and Blown Levees: The Rumors of Katrina

Hurricane Katrina gave life to numerous rumors, many if not most having racial implications. These can generally be placed into one of two groups: (1) those rumors "othering" Blacks as somehow "less worthy" due to their criminal, violent, or welfare-driven natures, or (2) those rumors suggesting that White authority (i.e., "the government") purposefully acted to the detriment of Blacks in need. From those two categories, we will introduce and analyze the two rumors most discussed by our interviewees as illustrative of the ways in which the race-rumor intersection impacted how survivors experienced the storm and its aftermath. These rumors include the "Marauding Gangs" rumor and the "Blown Levees" rumor.

Marauding Blacks: What Whites Perceived as the Real Threat

The early stories were terrifying: with flood waters still covering most of the city, gangs of heavily armed and clearly dangerous young Black men were roaming the streets of New Orleans, shooting and stabbing people, taking over their homes and stealing everything in sight before firing upon military and rescue helicopters.[25] In the Superdome, where citizens had been erroneously led to believe they would find safe shelter, similar gangs were raping little girls and beating up old men. Shocked citizens across the country watched, listened to, and read the accounts of the chaos *The New York Times's* Maureen Dowd[26] described with much shame: "America is once more plunged into a snake pit of anarchy, death, looting, raping, marauding thugs, suffering innocents, a shattered infrastructure, a gutted police force, insufficient troop levels and criminally negligent government planning." For many of our White interviewees who evacuated, who had been told stories from various others, there was no mistaking who the perpetrators of this anarchy were. As one fifty-five-year-old White male explained: "And, one policeman explained to me, he said, 'Don't stop because they had car-jacked twelve people—because they knew that was the only way out of the city— they'd stop you.'"

This respondent spoke in coded language, but it was clear to the interviewer what he meant when he spoke of "them." When asked to clarify who "they" were, the respondent described Black men. Regardless of the validity of the claim that "they" were car-jacking motorists, both the actions of the police officer and the respondent reflected that "reality." As a result of the police officer's belief in the dangerous Black man,[27] he took to telling others about the danger. Similarly, the respondent sped out of town with the windows rolled up despite the heat. In an attempt to ascertain whether there was a first-hand experience with car-jackers, the researcher asked a follow-up question and received the following response:

Did you see anything when you were getting out? Any car-jackings? Any . . .

No. There were people on the road, you know what I mean? This was about eleven or twelve o'clock during the day, so I guess the people that do that sort of thing don't strike too much during the light of day. And, I think the police were getting up to it.

In this quote, the respondent resolves dissonance concerning his hyperreality[28] of dangerous Black men with his lack of viewing any of "the people who do that sort of thing" by explaining that car-jackings don't happen during daylight hours and that the police had probably suppressed the incidents. How or why the police would disclose this information to the respondent but keep it from others was not discussed.

The rumor of the car-jackings rang true not just with our respondent, but also with Fox News. On the evening of August 30, Fox issued an "alert" as talk show host Alan Colmes reiterated reports of "robberies, rapes, car-jackings, riots and murder. Violent gangs are roaming the streets at night, hidden by the cover of darkness."[29] The race of these alleged marauders was never in doubt—words like "gangs" and "hidden by the cover of darkness" accompanied visuals of distraught, often desperate victims, most of whom were Black. If one missed the association, several reports were more blatant, including the now infamous *Yahoo! News* photographs that showed a Black man after he had "looted" supplies as opposed to a White couple that had "found" free groceries.[30]

Rumors did not merely circulate about Blacks in the city or at the much-publicized Superdome and convention center sites. White evacuees at other shelters often expressed concern over the Blacks in their midst. The following forty-six-year-old White male told another variation of the "dangerous Black man"[31] narrative in recounting this rumor he had heard. When the researcher asked if there had been anything at the National Guard base requiring an abundance of military and civilian police officers, the respondent reported that many people had been robbed and that some people had gotten out of hand. When pressed, the only problematic activity that the respondent had actually *witnessed* was complaining about the conditions on the base.

There have been some things here. They had some people who got out of hand.

Who got out of hand?

Some of the evacuees did.

What did they look like?

They were Black. I'm not prejudiced or anything, but a lot of them were Black. They complained quite a bit.

What happened?

They had various things. There was arguing, that kind of stuff. And, a lot of people were fussing.

What kind of things have you seen?

There's been some thefts, there's been some, uh, a lot of complaints.

Have you seen any thefts?

I have not seen it myself, no, but I heard a lot about it.

Despite this respondent's statement that he is not prejudiced, his perception of reality seems to be shaped by the long-standing narrative that Blacks are criminals. He witnesses Black people complaining and "fussing," and has also heard of some thefts. He believes the stories about thefts despite not having first-hand experience of them. His reality of thefts was likely buoyed by both a cultural image of the Black man as criminal[32] and also by his witnessing of what he describes as fussing on the part of Black evacuees. It should be noted that Black evacuees at the same shelter did not repeat the same rumor; for them, the blatant military presence was unwarranted.

In the instance of Hurricane Katrina, the cultural narratives suggesting Blacks are inherently dangerous led to rumors that fed, and were fed by, media reports. Several joined *The New York Times* and Fox News in early misreporting. The *Herald Sun News* wrote, "Gangs stalked the tourists and women were threatened with rape."[33] The *Los Angeles Times* reported that the National Guard was being positioned on rooftops because the snipers had become such a problem.[34] While there may be some truth to these stories of lawlessness, after several months of investigation, the majority appear to be baseless rumors; reporters and researchers alike have had difficulty in finding people with first-hand reports of violence. Now, in retrospect, many media outlets have corrected the assertions they made in the days following the first storm. For example, Carr, of *The New York Times,* found the following:

> But many instances in the lurid libretto of widespread murder, carjacking, rape, and assaults that filled the airwaves and newspapers have yet to be established or proved, as far as anyone can determine. And many of the urban legends that sprang up—the systematic rape of children, the slitting of a seven-year-old's throat—so far seem to be just that.[35]

In contrast, the "gangs of Black men are running amok" rumor mill did not seem to work the same way for many of our White respondents who remained in New Orleans. Several spoke of cooperation even though they were in the city where the bulk of violent and lawless stories were being reported. The following seventy-six-year-old White male speaks of a neighbor who evacuated people by boat: "He said he could help people. He had a boat full of gasoline cans. The first responders were really the volunteer boat-people of New Orleans. Those were the first ones that did some good there with their boats loaded up."

Whether or not the respondent believes that there exists a close association between violence and Black men is not entirely obvious.[36] He did, however, feel that the media reports of violence were exaggerated, and he believes they were exaggerated at the expense of New Orleans's image. He is quoted as saying:

> That, that really bugged me. And, I'm blaming the media. But, look, it's their job to report, number one. Number two, what you going to report? Dull stuff? But, that's not the whole story. That really bugged me. It made an image, a terrible image, worse than it really was.

Most of our White respondents who did not evacuate had responses that were similar to the one quoted here. White evacuees were much more likely to articulate narratives of dangerous Black men than were White survivors who stayed in New Orleans. We believe the difference occurred because those who were in the city had to negotiate their first-hand experiences of cooperation with the contrasting images they saw in the media. The White respondents who left were more likely to let racialized rumors and second-hand knowledge influence the construction of their reality. These were the stories, after all, that—quite unlike the dominant rumor in the Black community that the levees had been intentionally blown—resonated with the media and took on lives of their own. In *Rumors, Race and Riots*, Terry Ann Knopf explains that racial bias in the media has implications for the reception and regurgitation of rumors. According to Knopf, the press has often shaded the news:

> Numerous instances were uncovered where the "white version" of events was impulsively, if not automatically, adopted by the press—thereby becoming the only "official version" of those events. All too often, and on the basis of virtually no evidence, blacks were incorrectly faulted as the aggressors and main perpetrators of the violence. The tendency on the part of the press, as well as other groups in positions of authority, to echo rumors found in the white community—in the face of no evidence, insubstantial evidence, or even contradictory evidence—amounts to a clear and unmistakable bias.[37]

Because the rumors involving dangerous Black men at large were easily reconciled with the collective consciousness of a largely White-owned and -staffed mass media and members of the White community, these unsubstantiated stories convinced White evacuees there was much to fear and journalists there was much to "report."

They Blew Up the Levees: Black Reality Concerning White Authority

In our research, nowhere did we see as decisive a racial divide as when the topic of the levees being intentionally destroyed came up. It was widely reported by the mainstream media that the levees in and around New Orleans had failed and/or been breached. However, while the image of dangerous Black men haunted the White imagination during and after Hurricane Katrina, Blacks were negotiating a similarly frightening narrative: that of an abusive and racist government taking aim at the city's Black residents. Perhaps nowhere was this concern more clearly articulated than in the belief, held by many Blacks in the New Orleans area, that the levees protecting the city—especially those protecting Black neighborhoods—had been intentionally destroyed during the storm.

To most Whites, including those in the state and federal government and corporate mass media, this contention was a manifestation of hyper-paranoia on the part of a devastated populace. They immediately dismissed the idea as ludicrous. However, for Blacks in the Mississippi Delta region, the thought of government officials blowing up the levees above the Lower Ninth Ward in order to protect the central business district and richer, Whiter neighborhoods was more than idle conjecture; it was history repeating itself.[38] Though most Blacks in the Delta were not alive when the Great Mississippi Flood of 1927 occurred, the majority have heard or read about the devastation. Black communities were destroyed and Black lives were lost due to the decisions of those in power.

In 1927, ineptitude, greed, and neglect fostered the conditions that eventually allowed the Mississippi River's floodwaters to do the damage they did. For example, New Orleans was never in any danger of flooding since many levees had broken upstream. Nevertheless, bankers and businesspeople of the city dynamited the levees downstream of their city in order to protect their investments. As a result, 10,000 residents of New Orleans, most of them Black, were flooded from their homes. With only a few exceptions, the displaced residents were never compensated for their losses.[39]

The flood of 1927 is a marker in terms of collective memory for Gulf Coast Blacks. The stories of Blacks being rounded up and forced to work at gunpoint on broken levees along the Mississippi River have been told for generations.[40] Blacks today know that many of their ancestors lost their homes or their lives in that flood and that levees around New Orleans were blown in order to protect the business district—resulting in the displacement of thousands.[41]

Just as racial stereotypes informed how Whites negotiated rumors during Katrina, history influenced how Blacks responded. The following forty-two-year-old Black male demonstrates how his knowledge of the previous flood influences his interpretation of stories around Hurricane Katrina. "I heard they blew up them levees. You know, they did that before, right? But, I tell you what, ain't no accident them levees broke [following Hurricane Katrina] and it ain't no accident Black folk were left to die."

In this case, the respondent is able to believe that the levees were intentionally destroyed in 2005 because of the documented intentional destruction in 1927. His experience of current events is informed by what he perceives as plausibility: to his mind, the systematic targeting of Blacks by White authority (blowing the levees) and the deadly disenfranchisement of Blacks (leaving them behind to die) make sense because they align with historical facts.

As with White respondents and dangerous Black men, we were unable to find a Black respondent with conclusive first-hand experience of the dynamited levees. We did, however, interview the following forty-something-year-old Black man who reports having heard the explosion that destroyed the levee protecting the Lower Ninth Ward.

> I'm telling you, I heard it blow. It was an explosion and the water rushed in. I couldn't get out anymore. I ended up on my roof. But no . . . no one's gonna tell me they didn't blow them levees. I was there! I heard it. I was there. And no levee breaking sounds like that. They blew 'em before, and they blew 'em now. And they don't give a damn 'cause they know no one's gonna listen to us.

The above respondent concludes his comment with an important point: he feels that beyond a shadow of a doubt, he *knows* the levees above the Ninth Ward were blown and that those in authority are not likely to consider his claims. Despite the assumption that the U.S. mass media will jump on any sensational story, that is not actually the case. With the exception of when Louis Farrakhan announced he believed the levees had been destroyed on purpose, the levees-blown rumor circulating in Black communities barely registered on the radar screen of the mainstream media.[42]

While conspiracy theories are often attributed to the most destitute (and therefore desperate) members of a society, one of the more striking attributes of the levees conspiracy theory is that it seems to cross class lines. For instance, the following interviewee, a fifty-four-year-old Black female, is highly educated, solidly middle-class to upper middle-class, and a leader in the New Orleans Black community, yet she finds the conspiracy theory quite believable:

> Oh, I don't know [if the levees were blown], but it wouldn't surprise me. From what I've seen and heard, yeah, they very well may have. See, this is New Orleans and we have a unique history, a unique culture, lots of different people mix

here. But never forget. This is still the South. And when it comes down to it, who do you think they're going to protect?

For many Whites, the contention that the levees were intentionally destroyed is absurd and is not supported by factual evidence—the rumor was a non-starter in White communities. It's non-relevance, then, with the mainstream press is hardly a surprise. Nevertheless, the Blacks we interviewed were not nearly as quick to dismiss the idea. If it happened before, they wonder, and the same power relations are in place as were in place eighty years ago, why not this time?

What both Blacks and Whites shared with us was not only their acceptance of these racialized rumors as "fact," but also their willingness to base decisions on these unsubstantiated stories. In the case of Whites negotiating the "dangerous Black men rumors," many White respondents spoke of areas they avoided at shelters and actions they took as a direct result of fearing what they had heard about in the rumors. They had not witnessed this violent behavior themselves but articulated such strong belief that it was occurring just beyond their purview that their actions were dictated by it. One young White woman had agreed to pretend she was engaged to one of our White male respondents because she had been told some young men of color (three Blacks, one Latino) might rape her. By claiming to be engaged, she was allowed to be housed with the White respondent and gained a protector. For many White respondents, the fear reflected in the dangerous Black man rumor was profound and persuasive.

Similarly, some of our Black respondents voiced skepticism about attempting to rebuild in their predominately Black neighborhoods because they believed White authority flooded those areas on purpose to force them out and would, therefore, never provide the assistance they needed to reconstruct their lives. A twenty-five-year-old Black woman formerly residing in the Lower Ninth Ward claims, "They cracked those levees. They knew what they were doing. And now I don't know what I'm going to do. My house is gone—how do I rebuild on $2,000?"[43] For this young woman, and many of her neighbors, their frustrations and their reticence to rebuild is informed by their conviction that the levees *were* intentionally destroyed, that New Orleans is a city that doesn't really want her kind.

CONCLUSION

In this chapter we have attempted to examine how race, rumor, and collective memory collided during and after Hurricane Katrina and how that collision helped define the catastrophe. To our minds, whether or not respective rumors are eventually legitimized as primarily factual or written off as mostly fictional is not the point. The point, rather, is that the chaos of Katrina was heightened by race-based speculation and that much can and should be learned by the negotiation of that speculation. For a number of our White interviewees, this dynamic often resulted in "othering" Blacks as menaces and as threats. This image of Blacks, especially Black men, has a long history—as long as the history of the country itself—and despite progress in race relations, that cultural narrative appears to still be well ingrained in the collective memory of the White community. For Blacks, rumors supporting the "need" to fear White authority quickly arose and despite relatively little attention from the media, remain on the minds of many Blacks in the area. The collective memory of victimization at the hands of White slaveholders, politicians, and law enforcement officials have shaped Black perspectives in the wake of Katrina.

These findings highlight the need for consideration—and possibly further investigation—of at least two points:

The mass media played a *major* role in propagating certain rumors and mitigating others, consequently presenting the concerns of the White community as both real and normative and once again neglecting the concerns of the Black community. We only addressed two of these rumors in any depth here; there were dozens of others. Speculative journalism is probably not going away anytime soon[44] but perhaps the type of race-based rumor-mongering we saw with Hurricane Katrina can be curtailed. If the journalists themselves are not going to demand a standard of evidence before reporting something as "news," it rests with us—the consumers, researchers, and politicians—to view news with an increasingly critical eye before relying on what is reported to make decisions.

Rumors and catastrophes, together, may provide a good litmus test so far for race relations in the United States. With Hurricane Katrina, we saw examples of tremendous cooperation but also of considerable tension and anxiety across racial lines. Crises strip away the illusions of politeness in which the post–Civil Rights era of "tolerance" has cloaked us, as a society. In a crisis, one rarely has the time, energy, or motivation to be polite. As a result, people who had convinced themselves and others that they held no preconceived assumptions about a race different from their own found themselves paying heed to, and propagating, racialized rumors. Rumors rely on deep-seated cultural narratives to survive; crises bring such raw narratives to the surface.[45] One of the stories of Hurricane Katrina, perhaps, is that our emphasis on tolerance has inadvertently lead us away from the difficult discussions that foster true understanding.

NOTES

1. We would like to thank the Natural Hazards Center and the Department of Sociology the University of Colorado at Boulder, for funding this research. Also, thanks to Kathleen Tierney, Tom Mayer, Polly McLean, and Elizabeth Skewes for your guidance, assistance, and support.

2. *Associated Press,* September 1, 2005.

3. For the purposes of this chapter, we are focusing primarily on the media coverage of, and rumors surrounding, Hurricane Katrina. However, the scope of our overall research into the crises affecting the Gulf Coast in the fall of 2005 includes examining Hurricane Rita.

4. The authors acknowledge that those directly impacted by Hurricane Katrina represent a multiplicity of races and ethnicities other than "Black" or "White." The purpose of this research, primarily, is to investigate Black-White relations during and after Katrina, and how those relations were impacted by the decisions of media organizations. However, we do not wish to imply that this was an event that impacted Blacks and Whites exclusively, or that the experiences and concerns of other racial and ethnic groups do not merit investigation.

5. Eduardo Bonilla-Silva, *Racism Without Racists: Color-Blind Racism and the Persistence of Racial Inequality in the United States* (Lanham, Md.: Rowman & Littlefield, 2003), 4–11.

6. Michael Eric Dyson, "Denying a racist past slows US policy," *The Age,* December 28, 2002, <http://www.theage.com.au/articles/2002/12/27/1040511174476.html>, (September 9, 2004).

7. David J. Jacobsen, *The Affairs of Dame Rumor* (New York: Rinehart, 1948), 64.

8. Terry Ann Knopf, *Rumors, Race and Riots* (New Brunswick, NJ: Transaction Publishers, 2006), 18–20.

9. Kenneth M. Stamp, ed. *The Causes of the Civil War* (Englewood Cliffs, NJ: Spectrum, 1961), 5.

10. Knopf, *Rumors, Race and Riots*, 33–44, 48–58.

11. Gary Alan Fine and Patricia A. Turner, *Whispers on the Color Line: Rumor and Race in America* (Berkeley: University of California Press, 2001), 50.

12. Charles J. Ogletree, *All Deliberate Speed* (New York: W.W. Norton & Company, 2004), 290–94.

13. Fine and Turner, *Whispers on the Color Line: Rumor and Race in America,* 11.

14. James Carey, "A Cultural Approach to Communication," *Communication* 2 (1975): 1–22.

15. Michael Eric Dyson, *Race Rules: Navigating the Color Line* (New York: Vintage/Random House, 1997), 111–15.

16. bell hooks, *Reel to Real: Race, Sex and Class at the Movies* (New York: Routledge, 1996), 69–76.

17. Donald Bogle, *Prime Time Blues: African Americans on Network Television* (New York: Farrar, Straus and Giroux, 2001), 32–41.

18. Herman Gray, *Watching Race: Television and the Struggle for Blackness* (Minneapolis: University of Minnesota Press, 1995), 73–79.

19. Vincent F. Rocchio, *Reel Racism: Confronting Hollywood's Construction of Afro-American Culture* (Boulder, CO: Westview, 2000), 23–25.

20. David R. Roediger, *Colored White: Transcending the Racial Past* (Berkeley: University of California Press, 2002), 56–67.

21. K. Sue Jewell, *From Mammy to Miss America and Beyond: Cultural Images and the Shaping of US Social Policy* (New York: 1993), 183–207.

22. Robert M. Entmann and Andrew Rojecki, *The Black Image in the White Mind: Media and Race in America* (Chicago: University of Chicago Press, 2000), 209.

23. Speculative journalism as a practice is not new. However, the acceptance of, and time (in television and radio) and space (in print and on the Internet) devoted to reporting composed primarily of speculation have reached new proportions. For a discussion of the changing news culture in the United States, see Richard Campbell, Christopher R. Martin, and Bettina Fabos, eds., *Media and Culture: An Introduction to Mass Communication* (Boston/Bedford: St. Martin's, 2005), 156.

24. Entmann and Rojecki, *The Black Image in the White Mind: Media and Race in America*, 81–84.

25. *Associated Press,* September 1, 2005.

26. Maureen Dowd, "United States of Shame," *The New York Times,* September 3, 2005.

27. Barry Glassner, *The Culture of Fear* (New York: Basic Books, 1999), 107–28.

28. Jean Baudrillard, *Jean Baudrillard, Selected Writings*, ed. Mark Poster (Stanford: Stanford University Press, 1988).

29. Susannah Rosenblatt and James Rainey, "Katrina Rumors," *Los Angeles Times,* September 27, 2005.

30. Aaron Kinney, "'Looting' or 'Finding'?" *Salon.com*, September 1, 2005, <http://dir.salon.com/story/news/feature/2005/09/01/photo_controversy/index.html> (September 7, 2006).

31. Glassner, *The Culture of Fear*, 107–28.

32. Glassner, *The Culture of Fear*, 107–28.

33. Chris Tinkler and Daryl Passmore, "Rape Threat to Our Women," *Sun Herald News*, September 4, 2005.

34. Rosenblatt and Rainey, "Katrina Rumors."

35. David Carr, "More Horrible than Truth: News Reports," *The New York Times,* September 19, 2005.

36. At the beginning of the interview, this respondent volunteered that his opinions are a little bigoted. He had seen the media reports of violence in the Superdome, the stadium where many evacuees fled immediately following Hurricane Katrina, and in the surrounding areas. Still, he appears to balance his understanding of race and the reports he had seen on TV with his first-hand experiences during the storm.

37. Knopf, *Rumors, Race and Riots*, 69.

38. Michael Eric Dyson, *Come Hell or High Water: Hurricane Katrina and the Color of Disaster* (New York: Basic Civitas Books, 2006), 196–97.

39. John M. Barry, *Rising Tide: The Great Mississippi Flood of 1927 and How it Changed America* (New York: Simon and Schuster, 1998), 412–22.

40. Dyson, *Come Hell or High Water*, 196.

41. Pete Daniel, *Deep'n as It Come: The 1927 Mississippi Flood* (New York: Oxford University Press, 1977).

42. The authors collected well over 100 storm-related articles from sources such as *The New York Times*, the *Los Angeles Times,* the *Times-Picayune* (New Orleans), *The Washington Post,* the *Houston Chronicle*, *Time* magazine, and *Newsweek* and also reviewed hours of coverage from CNN, Fox News, and MSNBC. From the coverage produced by these mainstream media organizations, we found very few reports regarding the contention that the levees were intentionally destroyed. For example, on September 12, 2005, the *Los Angeles Times* reported that Louis Farrakan had made allegations that the levees surrounding predominately Black, poor neighborhoods in New Orleans may have been blown up on purpose.

43. The respondent is referring to the initial "FEMA check" victims of Hurricane Katrina had been promised. It should be noted that as of the date of the interview, a full seven months after the storm, this respondent reported she had not yet received any government assistance.

44. Compbell et al., *Media and Culture*, 156.

45. Knopf, *Rumors, Race and Riots*, 149–51.

Chapter Three

Reframing Crime in a Disaster

Perception, Reality, and Criminalization of Survival Tactics among African Americans in the Aftermath of Katrina

Hillary Potter[1]

Hurricane Katrina resulted in desperate measures by displaced, debilitated, and distressed residents in the Gulf Coast. One such response by many residents to the destructive consequences of Katrina, particularly in the New Orleans area,[2] was their involvement in activities considered to be criminal in nature and defined as crime by legal policy. News media accounts described acts of looting and violence. The research presented in this chapter is based on the context of residents' involvement in criminal activity and their reactions to legal intervention for criminal acts immediately following a natural disaster. Of particular interest is how residents redefined what is "criminal" subsequent to this form of devastation, and considering their perceptions of the government's assistance with survival resources—such as food and water, temporary lodging, and medical attention—that may affect them reframing it as their right to endure as best they can, including looting stores to supply themselves with items necessary for their subsistence. A significant consideration in this analysis is the importance of racial identification and the way race shapes the life experiences of the individuals. These factors impacted African American survivors' perceptions of their actions and the responses by law enforcement officials and other emergency workers toward African Americans in the immediate aftermath of the storm and in the temporary sheltering of the evacuees.

Largely, the purpose of this study was to tease out the perpetuation of racially based stereotypes of African Americans as related to crime, particularly since the media perpetuate these stereotypes.[3] Indeed, prior research has found that perceptions of crime among the general public are highly shaped or produced by information fed by many forms of media.[4] Because of these representations, particularly in the aftermath of Katrina and during the ensuing chaos in New Orleans that was incessantly presented on television news programs and in news print photography, giving voice to the evacuees who found themselves engaging in behaviors that would typically be deemed illegal was another purpose of this project. Interviews were primarily exploratory in nature, but queries were geared toward the questions sought to be answered through this research. That is, (1) When faced with the devastation of a natural disaster, how is crime reframed, redefined, and restructured among those committing criminal acts? and (2) How are these behaviors and perceptions affected by the participants' race/ethnicity and socioeconomic statuses, and their perceptions of how government officials respond to them based on these categories?

The contribution of the present study will be on the impact of environmental factors and race-based typecasting affecting criminality, rates of crime, and the ensuing response of official agencies. As Young writes:

> We pretty much ignore the involvement of Whites in run-of-the-mill crimes and in white collar crimes. It is almost as though White offenders are homogenized. Their behavior is viewed less as crime and more as unfortunate deviance, something that everyone engages in from time to time. This is behavior that is not really worthy of vilification. The harm and costs are downplayed. Thus, the criminality of Whites is either ignored or associated with behaviors that are barely criminal whereas the criminality of Blacks and Black criminals become the crime problem.[5]

The present study adds not only to the research literature on mainstream crime-causation theories, but, more specifically, to a critical theory of crime causation and control. Critical theories on crime and criminal law (including feminist criminology, critical race theory, critical race feminist theory, and Black feminist criminology[6]) place the intersections of race, ethnicity, gender, and socioeconomic status at the center of any analysis on criminal activity and responses by crime-processing system representatives. Accordingly, this project significantly aids in strengthening this scarcity in the criminology research.

STUDY SETTING

The original proposed setting for conducting the interviews and engaging in observation in the immediate aftermath of Hurricane Katrina was the city of

New Orleans. It was imperative that this research was to be performed as soon as possible in order to capture residents' close to real-time engagement in committing legally offensive and restricted behaviors in the context of a major catastrophe. However, as the days multiplied after the storm arrived to the Gulf Coast, the majority of New Orleans residents had been evacuated and access was essentially restricted to government officials and others aiding in the relief efforts. As such, it was deemed that it was the people my research assistant and I wished to speak with, not the city we wished to see, so the setting was changed to Baton Rouge, where we would spend time at a shelter interviewing evacuees. By September 7, 2005, I had received approval from the human subjects research committee at the University of Colorado at Boulder and secured funding for the project from the Quick Response Program of the Natural Hazards Center at the University of Colorado at Boulder. These funds are made available by the National Science Foundation and provided for social and behavioral scientists to quickly enter the field to conduct research within days or weeks of a natural disaster. The main research setting, we visited during September 15–17, 2005, was at the Baton Rouge River Center, where a temporary shelter had been set up to house Katrina evacuees. During our visit we received various accounts of the number of residents in the makeshift shelter, which ranged between 1,500 and 1,800 inhabitants housed, who resided in two large open areas furnished with cots.

A qualitative approach to answer the research questions provided a framework for a more exploratory and in-depth examination of the subject. Data were gathered from interviews with shelter residents, most of whom had resided in New Orleans at the time of the storm, and through participant observation within and around the shelter. Respondents were located by my research assistant and me immersing ourselves in areas of the study site where survivors were congregated and "public" access was allowed. In general, a "cold-calling" method was used, where individuals were approached in communal areas, engaged in a conversation about survival skills and/or criminal activity in light of the disaster, and ultimately asked if they would be interested in participating in a study on the subject. When potential interviewees agreed to be participants in the study, they were assured of (a) their anonymity, (b) that no identifying data were recorded, and (c) that only demographic information was documented. Using this format also allowed a speedy approval from the human subjects research committee, as it was important for us to enter the field as soon as possible. Thirty-six interviews were completed with adult (at least eighteen years old) evacuees. Of these, about two-thirds ($n = 23$) were African American men. Another two participants were African American women. The remainder of the sample was White, Latino, or Pacific Islander, which included five women and six men. Interestingly, I personally interviewed seventeen of the twenty-three Black men. While I approached seven of these men, the remaining ten interviewees approached me. Oftentimes, they approached to inquire who I was and what I was doing, since the other residents of the shelter and the shelter volunteers were recognizable to these men as *belonging* in the shelter. This chapter analyzes only the interviews conducted with the twenty-three African American men and the two African American women.

FINDINGS

Prior to the devastation caused by Katrina, many of the respondents considered their position in U.S. society as one that is situated at the lower ranks of the social hierarchy. They believed their life chances of being African Americans and *poor* African Americans positioned them to be unimportant, devalued, or undervalued, and a burden to society (particularly when in need of government assistance in the form of finances and housing). Respondents regularly shared stories of the racism they have experienced and witnessed throughout their lives. A thirty-seven-year-old male participant stated, "Chances are limited because of skin color. . . Whites over Blacks." Similarly, a forty-eight-year-old male respondent shared his take on racism when asked, "Do you think people in New Orleans were treated differently because of race or skin tone before the hurricane?" He responded with a disdainful comment because of the seeming ignorance of my comment: "You know it's a racist town! . . . They don't want us niggas around their neighborhoods."

The respondents in this study believed that because of their position in society as African Americans, the feeling that they are not supported and trusted by others (i.e., Whites) in society, and their inability to leave New Orleans after the effects of Katrina ravished the city, that they were left to care for themselves using any means necessary. A thirty-five-year-old respondent spoke of the desperation she witnessed among New Orleans residents, recounting that "as soon as they dropped food from the helicopters, people were snatching it up and not leaving any for anyone else." Accordingly, the respondents did indeed reframe acts of "looting" as *lawful*. As was evident in news media reports concerning these acts, individuals and groups seemed to rest on one of two sides of the debate about the utility of the looting that took place in the aftermath of Katrina, and may have further qualified their assessment of the acts by deeming what was allowed to be taken (e.g., food and water) and what was not allowed to be taken (e.g., guns and luxury items such as televisions and stereos). A twenty-six-year-old male eloquently summarized the schism among the U.S. citizenry regarding the subject of culpability for local, state, and federal governments and survivors ensnared in the hurricane-ravaged city of New Orleans:

> But like I told you, it's a give and go situation. It's a thin line between good and bad. Some people look at the government as the bad guys, some people look at the government as the good guys. Some people look at the pillagers as the bad guys, and some people look at the pillagers as the good guys. It depends on what side of the fence you are standing on.

One respondent, a thirty-five-year-old female, expressed her feelings during the rescue efforts of those trapped in New Orleans: "I felt like an outcast in the Convention Center and in the Superdome. When we went to the shelter in Cleborn, Texas, I finally felt like an American, like a citizen." Though the respondents in this study had been rescued or escaped from New Orleans and were being housed in the Baton Rouge shelter, they continued to face the burden of their racial status. Much of this was based on the rumors that emanated in the days following Katrina's landfall and the existing, pre-Katrina stereotypes about African Americans, particularly that of the fallacy of the "criminalblackman."[7] As Rome writes, "Mass media have played and will continue to play a crucial role in the way white Americans perceive African Americans. As a result of the overwhelming media focus on crime, drug use, gang violence, and other forms of anti-social behavior among African Americans, the media have fostered distorted and insidious public perceptions of African Americans."[8] Such beliefs that easily lead many to view "criminal" simultaneously with "African American man," seemingly affected the procedures and management of the temporary shelter.

For each of the aforementioned concerns, I provide a look into (a) the respondents' perceptions of official response by government agencies and agents to provide assistance, (b) the respondents' descriptions and reflections on the so-called illegal acts that took place after Katrina passed, and (c) the management of the shelter at the Baton Rouge River Center and the respondents' insights about their treatment.

Perceptions of Official Response to Assist

Many of the respondents believed the local, state, and federal government officials and the relevant agencies could have been swifter and more prudent in their response to assisting those who remained in New Orleans during and after Katrina (whether by choice, by circumstance, or by incapability). This is evident in a sampling of several of the respondents' reflections on their experiences of being in New Orleans after the storm:

> They responded terribly.

> They just left them [*sic*] there to die.

> It was a slow response.

> It was like a Third World country.

> I felt like some kind of cannibal. They lied and were arguing instead of saving people.

> They wasn't there. We didn't have no security.

> It reminded me of the old days when there was no law, no order . . . At the Superdome the police were afraid to come to the crowd.

Further, the respondents were asked about the police response specifically and in reference to their trust of law enforcement officials before and after Katrina. Three male interviewees responded with the following:

> *Never* trusted them. When I was a little boy I used to kick them!

> I didn't trust the police much before. . . that hasn't changed.

> No, I don't trust those fuckers!

A debate among politicians, stakeholders, academicians, and laypeople attempted to promote that the assistance, or lack thereof, afforded to individuals trapped in New Orleans was either color-blind or racist. The color-blind outlook makes the assumption that any paucity in government agencies aiding people with few means to leave the city prior to Katrina's wrath was due simply to government incompetence or lack of compassion, not to any blatant racially biased agenda that intimated that African Americans (the majority of the city's population at the time of Katrina) should be left in the city to perish because of White government officials' prejudices. Whether or not any government inaction was influenced by racist ideology, what is clear is that many of the respondents believed slow or poor official response to be racially motivated. A fifty-four-year-old male participant stated because of the large number of Blacks in the city at the time Katrina hit, "I think that's why they were slow to respond. If it was 70 percent White, they would have responded quicker." One of the other respondents, a thirty-five-year-old woman, reflected, "We have fifty states and every one [of the evacuees] should be placed right now. We don't have to live like this. But since we are Black and poor White trash, they forget about us." In ruminating about the issues of racism in the United States and the official response to Black residents of New Orleans, a fifty-five-year-old male respondent declared, "I done seen a lot of that [racism] in my life. I'm not really surprised [they didn't respond sooner]. That's what we get for being who we are. When this dies down, we will still be Black."

The Acts

The descriptions of the acts that would generally be considered illegal and criminal varied from collecting food, water, dry and clean clothes, and baby diapers (that is, items considered to be essential for survival) to taking items such as liquor, cigarettes, and electronics (that is, items often deemed as *non*essential). A thirty-five-year-old woman described her experiences with securing merchandise: "We had to break into the Riverwalk[9] to get ice and water, to get shoes, to get clothes, to get socks. We had to broke [*sic*] into Bath and Body Works and took soap." As can be gleaned from this respondent's use of the phrase "had to," the language used by the evacuees aided in leading them to reframe and justify their acts. Interestingly, a couple participants referred to their behaviors in a manner that would be indicative of running errands on an ordinary day, as demonstrated by a fifty-four-year-old male respondent when he replied, "I went to pick up some stuff."

In addition, respondents and other survivors they spoke of either engaged in breaking into and entering a store to secure goods—like the aforementioned account—or entering a store after it had already been breached. For example, a thirty-seven-year-old male reported, "There was a bunch of us [survivors] and the police broke into Wal-Mart and said, 'Go get what you want.'" A similar story of police assistance in securing food was relayed by a forty-seven-year-old man:

> People were dying of thirst. Drinking hot beer. Drinking hot water. With no generator, no power, no water, no electricity . . . the food was spoiling. The police was letting them in to get what they want. Shopping carts full, buggies full of liquor, cigarettes, drugs, pharmacies [*sic*], cold medicine. They didn't give a fuck. Whatever a person needed, they went in and take it. 'Cause they didn't care.

One participant tells the story of crossing paths with a neighbor in the chaos of the aftermath of Katrina. When the participant asked his neighbor which stores were open for business the neighbor replied, "*All* the stores are open!" In another instance, a fifty-year-old female respondent spoke of a store owner's generosity: "They had one decent man that opened up his store and told them to take whatever they want. 'Go ahead and take what you want.' The meat was no good then, after three days. The only thing I had gotten from there was water. I already had canned goods at home." This respondent believed that all the stores in the area should have employed such benevolence.

Limitations on Behaviors

As previously described, some respondents physically broke into stores, while others entered stores that had already been broken into or otherwise opened (for instance, doors and windows unsealed or broken by the force of the flood waters). However, a few respondents deliberately entered only those stores that were already accessible, as reported by a forty-eight-year-old male evacuee: "I didn't break into the stores. That's for them young fools."

While some of the respondents seized the opportunity to have items they lost because of the flooding or merchandise they could not otherwise afford (that is, "luxury" items), many respondents placed limitations on the materials they acquired. This is evident in the statement, "I didn't take beer, liquor, stereo equipment" (fifty-four-year-old male) and this twenty-six-year-old man's description of the behaviors among others:

> Some people were breaking in stores because they needed it. . .They needed water. They needed some food to eat. . .[But] some people wasn't even taking food, wasn't even taking stuff that they could survive off of. They taking cigarettes. They taking DVDs. What the hell you going to do with a DVD?

Some of these respondents were clearly bothered by the behaviors of other survivors and believed everyone should be limiting the types of items taken or, as depicted in the following account, limiting the number of items taken: "People turned into scavengers. Another lady had a young baby and we tried to steal him some Pampers[10] but couldn't. People should only take one and leave some for others. But people were walking out with their arms full."

Justification for Behaviors

Even though there was variance among the sample regarding what should or should not have been taken, as expected, a common theme among respondents regarding the otherwise illegal behavior of "stealing" or "looting" was that these behaviors were reframed as *survival tactics*. A sampling of the comments to the question (or similar question), "Why did you do what you did?" were:

> How was I to survive?

> Basically, we did what we needed to do.

> Even though there was dumb, ignorancy [*sic*], that was a survival issue.

I saw it as a survival tactic. We were desperate people.

I try to be a law-abiding citizen, obey the laws. I didn't like it . . . It was wrong, but I had to survive.

People was left without a choice. [The government] didn't care. Women with babies. . .what were they supposed to do?

The act of police officers breaking into stores and otherwise aiding New Orleans residents in attaining sustenance—as illustrated previously—only further justified the respondents' actions, as depicted in a twenty-seven-year-old male respondent's comment, "I don't consider them looters. You gonna throw it out anyway. I call it borrowing or helping in a time of need. If the police were stealin' how they gonna say we're looters?"

A twenty-six-year-old male participant elaborated on this concept of committing classically unlawful acts because of desperation by providing scenarios in his response:

Just because a person was stealing this and doing that and getting all this stuff, doesn't mean that they wasn't out there helping somebody . . . Some people didn't have no family outside of New Orleans. Some people didn't have no people to check on them. Some of the elderly didn't have nobody to check on them. You know if your family don't know the means to get in contact with somebody—with 25 million, 25 thousand, 50 thousand trying to get in touch with a person; so you're on hold and you can't get through—what would you do? Would you steal a car and go get your family member? Or would you sit there and say, "Well, I'm not going to steal this car 'cause it's a bad thing and I want to do the right thing. And it's a bad thing to steal this car, but ain't nobody around, and I see these keys and I know where they are at, and I know I can get to them and I know it got a full tank of gas. And I know the water ain't too too bad where my family member is. I know that I could get through there"? So what kind of decision do I make as a person, as a human being, trying to keep my morals? Do I keep my morals and stick to my guns? Or do I put it in my own hands and is that God making the way?

Undoubtedly, many respondents demonstrated or outwardly expressed remorse for their actions. This thirty-five-year-old female spoke of her feelings concerning the acts she committed in the pandemonium that ensued from Katrina:

I feel degraded. It's nothing to be proud of but I had to survive. It was either that or die. It was either that or be funky. I didn't want to be in those wet, damp clothes all day. I really don't feel good about it at all. And in the future, if I could, I would pay back every last penny for the stuff I took . . . Those were the choices we had. Those were the options we had. We had to go in Winn-Dixie and steal food to eat. We had to steal food so we could eat, like those in Iraq who are fighting for freedom.

Shelter Treatment

An unanticipated finding of this study was the way in which the temporary shelter was being operated and the resulting effect on the evacuees being housed there. Housing a large number of people in only two large sleeping areas of a facility not intentionally designed for sheltering people in need may indeed warrant security. This is evident in the thirty-five-year-old woman's response that "You don't know who is sleeping next to you. It's hard to live like that." However, the level of safety measures and the inconsistency in who faced security screening inclined me and the residents to believe these operations were likely based on racially-motivated biases. A forty-eight-year-old male participant reasoned, "It's racist in the way they sheltered us. I saw on the news Whites with barbeques. [In here,] it's the White trash of the White folks who got caught up because they were in a poor neighborhood." In particular, these biases were likely generated from the inordinate number of rumors spread after Katrina (many of which were later found to be untrue[11]) and the pre-existing stereotype of African Americans as a group to fear because of their violent and otherwise criminal tendencies.

Safety Measures

Entrance into the shelter was gained through one door, located at the front of the Baton Rouge River Center. The entrances were controlled by National Guard soldiers, most of whom were men. Each entrant was to pass through a free-standing metal detector and had to have her or his bags physically searched by a National Guard soldier. If an individual continued to trigger the metal detector, she or he was scanned with a hand-held metal detector to deem the entrant was not carrying anything that would be harmful to those inside the shelter (that is, contraband). Each of the National Guard members was armed with a rifle, which connected to a strap and draped over his or her chest or back, and a handgun, which was stored in a hip holster. Many of the respondents spoke of the National Guard's presence at the shelter without prompting, while others were asked questions such as, "Why is the National Guard here?" A forty-eight-year-old male respondent simply replied to this question with, "They here for us niggas!" This was the general sentiment among the African American respondents, that the Guard was there to maintain control over Black evacuees, many from New Orleans.

The secure measures in place affected the speed of being able to enter the facility. As it was a non-smoking building, residents had to leave the enclosed area to smoke cigarettes, but typically had difficulty withstanding the high temperatures outside; therefore there was a lot of movement in and out of the center. Several respondents commented, with disdain, on this process, including the fifty-year-old female respondent:

> Black refugees wait in line day in and day out. Look at the line. I think everyone should just go in. What do you need to be searched for every day? You know the people coming in there everyday. We ain't got not weapons, we ain't got no guns. It don't make no sense. The line is way down the street. You can spend the whole night waiting in line. . . Everybody going in the shelter. The same people come out, the same people coming in—except the people coming in on the bus [who haven't been here all day]. I don't understand that. If they've been there [in the shelter] they have tags[12] on; let them on in.

This same respondent was bothered by the restrictions placed on the items that could be taken into the facility, including the prohibition of alcohol, drugs, and cameras. She stated, "They don't want people to take pictures to see how it really is and what's going on. I have a camera in the car." During our time at the shelter, a large number of news media representatives were present. In reference to a photojournalist taking pictures prior to a presidential address,[13] the respondent continued, "See that lady? See! [And] they make me keep [my camera] in the car."

Another set of National Guard soldiers patrolled the perimeter of the building, carrying rifles in front of them, as opposed to the soldiers at the entrance check-in, who hung their rifles on their backs. Between these patrolling soldiers and those inside the entrance to the building, several of the respondents commented on the level of weaponry, the way it made the residents feel, and the implications of such a stance by the National Guard:

> I'm kind of nervous that the National Guard are around with AK-47s. And they wonder how kids get exposed to guns!

> They don't need to have M16s with children all around here.

> If [the National Guard] can't control [the shelter and the evacuees], they are going to start shooting. They don't have to have the big shotguns. They don't have to be standing in there with them. What, them telling me I'm violent? If they were really going to protect us, they should have this whole place surrounded. I come to the door and I'm greeted with a shotgun . . . It's just the guns that throw the whole thing off. Instead of them guarding the facility, they are ready to shoot anytime.

Assistance by Way of Captivity

An extension of the comments shared in the previous section highlights the multiple references to the shelter feeling as though it was a jail or prison as opposed to a place to assist law-abiding citizens who had been displaced from their homes due to a natural disaster. Comparisons made between criminal incarceration and disaster relief sheltering were based on personal experiences of the respondents having served time in prison and/or jail or on what they believed jail or prison life was like.

> It reminds me of being in jail . . . people walking around with the guns.

> It's like I'm back in jail all over again.

> We may be refugees, but we're not prisoners. We may be homeless, but we're not prisoners.

> Red Cross got beaucoup [a lot of] money. But we don't get three hot meals in here a day. You get three hot meals in a penitentiary. You get three hot meals in a jail. Why not here? And you're free.

The fifty-year-old female respondent continued on from her comments about the use of weapons by the National Guard monitoring the facility by, like the respondents' comments above, equating their operations with prison life:

> People are getting frustrated and tired . . . I think [the National Guard] are trying to see if anybody has drugs on them. Let [the residents] in; I don't understand that. Why should you go through the same thing everyday that you've been here? . . . We don't have no weapons on us. I don't have no weapons on me. We are not prisoners, but they are treating us like prisoners. Just because we're homeless, don't treat us like prisoners.

CONCLUSION

This chapter analyzed in-depth interviews conducted with Katrina evacuees and observations made at the Baton Rouge River Center approximately two weeks after the disaster. It offered evidence for the argument that New Orleans residents' survival tactics and the government's methods in aiding the evacuees were laden with racialized biases and stereotypes. These perceptions indisputably led to the unremitting criminalization of many African American evacuees. Admittedly, though many New Orleans survivors may have been engaged in acts that would generally be deemed illegal, this chapter argued that it is imperative to judiciously consider the types of acts and motivations for committing them (e.g., survival).

Getting individuals to disclose their involvement in criminal activity, especially acts that would not otherwise likely be discovered by police, is generally a difficult task. However, as witnessed by television news video clips on criminal activity (e.g., looting) engaged in by Katrina survivors, the rampant involvement in such activity among scores of people had, at least for the time being, ostensibly *standardized* the conduct. This may have enabled respondents to be more forthright about their so-called unlawful involvement than would otherwise be possible.

Indeed, there was alternative labeling of the "criminal activity" participated in by the respondents or by those they witnessed participating in these behaviors. As looting activities were continuously replayed in news outlets, African Americans were typecast as "criminal" and treated accordingly when they arrived at some shelters. Undoubtedly, these conditions are based on the life chances afforded African Americans in the United States. As Fishman argues, "We need to think seriously about the reality of life in America—a reality in which race strongly interjects itself into the images that whites and blacks hold of one another. In turn, race accentuates the sting of everyday oppression, as well as the sting of the oppression that colors the criminal justice system's differential treatment of blacks."[14]

Perceptions *are* important both for *and* about African Americans. Without a doubt, there are crime-related stereotypes when considering Black people and the poor. Rome suggests that "stereotyping African Americans as criminals feeds into denials of racism, with the parallel assumption that any problems faced by African Americans (or Hispanic Americans, American Indians, or Asian Americans) are their own fault."[15] The perpetuation of racial stereotypes often affects assistance afforded African Americans, whether it is in a natural disaster or in daily life in the United States.

Certainly, because of the impact of the disaster, emergency workers, including law enforcement officials, were confronted with a lack of resources and workforce to deal with crime, while simultaneously dealing with the effects of the disaster. However, among many New Orleans African American survivors of Katrina, there was a continued distrust of the police and criminal justice practices, which was evident prior to Katrina and was confirmed and exacerbated by police officer inaction and *their* (the officers') "survival tactics" during and after the storm. Further, respondents in the study also demonstrated the continued distrust by many African Americans of the government's desire to assist poor, Black people, and a continued distrust that (White) society's (pessimistic) beliefs about Black people will change.

Recommendations made to improve disaster policy should center on how to manage criminal activity in the aftermath as based on the offenders' perceptions of law enforcement intervention, their motivations for engaging in such behavior, and the nature and extent of the types of criminal activity more likely to be engaged in after a disaster. The practical benefits of the outcome of this study insist that aid by government entities must more adequately address crime-related acts following disastrous events. As with other disaster relief efforts, and what has already been advised by many, contingency plans must be in place to assist with evacuating individuals with few means to leave the area expected to be affected. By confronting this issue beforehand, much of the problem of "looting" and other criminal activity in the aftermath of a natural disaster will be immaterial. Effectively evacuating those (or at least a good portion of those) in impending danger will eliminate the *need* for individuals to resort to any means necessary to survive.

In the assistance provided to survivors in the aftermath of natural disasters, deferring to sociological implications is imperative. Disaster relief agents and agencies must necessarily take into account the stratified cultural, racial, and structural society in which we live within the United States. Seriously taking such heterogeneity and inequality into consideration should aid in the development and implementation of policies that are not focused on longstanding racialized and classed stereotypes and rumors.

NOTES

1. This chapter is based on a study, "Reframing Crime: Race, Gender, Class, Criminality, and Enforcement of Laws in a Natural Disaster," funded by the Natural Hazards Center, Institute of Behavioral Sciences, University of Colorado at Boulder, with funds contributed by the National Science Foundation.

2. While similar acts took place in other cities, like in Biloxi, Mississippi, the majority of the news media reports focused on the deviant behaviors of New Orleans residents.

3. Laura T. Fishman, "The Black Bogeyman and White Self-Righteousness," in *Images of Color, Images of Crime: Readings*, 3rd ed., eds. Coramae Richey Mann, Marjorie S. Zatz, and Nancy Rodriguez (Los Angeles: Roxbury Publishing Company, 2006), 197–211.

4. Dennis M. Rome, "The Social Construction of the African American Criminal Stereotype," in *Images of Color, Images of Crime: Readings*, eds. Coramae Richey Mann, Marjorie S. Zatz, and Nancy Rodriguez, 3rd ed. (Los Angeles: Roxbury Publishing Company, 2006), 83.

5. Vernetta Young, "Demythologizing the 'Criminalblackman': The Carnival Mirror," in *The Many Colors of Crime: Inequalities of Race, Ethnicity, and Crime in America*, eds. Ruth D. Peterson, Lauren J. Krivo, and John Hagan (New York: New York University Press, 2006), 65.

6. For an overview of Black feminist criminology, in particular, see "An Argument for Black Feminist Criminology: Understanding African American Women's Experi-

ences with Intimate Partner Abuse Using an Integrated Approach," *Feminist Criminology* 1, no. 2 (April 2006): 106–24.

7. Katheryn Russell, *The Color of Crime: Racial Hoaxes, White Fear, Black Protectionism, Police Harassment, and Other Microaggressions* (New York: New York University Press, 1998).

8. Rome, "The Social Construction of the African American Criminal Stereotype," 78.

9. The Riverwalk Marketplace is a shopping and dining center connected to the convention center.

10. A general term used for diapers is referring to this specific diaper brand name.

11. Susannah Rosenblatt and James Rainey, "Katrina Rumors," *Los Angeles Times*, September 27, 2005.

12. Each evacuee resident of the shelter was fitted with a brightly-colored wristband, used to identify those being serviced in the shelter.

13. An increased number of reporters and photographers were at the shelter before, during, and after President George W. Bush's televised address from New Orleans on the evening of September 15, 2005.

14. Fishman, "The Black Bogeyman and White Self-Righteousness," 208.

15. Rome, "The Social Construction of the African American Criminal Stereotype," 85.

Chapter Four

Cultural Differences in Perceptions of the Government and the Legal System

Hurricane Katrina Highlights What Has Been There All Along

Meera Adya[1]
Monica K. Miller
Julie A. Singer
Rebecca M. Thomas
Joshua B. Padilla

Perceptions of the government's response to Hurricane Katrina, as demonstrated by national surveys and public responses to the disaster, illustrate differences in the way members of minority groups view law enforcement and governmental actions as compared to members of the majority group.[2] The finding that minorities perceived the government's response in a much more negative light than Caucasians suggests that cultural differences are important in shaping perceptions and are worthy of research. This paper examines the varying expectations, perceptions, and beliefs that different cultural groups in the United States have toward the government and legal system and explores the implications for policy and future research.

The reactions to Hurricane Katrina highlight cultural differences in perceptions of the government and legal system; however, such disparate perceptions are a result of years of perceived cultural inequities in the legal system. These perceptions, unfortunately, are based on actual inequalities in the legal system. For instance, research has indicated that minorities, especially African Americans, are more often targeted for the death penalty than Caucasians[3] and often receive harsher punishment for minor felonies and misdemeanors.[4] Further, there are incidents in which minorities are sometimes unfairly excluded from jury duty.[5] Not surprisingly, public perceptions suggest that minorities do not receive fair treatment within the court system,[6] and it is believed that members of minority groups are unlikely to have equal access to the court system.[7] The government has also treated minority citizens poorly, through policies such as racial profiling[8] and using minorities as participants in studies of sexually transmitted diseases.[9] Finally, police officers have been accused of using excessive force against minorities in some high-profile cases such as the Rodney King case.[10] Given that there is a history of racial inequality throughout the legal system, it is not difficult to imagine or understand why different cultural groups would hold different views of the government and legal system. However, because beliefs about the justice system affect one's willingness to participate in the legal system (e.g., serve as jurors or report crimes to police), it is essential that researchers and policymakers enhance their understanding of cultural differences in perceptions and find ways to address perceived inequities. The analysis of the existing research will elucidate continuing differences in perceptions of governmental actors and should stimulate future research aimed at designing interventions that help minorities more effectively participate in the justice system in the United States.

To situate the discussion of culture and the legal system in current affairs, the first part of this chapter will explore the cultural differences in reactions to governmental response in the aftermath of Hurricane Katrina. The next section will review general conceptions of cultural differences in order to establish a foundation for a review of the literature. We then review the research literature on each of the three most commonly studied cultural groups in the United States (i.e., African Americans, Hispanics, and Asians) concerning cultural difference in perceptions of the legal system (e.g., courts and law enforcement). We follow with a look to the future by presenting policy recommendations and issues for future research based on the reviewed research. The chapter concludes that different cultural backgrounds can account for differences in perceptions of the legal system, which in turn present implications for legal participation, equal access, and justice.

HURRICANE KATRINA:
A CASE STUDY IN CULTURAL DIFFERENCES

Much of the discourse in the aftermath of Hurricane Katrina centered on the governmental response to the total devastation of New Orleans.[11] There has been significant dissatisfaction with the government's response, but African Americans across the country have had stronger reactions to the disaster in New Orleans and the Gulf Coast than have Caucasians.[12] African Americans appear more connected to what has happened, likely because many African Americans have family that currently live in the South or come from the South.[13] In fact, African Americans are almost twice as likely as Caucasians (43 percent vs. 22 percent) to say they personally know someone directly affected.[14] The disparate emotional impact is also clear: African Americans are much more likely than Caucasians to report feeling depressed and angry because of what has happened in hurricane-affected areas.[15] African Americans perceive the victims of the disaster and their plight differently than Caucasians do, and make harsher judgments of the federal government's response.[16] According to Sociologist Darnell M. Hunt of the University of California, Los Angeles's African American Studies department, finding an event in American history that has affected African Americans as Katrina has would require going back to slavery or the burning of African American towns.[17] Furthermore, the images of large numbers of African Americans being neglected and suffering in filth appear to tap into the personal experiences of injustice familiar to most African American people in society.[18]

In the week following the hurricane and flooding, African American public figures as diverse as the Rev. Jesse Jackson[19] and R & B singer Kanye West[20] expressed their views that race played a role in the response of the government to the devastation. Some African American leaders, however, were reluctant to cite race as a reason for delayed or inadequate government response, instead citing social class as the issue.[21] The African American Caucus of the United States Senate, the African American Leadership Forum, the National Urban League, and the National Association for the Advancement of Colored People (NAACP) jointly charged that the inadequate response was because most of the affected were poor.[22] Although class is the issue these organizations choose to focus on, it was clear that the vast majority of those poor were also non-Caucasians.

In the aftermath of the hurricane, many wealthy African Americans rallied to help victims, but again their actions and advice demonstrated a different perception of how that help should be dispensed.[23] Hip-hop performer Timbaland urged well-off African Americans to "take your money and do your own thing" rather than giving to relief organizations because "who knows where that money's going."[24] Such responses demonstrate the African American community's dissatisfaction with the relief efforts.

To illustrate the racial differences in perceptions of the governmental response to the hurricane, two independent polls were conducted by *USA Today/CNN/Gallup*[25] and the Pew Research Center for the People and The Press.[26] In the Pew poll, 85 percent of African Americans felt President Bush could have done more to get relief efforts moving, while only 63 percent of Caucasians felt the same.[27] Both studies found that more than six in ten African Americans believe that the slow response to the hurricane was because the vast majority of victims were poor and African American.[28] On the other hand, nine out of ten non-Hispanic whites believe neither race nor poverty were factors in the government's response.[29] African Americans also hold more sympathetic attitudes toward the people who became stranded by the flooding in New Orleans.[30] When asked who is responsible for people being trapped in New Orleans, African Americans hold the federal government accountable more than Caucasians, while Caucasians give the most responsibility to the residents themselves.[31] In addition, Caucasians have much harsher attitudes toward people who took things from homes or businesses after the hurricane, as Caucasians were more likely to characterize these behaviors as criminal.[32]

The crisis in New Orleans, sparked by a natural disaster of staggering proportions, highlighted racial differences in attitudes and perceptions of the government and justice system; however, many of these differences were pre-existing. Further, it is important to realize that more frequently occurring events such as victimization by crime contribute to racial differences in attitudes and perceptions of the criminal justice system and subsequent differential access to services and participation. A great deal of research, discussed throughout this chapter, reveals a host of cultural differences in perceptions and attitudes. It is essential to understand these differences if policymakers are to minimize inequities and promote justice for all citizens.

CULTURAL DIFFERENCES GENERALLY

A person's perception of the world is heavily influenced by their culture, traditions, and customs passed on from their heritage.[33] There are two primary ways in which cultures are conceptualized. One way is to make a distinction between individualistic and collectivist cultures.[34] In individualistic cultures such as the United States, people are concerned with individual accomplishment and personal accountability.[35] In contrast, people in collectivistic cultures such as China, are more concerned with group accomplishments (e.g., family success) and cohesion.[36]

The other way in which culture is conceptualized is by using the term "culture" as a synonym for race. This is because of the current acknowledgment by many scientists that race does not exist as a biological category, and is a social construction used to categorize people of different backgrounds.[37] The goal of this chapter is to examine literature that illustrates how different backgrounds or cultures lead to a difference in attitudes that affect how members of different cultures perceive and interact with the law.

CULTURAL DIFFERENCES IN
PERCEPTIONS OF THE LEGAL SYSTEM

The way in which people perceive the law (e.g., judges, lawyers, law enforcement) influences the way they interact with the system.[38] Because the courts and legal authorities have traditionally been considered "White" institutions, members of ethnic groups have developed different attitudes toward the law than have Caucasians.[39] Researchers have investigated and established these differences among three of the primary ethnic groups: African Americans, Hispanics, and Asian Americans.[40]

Studies Involving African Americans

African Americans' perceptions of the law and legal authorities have been well researched over the past four decades.[41] Several important distinctions in perceptions between African Americans and Caucasians have been found.[42] These differences have the potential to severely impact how African Americans perceive and react toward the courts and law enforcement officials.[43] What follows is an overview of literature that has found that African Americans in general have less favorable perceptions of the police and the courts than Caucasians.

Police

Research investigating the differences between African Americans and Caucasians concerning perceptions of the police has focused on three primary areas, (a) general perceptions of the police,[44] (b) police use of lethal force,[45] and (c) police misconduct.[46] In each of these domains African Americans consistently have less favorable views of the police.[47] Research investigating differences within the African American community has produced some interesting insights into the underlying factors that drive these attitudes.[48]

Several studies have consistently found that African Americans have less favorable views than Caucasians of the police in general.[49] Researchers analyzing a CNN/*USA Today*/Gallop Race Relations Survey and the NBC News/*The Wall Street Journal* Survey in 1998 found that African Americans are more likely than Caucasians to perceive racial disparities in policing, with African Americans feeling as though they are the targets of the police.[50] These anecdotal findings are complemented by experimental laboratory research. For example, one study recreated scenes of an officer giving someone a traffic ticket. In some scenes the officer was Caucasian, while in other scenes, the officer was a minority. Similarly, the race of the violator was also manipulated.[51] The results revealed that, regardless of the police officer's ethnicity, African Americans rated the police less positively than Caucasians.[52]

To get an idea of how African Americans compare the police to other social institutions, researchers have asked survey respondents to rank the favorability of fifteen different institutions: the U.S. FBI, local police, AMA, Congress, Supreme Court, the press, CIA, NAM, AFL-CIO, CORE, NAACP,

ACLU, Russia, John Birch Society, and the Ku Klux Klan.[53] African American respondents between the ages of eighteen to thirty-four, and those older than fifty years of age rated the local police twelfth and eleventh respectively, indicating that respondents did not have favorable impressions of their local police.[54] These studies are in line with countless replications, which consistently find that African Americans have unfavorable views of the police.[55] As such, researchers have expanded their focus to examine how specific acts of policing influence these negative attitudes.

One of the specific behaviors of interest lies in the differences between African Americans and Caucasians in justifying police use of force. Research has found that African Americans are less likely than Caucasians to endorse the use of deadly force for both violent and nonviolent suspects who were fleeing the scene.[56] Similarly, an analysis of the 1994 General Social Survey found that African Americans were 73.3 percent less likely to believe that there were any reasons to justify police use of force.[57] When socioeconomic status of the respondent was included in their analysis, it was found that there are differences within the African American community in their support of police use of force.[58] The exact reason why individuals of lower socioeconomic status (hereafter, "SES") from both ethnicities harbor unfavorable views of police use of force was not investigated in this study. However, research yet to be discussed[59] suggests that contact with the police plays a significant role in shaping attitudes. However, as for the current discussion on African American's perceptions of police use of force, the research cited above highlights how African Americans are less likely than Caucasians of similar status to support police use of force, even when controlling for socioeconomic factors.

Another specific area in which research shows a difference in perception between African Americans and Caucasians is perceptions of police misconduct. For example, researchers have compared the perceptions of police misconduct of several ethnicities and found that African Americans are the most likely American minority to believe that police misconduct occurs[60] and to believe that they are frequent targets.[61] Similarly, earlier research found that African Americans are more likely than Caucasians to report personal experiences with discriminatory police mistreatment.[62] The researchers examined the influence of personal contact in an attempt to explain why African Americans have less favorable views of the police than the Caucasians.[63] The study found that people of lower SES report significantly more contact with the police than middle-class people, leading the researchers to conclude that the more negative views of African Americans of lower SES can in part be explained by increased contact with police.[64] Further analysis of this "contact hypothesis" will be discussed later.

The Courts

Research investigating the differences between African Americans' and Caucasians' perceptions of the court system has focused primarily on (a) general perceptions of the court system,[65] (b) the racial dynamics of juries,[66] and (c) attitudes about capital punishment.[67] Just as with law enforcement, research has found that African Americans have less favorable views of the legal system, influencing them to be skeptical of the courts.[68]

Research has consistently found that African Americans have unfavorable views of the courts. For example, a recent study found that African Americans are less likely than Caucasians to believe the Mississippi state judiciary is fair.[69] In addition, research examining how race and SES influence perceptions of the United States court system found that middle-class African Americans are the group most concerned with fair treatment and equality in the courts.[70] This can be seen in research looking at cultural variability in assigning attributions to deviant behavior.[71] This research examined how African Americans judge fairness of the legal system.[72] While past studies conducted with Caucasians found that this group tends to focus their judgments of fairness based on the intent of the criminal, the more recent study conducted with African Americans found that this group was likely to focus their judgment on environmental factors to explain bad behavior.[73] These studies illustrate a general skepticism among African Americans about the fairness of the U.S. legal system. Each of these studies found that African Americans have more negative views of the courts as compared to other ethnic groups[74] as well as the general public.[75]

This skepticism of the courts is also related to African Americans' willingness and ability to participate in juries.[76] Researchers examining jury composition found that African Americans are severely underrepresented in jury booths across the nation.[77] One reason is that criteria required for jury duty in many states (e.g., requiring jurors to be registered to vote) creates obstacles for African Americans to participate.[78] One study in New Jersey found that some African Americans (and Hispanics) did not register to vote specifically because they did not *want* to be called as jurors.[79] Because minorities are underrepresented on juries, decisions reached by juries may discriminate against minorities.[80] Underrepresentation of African Americans on juries can then exacerbate the perception that the court is a "White" institution, thus leading to skepticism as to whether the American legal system is truly colorblind and fair to minorities.

Similarly, skepticism as to the fairness of the courts influences African Americans to be less willing than Caucasians to support capital punishment.[81] For example, research has found that African Americans are 68.8 percent less likely to support capital punishment as compared to Caucasians.[82] This distrust harbored by African Americans toward the courts' application of capital punishment is justified, as studies have found disturbing patterns of racism.[83] When the victim of a murder is Caucasian, an African American is significantly more likely than a Caucasian to be charged with a capital crime by a prosecutor.[84] African Americans are aware of this disparity in the courts, which leads them to use an alternative set of standards when forming attitudes toward capital punishment.[85] Research has found that African Americans' reasoning for endorsing the death penalty focused on whether death was an appropriate sentence, whereas Caucasians focused on the intent of the criminal.[86] The attention given by African Americans to the appropriateness of the sentence is an indication of their skepticism of the court. African Americans are aware of racial discrepancies that occur in the American legal system and that awareness manifests itself in skepticism of the court.[87] With empirical evidence supporting their fears, it is apparent why African Americans have a negative view of the American court system.

Theoretical Explanations and Conclusions

Researchers attempting to explain why African Americans have less favorable views than Caucasians about the law have proposed three reasons.[88] The first explanation is based on SES.[89] Researchers looking at "high" crime areas and "low" crime areas in Atlanta, Georgia, and Washington, D.C., found that people who reported higher negative attitudes toward the police were more often those in high crime areas, those with lower incomes, and who were single, separated, or divorced.[90] The fact that this pattern holds for single, separated, and divorced people indicates that socio-economic conditions influence people's attitudes toward the police beyond their ethnicity, bearing in mind that minorities are overrepresented in the lower SES.[91]

The second explanation focuses on police contact.[92] As some of the research discussed above has indicated, people who have more experience with the police are more likely to develop negative views toward the police.[93] Research investigating the influence of contact has continuously found this trend, regardless of whether the contact was experienced personally or vicariously through the stories of others.[94] Therefore, simply hearing of stories of police misconduct may lead to the creation of negative attitudes toward the legal system, independent of actual contact with the police.

The third explanation focuses on how African Americans are socialized to view the police.[95] One researcher found that African American males are taught at a young age to question legal authority.[96] Constant exposure to the unfair nature of the courts creates a delegitimization of the legal system, conceptualizing it as a "White" institution.[97] John Davis proposes that this leads minority groups who feel persecuted by the majority group (Caucasians) to raise their children to perceive the law enforcement institutions with cynicism.[98]

Each of these explanations provide researchers with insight into the factors that lead African Americans to have less favorable attitudes toward law enforcement officials and the courts.[99] However, the influence of SES, contact with the police, and socialization and how these three factors work together to shape attitudes has yet to be fully examined. Although attitudes and perceptions are complex phenomena that are difficult to explain, researchers have successfully demonstrated that Caucasians and African Americans do hold different attitudes and perceptions of the legal system.

Studies with Hispanic Populations

As the number of Hispanics immigrating to the United States has increased in the last twenty years, so too has research investigating the Hispanic perspective on the U.S. legal system.[100] In comparison with studies involving African Americans, research investigating the Hispanic perspective has been relatively limited.[101] However, enough research has been conducted to infer that many of the same factors that drive the attitudes of African Americans are influential in the Hispanic community.[102] What follows is an overview of the research that has been conducted examining Hispanics' view of police and the courts.

Police

Research investigating the Hispanic perspective of the police has focused on two areas, (a) general attitudes toward the police,[103] and (b) experience with police misconduct.[104] Although there are only a handful of these studies to analyze, there is enough available research to draw conclusions as to attitudes of Hispanics toward the police.

An analysis of the 1979 National Crime Survey showed that, compared to the general population, Hispanics felt the police do not have the ability to reduce the incidence of crime, felt they had inadequate police protection, and generally evaluated the police less favorably.[105] In a similar study, the same researcher surveyed 312 Hispanics throughout Texas examining perspectives on state legal authorities.[106] Their ratings indicated that the respondents felt the police officers had bad attitudes, exhibited poor response times, and discriminated against Hispanics.[107] Similarly, in a comparison across ethnicities in a small city, researchers found that Hispanics as a group had the lowest ratings of satisfaction with the police.[108] Specifically, only 57 percent were satisfied with the legal authorities, as compared to 93 percent of Caucasians.[109]

One study that has been conducted which looked at Hispanics' experience with police misconduct involved surveying 1,792 residents across all cultures living in metropolitan areas.[110] It was found that Hispanics were more likely than Caucasians to believe that police abuse frequently occurs and is a very common phenomenon.[111] In addition, Hispanics were significantly more likely than Caucasians to report personal and vicarious experience with police abuse.[112] These findings suggest that, as with African Americans, Hispanics feel that the police discriminate against them. However, this distrust of legal authorities does not appear to carry over to attitudes toward the legal system.

Courts

Research investigating Hispanic perceptions of the courts has generally found that Hispanics and Caucasians have similar attitudes about the fairness of the U.S. legal system. For example, research has found that Hispanics have similar attitudes toward the courts as the overall general public.[113] The few studies that do not find similar levels of satisfaction involve examining recent (or illegal) immigrants' perceptions of the legal system.[114] These studies evince what is termed a "bio-focal lens": immigrants who have had contact with immigration officials have slightly less favorable views of legal authorities, but nevertheless have an overall positive view of the U.S. courts.[115] Researchers suggest this is because the legal system in the United States is viewed as an improvement as compared to the judicial system in their country of origin.[116]

The results of the research discussed in this section may seem to be contradictory. How can Hispanics hold unfavorable views of the police, while maintaining positive views of the legal system? As we will see in the section comparing the perceptions of several cultures, although Hispanics are more likely to have negative views toward the police than Caucasians, their perceptions of the police are closer to those of Caucasians than of African Americans. Before looking at those multicultural comparisons, one other minority group, Asian Americans, has been given some attention in the research on cultural differences in perceptions of the legal system.

Studies with Asian Americans

Just as there are relatively few studies examine that Hispanic views toward the law as compared to African Americans, there are relatively few studies that examine Asian views toward the law as compared to Hispanics. Similarly, as with Hispanics, the term "Asians" is a broad category encompassing several ethnic groups from eastern Asia and the Pacific islands.[117] Because "Asians" is the label used by American society to categorize these groups, this review article will do the same. When conducting a literature search for studies addressing how Asians perceive the legal system, the authors were only able to locate four studies that have systematically examined how Asians view the court system as compared to other cultural groups. Therefore, each of these studies, including two conducted in Canada, will be included in the analysis.

American Studies: Asian Perspectives of the Police and the Courts

Two studies were conducted examining Asians' view toward the American courts.[118] Research on the Hawaiian justice system examined the sentencing rates between Caucasian and minority juvenile offenders in 3,000 cases from 1980 to 1986.[119] It was found that Hawaiian, Filipino, Asian, and Samoan offenders were overrepresented as defendants in juvenile courts as compared to their proportion of the state population.[120] In addition, it was found that Hawaiians and Samoans receive longer sentences than Caucasian youth for identical crimes.[121] This study establishes the same trend for Asians in Hawaii that has been consistently found for African Americans and Hispanics throughout the country: minorities are more likely to be jailed and receive longer sentences than their Caucasian counterparts.[122]

In an attempt to gain insight into how Asians experience the court, researchers examined the way in which Vietnamese and Hmong litigants use their culture as a defense strategy in civil and criminal cases.[123] They found that the primary complaint among the defendants revolved around complications with language, proposing that it was the basis for disputes with police, court interpreters, prosecutors, judges, and counsel for the defendant.[124] For example, inadequate or improper presentation of Miranda rights can cause minorities to feel threatened, as if they have suddenly lost all of their privileges as a citizen, and can lead to altercations that compound their legal problem.[125]

These studies suggest that there is discrimination toward Asians occurring in American courts,[126] yet there have not been any studies conducted in the United States to determine if Asians perceive such discrimination, and whether it influences how they interact with the legal system. To accomplish this, it is necessary to review research that has been conducted in Canada, as some Canadian researchers have investigated this research question. While the legal systems of the United States and Canada differ to some degree, as certainly does the social policy and resultant sociopolitical context, the studies are still informative and highlight the need for more research to be done here in the United States.

Canadian Studies: Asian Perspectives of the Police and the Courts

The first Canadian study surveyed Chinese community leaders to examine their perceptions of three major aspects of the criminal justice system: the law

and the legal system, access to legal services, and their willingness to participate in the legal system.[127] In addition, respondents were questioned about
the level of participation of Chinese members of the community in the criminal justice process.[128] With respect to the aspect of the law, it was found that
about half the respondents disagreed with the notion that the laws in Canada
were consistent with the principles of equality, around three quarters agreed
with the idea that systemic racism is present, and over 80 percent believe reform is necessary.[129] With respect to access to legal services, slightly over half
disagreed with the proposition that lawyers are culturally sensitive, whereas
slightly under a half agreed that culturally appropriate services were available
to those who need it.[130] Finally, when asked about the level of participation
by Chinese community members in the criminal justice system, 80 percent
did not feel that Chinese people were well informed about crime policies, and
about 66 percent felt that minority employees are inadequately represented in
Canadian criminal justice agencies.[131] Overall, the results of the survey
demonstrate that Chinese community leaders are critical of many aspects of
the justice system. When the Chinese population looks to these leaders to understand the law, it is safe to assume that the skepticism harbored by the leaders is transferred to the public, influencing Asians to become detached from
the Canadian legal process.

Other Canadian studies on Asian perceptions of the legal system applied
the contact hypothesis, often used to explain American minorities' unfavorable views of the legal system.[132] One study examined how negative interactions with legal officials influenced the perception of Canadian residents of
Chinese, African, and White ethnic origins.[133] It was found that increased
contacts with the criminal justice system differentially affected the perceptions of the three ethnicities.[134] To be more precise, increased contacts with
police increase the perceptions of injustice for all ethnic groups, but more so
for Blacks than for Caucasians or Asians.[135]

By examining the literature reviewed in this section, it is clear that the experience of Asian minorities is similar to that of Hispanics.[136] Empirical research has found that Asians are discriminated against by Western courts (in
the United States and Canada).[137] It is also evident that the Chinese community is aware and willing to report that they are not treated equally,[138] yet
when it comes to contact, Asians are not as willing as African Americans to
generalize their experiences with legal authorities to the legal system in general.[139] For an explanation why contact with the legal system was ineffective
in altering the Asian perception, it helps to look at research being conducted
in the United States that examines how minorities differ from each other in
their perception of the law.[140] In particular, researchers describe a racial hierarchy, with minorities differing in their endorsement of the legal system.[141]

Multicultural Comparisons of Caucasians, Hispanics, and African Americans

Studies that have compared ethnic groups have found evidence of a racial hierarchy among the three largest ethnic groups' perceptions of the law.[142] Specifically, it appears that African Americans view the police and the legal system negatively, Caucasians view the police and legal system positively, and Hispanics falling in between the two.[143] For example, data was analyzed from the U.S. Sentencing Commission, comparing the outcomes for African American, Hispanics, and Caucasians charged with drug crimes (involving cocaine, marijuana, or opiates).[144] It was found that African Americans received longer prison sentences than Caucasians, while this was not true for Hispanics.[145]

Similarly, research on police misconduct found that African Americans were more likely than Caucasians to say that police misconduct occurs "very often."[146] Hispanics also were more extreme in their views, but the Caucasian-Hispanic gap was less than that of African American–Caucasian gap.[147] The researchers concluded that the social hierarchy of race places Caucasians at the top, African Americans at the bottom, and Hispanics — racially white but ethnically different — in the middle.[148]

Beyond overall perceptions of the legal system, there is also evidence that this racial hierarchy manifests itself in the attitudes of the minority group members.[149] Researchers have analyzed several national polls (e.g., Hearst National Survey on the Courts) and found that African American respondents judge the courts differently than Hispanics and Caucasians.[150] African Americans are most likely to be influenced by perceptions of fairness and equality, whereas Hispanics and Caucasians are more concerned with the quality of treatment a person receives in the court.[151]

Taken together, these studies illustrate how cultural factors are able to influence how a person perceives and interacts with the court.[152] These studies all suggest that American society is hierarchical.[153] An individual's position in this hierarchy influences not only the amount of contact one has with the law, but also the type of contact one has with the law.[154] The reasons for the existence of this hierarchy may lie in the explanations given for African Americans' negative attitudes toward the law.[155] Factors such as contact and socialization may be influencing this trend.[156] However, currently, there is not enough cross-cultural analysis to draw substantiated conclusions.

POLICY RECOMMENDATIONS

As this research on different ethnic groups shows, society needs to address cultural differences in behavior and in perceptions different ethnic groups may have toward the legal system. Policymakers need to eliminate policies that make this issue worse, such as the use of racial profiling by the police, as well as adopt new policies that will improve the system. After all, mistrust in the legal system keeps people from participating in the legal system; they may not report for jury service, they may be hesitant to report crimes, and they may not want to testify as a witness to a crime they witnessed.

Researchers need to delve into the reasons for the mistrust that some groups may have and implement policy change that will allow these citizens to trust their legal system. An example of such policy change would be to actively encourage more minorities to sit on juries. In Pennsylvania, for example, it was shown that adults in African American neighborhoods were half as likely to be summoned for jury duty than those in Caucasian neighborhoods, prompting the development of a bill that would that would expand Pennsylvania's juror source lists to include state income tax and welfare records in order to close gaps in the master jury list.[157] People who have served on juries report having more positive attitudes toward the legal system.[158] If more minorities are given the opportunity to serve as jurors, it may change their perceptions of the legal system and allow them to see it in a positive light. Another example of a policy change would be to actively recruit more minorities toward employment in law enforcement or as lawyers. Affirmative action policies have been implemented to ensure that job applicants in many fields, including those applying for jobs in law and law enforcement, are not discriminated against for any reason, including ethnic origin.[159] In becoming more visible members of the legal system, members of minority groups may help to eliminate the feeling within their communities that the system is a "system of Whites" and lead them to have greater trust in the fairness of the system. Another policy change that may alter views would be to offer more civics classes within schools to socialize children to the legal system. This greater familiarity with the legal process may lead youth to have more positive views of the legal system and the government in general.

Above all, the most important policy change should be greater governmental support of research that fills in these knowledge gaps. Governmental support could come in the form of grant money, sponsored initiatives, and acknowledgment that this research is an important component in making our legal system better. There is much research to be done to determine how to change negative perceptions and prevent real and imagined inequalities from occurring.

FUTURE RESEARCH

Future policy should be informed by solid research. This review of the existing literature has revealed that there are a number of gaps in our knowledge base. Most research has focused on African Americans' experiences with the law, but has not spent much attention on other ethnic groups' interactions. Specifically, there have been many explanations given for why African Americans may view the legal system in a particular way, but no research has been done which extends this explanation of views to other minority groups. Research which put African Americans, Hispanics, and Caucasians in a hierarchy based on their attitudes toward the police[160] (Caucasians being most positive, African Americans most negative, and Hispanics in the middle) is an interesting theory, but does not account for the attitudes of Asians, Middle Easterners, or any other minority groups. Further, it can be generally stated that there are gaps in the literature in three particular areas: views of Asians, Hispanics, and those from Middle Eastern countries, all of which will be explored in more detail below.

Few studies have been conducted on the interactions of Asians and Asian Americans with law enforcement.[161] More studies have been conducted in Canada than the United States; however, it could be argued that our legal system varies from Canada's on a number of important points. Additionally, future research needs to tie in both research on Asian values and the socialization of these values into children so that we have a better understanding of why Asians perceive legal institutions in the manner that they do. The integration of this knowledge would better suggest which legal interventions would be most effective in accommodating cultural needs and increasing the effectiveness of legal policy.

The literature on Hispanic perceptions of the legal system is not as developed as that with African Americans. Also, many studies use specific cultural samples (Mexican Americans, Cuban Americans) and generalize the findings to all Hispanics without acknowledging the vast differences among all of these groups. Future studies should note these limitations and compare perceptions of the legal system between Hispanic groups and see if there are emerging differences.

There is virtually no literature on the experiences of minorities from Middle Eastern countries. Especially after events such as the terrorist attacks of September 11, 2001, these minorities have been increasingly singled out and seen with suspicion by law enforcement officials. Many have felt targeted because of their skin color or dress. However, there has been no systematic research looking at this stereotyping and the subsequent attitudes of individuals from the Middle East toward the legal system and law enforcement.

Research has suggested that minorities view our legal system as a "White institution" which does not serve their needs, only those of the White majority.[162] However, we as yet do not understand all of the reasons why some members of society feel this way. If there is, as some have argued,[163] a social hierarchy in our country, then more research should be done which explains these differing negative attitudes toward law enforcement. As stated previously, understanding the reasons for these feelings of unfair treatment will help us in the future to design better legal interventions or modify existing ones which currently serve to reinforce this feeling of neglect.

Research in the procedural justice arena has shown that when people perceive the procedures that the police and the courts use in dealing with them as fair, they are more likely to report the entire experience more favorably.[164] This holds true even when they do not receive the outcome they wanted.[165] In terms of defining a fair procedure, there appear to be some ethnic differences. Specifically, Caucasians and African Americans rely on trust and treatment with respect while Hispanics focus on evidence of neutrality,, however, all people interviewed focused most on questions of procedure and process.[166] Importantly, if people feel that legal authorities are polite and respectful and treat everyone in the community fairly, they will be more supportive of law and legal authorities.[167] Additional research needs to be conducted that examines how these procedural justice findings can be implemented within the legal system so that procedures are perceived as fair, which will then improve how the system itself is being perceived.

Finally, additional research is needed to support the assertion that differing perceptions of law enforcement are a result of differential socialization of minorities and the majority group.[168] Because there is limited research in this area, further studies are needed to determine which differences truly exist and how they arise. In this way, interactions between minority and majority groups within the law enforcement context will be better understood so that stereotypes or misinformed policy do not adversely affect interactions between the police and the policed.

CONCLUSION

Although differential reactions to Hurricane Katrina serve as an illustration of cultural differences in perceptions of the government and legal system, such differences affect perceptions of everyday interactions as well. Cultural differences in beliefs and perceptions about the government and the legal system have important implications for those who have the power to decide policy and legislation. Viewing the interaction of citizens with the legal system through the perspective of the legal actors is only part of understanding how and why citizens interact with the legal system the way they do. As this chapter has shown, the same event with the same legal actors can result in disparate reactions from the citizen involved depending on the cultural background of the citizen. The legal system is meant to be a resource for all members of our society to seek and ensure justice. To do so, the legal system must represent all members of society in such a way that al! members feel served by it. Understanding why some members of society may feel ill-served by their system of justice will serve as a foundation from which a more inclusive and just system can be fashioned.

NOTES

1. This chapter reprinted by permission of *Journal of Law and Social Challenges*, University of San Francisco School of Law 8 (Fall 2006).

2. See, e.g., Susan Page and Maria Puente, "Poll Shows Racial Ddivide on Storm Response," *USA Today*, September 12, 2005, http://www.usatoday.com/news/nation/2005-09-12-katrina-poll_x.htm; The Pew Research Center for People and the Press, "Two-in-Three Critical of Bush's Relief Efforts: Huge Racial Divide over Katrina and Its Consequences," September 8, 2005, http://people-press.org/reports/display.php3?ReportID=255.

3. U.S. Department of Justice, *The Federal Death Penalty System: A Statistical Survey* (Washington, D.C.: 2000), http://www.usdoj.gov/dag/pubdoc/_dp_survey_final.pdf. In *McCleskey v. Kemp*, 107 S.Ct. 1756 (1987), McCleskey supported his claim of racial discrimination with a study conducted by Professor David C. Baldus, George Woodworth, and Charles Pulaski. The study found that the death penalty was given in 8 percent of cases involving both a Caucasian defendant and a Caucasian victim. When the defendant was Black and the victim White, the application of the death penalty rose to 22 percent, and when both the victim and defendant where Black, the death penalty was given in only 1 percent of cases. The study also found that prosecutors sought the death penalty disproportionately. In cases with a Black defendant and a White victim, the death penalty was sought in 70 percent of cases. When both the victim and defendant were White, only 32 percent were pursued as death penalty cases and only 15 percent when both were Black. For cases involving White defendants and black victims, only 19 percent involved the prosecution seeking the death penalty. In the end, Blacks are more likely than Whites to receive the death penalty and Blacks killing Whites have the greatest likelihood of receiving the death penalty. A study conducted by the U.S. Department of Justice came similar to conclusions. At the time of the writing of this chapter, 18 people are on federal death row; 16 of them are either African American, Hispanic, or Asian. During the five-year period from 1995 to 2000, 80 percent of federal capital cases recommended for prosecution seeking the death penalty involved people of color and 72 percent of cases approved for death penalty prosecution involved minority defendants.

4. Lawrence S. Wrightsman, Edie Greene, Michael T. Nietzel, and William H. Fortune, *Psychology and the Legal System* (Belmont, CA: Wadsworth, 2000), 18. A 1996 study conducted by C. J. Levy of persons convicted of misdemeanors or minor felonies between 1990 and 1992 found that a third of the minority defendants would have received more lenient jail sentences if they had been White.

5. *Miller-El v. Cockrell*, Supreme Court of the United States, 537 U.S. 322 (2003). The now infamous "Texas shuffle" was used to keep African Americans from serving on juries. In the opinion *Miller-El v. Cockrell*, Justice Souter noted that Black jurors were questioned more aggressively about the death penalty, and the pool was "shuffled" at least twice by prosecutors, apparently to increase the chances Whites would be selected. See also, Brian H. Bornstein, Monica K. Miller, Robert J. Nemeth, Greg L. Page, and Sara M. Musil, "Juror Reactions to Jury Duty: Perceptions of the System and Potential Stressors," *Behavioral Sciences and the Law* 23, no. 3 (2005): 321. In a survey of jurors, 83 percent felt that juries *should* reflect the ethnic diversity of the community, only 36 percent felt that their jury *did* reflect that diversity.

6. National Center for State Courts (NCSC), *How the Public Views the State Courts: A 1999 National Survey* (Williamsburg, VA: National Center for State Courts, 1999). The 1999 NCSC report was based on the results of 1,826 telephone interviews with a sample that represented the ethnic mix of the country. The participants generally agreed that juries do not adequately represent the community, and that people who are wealthy, Caucasian, or English speaking get better treatment than people who lack these characteristics. For example, participants were asked "What kind of treatment do various groups receive from the courts?" and were given the options: "far better treatment," "somewhat better treatment," "same treatment," "somewhat worse treatment," and "far worse treatment." Eighty percent of participants believed that wealthy people received "far better" or "better" treatment, and 55 percent of the participants felt that non-English-speaking people received "somewhat" or "far worse" treatment in the courts.

7. Bornstein, *Juror Reactions*, 321. In a survey of jurors, 59 percent of respondents agreed that immigrants may be less likely to use the court system, 49 percent agreed that minority litigants have difficulty affording representation, and 76 percent agreed that income affects the quality of legal representation.

8. Curt R. Bartol and Anne M. Bartol, *Psychology and the Law: Theory, Research, and Application* (Belmont, CA: Wadsworth, 2004), 477–79. A 1999 Gallup Poll revealed that 72 percent of African American males between eighteen and thirty-four believed they had been stopped by officers because of their race while only 6 percent of non-Hispanic Caucasians believed the same. The African American males described being stopped for minor traffic violations, such as under-inflated tires, and then being asked to consent to a search. Drug-courier profiling is also a type of racial profiling, used to identify suspected drug couriers in airports and other border-crossing stops.

9. See the U.S. Department of Health and Human Services, The Centers for Disease Control and Prevention, The National Center for HIV, STD, and TB Prevention, *Tuskegee Syphilis Study* (2005), http://www.cdc.gov/nchstp/od/tuskegee/, for complete history of the study. In short, the study involved 600 African American men in Macon County, Alabama, 399 infected with syphilis and 201 noninfected men. Researchers told the men they were being treated for "bad blood," and they were not given the proper treatment needed to cure their illness. In exchange for taking part in the study, the men received free medical exams, free meals, and burial insurance. The study went on for forty years, although originally slated for six months, causing needless suffering in the subjects. This study prompted research ethics reforms.

10. Wrightsman et al., *Psychology and the Legal System*, 162. Rodney King was stopped after a chase through a Los Angeles suburb, shot with a 50,000-volt stun gun, then beat and kicked by three police officers. King was hospitalized with serious injuries including multiple skull fractures, a broken ankle, a cracked cheekbone, and internal injuries. The incident was witnessed and video taped, the broadcast of which caused riots to break out in African American neighborhoods in Los Angeles.

11. Wrightsman et al., *Psychology and the Legal System*, 162.

12. Wrightsman et al., *Psychology and the Legal System*, 162.

13. Page and Puente, "Poll Shows Racial Divide."

14. Pew, "Two-In-Three Critical."

15. Pew, "Two-In-Three Critical." That is not to say that non–African Americans were not affected. Seventy five percent of those surveyed say they are following news of Katrina closely; only the 9/11 terrorist attacks and the start of the war in Iraq have attracted more of America's attention in recent memory (Pew, 2005). The hurricane has had a psychological impact on the entire American public, with 58 percent of respondents, regardless of race, saying they have felt depressed over what has happened (Pew, 2005) and 98 percent saying they felt sadness as they watched events unfold on television (Page and Puente, 2005).

16. Pew, "Two-in-Three Critical."

17. *CBS News*, "Blacks Rally Around Katrina Cause: Hurricane Inspires Record Outpouring of Aid in Black America," September 9, 2005, available at http://www.cbsnews.com/stories/2005/09/09/katrina/main829498.shtml.

18. *CBS News*, "Blacks Rally."

19. *CBS News*, "Race an Issue in Katrina Response," September 3, 2005, available at http://www.cbsnews.com/stories/2005/09/03/katrina/main814623.shtml.

20. *CBS News*, "Rapper Blasts Bush Over Katrina: Kanye West Says Bush 'Doesn't Care About Black People' on Telethon," September 3, 2005, available at http://www.cbsnews.com/stories/2005/09/03/katrina/main814636.shtml.

21. *CBS News*, "Race an Issue."

22. *CNN.com*, September 2, 2005.

23. *CBS News*, "Blacks Rally."

24. *CBS News*, "Blacks Rally."

25. Page and Puente, "Poll Shows Racial Divide."

26. Pew, "Two-in-Three Critical."

27. Pew, "Two-in-Three Critical."

28. Page and Puente, "Poll Shows Racial Divide"; Pew, "Two-in-Three Critical."

29. Page and Puente, "Poll Shows Racial Divide"; Pew, "Two-in-Three Critical." In addition, in the *USA Today*/CNN/Gallop poll, almost three quarters (72 percent) of African American respondents say that George Bush does not care about African American people, while only about one-quarter (26 percent) of White respondents agree.

30. Pew, "Two-in-Three Critical."

31. Pew, "Two-in-Three Critical." An overwhelming majority of African Americans (77 percent) say most of those who stayed behind did so because they did not have a way to leave the city, as opposed to wanting to stay (16 percent); agreement to

these items for Caucasians was much different (58 percent and 32 percent respectively).

32. Pew, "Two-in-Three Critical." 57 percent of African Americans characterize people who took things from homes and businesses as mostly ordinary people trying to survive during an emergency. Just 38 percent of Caucasians agree, with 37 percent saying those who took things were criminals taking advantage of the situation. In response to pictures of looters, 77 percent of African Americans characterize them as desperate people trying to survive, while 50 percent of Caucasians characterize them as criminals.

33. B. James Starr, Lloyd R. Sloan, and Tarl R. Kudrick, "Just Deserts: African American Judgments of Justice in Stories of Varying Cultural Relevance," *Cross-Cultural Research* 31, no. 2 (1997): 137–54.

34. John W. Berry, Ype H. Poortinga, Marshall H. Segall, and Pierre R. Dasen, *Cross-Cultural Psychology: Research and Applications* (Toronto: Cambridge University Press, 1992).

35. Berry et al., *Cross-Cultural Psychology,* 66.

36. Berry et al., *Cross-Cultural Psychology,* 66.

37. See generally Audrey Smedley and Brian D. Smedley, "Race as Biology Is Fiction, Racism as a Social Problem Is Real: Anthropological and Historical Perspectives on the Social Construction of Race," *American Psychologist* 60, no. 1 (2005): 16–26. But see Genetics for the Human Race (Special Issue), *Nature Genetics* 36, no. 1 (2004): 1–60, where scientists argue about the possible legitimacy and merits to considering the biological basis for race.

38. Tom R. Tyler, "Public Trust and Confidence in Legal Authorities: What Do Majority and Minority Group Members Want from the Law and Legal Institutions," *Behavioral Sciences and the Law* 19, no. 2 (2001): 215–35.

39. John A. Davis, "Justification for No Obligation: Views of African American Males toward Crime and the Criminal Law," *Issues in Criminology* 9 (1974): 69–87.

40. Other groups have not been researched to any degree, and so will not be discussed in this paper.

41. See generally Charles W. Peek, Jon P. Alston, and George D. Lowe, "Comparative Evaluation of the Local Police," *The Public Opinion Quarterly* 42, no. 3 (1978): 370–79; Ronald Weitzer and Steven A. Tuch, "Race and Perceptions of Misconduct," *Social Problems* 51, no. 3 (2004): 305–25.

42. See generally Berry et al., *Cross-Cultural Psychology,* 33; Deane C. Wiley, "Black and White Differences in the Perception of Justice," *Behavioral Sciences and the Law* 19, no. 5–6 (2001): 649–55; Peek et al., "Comparative Evaluation"; Francis T. Cullen, Liquin Cao, James Frank, Robert H. Langworthy, Sandra L. Browning, Renee Kopache, and Thomas J. Stevenson, "'Stop or I'll Shoot:' Racial Differences in Support for Police Use of Deadly Force," *American Behavioral Scientist* 39, no. 4 (1996): 449–60.

43. See generally Robert L. Young, "Race, Conceptions of Crime and Justice, and Support for the Death Penalty," *Social Psychology Quarterly* 54, no. 1 (1991): 67–75.

44. See generally Ronald Weitzer and Steven A. Tuch, "Race, Class, and Perceptions of Discrimination by the Police," *Crime and Delinquency* 45, no. 4 (1999): 494–507.

45. See generally Cullen et al., "'Stop or I'll Shoot.'"

46. See generally Weitzer and Tuch, "Race and Perceptions of Misconduct."

47. See generally Weitzer and Tuch, "Race and Perceptions of Misconduct."

48. See generally Young, "Support for Death Penalty."

49. See generally Weitzer and Tuch, "Race and Perceptions of Misconduct"; Wiley, "Perceptions of Justice"; Peek et al., "Comparative Evaluation"; Cullen et al., "'Stop or I'll Shoot.'"

50. Weitzer and Tuch, "Perceptions of Discrimination," 502.

51. See generally, Wiley, "Perception of Justice."

52. Wiley, "Perception of Justice," 653.

53. Peek et al., "Comparative Evaluation," 371.

54. Peek et al., "Comparative Evaluation," 374.

55. See generally Weitzer and Tuch, "Perceptions of Discrimination"; Wiley, "Perceptions of Justice"; Peek et al., "Comparative Evaluation."

56. Cullen et al., "'Stop or I'll Shoot,'" 456.

57. Shaheen Halim and Beverly L. Stiles, "Differential Support for Police Use of Force, the Death Penalty, and Perceived Harshness of the Courts: Effects of Race, Gender, and Region," *Criminal Justice and Behavior* 28, no. 1 (2001): 3–23.

58. Wilson and Dunham found that middle-class African Americans show similar levels of support for police use of force as Caucasians in general (regardless of class), however still express less support for police use of force than middle-class Caucasians. George Wilson and Roger Dunham, "Race, Class, and Attitudes Toward Crime Control: The Views of the African American Middle Class," *Criminal Justice and Behavior* 28, no. 3 (2001): 259–78.

59. For example, Cecilia Menjívar and Cynthia L. Bejarano, "Latino Immigrants' Perception of Crime and Police Authorities in the United States: A Case Study from the Phoenix Metropolitan Area," *Ethnic and Racial Studies* 27, no. 1 (2004): 120–48.

60. Weitzer and Tuch, "Race and Perceptions of Misconduct," 314.

61. Weitzer and Tuch, "Race and Perceptions of Misconduct," 320.

62. Weitzer and Tuch, "Perceptions of Discrimination," 502.

63. Weitzer and Tuch, "Perceptions of Discrimination," 502.

64. Weitzer and Tuch, "Perceptions of Discrimination," 502.

65. See generally Richard R.W. Brooks and Haekyung Jeon-Slaughter, "Race, Income and Perceptions of the United States Court System," *Behavioral Sciences and the Law* 19, no. 2 (2001): 249–64.

66. See generally Hiroshi Fukarai, Edgar W. Butler, and Jo-Ellan Huebner-Dimitrius, "Spatial and Racial Imbalances in Voter Registration and Jury Selection," *Sociology and Social Research* 72, no. 1 (1987): 33–83.

67. See generally Young, "Support for Death Penalty."

68. See generally L. Marvin Overby, Robert D. Brown, and John M. Bruce, "Race, Political Empowerment, and Minority Perceptions of Judicial Fairness," *Social Science Quarterly* 86, no. 2 (2005): 444–62; Brooks and Jeon-Slaughter, "Perceptions of the Court System."

69. Overby et al., "Political Empowerment," 456.

70. Brooks and Jeon-Slaughter, "Perceptions of the Court System," 261.

71. Starr et al., "Just Deserts," 153.

72. Starr et al., "Just Deserts," 153.

73. Starr et al., "Just Deserts," 153–54.

74. Brooks and Jeon-Slaughter, "Perceptions of the Court System," 228.

75. Starr et al., "Just Deserts," 152.

76. See generally Hiroshi Fukurai, Edgar W. Butler, and Richard Krooth, "Where Did the Black Jurors Go? A Theoretical Synthesis of Racial Disenfranchisement in the Jury System and Jury Selection," *Journal of Black Studies* 22, no. 2 (1991): 196–215.

77. Fukarai et al., "Spatial and Racial Imbalances," 33.

78. Fukarai et al., "Black Jurors," 198.

79. National Center for the State Courts, *Race and Ethnic Fairness* (1992), http://www.ncsconline.org/Projects_Initiatives/REFI/NJ2REB.htm.

80. National Center for the State Courts, *Race and Ethnic Fairness.*

81. See generally Young, "Support for Death Penalty," 42.

82. Halim and Stiles, "Differential Support," 19.

83. For example, Thomas J. Keil and Gennaro F. Vito, "Race and the Death Penalty in Kentucky Murder Trials: 1976–1991," *American Journal of Criminal Justice* 20 (1995).

84. Keil and Vito, "Race and the Death Penalty," 34.

85. See generally Young, "Support for Death Penalty."

86. Young, "Support for Death Penalty," 72.

87. Young, "Support for Death Penalty," 72.

88. See generally Keith D. Parker, Anne B. Onyekwuluje, and Komanduri S. Murty, "African-Americans' Attitudes toward the Local Police: A Multivariate Analysis," *Journal of Black Studies* 25, no. 3 (1995): 396–409; Weitzer and Tuch, "Perceptions of Discrimination"; Davis, "Justification for No Obligation."

89. Parker et al., "African-Americans' Attitudes."

90. Parker et al., "African-Americans' Attitudes," 403.

91. Parker et al., "African-Americans' Attitudes," 403.

92. See generally Weitzer and Tuch, "Perceptions of Discrimination"; Menjívar and Bejarano, "Latino Immigrants' Perceptions."

93. Weitzer and Tuch, "Perceptions of Discrimination," 502.

94. Menjívar and Bejarano, "Latino Immigrants' Perceptions," 139.

95. See generally Davis, "Justification for No Obligation."

96. Davis, "Justification for No Obligation."

97. Davis, "Justification for No Obligation," 79.

98. Davis, "Justification for No Obligation," 81.

99. See generally Parker et al., "African-Americans' Attitudes"; Weitzer and Tuch, "Perceptions of Discrimination"; Davis, "Justification for No Obligation."

100. For example, Weitzer and Tuch, "Race and Perceptions of Misconduct"; David L. Carter, "Hispanic Interaction with the Criminal Justice System in Texas: Experiences, Attitudes, and Perceptions," *Journal of Criminal Justice* 11, (1983): 213–27.

101. See generally Weitzer and Tuch, "Race and Perceptions of Misconduct."

102. References to Hispanic culture refer to the general category applied to immigrants from Latin nations. Although there is great diversity between the many ethnic-

ities that encompass this category, they do all share a common identity that is recognized socially among American society.

103. See generally Carter, "Hispanic Interaction."

104. See generally Weitzer and Tuch, "Race and Perceptions of Misconduct."

105. See generally Carter, "Hispanic Interaction."

106. See generally David L. Carter, "Hispanic Perception of Police Performance: An Empirical Assessment," *Journal of Criminal Justice* 13(1985): 487–500.

107. Carter, "Hispanic Perception of Police," 497–98.

108. Venessa Garcia and Liqun Cao, "Race and Satisfaction with Police in a Small City," *Journal of Criminal Justice* 33(2005): 191–96.

109. Garcia and Cao, "Race and Satisfaction," 195. Although Carter's sample in Texas was primarily of Mexican origin, Garcia and Cao's sample in the small northeastern town was probably more diverse, giving researchers the confidence to conclude that Hispanics in general have less favorable views of the police in general than do Caucasians.

110. Weitzer and Tuch, "Race and Perceptions of Misconduct," 310

111. Weitzer and Tuch, "Race and Perceptions of Misconduct," 320.

112. Weitzer and Tuch, "Race and Perceptions of Misconduct," 320.

113. Rodolfo O. de la Garza, and Louis DeSipio, "A Satisfied Clientele Seeking More Diverse Services: Latinos and the Courts," *Behavioral Sciences and the Law* 19 (2001): 237–48.

114. For example, Menjívar and Bejarano, "Latino Immigrants' Perceptions."

115. Menjívar and Bejarano, "Latino Immigrants' Perceptions," 130.

116. Menjívar and Bejarano, "Latino Immigrants' Perceptions,"131.

117. See generally John M. MacDonald, "The Effect of Ethnicity on Juvenile Court Decision Making in Hawaii," *Youth and Society* 35(2003): 243–63.

118. MacDonald, "Effect of Ethnicity"; Randall R. Berger and Jeremy Hein, "Immigrants, Culture, and American Courts: A Typology of Legal Strategies and Issues in Cases Involving Vietnamese and Hmong Litigants," *Criminal Justice Review* 26 (2001): 38–61.

119. MacDonald, "Effect of Ethnicity," 244.

120. MacDonald, "Effect of Ethnicity," 254.

121. MacDonald, "Effect of Ethnicity," 258.

122. MacDonald, "Effect of Ethnicity," 254–55.

123. Berger and Hein, "Immigrants, Culture, and American Courts," 41.

124. Berger and Hein, "Immigrants, Culture, and American Courts," 57.

125. Berger and Hein, "Immigrants, Culture, and American Courts," 55–56.

126. See generally Berger and Hein, "Immigrants, Culture, and American Courts"; MacDonald, "Effect of Ethnicity."

127. Henry P.H. Chow, "The Chinese Community Leaders' Perceptions of the Criminal Justice System," *Canadian Journal of Criminology* 38, no. 4 (1996): 477–84.

128. Chow, "Chinese Community."

129. Chow, "Chinese Community," 479.

130. Chow, "Chinese Community," 482.

131. Chow, "Chinese Community," 482.

132. Weitzer and Tuch, "Perceptions of Discrimination," 502.

133. Scot Wortley, "Justice for All? Race and Perceptions of Bias in the Ontario Criminal Justice System: A Toronto Survey," *Canadian Journal of Criminology* 38, no. 4 (1996): 439–68.

134. Wortley, "Justice for All?" 448.

135. Wortley, "Justice for All?" 458.

136. See generally Wortley, "Justice for All?"

137. See generally MacDonald, "Effect of Ethnicity"; Berger and Hein, "Immigrants, Culture, and American Courts"; Chow, "Chinese Community"; Wortley, "Justice for All?"

138. Wortley, "Justice for All?"

139. Wortley, "Justice for All?"

140. For example, Weitzer and Tuch, "Race and Perceptions of Misconduct," 321.

141. Weitzer and Tuch, "Race and Perceptions of Misconduct," 321.

142. Weitzer and Tuch, "Race and Perceptions of Misconduct," 321.

143. Weitzer and Tuch, "Race and Perceptions of Misconduct," 321.

144. Christopher G. Hebert, "Sentencing Outcomes of Black, Hispanic, and White Males Convicted under Federal Sentencing Guidelines," *Criminal Justice Review* 22, no. 2 (1997): 133–56.

145. Hebert, "Sentencing Outcomes."

146. Weitzer and Tuch, "Race and Perceptions of Misconduct," 321.

147. Weitzer and Tuch, "Race and Perceptions of Misconduct," 321.

148. Weitzer and Tuch, "Race and Perceptions of Misconduct," 321.

149. See generally Tyler, "Public Trust."

150. Tyler, "Public Trust."

151. Tyler, "Public Trust," 228.

152. See generally Weitzer and Tuch, "Race and Perceptions of Misconduct," 321; Hebert, "Sentencing Outcomes"; Tyler, "Public Trust."

153. See generally Hebert, "Sentencing Outcomes"; Tyler, "Public Trust."

154. Hebert, "Sentencing Outcomes"; Tyler, "Public Trust."

155. See generally Parker et al., "African-Americans' Attitudes"; Weitzer and Tuch, "Perceptions of Discrimination," 502; Davis, "Justification for No Obligation."

156. Parker et al., "African-Americans' Attitudes"; Weitzer and Tuch, "Perceptions of Discrimination," 502; Davis, "Justification for No Obligation."

157. National Center for State Courts, *Jur-E Bulletin*, October 12, 2005, http://www.ncsconline.org/WC/Publications/KIS_JurInnJurEPub05.pdf.

158. See generally Brian L. Cutler, "Judging Jury Service: Results of the North Carolina Administrative Office of the Courts *Juror* Survey," *Behavioral Sciences and the Law* 19, no. 2 (2001): 305–20.

159. Michael A. Fletcher, "Affirmative Action Tops NAACP List," *Washington Post*, July 14, 1998, http://www.washingtonpost.com.

160. Weitzer and Tuch, "Race and Perceptions of Misconduct."

161. See generally MacDonald, "Effect of Ethnicity"; Berger and Hein, "Immigrants, Culture, and American Courts"; Chow, "Chinese Community"; Weitzer and Tuch, "Perceptions of Discrimination"; Wortley, "Justice for All?"

162. Davis, "Justification for No Obligation," 75.

163. See generally Weitzer and Tuch, "Race and Perceptions of Misconduct."

164. See generally Tyler, "Public Trust."

165. Tyler, "Public Trust."

166. Tyler, "Public Trust," 232.

167. Tyler, "Public Trust," 234.

168. See generally Davis, "Justification for No Obligation."

Part Two

CULTURE AND COMMUNITY

Chapter Five

From "Gateway to the Americas" to the "Chocolate City"

The Racialization of Latinos in New Orleans

Nicole Trujillo-Pagán

In the days and weeks following Hurricanes Katrina and Rita, the media constructed the disaster in Black-and-White terms and largely ignored the city's Latino population. When it did consider Latinos, the media characterized them as a new population that threatened the city in several ways. This chapter argues that media excluded Latinos from its characterizations of evacuees and racialized the Latino population as invaders. The implications of this coverage were that the media failed to draw attention to Latinos as evacuees, which promoted Latinos' vulnerability and exclusion from recovery efforts. Instead, the media's constructions of Latinos as an "army of aliens" that threatened the "Chocolate City" intensified the racial tensions surrounding the disaster.

Latinos have had important historic, economic, and cultural roles in New Orleans. For instance, in the post–World War II era, New Orleans Mayor De-Lesseps S. Morrison initiated a program to promote Latin American trade through New Orleans. Under Morrison's leadership, the city dubbed itself the "Gateway to the Americas" and the flow of goods and immigrants to New Orleans increased. In 1992, Beatrice Rodriguez Owsley wrote that the phrase "Gateway to the Americas" had resurfaced "to symbolize the city's emergence as a leading port for Latin American trade" and she catalogued oral histories from another wave of Latino business owners who had followed the trade of goods into the city during the 1970s and 1980s. As recently as July

2005, *Hispanic Trends* reported that the Hispanic Chamber of Commerce in New Orleans was "working to make New Orleans the next big gateway to Latin America." Even immediately following Hurricane Katrina, on September 6, 2005, Wynton Marsalis dubbed New Orleans the "original melting pot."[1] Ironically, in October 2005, the image of New Orleans as an ideal "Gateway to the Americas" was threatened by New Orleans Mayor Ray Nagin who worried about preventing the city from being "overrun" by Latino immigrants. In a subsequent public speech, he dubbed New Orleans the "Chocolate City" and promised to recover both the city and the racial demographic of a Black-majority city. What distinguished the perception of New Orleans as the "Gateway to the Americas" and as the "Chocolate City" was that after Hurricane Katrina, Latinos came to embody many anxieties about how New Orleans would recover. These perceptions obscured Latinos in the ways it imagined the pre-disaster city, reintroduced Latinos as a demographic and cultural force that threatened the city's ability to duplicate itself as it had been before the disaster, and imposed a homogeneous understanding of Latinos as low-wage workers.

The history of Latinos in New Orleans contrasted with Mayor Nagin's comments about New Orleans. Latino immigration to the city had increased not only after Hurricane Katrina, but also during the late 1990s and early 2000s.[2] Latinos perceived Nagin's comments as an intensification of Hurricane Katrina's devastating impact on their communities. In contrast to Nagin's comments, Latinos emphasized their history and "place" in New Orleans and drew attention to how their communities were impacted by Hurricane Katrina. For example, some Latinos who lost their homes and businesses felt they were excluded from federal contracts and representation on Nagin's administration (despite the presence of a Latino on the "Bring New Orleans Back" Commission). Their perception of being "vulnerable" within the city's recovery was a product of physical damages they sustained and their fears about potential exclusion from equitable access toward recovery and access to relief resources. Latino business owners and workers alike shared the experience of a racialized recovery. In this way, Latinos' experience of the post-impact phase of recovery paralleled the Black community's experience of racial exclusion.

This chapter explores the ways in which broader structural vulnerabilities, including migrant generation, familiarity with the city's bureaucratic structure, place of residence, and legal status can impact the experience of a disaster. It argues for attention to the broader perceptions of Latinos, which, bolstered by the media, promoted the vulnerability of Latino communities within New Orleans. As a result, this chapter addresses both the resident Latino community of New Orleans and the migrant Latino community that was heavily involved in disaster recovery work. It finds that both resident and migrant Latinos were affected by broader racializations of the Latino community that local and federal relief workers relied upon in their disaster management plans and activities. On the one hand, relief workers consistently argued that they "hadn't seen any Latinos" in the New Orleans area. On the other hand, Mayor Nagin worried about the rapid and concentrated influx of Latino migrants to the city, which led the media to reconstruct Latinos' visibility as a recent and controversial population in the city. Relief workers, politicians, and the media participated in racializing New Orleans's Latinos in ways that emphasized newcomers as predators and intensified Latino Katrina survivors' sense of being vulnerable, invisible, and "ignored."

"Racialization" is used to refer to the concept of "racial formation processes" developed in 1986 by Michael Omi and Howard Winant, which they define as "the sociohistorical process by which racial categories are created, inhabited, transformed, and destroyed."[3] They argue that these processes involve a relationship between the *structure of inequality* and the *representation of racial dynamics*. This perspective's emphasis on inequality and representation is particularly useful for historizing the changing role of Latinos within New Orleans's race relation and it raises unique questions for how Latinos have been considered both a racial *and* an ethnicity group. Although the 2000 U.S. Census attempted to resolve this dilemma through a separate "Hispanic/Latino-origin" question, the case of New Orleans demonstrated how broader racializations, and more specifically the "otherization" involved in racial subordination, developed at the local level and within the condensed period of months following Hurricane Katrina.

METHOD

Following Omi and Winant, this chapter traces the relationship between the structure of inequality and the representation of racial dynamics. This chapter accomplishes these goals by first emphasizing a variety of institutions that recreated Latinos as an ethnic/racial group in a post-Katrina New Orleans. It presents a comparative historical analysis of Latinos in pre- and post-Katrina New Orleans to argue that Latinos and their history in the city were largely ignored in pre-Katrina New Orleans, which bolstered their early invisibility during the immediate post-impact phases of the hurricane and their subsequent political vulnerability in recovery efforts. The chapter then considers representations promoted by the media.

The chapter pursues several methodologies to frame its analysis. In its first section, the chapter contextualizes Latinos' political, economic, and social relationship to New Orleans. It draws from unpublished manuscripts and U.S. Census data to assess the structural location of a diverse Latino population that included a mature Central American Latino population, a settled Cuban population, and recent waves of Latino immigration during the 1990s from both Central America and Mexico. The chapter also uses Mid-City (see Figure 5.1) as a case study to demonstrate how Latinos' experience in the city was informed by racial discrimination. Mid-City (Orleans Parish Census tract 65) is an area on the northwestern side of the city and contained a population that was 17 percent "Hispanic or Latino" according to the 2000 U.S. Census.

In its second section, the chapter analyzes media coverage to explore the ways in which Latinos were described following the hurricane. This section draws from a Lexis-Nexis search of articles whose main subject was "New Orleans" and that included at least some mention of "Latino," "Hispanic," "Mexican," "Honduran," and/or "immigrants" within the same article. The analysis was based on articles over 100 words in length and excluded short summaries, "briefs," "news in 90 seconds," and headline-type articles. In an attempt to emphasize coverage that would enjoy a wider audience, the analysis included editorials but excluded letters to the editor. This method resulted in eighty-six articles from both printed and online media sources, which included a few limited summaries of television and radio coverage. Articles were coded for narrative phrasing that described Latino individuals and/or

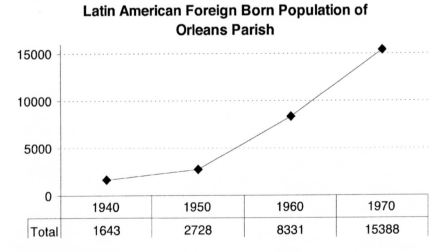

Latin American Foreign Born Population of Orleans Parish

	1940	1950	1960	1970
Total	1643	2728	8331	15388

Data: U.S. Census.

Figure 5.1.

Latinos as a population and excluded direct quotes from interviewees. Phrases were grouped by similarity to produce general categories of concerns relating to Latino individuals and/or populations. This analysis found that media coverage did pay some limited attention to Latino evacuees but overwhelmingly constructed Latinos as recent migrants to New Orleans. It also found that media coverage often constructed Latinos as a threatening force in the city's recovery. In this way, the media racialized a diverse community as "outsiders" and reproduced the presumption that Latinos took jobs away from non-Latinos who resided in New Orleans prior to Hurricane Katrina.

GATEWAY TO THE AMERICAS

In New Orleans, Latinos have enjoyed a longer history of entrepreneurial success that complicates their status as an ethnic or racial minority. In the limited published scholarship on Latinos in New Orleans, Beatriz Rodriguez Owsley points out that Latinos had doubled their rates of business ownership in the period from 1972 to 1982. Her oral histories demonstrate these businesses were concentrated in the Greater New Orleans area and their success depended on a growing Latino market. Rodriguez's oral histories also demonstrate that many Latino entrepreneurs were Cuban or Honduran and had arrived in New Orleans through social and commercial networks that resulted from trade between New Orleans and Latin America.[4] The post-1970s growth in the Latino population was part of a wave of immigration that had begun in the 1950s[5] and that relied on important commercial and social ties developed in the early twentieth century.

Despite the diversity of a community that could trace its history to the early twentieth century and even the Spanish colonial period, the contemporary Latino population owes a significant part of its history to commercial relationships between New Orleans and Latin America. The large Honduran population that settled in New Orleans resulted in part from a commercial relationship to the banana trade. Hondurans from La Ceiba often migrated as clerks and managers for the United Fruit Company and the Standard Fruit Company. The implications this trade had on the development of Honduran migration to New Orleans is suggested by U.S. Census data, which confirm that the number of "persons born in Central America" who lived in Louisiana grew from 100 persons in 1890 to 1,023 persons in 1930. Their occupations and commercial interests also drew Honduran immigrants into a larger relationship between Central America and the United States, which included Standard Fruit's expansion into Nicaragua, Mexico, and Haiti. For instance, once settled in New Orleans, former Honduran president Manuel Bonilla supported Samuel Zumurray's invasion through La Ceiba in 1911.[6] Although the role that other Honduran migrants played in the broader relationship between New Orleans and La Ceiba is unclear, this relationship had far-reaching and profound implications on immigrants' relationship to both Honduras and other Central American immigrants.[7] In Honduras, these immigrants held higher status than those who worked on plantations in La Ceiba to increase banana production. In New Orleans, these migrants became central to the development of Latino *colonias* in the Mid-City area.

A second, but equally as important, influence on the development of Mid-City was the wave of political refugees in the city. Among refugee waves of immigration to New Orleans, perhaps the most notable was that of Cubans who, although never appearing to outnumber Hondurans, was facilitated by the active involvement of organizations like the Catholic Cuban Center.[8] Politically motivated migrations continued throughout the 1970s as migration intensified and expanded to include greater numbers of Central American (Nicaraguans, Salvadorans, Guatemalans) and Cuban immigrants. Although there are few data on the influence of these waves on the broader Latino population of New Orleans, Luis Emilio Henao provided a comprehensive snapshot of the Latino population in 1982. He wrote that "the Hispanic population provides a great deal of the *manual* labor in the industrial and construction areas. This number was increased with the arrival of numerous non-skilled Cuban refugees." Henao also cited a 1973 report on the "Profile of Poverty in New Orleans" that found 50 percent of Latinos in metropolitan New Orleans were "laborers belonging to the lower class."[9] Despite his contradictory evidence on occupational concentration, Henao suggested that poverty among Latinos in Louisiana was low in comparison to Whites. He wrote Latino poverty in New Orleans was concentrated among female-headed households in the Irish Channel, which he estimated were 58 percent of all families in that area.[10]

Latino organizations and consulates provided estimates of the Latino population from the 1960s to the present and consistently argued that the U.S. Census significantly undercounted the Latino population. Similarly, Henao cited a 1980 study that found "only 75.5 percent of the Hispanics had received the form and that not all had answered it. The 13 percent of those who didn't receive the census form, added to the 7.1 percent who had received it but had not answered it, gives us a significant percentage of 20.8 percent of the Spanish population who were excluded from the census of 1980."[11] Estimations of the Latino population's size were particularly sensitive to the small proportions of Latinos in the city. As a result, various analyses produced throughout the 1970s and 1980s presented a mixed and sometimes contradictory profile of the Latino community. Nonetheless, Mid-City was one of several neighborhoods where Latinos settled, which Henao had considered to be "a section of middle and lower class people. It became an area of residential transition for the Hispanics, especially for those who worked in commerce."[12] The transient nature of Latinos in Mid-City meant its residents recognized many of the changing dynamics that had influenced the broader population during the 1980s and 1990s. For instance, in my interviews with Latino residents of Mid-City, they provided contradictory reports of how their neighborhood had changed recently but confirmed their neighborhood was in a period of transition. These residents included those who had enjoyed some degree of social mobility and had already moved out of Mid-City to nearby suburbs like Kenner.

The Latino population in Louisiana continued to grow after 1980, which is confirmed by U.S. Census samples demonstrating a 71 percent increase from 70,523 in 1980 to 99,699 persons in 1990.[13] An important part of this growth resulted from Latino outmigration to areas surrounding New Orleans, such as Kenner in Jefferson Parish. Blanca Rosa Morales Medina observes that from 1980 to 1990, Latinos' growth rate was 20 percent within Jefferson Parish while the area's overall population declined. Medina also notes that the Latino population in Orleans parish decreased during the same period and speculates that "the Hispanic population is migrating from Orleans to Jefferson."[14] This migration was an aspect of social mobility. For instance, earlier, in 1982, Henao had warned that "the Hispanic population which has continued to live in New Orleans Parish is the population of least economic resources."[15] Although the Latino population living in Orleans parish was relatively small and had fewer economic resources, it remained sizeable enough to maintain a community that supported businesses in areas like Mid-City. By 2000, the U.S. Census demonstrated that Mid-City had retained an important population of Latinos within Orleans parish.[16]

The history of Central American and Caribbean groups in New Orleans demonstrates several important features of the pre-Katrina Latino community. First, many Latinos who migrated to New Orleans were political exiles who sought to influence politics within their sending societies. These migrants made the Latino community within New Orleans seem tenuous because immigrants often returned to their sending societies once political tensions in their sending countries had been resolved. Political exiles coexisted with commercial migrants who often maintained homes in Honduras and traveled back and forth to New Orleans. On the other hand, political tensions were not always resolved. Poorer Latinos were also limited in their ability to travel back and forth from their country of origin. Latinos who remained in the city were sufficiently diverse to promote what some later Latino immigrants considered a "dispersed" and "disunited" community. This community also included a newer wave of post-2000 Latino migration to New Orleans that had barely begun to incorporate in New Orleans by the time Hurricane Katrina devastated the city.

Although Beatrice Rodriguez Owsley's oral histories stands as one of the only published studies of Latinos in New Orleans, Latinos who had lived in Mid-City remembered how they had individually arrived in New Orleans as they walked amidst their wet and mold-encrusted belongings. Their narratives of migration often began with reference to the banana trade or their role in promoting New Orleans' recovery after Hurricane Betsy. These migrants' continual mention of Latinos' role in New Orleanian history seemed to insist that they had already played an important and positive role in the city's development and expansion and had created "place" in the city. For instance, they overwhelmingly referred to New Orleans rather than Honduras in relating their stories.

After Hurricane Katrina, many Honduran residents of Mid-City remembered a variety of early experiences in the New Orleans area that reflected their ambivalence toward the city's race relations. On the one hand, some residents discussed the confusion they felt when they boarded the city's buses and didn't know where to sit. Migrants who had arrived in the 1930s and 1940s described segregation with apparent surprise and disbelief. When I asked where they sat, they described their choice to sit "at the front of the bus" as a refusal to participate in Jim Crow segregation. When I asked migrants how the city had treated them, they claimed that the city "didn't know" Latin Americans and exempted them from race-based segregation. On the other hand, many ignored how their settlement in Mid-City could have reflected residential segregation in New Orleans. When I asked about how their Afro-Honduran and Afro-Cuban compatriots fared, they insisted "we're all Latino." When I asked Afro-Hondurans about their experiences with discrimination, they claimed they were often assumed to be African American by other city residents and discussed individualized struggles against discrimination in their mixed-race families and workplaces.

Hondurans who had lived in Mid-City reflected the dynamics of Latino communities within a *colonia.* As I walked the streets of Mid-City in October 2005, I found that only a few of its residents were among the early twentieth century wave of migrants. These migrants lived amongst second-generation New Orleanians like Gus[17] and June who reclaimed Mid-City by relating stories of their parents who had first arrived in the area from Honduras and Cuba. Their stories differed from those of the majority of Mid-City Latino residents who related migration experiences from Honduras during the 1970s and 1980s. In turn, these migrants had witnessed subsequent waves of Latino immigration from Nicaragua, Salvador, and Guatemala during the

1990s. For instance, despite the broader growth in number and diversity of Latinos, many emphasized the increasing numbers of African Americans when they discussed recent changes in the Mid-City population. In contrast, second-generation Latinos believed changes in the neighborhood were a product of more recent gentrification following the opening of the nearby streetcar, which provided better access to downtown New Orleans.

Mid-City's diverse population reflected how an internally stratified community was affected by Hurricane Katrina. Mid-City residents' homes included some newer, elevated houses and a large number of older wooden structures that were approximately sixty to seventy years old and had been clearly compromised by Hurricane Katrina. Nonetheless, despite this diversity within Mid-City, the Latino community maintained social ties to other Latinos outside of the area. For example, more recent Mid-City Latino immigrants rented properties from earlier Latino residents who had eventually purchased their homes in the neighborhood and moved to areas like Kenner and Lakeview. When I interviewed these earlier Latino immigrants who visited their rental properties, they told me how leaving Mid-City was part of "moving up" and realizing their "American Dream." Their narratives also differed within the migrant generation.

Arnaldo and Juan are both first-generation Honduran immigrants who reflected different socioeconomic trajectories. Arnaldo and Juan had arrived in Mid-City in the late 1970s but Arnaldo had moved to nearby Metairie over five years ago. Juan lived alone in Mid-City and had refused to evacuate because "they are always announcing hurricanes and I didn't think this one would be any different." Juan was soft-spoken, related his story with a sense of confidence and pride, and claimed his place in the city through his narrative about the disaster. He explained that he had remained in his home and, when the water began to rise, climbed into the attic. He eventually found a saw in the attic and saw himself as resourceful when he used the saw to break through to his roof. He remained on his roof for three days in the company of his dogs. Juan was similarly proud of his dog, which he used to complement his own resourcefulness. Juan explained that his dog was "clever" in climbing onto a floating object to regain his position on the roof despite several falls into the water. Juan repeatedly challenged my questions about evacuation with his responses. "Why should I ever have to leave my home?" he countered. Juan explained that accepting the threat implied by storm warnings and "running from the storm" would have meant that he could not overcome obstacles. He felt "if I believe something bad will happen, then it will happen." In Juan's narrative about staying on his roof, believing he was vulnerable was tantamount to increasing the possibility of a negative outcome. Rather than fear, Juan was proud of his ability to endure the storm and remain in his home. He not only found a saw and broke through his roof, but he also joined his neighbors on boats they used to search a nearby Winn-Dixie store for food. Juan had not wanted to leave his home or evacuate. He returned as soon as the city allowed him reentry despite the fact that the area had been largely abandoned and lacked electricity. Once he returned, he immediately began repairs.

In contrast, Arnaldo lived in nearby Metairie and had evacuated the city. Despite making a different set of choices, Arnaldo never expressed surprise at those his brother had made. Instead, Arnaldo continually looked over at me for validation and laughed at each episode in Juan's story of conquest over adversity. Later, Arnaldo drove me to Lakeview to demonstrate that even the "rich" in "rich homes" could not control the effects of the disaster. Despite the fact that Arnaldo no longer lived in Mid-City, he was very proud of the area and seemed to know everyone we passed on a first-name basis. Even as he pointed out several Cuban-owned businesses in the area, Arnaldo insisted that *"los Hondureños siempre han mandado aqui"* ("Hondurans have always decided what happens here."). He pointed out more recent Nicaraguan, Salvadoran, and Guatemalan immigrants as we passed them on the streets but did not want to stop or introduce me to them because, he explained, "They didn't know the history of the area."

Walking through Mid-City, I confirmed that more recent Latino migrants were more likely to be poorer and undocumented. Among these, many Hondurans had arrived in New Orleans in the late-1990s after Hurricane Mitch. I spoke to Teresa as she worked with her father and Eulalio who were gutting the home of their employers. Teresa, a Honduran immigrant who had lived through Hurricane Mitch in Honduras, lived with her father and brother in a trailer in Kenner where they stayed during the hurricane. When I asked Teresa about whether she was concerned about the increased numbers of immigration officials in the area, she explained that they had worked alongside her. Although the temporary protected status that Honduran and other Central American immigrants enjoyed had ended for those arriving after 2001, Teresa seemed happy about rumors that Hondurans would soon receive an amnesty for enduring the storm and aiding in the recovery efforts. Teresa explained that many recent Latino immigrants I had passed on the street had evacuated to Texas and were visiting Mid-City to collect their belongings and share their stories with their neighbors. Although they were frequently disoriented when I asked these recent immigrants whether they planned to return to New Orleans, Teresa felt confident that they would. After all, she explained, "There's lots of work."

The Mid-City Latino population demonstrated several important features. First, it demonstrated that older waves of Honduran immigrants viewed moving out of Mid-City housing as an aspect of social mobility. Second, the Latino population that lived in Mid-City was stratified based on migrant generation. In addition to the early twentieth century wave of Honduran and Cuban immigrants, many 1970s and 1980s Honduran immigrants who lived in Mid-City felt they had turned the neighborhood into a community. Although these immigrants recognized Mid-City was in a period of transition, they considered recent wave of Latino immigrants to be marginal to "their community." Third, the 1970s-1980s Honduran migrants viewed their move to areas like Kenner as a reproduction of this stratification. For example, Ricardo is a Honduran immigrant who maintained his Mid-City home as a rental property after purchasing a home in Kenner only three weeks before Hurricane Katrina. He explained that the outmigration of Latinos from Mid-City to Kenner began in the 1990s and that more "well to do" Latino immigrants in Kenner lived closer to the border with Orleans parish than recent migrants who were poorer. Finally, more recent migrants like Teresa and Eulalio were more likely to rent and to discuss legal status.

RACIALIZATION

Recent Latino immigrants to New Orleans and Kenner had not fully integrated into more established networks and communities and were largely invisible in the weeks and months following Hurricane Katrina. Instead, the media emphasized Latino workers who migrated after the storm to take jobs in recovery. Although the media stopped short of comparing Latinos' role in the city to looting, it did project a new image of Latinos as an "army of aliens," questioned Latinos' entitlement to work and be in the city, and repeatedly raised concerns about the long-term implications of this migration on the city's culture and demographics.[18] The following sections analyze themes in this coverage to understand the ways in which the media has represented Latinos in New Orleans following Hurricane Katrina.

The media rarely provided a rich sense of who Latinos were or what they had experienced. In the weeks following Hurricane Katrina, the coverage of Latinos in New Orleans was brief and limited. Local papers in Houston and San Antonio discussed individual narratives of evacuation in sympathetic tones that promoted their readers' understanding of new arrivals. For example, the local *San Antonio Express News* explained its hope was "that these stories will introduce our new neighbors to the community where they might choose to stay."[19] Nonetheless, even these early articles were preoccupied with legal status and characterized evacuees who had not passed inspection upon entry into the United States in negative terms that included having "crept" across the border.[20] International media outlets in Australia, England, and throughout Latin America also focused on the status issue by emphasizing how undocumented Latino evacuees feared officials and deportation and the consequences this fear had in terms of patterning Latinos' failure to evacuate and/or seek relief. In these narratives, Latinos were persistently constructed as victims who were "terrified," "consumed by worry and fear," "ineligible for most aid," and "very frustrated."[21] The articles reinforced this passive characterization by describing Latino evacuees' behaviors in terms that included "staying in flooded homes to guard belongings," "sneaking in" to shelters, "slip[ping] out" in the morning, and "praying they won't be noticed."[22] One article in the *Washington Post* imposed the reporter's interest in body language rather than how evacuees understood their own experience: the evacuee's "body language said it all. Eyes down, arms folded, back slumped, he had the visage of a defeated man."[23] Although the media constructed Latino evacuees largely as defeated victims, one article in a Houston paper was an exception. It suggested Latinos had acted in the midst of the disaster when it documented one evacuee's experience "delivering food and water to neighbors also struggling to survive."[24] Another exception was one article that suggested Latinos' experience was patterned by forces beyond immigration status when it noted "illegal immigrants live in the hardest-hit areas."[25]

Two early articles considered whether Latinos would become the "replacement work force" for recovery.[26] Their emphasis on Latinos as "replacement" workers provided the earliest suggestion that Latinos might displace native workers. Although one of the articles considered how Latinos' potential role in recovery work would reproduce their poverty within New Orleans, other articles shared a general inability to understand how poverty, legal status, and racialization reinforced each other. In other words, media coverage emphasized Latinos as marginal workers and ignored the population's historically productive social role in New Orleans. Instead, the coverage described how immigrant workers "descended," "poured into," "appeared throughout," and changed "the complexion" of the city.[27] Several articles insisted that Latinos were "transforming the city's demographics."[28] Reinforcing the characterization of Latino workers' growth in the city as a problem, one writer explained that the "recent and sudden influx of immigrants seems a little too much, too fast."[29] In other words, the media simultaneously characterized Latinos as passive victims and a Katrina-like force that displaced "working-class black residents."[30] For instance, one article blamed federal authorities who "opened the gates" for "a new flood."[31] Ironically, this article was the only incidence of any coverage that considered how recovery workers were not only immigrants, but also native-born migrants from surrounding areas like Georgia and Texas.

The issue of labor was a central one for the media and for Latinos. The media overwhelmingly reduced Latinos' experience in a devastated city to labor issues. While many articles documented cases of wage fraud among "this marginalized sector of unfortunates" and some considered the deplorable housing conditions Latino workers faced, many others claimed Latinos were seen as "usurpers" and promoted a concern about the city's reliance on Latino workers.[32] For instance, an October 2005 article in the *Los Angeles Times* suggested Latinos "may be the new service class in New Orleans" and pointed out that "for decades, the city's low-wage service industry was dominated by African Americans, many of whom lived in the areas hardest hit by Hurricane Katrina and evacuated to other cities."[33] This article constructed Latinos as "job takers" and ignored their economic role in creating jobs. For instance, worrying about Latinos' departure from California to New Orleans, one writer explained that "for every agriculture job that is lost, 3.5 jobs are lost as well in related areas, such as packing and transportation."[34] In this way, the media created Latinos as another force threatening to permanently displace a vulnerable population that was further weakened by Hurricane Katrina. Broadening the class implications of Latino immigration onto homeowners, one article suggested Latino migrants would stay because "they can buy distressed property pretty cheaply."[35]

The myriad ways media understood the role of Latino labor in New Orleans refracted not only social issues in recovery, but also broader concerns about the centrality of Latino labor in the United States. For instance, in October 2005, one writer claimed that Latinos had "been so warmly received by contractors that many of them say they plan to stay, save money, buy homes, and put down roots in the Big Easy."[36] This article exemplified media's use of labor to refract broader concerns about the economic impact of Latino migration. By November 2005, another writer worried about Latinos' migration from other areas in the United States and warned "the grape pickers are leaving northern California, and the grapes are left hanging on the vines. You'll feel the effect when you uncork a bottle of wine next year or the year after that."[37] Media's concern with Latinos' movement was heightened by December when the same writer claimed "it's not just the grapes that are being lost on the vines. Citrus growers in Arizona and lettuce and almond farmers across the nation are feeling the effects as well. There are anecdotal situations where lettuce farmers, short 200 workers to bring in a crop, fear going under, losing the farm to less expensive imported produce from China, Canada and Mexico."[38] This writer suggested that reliance on Latino laborers not only threatened a particular city's culture and demographics, but any attempts to develop a broader industry based on Latino labor.

The media suggested Latinos were an unreliable labor force and expanded this concern to a central issue in New Orleans' recovery: culture. Often, the media contrasted music, food, and even patterns of socializing to distinguish the effects of Latino migration in the city. For instance, Lovato's 2005 piece entitled the "Latinization of the New New Orleans" claimed that "the new New Orleans [is] a city on the verge of a radical Latinization that is transforming other urban landscapes in the country." In the post-Katrina context, the terms of this transformation were often understood to imply displacement. For instance, one writer claimed "the perennial sounds of New Orleans jazz have been replaced at work sites by cumbias and norteñas blaring from work-crew boom boxes."[39] Media coverage reproduced concerns about "Whose city is this going to become?" and repeatedly contrasted "undocumented workers," who overwhelmingly come from the Americas, with "American workers."[40] This exclusionary phrasing implies Latinos are not only foreign to "America" but also potentially cast them as un-American. For example, the media rarely distinguished "local" from non-local workers. In this way, the media obscured Latinos as a growing population that included many local, that is, pre-Katrina residents and ignored Latinos' historic influence on the city.

The media coverage beginning in mid-October 2005 portrayed Latinos as a unique "army of aliens" who that would recover New Orleans and put it "on its way to becoming a largely brown city."[41] This coverage not only ignored significant diversity among post-Katrina Latino migrants but also reproduced what Ana María Ochoa Gautier called "the historic game of locating one history of excluded people against another."[42] For instance, only two of eighty-six articles recognized that many Latino residents of New Orleans had returned for work in recovery jobs. None recognized that many Afro-Latinos lived in New Orleans, had been integrated within African American communities, and had potentially experienced the aftermath of Hurricane Katrina in ways that reflected the racial dynamics of the city. Having ignored these dynamics, the media did not address the ways Afro-Latinos' experience of the disaster may have differed from that of their African American and Latino counterparts. The media's homogenized racialization of Latinos was mirrored by officials' actions at shelters. For instance, several articles commented on an incident in Long Beach, Mississippi, where sheriff's deputies entered a Red Cross shelter and "demanded identification from dozens of people who *looked* Hispanic. . .They were concerned that the shelter was being used to house out-of-town construction workers."[43] One article that did attempt to distinguish Latinos protested Nagin's homogenization of Latinos as "Mexicans" and centered on physical attributes. Nonetheless, it assumed the social meanings attributed to physical attributes and promoted an immigrant-native minority distinction by contrasting "an almond-eyed, Mayan-faced, 4-foot-2-inch undocumented immigrant from Guatemala, and. . .a shaven-headed, tattooed, 6-foot-3-inch U.S. citizen and former Chicano gang member."[44]

Despite a variety of legal statuses, the media emphasized legal status to identify, distinguish, and criminalize Latino workers as a group. For instance, local coverage of "one of the largest raids since thousands of Hispanic workers flocked to New Orleans following Hurricane Katrina" included the claim that "at least a dozen had violent criminal backgrounds in Central America."[45] Ironically, the article pursued its subtle conflation of legal status with criminality by quoting an Immigration and Customs Enforcement (ICE) official. The writer relayed claims that ICE was "overzealously enforcing immigration laws after Katrina" but quoted the ICE official who defended the agency, explaining that "we're concerned about the bad guy; we want to catch the bad guy, the guy with a criminal record who might break the law or present a threat to public safety. . .We're not that concerned with the Sheetrocker." In this way, the article promoted an ambiguous distinction between "bad" Latinos who may pose a threat to public safety and "good" Latinos who are defined by their work. The article's coverage of the forty arrests promoted the impression that there are many criminals among the recent Latino migrants. Similarly, several weeks later, the *Times Picayune* again quoted an ICE agent who explained that their round-up of sixty-eight illegal immigrants over the April 1, 2005, weekend targeted "violent, criminal" immigrants.[46] Reflecting the trend in perception, the *Times Picayune* covered the May 2006 rally in New Orleans by including a quote from an organizer who said undocumented Latinos should not be treated as criminals.[47]

The media are a site of discourse and their representation of Latinos is politically significant.[48] It is also an important influence on racial attitudes and therefore influences Latino migrants' reception in New Orleans. In many ways, it not only reflects the unique conditions and context recent migrants faced, but also presents a version of the population for non-Latinos who struggle to recover New Orleans. Within the city, the media frame a context that can either promote or inhibit a positive reception for Latino migrants. Indeed, the ways in which other cities initially portrayed Latino evacuees explicitly attempted to welcome Latino evacuees and "introduce" residents to the new migrants. In New Orleans, however, this reception was influenced by the media's emphasis on Latinos' legal status, criminality, and potential role in displacing pre-Katrina residents and New Orleanian culture. In this way, the media ignored the pre-Katrina "gumbo" and recast Latinos as a force that could potentially "overrun" the city's plans for recovery.

CONCLUSION

This chapter highlighted the importance of a historical perspective to maintain and nurture the diversity of communities affected by natural events like hurricanes. It argued that the absence of a historical perspective facilitated the reproduction of discriminatory approaches toward vulnerable populations by both non-Latino residents and government officials. The chapter's analysis underscored how vulnerable populations were quickly racialized and became scapegoats within the context of a disaster and demonstrated that racialization is a critical aspect of the Latino experience in New Orleans. It found that Latinos' racialization resulted from nativism, an inadequate federal disaster management policy that could address Latinos' needs, segmented labor markets that discriminate against Latinos, and persistent social marginalization. It also elucidated central issues surrounding race and immigration, that is, racialized immigration. It demonstrated that this racialization made Latinos particularly vulnerable in the broader socioeconomic recovery following Hurricane Katrina.

The post-Katrina period of New Orleans' history coincides with national debates over immigration reform. Tensions that arose between local and federal governments in relation to the Hurricane Katrina disaster were reproduced in the case of Latino migrants. For example, President Bush's decision to suspend the Davis-Bacon Act again collided with local desires when large contracts and migration resulted. In turn, local government struggled to regain control over recovery plans. In this context, New Orleans Mayor Nagin portrayed the city as a victim that was being "overrun" by "Mexican" workers. Indeed, the city is not powerless in how it responds to the Latino migrants who have been a critical force in recovering the city. For instance, New Orleans's major newspaper, the *Times Picayune,* continues to influence the context in which Latino migrants are understood and treated.

Despite official counts of the Latino population in the greater New Orleans area, Latinos had already developed a rich and productive history and "place" in New Orleans. Their contributions to the New Orleans "gumbo" seemed to disappear in media coverage on Latinos in New Orleans. The media also failed to follow up in any systematic way on the ways in which Latino evacuees may or may not have recovered their lives. Instead, the media emphasized new Latino migrants and frequently cast them as "aliens" who could potentially recreate criminality in the city and displace a revisionist pre-Katrina New Orleans culture.

In much the same way that neighborhood histories like those of Mid-City seem reduced to post-hurricane debris, Latino residents' struggles, difficulties, and community were summarily dismissed by the media. What remains is the version of Latinos as "others," which reproduces the inequality that feeds Latinos' poor socioeconomic status. The political and cultural consequences of this otherization are evident in the media coverage of exploited workers, inadequate legal protections, and harassment by police and immigration officials.

NOTES

1. Wynton Marsalis, "Marsalis on Katrina's 'Race/Class' Issue," *EUR Web,* September 6, 2005, http://www.eurweb.com/printable.cfm?id=22179.

2. Katherine Donato, Nicole Trujillo-Pagán, Carl L. Bankston, III, and Audrey Singer, "Reconstructing New Orleans after Katrina: The Emergence of an Immigrant Labor Market," in *The Sociology of Katrina: Perspectives on a Modern Catastrophe,* eds. David Brunsma, David Overfelt, and Steve Picou (Lanham, MD: Rowman & Littlefield, *Forthcoming*).

3. Michael Omi and Howard Winant, *Racial Formation in the United States: From the 1960s to the 1990s,* 2nd ed. (New York: Routledge, 1994), 55.

4. Beatrice Rodriguez Owsley, *The Hispanic-American Entrepreneur: An Oral History of the American Dream* (New York: Twayne Publishers, 1992).

5. U.S. Census data in Elmer Lamar Ross, "Factors in Residence Patterns among Latin Americans in New Orleans: A Study in Urban Anthropological Methodology" (Ph.D. diss, University of Georgia, 1973), 5.

6. Allen Johnson, Jr. "A Fruitful Relationship," *Gambit* 19(December 1, 1998): 23.

7. Mark Moberg, "Crown Colony as Banana Republic: The United Fruit Company in British Honduras, 1900–1920," *Journal of Latin American Studies* 28, no. 2 (1996): 357–81; Steve Marquardt, "'Green Havoc': Panama Disease, Environmental Change, and Labor Process in the Central American Banana Industry," *The American Historical Review* 106, no. 1 (2001): 49–80.

8. Luis Emilio Henao, *The Hispanics in Louisiana* (New Orleans: Latin American Apostolate, 1982).

9. Henao, *Hispanics in Louisiana,* 29.

10. Henao, *Hispanics in Louisiana,* 29.

11. Henao, *Hispanics in Louisiana,* 26.

12. Henao, *Hispanics in Louisiana,* 22

13. Contradicted by http://www.state.la.us/opb/labench/demo6.gif.

14. Blanca Rosa Morales Medina, "Diversity in Mainstream Suburbia: An Investigation into the Social and Economic Conditions of the Hispanic Population of Jefferson Parish, Louisiana" (Master's thesis, University of New Orleans, 1998), 6.

15. Henao, *Hispanics in Louisiana,* 27.

16. According to the 2000 U.S. Census, "Hispanic or Latino" comprised 17 percent of Orleans Parish Census tract 65.

17. Formal names represent pseudonyms assigned to protect confidentiality.

18. Roberto Lovato, "The Latinization of the New New Orleans," *New America Media,* October 18, 2005, http://crm.ncmonline.com/news/view_article.html?article_id=fa92e2c88a63985418da75582292b5c7.

19. Lety Laurel, "Faces of Katrina," *San Antonio Express-News,* September 8, 2005, 2B.

20. Darryl Fears, "For Illegal Immigrants, Some Aid Is Too Risky; Fears Abound as Government Won't Promise Immunity from Deportation," *The Washington Post,* September 20, 2005, A06.

21. Reuters News Service, "Katrina's Aftermath: Uprooted Hispanic Immigrants Ask What to Do after Katrina. New Orleans Was Home to One of America's Largest Populations from Honduras, Mexico," *The Houston Chronicle,* September 12, 2005; Fears, "For Illegal Immigrants"; Associated Press, "Illegals Go Their Own Way," *Herald Sun,* September 10, 2005, 19.

22. Associated Press, "Illegals Go Their Own Way."

23. Fears, "For Illegal Immigrants."

24. Laurel, "Faces of Katrina."

25. Associated Press, "Illegals Go Their Own Way."

26. Patrick Osio, Jr., "Americans can Fill Immigrants' Jobs," *The San Diego Union-Tribune,* September 26, 2005, B-7; Raul A Reyes, "Katrina's Next Expose: Immigration Woes," *USA Today,* October 14, 2005.

27. Peter Pae, "Immigrants Rush to New Orleans as Contractors Fight for Workers," *Los Angeles Times,* October 10, 2005; Penny Brown. Roberts, "Hispanic Workers Likely to Affect N.O. Culture," *theadvocate.com,* May 6, 2006, http://www.2theadvocate.com/news/2758411.html?showAll=y; Sam Quinones, "Migrants Find a Gold Rush in New Orleans," *Los Angeles Times,* April 4, 2006; Hernán Rozemberg, "The Changing Face of the Gulf Coast Work Force," *San Antonio Express-News,* March 19, 2006; Saundra Amrhein, "In Big Easy Cleanup, 'Us' vs. 'Them,'" *St. Petersburg Times,* October 23, 2005, 1A; Arian Campo-Flores, "A New Spice in the Gumbo: Will Latino Day Laborers Locating in New Orleans Change its Complexion?" *Newsweek,* December 5, 2005.

28. Reyes, "Katrina's Next Expose"; Roberts, "Hispanic Workers Likely to Affect N.O. Culture"; Ruben Navarrette, Jr., "The Language of Race," *San Diego Union-Tribune,* January 22, 2006.

29. Amrhein, "In Big Easy Cleanup."

30. Amrhein, "In Big Easy Cleanup."

31. Roberts, "Hispanic Workers Likely to Affect N.O. Culture."

32. Lloyd Williams, "The No Latino Left Behind Act: Last One out of Mexico Turn-off the Lights," *New York Beacon,* April 13–19, 2006, 13(15), 8; Quinones, "Migrants Find a Gold Rush in New Orleans."

33. Pae, "Immigrants Rush to New Orleans."

34. Victor Landa, "Labor, Not Border, Decides U.S. Churn," *San Antonio Express-News,* December 12, 2005, 5B.

35. Pae, "Immigrants Rush to New Orleans."

36. Navarrette, "The Language of Race."

37. Victor Landa, "Conned and Mistreated in Katrina's Wake," *San Antonio Express-News,* November 20, 2005, 3H.

38. Landa, "Labor, Not Border, Decides U.S. Churn."

39. Landa, "Labor, Not Border, Decides U.S. Churn."

40. Amrhein, "In Big Easy Cleanup"; Leslie Eaton, "Study Sees Increase in Illegal Hispanic Workers in New Orleans," *New York Times*, June 8, 2006, 16; Anderson, 2006.

41. Lovato, "The Latinization of the New New Orleans"; Navarrette, "The Language of Race."

42. Ana María Ochoa Gautier, "Nueva Orleáns, La Permeable Margen Norte del Caribe," *Nueva Sociedad* 201(January/February 2006), 70.

43. Mary Lou Pickel, "Immigrant Workers Rile New Orleans: Rules Shelved, Crews Labor for Meager Pay," *Atlanta Journal-Constitution*, October 19, 2005, 1A.

44. Lovato, "The Latinization of the New New Orleans."

45. James Varney, "40 Jailed in Raid on Immigrants: But Legal Groups Say City Needs Workers," *Times-Picayune,* March 18, 2006.

46. West Bank Bureau, "68 Immigrants Rounded Up, Arrested," *Times-Picayune,* April 7, 2006.

47. Leslie Williams, "Thousands Hold Rally for Immigrant Rights: Hispanic Demonstrators March Through CBD," *Times-Picayune,* May 2, 2006.

48. Leo R. Chavez, *Covering Immigration: Popular Images and the Politics of the Nation*, Berkeley (University of California Press, 2001).

Chapter Six

Saxophones, Trumpets, and Hurricanes

The Cultural Restructuring of New Orleans

Susan C. Pearce

CULTURE MATTERS

In the 2006 Hollywood film *Take the Lead,* a contentious exchange of words takes place between local ballroom dance teacher Pierre Dulaine and a South Bronx, New York, high school teacher. Offering to teach dance to the low-achieving students in detention, Dulaine explains, "Life for me is *dance*." To this, the recalcitrant principal responds argumentatively, "Life for these kids is like a hustle to stay alive and a fight to make ends meet, *not* ballroom dancing."[1]

Are the creative arts at all relevant in social environments when the stakes of daily realities are life and death? Has the music stopped for post-Katrina New Orleans? Like the South Bronx, the city of New Orleans has continued to house the deep intergenerational pockets of poverty that stem from the country's continued racial disparities and structural legacies of slavery. In fact, many of the exposés of race, poverty, and disempowerment that echoed throughout the mass-mediated public sphere since Hurricane Katrina hit shore in August 2005 have elaborated the *structural* histories and current realities of our system—and rightfully so. Through its analysis of 2000 decennial Census figures, for example, The Brookings Institution reports that New Orleans ranked sixth in the list of poorest cities among the 100 largest metropolitan areas in the United States. The median household income for the city's residents was 96th among these 100 metropolitan areas.

Poverty statistics revealed glaring racial disparities in the city; in the year 2000, 84 percent of the impoverished population of New Orleans was Black. A place that once boasted racially integrated neighborhoods had gradually begun to resemble the hypersegregated northern environs of Detroit and Chicago.[2] Before Katrina, the city's public structures—from the school system to the criminal justice system—were failing to meet public needs, and affected the poor and people of color most directly. These structural injustices came to public attention starkly through the journalistic accounts of the storm's aftermath.

A second, complementary side to the story of race, empowerment, and Katrina is located in that empirically elusive arena of *culture*, and has its roots in the creative agency of generations of people of African descent. It is the story of the musical legacy of the city of New Orleans—which includes zydeco, blues, and funk, among others, and the subject of this chapter—jazz. As it turns out, the world of jazz has infused itself into the post-Katrina civil-society public discourse over structural injustices and the struggle to recover, but has yet to resonate at the larger level of the state. This chapter investigates the "meaning reconstruction" that is integral to the infrastructural reconstruction of New Orleans after September 2005, with a focus on the legacy of New Orleans as a key jazz mecca. Using media and document analysis in an ethnographic style, I pose questions about empowerment and disempowerment as experienced in relation to jazz music and "race." My research materials include newspaper, magazine, and Web-based articles, radio broadcasts, performances, musical recordings, and documentary film.

DISENTANGLING CULTURE AND STRUCTURE

LOOPING: in acid jazz, a continuously building entanglement of old jazz tunes that are repeatedly played (looped), adding layers of improvised sounds

The exchange previously recounted between Pierre Dulaine and the South Bronx teacher exemplifies an age-old tension within the social sciences between the "survival" structural components of life—such as finding subsistence—and that of culture. The latter, in conventional Marxian terms, was "epiphenomenal"—it was the icing on the cake at the base of societal life, but not the core ingredient within the batter of society. Paramount to the task of emancipation, according to Marx, is to be attentive to people's material conditions rather than, for example, the world of ideas.[3]

Writing within the Marxian tradition, but with a more nuanced appreciation of culture, Frankfurt School theorist Theodor Adorno wrote a social critique of the world of jazz during its heyday as a popular, mass form in the 1930s.[4] Aspects of Adorno's essay have been justifiably criticized as dismissive, condescending, and even racist. One concern of his essay that might continue to inform our cultural criticism today, however, was Adorno's attempt to excavate the meaning of jazz composition and performance as it relates to actual social power. In Marxian terms, Adorno suggested that the music represented a false consciousness of emancipation, through its innovative rhythmic structure and individuality of melodies. Were African Americans simply being used as props by the actual power-holders, presenting an illusion of emancipation when they continued to be enslaved to their masters in the commodified world of entertainment?[5] At that time, Adorno could not anticipate the movement of jazz away from the core repertoire of popular music into an "art music" scene. Nor did he seem to foresee the varieties of styles and forms into which jazz would eventually modulate, fusing with other musical genres. Further, he did not predict how this music would take root in the societies of oppressive state communism, where musicians and audiences appreciated it as a form of uninhibited individual expression. Thus, attempts to answer his question face new complexities.

In more recent years, sociologists of culture have challenged the conceptualization of (structural) base and (cultural) superstructure as an oppositional scheme, as well as the assumption that some expressions of culture are necessarily anti-emancipatory. Moreover, researchers have illustrated the power of culture to influence structure, and to behave in structural ways.[6] Building upon the incomplete project of Max Weber on the sociology of music, Alan Turley has argued that the musician performs an exemplary role as an agent within societies, illustrating that culture plays a relatively autonomous part in social life.[7]

The jazz-related public conversations and activities surrounding post-Katrina New Orleans provide an opportunity to examine both the structure/culture question and the relationship between culture and social power in U.S. race relations. Adorno's pointed questions about African American social power can be both challenged and extended in investigating the meaning of jazz for the embattled city of New Orleans. The intrinsic style of the jazz form provides a lesson in the relationship between structure and agency, in fact. Despite the flexibility of improvisation (called "blowing" in the genre), jazz pieces are highly structured, both rhythmically and melodically, and blowing is rooted in those structures, which it also helps to transform. Looping takes this further, sampling old tunes and adding more improvisations on top. Thus, even the structures do not stand still.

A PLACE-BASED MUSIC

QUOTING: an unexpected incorporation of a well-known tune in the middle of a solo.

Jazz historians generally consider New Orleans to be the birthplace of jazz. The city has been described as "the first of the major American urban settings where conditions were favourable for advances in the development of jazz."[8] Those conditions included—perhaps first and foremost—the blending of its diverse resident cultures. Situated at the intersection of major waterways, the city received population inflows from multiple directions. Around 1900, jazz first began to emerge in the city as a new, innovative fusion of other music forms. Prominent among these was that of the blues, a form originating in the Mississippi Delta and offering a welcome cultural freedom from the degradation of minstrel singing. The other major source was ragtime, a syncopated popular music that had been nurtured in African American communities in the cities of the Midwest.

The city of New Orleans boasted a particularly fertile ground for the birth of a new music. As Turley notes, "A city is socially divided into racial, ethnic, and class communities from which musicians come; musicians then create their own community of music performance, composition, and identity."[9] And the creative potential that arises when multiple cultures interact and blend in urban areas leads to the birth of new musical styles and genres. In a city known for "creolization" of its various populations (indigenous, colonist, and forced migrant), New Orleans jazz reflected and was fed by this rich cultural mix. The new musical genre blended influences from the city's Spanish, French, Caribbean, and West African cultures, among others. Clearly, some key mixtures were due to force: first, that of transatlantic slavery, and second, that of post–Civil War Jim Crow segregation laws—where lighter skin Creoles were legally declared to be "Negroes," and required to live in the same neighborhoods with those who had darker skin. Early New Orleans jazz was played in the style of "trad," now known as Dixieland, featuring a 4/4 beat and a strong presence of brass instruments, with the three lead instruments devoted to creating melodic improvisations. A characteristic feature of the New Orleans music was the jazz funeral, which drew from a tradition that predated jazz: the marching brass band. The band would provide comfort for the bereaved family through its street performances. The jazz funeral took on a particular form:

> The procession begins with the playing of the dirge, a slow, mournful, solemn
> tempo that expresses a somber respect for the deceased. At a certain point, the

procession picks up the tempo and energy in celebration of the positive accomplishments of the individual and an acknowledgment of his or her zest for life.[10]

FREE: improvisation that pays no attention to chord changes in the piece

More controversial than the question of the birthplace of jazz has been a long-running debate among music historians and jazz specialists over the music's essential musical and ethnic roots. While this debate, which is far from settled, cannot be resolved here, its concerns do inform this analysis. The debate delves into issues of racial or ethnic "essence" and questions such as the extent to which West African rhythmic improvisational structures, call and response traditions, and other African influences inspired the music's development. Since the music is no longer located in one ethnic community, and members of many ethnic groups are among the composers and performers of jazz, is it "Black" music?[11] Social science now discounts "essential" definitions of racial groups, and has investigated how past assumptions about Blackness and Whiteness were based in racist assumptions, as exemplified in the recent research of Bruce Baum.[12] Orville Lee has written that race is "a durable social fact that lacks immutable form."[13] Therefore, a quest to locate this cultural form (jazz) in one racial group (Americans of African descent) risks such essentialism—and is thus an *anti*-progressive move. On the other hand, locating the invention of jazz at a multicultural intersection risks diffusing attention (and credit) from the centrality of African Americans in the music's legacy. The British scholar Paul Gilroy warns against the latter and suggests that identity be considered "neither as a fixed essence nor as a vague and utterly contingent construction."[14] This will be our approach here.

An analysis of the complex relationships between the culture of New Orleans, jazz music, and African American empowerment needs to strike a balance between an awareness of the multicultural strains at the heart of the music's beginnings and the critical roles that African American musicians, composers, and audiences have played in producing and reproducing the genre.

THE NEIGHBORHOODS

ROOT: the basic pitch of the jazz chord

New Orleans jazz, in fact, was rooted in neighborhoods. The jazz form arose organically within and across neighborhoods, and the performance spaces and musicians were able to place their own local stamps on the compositions that resulted. The neighborhood of Tremé, for example, where French-speaking

Creoles of color lived, historically prided itself on one of the highest concentrations of jazz parades in the city. Within Tremé was Congo Square. Originally located outside the fortified walls, this was a famed location where the enslaved would freely perform African music and dance on Sunday afternoons. Both the Sixth and Seventh Wards were also the neighborhoods of Creoles of color, and were home to a number of famous musicians. Early jazz composer Jelly Roll Morton, for one, lived in the Seventh Ward.

The Eighth and Ninth Wards were working-class African American neighborhoods at the beginning of the twentieth century, and the site of Woodmen of the World Hall, which was one of the earliest jazz performance clubs. The neighborhood of Carrollton and Black Pearl was an African American neighborhood where blues and gospel music were frequently performed, and from which early jazz may have "quoted." The red-light district of Storyville was known for a wealth of jazz clubs and restaurants where the music was nurtured. Adjacent to Storyville, the Tango Belt was replete with commercial jazz establishments, including three large theaters, cabarets, and nightclubs. Back o' Town was the birthplace of Louis Armstrong, an African American neighborhood with saloons, vaudeville theaters, and the Parisian Garden room, which was a middle-class ballroom. Jazz also took root in White neighborhoods such as the Irish Channel and the West End. Finally, the riverboats sailing from New Orleans extended the neighborhoods by carrying jazz performance out of the city.[15]

Although communities lost buildings and historic character to twentieth-century development or highway construction, a number of historic structures remained. After several name changes, Congo Square recovered its original name and continues to be a popular performance space in the early twenty-first century. Additionally, jazz performance has maintained its grassroots, locally embedded character, with most New Orleans–bred musicians choosing to remain in the city rather than relocate. The jazz funeral processions continued at the neighborhood level. And through the years, jazz evolved as one of the city's key tourist attractions. Throughout this history, people of African descent emerged as carriers, performers, composers, teachers, and technicians. A number of New Orleans "jazz families" now exist, passing the tradition from generation to generation. Jazz became infused within the daily social lives of people of African descent as one expression of community pride and collective memory—thus, the concept of "root" has become relevant to life on this side of the Atlantic. By understanding the rootedness in the neighborhoods, the networks, and the families, as well as the African-inspired forms, it is possible to map strong relationships between jazz and African American cultural practices as an alternative to attempting to locate an essential "Blackness" in the music.

GO OUT: to take the final chorus and end the piece

The 2005 storm's damage was felt most intensely in neighborhoods of the poor and non-White residents, forcing them with no alternative other than to "go out"—often in mass transportation rescue efforts. Although the storm was no respecter of race or class, post-storm reports suggest that people of African descent, renters, and the poor had higher odds of living in areas that were damaged by the storm.[16] Among the hardest hit from heavy floodwaters were precisely the neighborhoods that nurtured early jazz—including Storyville, the Tango Belt, and the Sixth, Seventh, Eighth, and Ninth Wards. Ninth Ward residents were much less likely to have private vehicles than those in higher-income areas, affecting the community's ability to evacuate. Neighborhoods saw major population losses, demolished houses, the closing of small businesses, the destruction of music venues and studios, and the out-migration of musicians.

The Lower Ninth Ward, one of the city's less-privileged neighborhoods, was among the most devastated. One year later, those few residents who have remained or returned referred to the area as a ghost town.[17] The neighborhood was the subject of post-Katrina media reports that focused on its crime, poverty, and urban blight before the storm. The future fate of neighborhoods such as the Ninth Ward remains unknown, as many residents have not yet returned, and many may never return. Additionally, the city is not giving priority to low-income housing construction or the reconstruction of neighborhoods such as the Ninth Ward. As of July 1, 2006, the Orleans parish consisted of only 48 percent of its pre-Katrina population.[18] Evacuees' decision-making about whether to return hinged not only on the city's ability to rebound, but on the evacuees' experiences in their new homes. A recent journalistic report suggested that trends varied across locations: evacuees in Atlanta had largely settled in, found work, were beginning to buy houses, and were optimistic about moving forward with their lives. On the other hand, evacuees in Houston were still facing continued struggles, including arguments with the Federal Emergency Management Agency (FEMA).[19]

New Orleans musician-in-exile Cyril Neville referred to post-Katrina New Orleans as "a spiritless body, and that's all it's going to be without those people from the sixth, seventh, eighth and ninth wards."[20] Music is always embodied, and cannot return in full force without its audiences, performers, memories, and communities, whose experiences inspire and inform the composition. One year after the storm, *The New York Times* reported that "tens of thousands in the African-American working-class backbone remain unable to return."[21] Neville continued:

Regardless of your point of view with respect to the motivations or competence of our government, the events of the past few months have combined to wipe out an entire community and culture. It will take a lot more than new buildings, roads and an upgraded levee system to repair what has been lost. As fellow Americans, our contributions can only stop when the family and community bonds and traditions that have been shattered by this natural and government-engineered disaster have been restored.[22]

This reality that the music is deeply rooted in the local community level resounded in a May 2006 seminar at Tulane University, where a panel discussion on the rebirth of the city's culture featured jazz musicians Michael White, David Torkanowsky, and Ellis Marsalis. A prominent theme of the panel was the embodiment of the musical legacy of jazz in the family and neighborhood. Ellis Marsalis expressed his concern: "I have only had one question that I continually ask generally, and that is, 'Who's going to teach the kids to play the music?' I hope that in the rebirth of New Orleans, that a certain level of respect comes towards younger students learning music in a little more formal way without the exclusion . . . [of jazz]."[23] Intergenerational networks have played key roles in keeping the craft alive. Jazz pianist David Torkanowsky spoke of the need to look backward, and take care of the village elders who have passed on the music through oral tradition, since jazz was not taught formally in its formative years: "It was dealt with in sessions and listing to records, and going to hear this cat play and sneaking into clubs under age . . . I'm not going to say it's continued with the strength that it has in the past, but with Katrina, we have experienced a palpable disconnect which can never be repaired to what it was."[24]

A closely related discourse regarding public action is the attention to jazz places. The particular dependency of jazz music to the physical places where it is performed has been explored by sociologist Howard Becker, who writes that "the availability of places for the performance of jazz depended on the viability and profitability of such places."[25] In October 2005, the Lakeview neighborhood suddenly found a beloved jazz site, the Naval Brigade Hall, demolished by firefighters from out of town in a matter of hours. This 102-year-old brick building had more recently served as a music school. Although the building had been declared uninhabitable by the city, the firefighters were not aware of relevant city regulations that might have spared the building. In response, a coalition of neighborhood groups, Save Our Neighborhoods, was organized to prevent future occurrences. Group member Bari Landry commented, "People who didn't know this city destroyed an important part of jazz history. It's gone."[26] In neighborhoods such as the Ninth Ward, however, this type of mobilization is near impossible, with such a sparse population base and few amenities.

The well-known Preservation Hall, located in a structure that was built in 1750, closed for several months following the floods, opened in December

2005 to disappointing attendance, closed again, and reopened in 2006. The hall is dedicated to preserving the "New Orleans style" of jazz, and had attracted daily crowds of tourists to its concerts since 1961.[27] A handful of other jazz venues have also reopened. Since September 2005, new places have been added to the collective memory repertoire through the medium of jazz: The 1.5-mile jazz funeral procession to commemorate the first anniversary of Katrina marched from the Ernest N. Morial Convention Center to the Louisiana Superdome—the notorious location for displaced residents in the immediate aftermath of the storm, remembered for its atmosphere of chaos. In 2006, the National Trust for Historic Preservation and the Preservation Resource Center of New Orleans announced that all twenty of New Orleans historic districts were on an endangered list. Spokesperson Kevin Mercadel charged, "Destruction of our historic neighborhoods is avoidable, unnecessary, and largely irreversible—and that would be tragic. The choice before us is urban change by destruction or urban change by integration with the past."[28]

THE MUSICIANS

PICKUP: a phrase just before the first bar
DISSONANCE: harsh clashes between musical sounds

Listen carefully and you will hear the music emerge. First, it will rise from the streets. Then, in the French Quarter it will become louder. You will hear it in the visitor centers and the small clubs. Later, you will hear the parades, the jazz funerals, and the unbridled celebrations. . . . Listen up. The band is about to play."

—John Quirk, Superintendent, New Orleans Jazz
National Historical Park, September 7, 2005[29]

Complementing the anger and disillusionment expressed by Cyril Neville has been a parallel insistence throughout the city (and beyond) that "the music must go on." In an early pre-storm interview, New Orleans Mayor Ray Nagin stated, "New Orleanians keep telling us don't be surprised if you hear jazz music playing in the French Quarter in the not too distant future."[30] This optimism did not always run counter to the bleak picture painted by Neville, and in some instances continued the theme of the intersections of culture/structure/agency. Singer Bette Midler put words around we-will-rise-again sentiment during the September 17, 2005, Higher Ground Hurricane Relief Benefit Concert organized by the Jazz at Lincoln Center program in New York City. Recounting her memories of her feelings after her childhood house burned to the ground, she belted out the Peggy Lee classic, "Is that all there is? If that's all there is my friends, then let's keep dancing."[31]

The Higher Ground Concert recalled both the historical legacy of jazz the collective memory of the city's repeated experience of rebuilding after tragedies—placing Katrina as only one in a series. More resistant tones resonated in the evening's tunes as well. Jazz singer Jon Hendricks, for example, expressed his political anger with the current situation through the song "Tell Me the Truth," in which he sang the lines "Nowadays, wrong is right, down is up, black is white, bad is good, truth is a lie."[32] At the time, the public was learning about the dire situations faced by poor evacuees, competence and management issues within FEMA, and the unequal life chances faced by people of African descent trapped by the storm. Jazz trumpeter Wynton Marsalis, artistic director of the Jazz at Lincoln Center program, closed the evening with a piece by Duke Ellington, played in a jazz-funeral style, following its traditional progression from a mourning mood to a more hopeful, upbeat tempo. Three days later, on September 20, musicians gathered at New York's Madison Square Garden for another benefit, "From The Big Apple to The Big Easy," which also featured a star-studded lineup.

In the wake of tragedy, Superintendent John Quirk of the New Orleans Jazz National Historical Park explained the sentiment of musicians as the following: "Jazz musicians do not dwell upon disappointment. Their art requires the quick transformation of such emotions into recipe ingredients for new sounds."[33] This sentiment reverberated in the decision to continue with two of the city's most popular annual events in 2006: the Mardi Gras celebration in February and the New Orleans Jazz and Heritage Festival in May and June. In contrast to a more modest-scale Mardi Gras event, the Jazz and Heritage Festival took a bolder approach. David Oestreicher, chair of the festival's governing board, said that they would aim for "a world-shaking event . . . .We think that we will be the watershed event that will jump-start the tourist economy for this part of the world."[34] And in the summer of 2006, New Orleans hosted at least three other annual music events that usually draw tourists to the city, including the International Piano Competition, French Quarter Fest, and Satchmo Summerfest. The French Quarter Fest drew 350,000 people, a number that pleased the organizers, although it was down from 500,000 in 2005.[35]

New Orleans native Wynton Marsalis has emerged as an especially active leader among the music community by organizing benefits and other relief efforts. In April 2006, Marsalis led the performance of the new composition "Congo Square," which he co-wrote with Ghanaian drummer Yacub Addy, at the original Congo Square in the city. Incorporating call-and-response styles from both traditional Ghanaian and jazz genres, the vocals in the piece drew a link between the square's history and Katrina.

The depth of the tragedy's effect on the music industry, however, is reflected in the many musicians forced into exile, creating a new diaspora. A new musical history is likely being written through this diaspora, resulting in compositions, new partnerships, and musical mixes. The diaspora provided the inspiration for filmmaker Robert Mugge's new documentary film, "New Orleans Music in Exile," which featured musicians now living in Austin, Houston, Memphis, and Lafayette. The cast of characters includes Dr. John, Irma Thomas, Cyril Neville, Eddie Bo, Theresa Andersson, The Iguanas, Re-Birth Brass Band, Jon Cleary, Papa Mali, World Leader Pretend, and others.

More immediately, displaced musicians were focused on making a living and supporting the recovery of their former home city through benefit concerts. Instruments, recording studios, equipment, and performance spaces were among the innumerable casualties of the storm. Post-storm online blogs and websites were replete with musicians requesting donations and assistance securing gigs in their new locations—offering virtual ethnographic materials on the extent to which New Orleans depended on its vast networks of musicians, and vice versa. One website hosted requests from musicians living in thirty-five states representing almost every region of the United States, with a particular concentration in Louisiana and Texas. In response, a number of new and preexisting organizations are providing assistance with instrument replacement and related needs. The Tipitina's Foundation, which organizes annual benefits to provide musical instruments for public schools, created a post-Katrina artist relief initiative, offering assistance with housing, musical instruments, and other needs of local musicians. The extent of the need can partly be measured by the level of demand expressed by musicians: The organization MusicCares, which also offers assistance to musicians, created a special Hurricane Relief Fund, and had 800 musicians in its pipeline requesting assistance in May of 2006.

The seemingly unending roster of benefit concerts, from the New Orleans region to cities such as Frankfurt, Germany, offers clear examples of the agency of jazz music in relation to civil society mobilization. This mobilization brought culture (music) to the aid of infrastructural needs, since many proceeds were distributed to the Red Cross, the Tipitina's Foundation, and other organizations involved in the rebuilding efforts. One of the more popular recipients of funds is Habitat for Humanity, a nonprofit organization that builds affordable houses with home ownership opportunity. This organization initiated a Musicians' Village project for the Upper Ninth Ward in New Orleans, to provide houses for musicians in hopes of attracting them back to the city. The project's partners in the music community include Harry Connick, Jr., Ellis Marsalis, and his son jazz saxophonist Branford Marsalis.

The live performances operated at a deeper level than the charitable purpose, however; they were embodied gatherings that brought musicians face to face with audiences, and they became sites of resistance, critique, and emotional expression. As emotion-laden sites, the performances collected the shared mixed moods of sorrow, anger, desperation, and hope, serving simultaneously as emotional release and political challenge. One singer at a large benefit combined these two facets in one performance as he belted the classic New Orleans anthem "When the Saints Go Marching In" while wearing at T-shirt bearing the slogan "Ethnic Cleansing in New Orleans." Politics were not omnipresent in the performances, however. In a Virginia concert just following the first anniversary of the storm, the touring Preservation Hall Jazz Band celebrated New Orleans through its program, yet abstained from explicit political statements.

MODULATION: moving to a new key

One step removed from the embodied form were the mass-mediated performances that reached national and international audiences—benefit broadcasts, radio playlists, specially produced programs—and new recordings. The label Putamayo, for example, known for its compilations of world music, had a previously produced New Orleans and a Mississippi Blues Collection, and announced that the proceeds from these sales would go to the Tipitina's Foundation and Habitat for Humanity, respectively. The exile has resulted in at least one big-name collaboration: jazz pianist and singer Allen Toussaint wound up in New York City, where he teamed up with musician Elvis Costello to produce the new recording, *The River in Reverse*. Toussaint lost his recording studio and equipment, his grand piano, and the gold records he had been awarded for his music in the flood. He was nevertheless able to invoke humor into the situation. During a 2006 program with Elvis Costello and popstar Mika Nakashima in Japan, Toussaint joked to reporters, "Well, I must say that Katrina was supposed to be a tragedy, but Katrina turned out in being [*sic*] a great booking agent."[36] Audiences filled concert halls and stadiums throughout the diaspora.

In September 2005 and following, memories of the Great Mississippi Flood of 1927 made a prominent appearance in frequent live and recorded performances of the Randy Newman song "Louisiana 1927." Among the bitter memories of that particular rescue effort was the camp in Greenville, Mississippi, where thousands of African American evacuees were housed. Quartered in a separate facility at the levee with bare necessities for living conditions, evacuees were guarded at gunpoint, forced to do manual labor, tagged for food rations only if they had done sufficient work, and beaten, while Whites were housed in hotels and other buildings in the town.[37] This flood was commemorated in numerous folk songs. Randy Newman's more recent rendition of the story recounted, "The river rose all day, the river rose all night. Some people got lost in the flood, some people got away alright [*sic*]. Louisiana, Louisiana.

They're trying to wash us away, they're trying to wash us away."[38] Replayed in the post-Katrina context, this piece resonated with residents' and evacuees' anger that governmental powers had failed them.

New pieces composed out of the tragedy are already inscribing the event into social memory, and are weaving their way into the repertoire of New Orleans theme music. John Autin's new song "I Miss my Darlin' New Orleans" recalls the Louis Armstrong classic, "Do You Know What It Means to Miss New Orleans?," a song that also received frequent airplay after Katrina. Despite the mournful tributes and the we-will-rise-again optimism of much of the music, many of the new compositions took on a particular political dissonance, and the anger seemed to mount with each month of inaction. Prior to the storm, "Do You Know What It Means to Miss New Orleans?" was often placed in the category of tourist "camp," but the piece went through a meaning translation due to the dire level of devastation and disappointment with the powers that be. This song was included on the new benefit album, *Our New Orleans*. A spoken-word version of this sentimental piece adds the phrase "while the current administration still wallows in procrastination a year later," and recites a litany of names from New Orleans jazz history.[39]

One CD produced following the storm, entitled *New Orleans Will Rise Again*, featured the image of a fist of a person of color, tightly clenching a red bandana, wrist braceleted with Mardi Gras beads. Among the songs in this compilation is a composition by The Brotherhood, "The Monkey that Became President." The song voices a shared derision toward Washington, D.C., with the words, "You hear those people making monkeys out of you and me." The image of the clenched fist, common in revolutionary struggles, has a cross-over purpose in jazz: it is an on-stage signal for the beginning the "out" chorus, the final chorus of the piece. Dissonance also made an appearance on the airwaves *between* the songs. On the first anniversary of the storm, WWOZ disc jockey Kathleen Lee explained her hesitation over whether to use her broadcast role to help her fellow New Orleanians to forget the tragedy by remaining silent about Katrina on the air. In the end, she decided that she felt compelled to speak about the continuing struggles of her city, and announced to listeners, "Help has been *dreadfully* slow to come." She pleaded with listeners beyond the crescent city to contact their political representatives to remember New Orleans.

CULTURE AND STRUCTURE *REDUX*

SUBSTITUTION: inserting a new chord in place of the existing chord

Conversations about the relationship between culture and structure, common in the halls of academia, have entered the vernacular public discourse over the meanings of post-Katrina reconstruction. Those making a case for the protection of culture as a structural concern included New Orleans writer Andrew Cordescu. He bemoaned that "New Orleans will be rebuilt, but it will never again be the city I know and love. I often compared it to Venice because of its beauty and tenuousness, its love of music, art, and carnival."[40] Like New Orleans, Venice is precariously perched on intertwining bodies of water. Yet unlike Venice, Cordescu observed, the nation (and world) failed to focus its engineering genius on how to protect and preserve the cultural treasure at the mouth of the Mississippi River. Cordescu's sad essay "Love Note to New Orleans" resounds with feelings of dread over the unrecoverable loss of a place whose soul had been stolen overnight.

In its analysis of the post-Katrina crisis, the Brookings Institution articulated the integral relationship of culture, infrastructure, and social power in its following recommendation—and jazz in particular makes an appearance:

> New Orleans must be rebuilt because it is unthinkable not to rebuild the nation's thirty-first-largest city and forty-forth-largest metropolitan area—a metropolis whose port has for 200 years linked the Mississippi River Valley to the wider world; . . . and whose rich traditions of racial integration have given the world pink and green Creole houses, crawfish *etouffee*, and jazz funerals. New Orleans has the potential, in this respect, to rise again as a paragon of urban resilience, racial integration, and economic reinvention—and it must.[41]

Nick Spitzer, producer/host of American Routes at Public Radio International, expressed a related concern over the culture/infrastructure dichotomy during the May 2006 panel discussion at Tulane University. He made the case that in New Orleans there is an actual historical relationship between the musician and the physical built environment in an embodied, material form. Jazz musicians in New Orleans—even those in well-known bands such as that of Louis Armstrong—worked construction by day and played music by night. The day job is even sanctified in the jazz lexicon, where it is called a "hame." Musicians worked as plasterers, bricklayers, lathers, and carpenters. Structurally speaking, the city depended upon these men for their skilled labor *and* their music. Spitzer commented that "these are real organic relationships that I think are difficult for governments, foundations, and corporations to address."[42] He called for a rethinking of the concept of infrastructure:

> The debate in the driveway, in the street, in the city has been increasingly, "How are we going to fix the infrastructure?" "We've got to fix this infrastructure." Native New Orleanians wouldn't have stayed here, and so many people wouldn't have come here if they thought the infrastructure was great. Let's face

it. The infrastructure here in *American* terms is not great. But what is great are
these sets of cultural intangibles, these relationships . . . So the question is, how
do we address a place where the culture *is* the infrastructure? That's why the
city's loved.[43]

In addition to these relationships between the music and the built environment is another cultural engagement with structure: the economics of jazz—
production, performance, and consumption. This returns us to Adorno's concerns over empowerment, race, and the jazz industry. For years, contrasts
have been made between jazz in New York as a commodified industry and
jazz in New Orleans as a purer form of cultural heritage. This contrast did not
sit well with Harlem Renaissance writer and poet Langston Hughes, who argued, "What do you think Tony Jackson and Jelly Roll Morton and King
Oliver and Louis Armstrong were playing for? Peanuts? No, money, even in
Dixieland. They were communicating for money. For fun, too—because they
had fun. But the money helped the fun along."[44] If the assumption has been
that the production-consumption enterprise, and the medium of money, pol-
lutes the music's cultural purity, the reality is that jazz was always, already
commercial. In New Orleans, jazz is about culture *and* business. Even as jazz
is embedded into an identity consciousness in New Orleans as a source of
community pride, it also serves as a means to earn a living—or add to a primary living. Music helped solidify the city's economic base. As the top industry, tourism had been responsible for 35 percent of the city's annual operating budget, or $210 million.[45] Thus, the second major blow to New Orleans
since Katrina was the severe loss of tourism.

We might continue Adorno's critical point of reference—the relationship of
jazz to social power and commodification—without reproducing his (admittedly outdated) condescension. Clearly, a description of empowerment of jazz
in African American life must simultaneously acknowledge the fact that the
form (in a city like New Orleans and elsewhere) does serve to enrich institutions and individuals who are external to African American communities.
There is no question that enrichment is shared by some members of an
African American elite. Proponents of the craft are aware that it is the rare
musician who will be enriched by learning the music, but the music has provided a bedrock of employment. New Orleans jazz clarinetist Michael White
promotes the craft as a counter-poverty measure:

In the music business it's very hard to be successful and make it in the pop music world or the hip hop world or the classical world. But almost any New Orleans kid of any ability and level can make it in the brass band, make money,
gain respect . . . . Jazz, among many other things, has been sort of an alternative
or social cure to unemployment and crime.[46]

Without moving into any larger claims for the music's contribution to fully experienced, shared social power, White is reporting on a dependence that the community has developed on the music as a potential leveler of social inequalities.

CONCLUSION

OUT-HEAD: the final chorus, where the tune returns to the original theme

What then of culture (jazz), structure, social power, and New Orleans? As demonstrated here, the jazz form is more than icing on the New Orleans cake. It is integrated into community structures, formal and informal educational systems, generational relationships within families, a lively local industry, and physical structures. The city continues to view itself not only as a carrier of jazz history but to the continued production of the craft. A WWOZ radio disc jockey refers to New Orleans as "the jazz corner of the world."[47] Countering observers who view the city as having now been "purged" of its social problems, this account illustrates the base that neighborhoods provided for the music, which offered its own structural contributions as a key industry for the city—a mutually beneficial, cyclical relationship.

The case of New Orleans and its jazz heritage offers a clear example of the relationship between culture and structure. Culture, in this example, operates as (1) a set of practices as well as symbolic content, (2) a relatively autonomous phenomenon that nevertheless converses with economics (through consumption and production), and (3) the ongoing activities of "social agents," such as the improvisational work of musicians, and is embodied in communities of people, which the music mirrors, engages, and changes. If its purity is indeed polluted through its function as a commodity in Marxian terms, or as a tool of a means-ends rationality in Weberian terms, it simultaneously provides its own intrinsic meaning structure where other values are present. There is more than one relationship between the music and African American social power.

In fact, the music partially serves as a platform for social critique. The post-Katrina jazz discourse and performance scenes have been unusually active arenas of civil-society mobilization. The musical repertoires have been both mass-mediated and face-to-face sites of mourning and remembrance, we-will-rise-again defiance, and wrath over federal inaction. The discourses engaged in conversation about the social-structural institutions of housing, development, industry, economy, city identity, education, and neighborhoods—in the context of African American social power. Through the benefits, the music has helped raise millions of dollars toward the rebuilding effort.

Despite this success, the charitable efforts of civil society will not be sufficient to the massive task of rebuilding. Civil society organizations cannot command the breadth or depth of resources, implementation power, or enduring nature of the state. Thus, the integration of the question of culture into the policy-making arena remains the task at hand. If the return of culture to the city becomes a priority, it implicates the rebuilding of lower-income neighborhoods, infusing music education into reconstructed school systems, preserving historic buildings, housing musicians, and bringing back the festivals.

OUTRO: coda, or additional ending

To me jazz is a montage of a dream deferred. A great big dream—yet to come—and always yet—to become ultimately and finally true."—Langston Hughes (1958:494)

NOTES

1. *Take the Lead* (film), directed by Liz Friedlander, screenplay by Dianne Houston, Tiara Blu Films production, released by New Line Cinema, 2006.

2. The Brookings Institution, "New Orleans after the Storm: Lessons from the Past, a Plan for the Future," Washington, DC: The Brookings Institution Metropolitan Policy Program, 2005, <http://www.brookings.edu/metro/pubs/20051012_NewOrleans.pdf>.

3. Karl Marx and Friedrich Engels, *The German Ideology: Including Theses on Feuerbach and Introduction to the Critique of Political Economy* (Amherst, NY: Prometheus Books [1932] 1998).

4. The "Frankfurt School" is the name given to the Institute of Social Research at the University of Frankfurt, Germany, which existed in exile from 1933 to 1953.

5. Theodor W. Adorno, "On Jazz," in *Essays on Music,* selected, with Introduction, Commentary, and Notes by Richard Leppert (Berkeley: University of California Press, [1936] 2002), 470–95.

6. Mark D. Jacobs and Nancy Weiss Hanrahan, eds., *The Blackwell Companion to the Sociology of Culture* (Malden, MA: Blackwell Publishing, 2005).

7. Alan C. Turley, "Max Weber and the Sociology of Music," *Sociological Forum* 16 (2001): 633–53.

8. Peter Townsend, *Jazz in American Culture* (Jackson: University Press of Mississippi, 2000), 4.

9. Turley, "Max Weber," 646.

10. City of New Orleans, "Remembrance, Renewal, and Rebirth Theme for City of New Orleans Hurricane Katrina Memorials," <http://www.cityofno.com/portal.aspx?portal=1&load=~/PortalModules/ViewPressRelease.ascx&itemid=3659>.

11. Nicholas M. Evans, *Writing Jazz* (New York: Garland Publishing, 2000), 1–20.

12. Bruce Baum, *The Rise and Fall of the Caucasian Race: A Political History of Racial Identity* (New York: New York University Press, 2006).

13. Orville Lee, "Race after the Cultural Turn," in *The Blackwell Companion to the Sociology of Culture,* eds. Mark D. Jacobs and Nancy Weiss Hanrahan (Malden, MA: Blackwell Publishing, 2005), 235.

14. Paul Gilroy, cited in Paul Austerlitz, *Kente Cloth to Jazz: A Matrix of Sound* (Middleton, CT: Wesleyan University Press, 2005), 25.

15. National Park Service New Orleans Jazz Historical Park, "New Orleans Jazz Neighborhood History Map," <http://www.nps.gov/jazz/Maps_neighborhoods.htm>.

16. John R. Logan, "The Impact of Katrina: Race and Class in Storm-Damaged Neighborhoods," Brown University Spatial Structures in the Social Sciences report (Providence, RI: Brown University, 2006), 7, <http://www.s4.brown.edu/Katrina/report.pdf>.

17. Gwen Filosa, "Lower 9 Residents Differ on Desire to Return," *The Times-Picayune,* August 24, 2006.

18. New Orleans Tourism Marketing Corporation, "New Orleans' Recovery as of August 2006," <http://neworleansonline.com/pr/releases/immediate/pr_Aug2006Recovery Update.pdf>.

19. Shaila Dewan, "Evacuees in Houston and Atlanta," *New York Times,* August 27, 2006.

20. Eddie Cockrell, "New Orleans Music in Exile," *Variety,* April 3, 2006, <http://www.variety.com/review/VE1117930122?categoryid=1023&cs=1>.

21. Adam Nossiter, "Outlines Emerge for a Shaken New Orleans," *New York Times,* August 27, 2006.

22. Cyril Neville, <http://www.cyrilneville.com/neville/>.

23. "Rebirth of New Orleans Music Culture" (Panel discussion at the seminar, "People, Places & Culture in New Orleans," Tulane University, New Orleans, Louisiana, June 1, 2006).

24. "Rebirth of New Orleans."

25. Howard S. Becker, "Jazz Places" (Paper given at the Albright-Knox Art Gallery, March 21, 2002), <http://buffaloreport.com/020401beckerjazzplaces.html>.

26. Margaret Foster, "In Sudden Demolition, New Orleans Loses its first Historic Building Since Katrina," *OnLine Preservation,* October 13 2005, <http://www.nationaltrust.org/magazine/archives/arc_news_2005/101305.htm>.

27. Glenn Astarita, "Post-Katrina Jazz in New Orleans," All About Jazz website, January 8, 2006, <http://www.allaboutjazz.com/php/article.php?id=20250>.

28. Kevin Mercadel, "Why Are New Orleans 20 Historic Districts on the National Trust Endangered List?" National Trust for Historic Preservation website, 2006, <http://www.nationaltrust.org/hurricane/mercadel.html>.

29. John Quirk, "Superintendent's Message—Hurricane Katrina," New Orleans Jazz National Historical Park website, September 7, 2005, <http://www.nps.gov/jazz/pphtml/newsdetail20340.html>.

30. CNN Larry King Live, Interview with Ray Nagin, September 14, 2005, <http://edition.cnn.com/TRANSCRIPTS/0509/14/lkl.01.html>.

31. "Higher Ground Hurricane Relief Benefit Concert," Jazz at Lincoln Center, September 17, 2005.

32. MSNBC.com, "Katrina Jazz Concert Strikes Political Tone," September 19, 2005, <http://www.msnbc.msn.com/id/9390988/>.

33. Quirk, "Superintendent's Message."

34. Keith Spera, "Planners Promise Bigger Jazzfest," WWOZ Radio website, November 12, 2005, <www.wwoz.org>.

35. French Quarter Festivals Inc. website, <http://fqfi.org/>.

36. *"Apres Vous*, M. Toussaint," *The Daily Yomiuri,* Japan, June 3, 2006, <http://www.elvis-costello.com/news/2006/06/apres_vous_m_toussaint.html>.

37. John M. Barry, *Rising Tide: The Great Mississippi Flood of 1927 and How it Changed America* (New York: Simon and Schuster, 1998), 311–17.

38. Randy Newman, <http://www.randynewman.com>.

39. G. Martinez, "Do You Know What It Is to Miss New Orleans?" (New arrangement), WWOZ Radio broadcast, August 29, 2006.

40. Andrew Cordescu, *New Orleans, Mon Amour: Twenty Years of Writings from the City* (Chapel Hill: Algonquin Books, 2006), 264.

41. Brookings Institution, "New Orleans After the Storm."

42. "Rebirth of New Orleans."

43. "Rebirth of New Orleans."

44. Langston Hughes, *The Langston Hughes Reader* (New York: George Braziller, 1958), 492.

45. New Orleans Tourism, "New Orleans' Recovery."

46. "Rebirth of New Orleans."

47. WWOZ Radio, August 27, 2006.

Chapter Seven

Prayer and Social Welfare in the Wake of Katrina

Race and Volunteerism in Disaster Response

Susan M. Sterett[1]

Jennifer A. Reich

EMERGENT ORGANIZATIONS, RACE, AND KATRINA IN DENVER

The news coverage of Hurricane Katrina in August and September of 2005 brought out an untold number of volunteers around the country. Many were horrified by what the images revealed about our polity. It is unusual to ship a disaster outside of the affected area, and most analyses of community building following disaster focus on efforts within the communities affected by the disaster.[2] However, Katrina was "spread all over the country." In Colorado about 400 evacuees arrived via flights the federal government organized; many others self-evacuated to the state. New organizations emerged in response to Katrina. In this chapter, we focus on one of the more prominent ones, the Colorado Coalition of Faith, which provided immediate assistance, and continued to provide volunteers and donations to evacuees for months after their arrival. The Coalition envisioned working toward goals beyond the settlement of Katrina evacuees in Colorado. Evacuees who relocated to distant cities after the flooding were disproportionately poor and Black. African American–led churches in the Denver metro area were quick to position themselves as advocates for the displaced, who they saw as "our people." In turn, their response brought local recognition to African American–led mixed race churches, including Baptist, Catholic, and nondenominational Christian

135

evangelical churches. Pastors in these churches were integrated into the state-led incident command system when evacuees first came to Denver and became leaders of the long-term recovery committee. Further, the pastors who assumed leadership over the response were not the leaders of the traditional Black churches, but were instead relatively young pastors who identified an opportunity to serve in what has been the racially segregated world of disaster response.[3]

We argue that although the response that included these Black churches was local, it unfolded in the context of national political conversations concerning race, disaster, and New Orleans. By the first week in September, the national government was vilified not only for bungling the immediate response to Katrina, but for neglecting the poor in New Orleans for decades.[4] Hopeful editorials imagined that Katrina would allow a new conversation about poverty in the United States,[5] with President Bush on September 15 announcing publicly that the United States would have to address decades of neglect.[6] We argue that this conversation about neglect of poor communities and communities of color, against a backdrop of general endorsement of diversity in the United States, set a context in which the usual disaster relief organizations, both governmental and charitable, could hear local claims concerning race. The professionalized charities that are part of the National Voluntary Organizations Active in Disaster (NVOAD) were accustomed to talking to each other. Inclusion into decision-making about local response to this disaster gave ministers hope that they could both affect disaster relief and receive support for longer-term projects. By examining the case of the Colorado Coalition of Faith, we explore how commitment to diversity can open space within voluntary organizations, while also showing the limits of such commitment. In total, commitment to diversity allowed for the provision of racially sensitive service, but could not change governmental spending priorities for the displaced. Furthermore, achieving ambitious goals of becoming long-term service providers required building capacity that could only partly be accomplished during one disaster. The professionalized charities are accustomed to working in a bureaucratic state that requires standardized procedures, including providing the same service to all and being able to account for all activities. The promise of a new voluntary organization is that it can provide the "heart" that is not part of standard operating procedures. Yet the promise of that fresh energy also makes a new organization difficult to integrate into the world of grants, contracts, and professional charity. The Black churches, which around the country are smaller and newer than the professionalized charities, have found it more difficult to tap into the funds made available for long-term service provision, including under the federal faith-based initiatives.[7]

This chapter is based on analysis of interviews, observations, and documents. We collected interview data in forty-five in-depth, open-ended interviews with professional charity workers, church leaders, volunteers, service providers, and government officials in Colorado. We also observed more than 150 hours of casework, coalition, and recovery committee meetings and volunteer trainings and meetings. We have also checked stories against newspaper representations, not least because newspaper representations figured in how people understood what they were doing. We begin by providing a framework for thinking about diversity in volunteerism. Building on this, we then use these data to chronicle the ways the response to the evacuees in Colorado unfolded, how coalition members were integrated, and the success and limits of their involvement, particularly as they strived for long-term resources and roles in state support of charitable work.

DIVERSITY TALK AND VOLUNTARISM

Community self-help has long been an important tradition in African American communities. African American traditions concerning racial solidarity have emphasized empowerment and responsibility. W.E.B. DuBois argued that the "talented tenth" bore a responsibility to work for the benefit of the race; only the most talented and educated had the skills and the commitment to work for the race.[8] DuBois argued, "The Negro Race, like all races, is going to be saved by its exceptional men."[9] Who, though, are the exceptional men? A disaster opens new opportunities, including for community leadership, and local churches in Denver saw the disaster that way. DuBois's quotation does not make clear whether he included women in this vision, and tension between African American women and men concerning leadership is longstanding, notably in churches.[10] One approach to leadership that appreciates the enormous contributions Black women have made defines leadership not only as appearing in public but doing the hard work of organizing and providing service.[11] African American women have long worked for community responsibility, embodied in the motto of club women in the late nineteenth and early twentieth century, "Lifting as we climb."[12] Women who were upwardly mobile believed they had an obligation to help others; that tradition continues in Black community work.[13]

However, it can be difficult to rely on community when many resources are well beyond the control of its members; many Katrina evacuees needed affordable housing, counseling for post-traumatic stress, and jobs.[14] Community self-help would need to include engaging broad public problems that no one voluntary organization controlled. Reflecting upon the different perceptions of the inequality Katrina revealed, political scientist Michael Dawson has argued that it is difficult for Black voluntary organizations, which he says are "at one of their weakest historic moments," to shape public discussion or policy. He argues that this is due to the "weakening of the voluntary associations and networks" which he says were built on "the already weakened social base."[15] Where communities can organize, they encounter local governments working with diminished resources and control.[16]

Despite the lack of access to policymaking Black community organizations face, and the ongoing persistence of racial inequality, American culture applauds diversity. The legal scholar Peter Schuck has argued that the United States is the first country in history to pursue racial and ethnic diversity rather than fear it.[17] Legally protected "diversity" includes a publicly stated commitment to inclusion in workplaces and schools across race, gender, national origins, and disability as well as a more generic appreciation for culinary or stylistic differences. Diversity, when broadly stated, commands allegiance across the political spectrum.[18] However, how one addresses concerns for diversity in the specific can be politically divisive. In addressing lack of diversity, one can approach it as an issue of inequality in public policy, and one can address it as a matter of voluntary inclusion, a much less politically charged understanding. In Colorado after Katrina, addressing diversity meant inclusion in voluntary organizations.

Working on diversity in community organizations rather than through state policy would seem to provide some hope for addressing the difficult problems of race and class. However, working across boundaries of class or race is still extremely challenging, as is building relationships that transcend the immediate volunteer activity. Despite good intentions, these efforts often fail.[19] What Paul Lichterman calls "customs in service" can prevent service across boundaries; people find it difficult to reflect upon and change their practices to work *with* those they mean to serve. Only if organizations rethink customs can connections among people "spiral outward," or genuinely engage people from different social worlds. Congregations tend to work on limited projects such as emergency food and shelter, which may not require long-term connection between those served and congregants.[20] Sociologist Robert Wuthnow points out that congregations and their members have multiple demands on both their time and money, making extensive commitments difficult.[21] Thus, the goal of the Black church leaders to serve the long-term needs of Katrina evacuees was particularly ambitious.

In Colorado, not only did volunteers have to work across class and race divisions after Katrina, they faced challenges not common in disaster response. Most disasters are shared between those serving and those receiving assistance; racial and class disparities in gaining assistance are local among people who may have experienced disaster differently, but who did experience it. Shipping Katrina out of state meant that volunteers and caseworkers were serving people who were not like themselves in the experience of disaster, regional culture, and often in class. Most research on emergent organizations focuses on communities addressing *their own* disasters.[22] The long-term evacuation of people from New Orleans and their settlement around the country made Katrina a local disaster in many cities, but the ordinary ties among community members did not always travel the distance between Denver and New Orleans. With good intentions and passion for the work, the volunteers were able to achieve some inclusion across boundaries of race, class, and voluntary and government work by focusing on the immediate needs and tasks presented. The primary emergent organization in Denver came together specifically to (a) serve African Americans in a way many did not believe the largely White professional charities could, (b) demonstrate God's love through service, and (c) develop capacity to work with the local homeless. In the following sections, we chronicle how this service unfolded.

RESPONSE: LOWRY AND THE BLACK CHURCHES

In Colorado, response to Katrina began Labor Day weekend, a week after the storm hit the Gulf Coast. Anticipating arrivals of evacuees sent by the federal government, Colorado's governor Bill Owens declared a state disaster on September 3.[23] On that same day, he issued an executive order that authorized state agencies to prepare housing for evacuees.[24] Both orders anticipated a federal emergency order for Colorado, issued September 5[25]; the orders smoothed the way for federal reimbursement for the approximately one million dollars spent to rehabilitate a dorm at Lowry, a former Air Force base in Denver that became a temporary shelter for evacuees, and to set up a reception center. Colorado is not subject to hurricanes, earthquakes, or tornados; it is forty-seventh of the fifty states in numbers of federal disasters declared. Without competing demands, state and local agencies, professional charities, and spontaneous volunteers mobilized quickly.

Most of our interviews with early responders in Colorado began with some account of where they were during Labor Day weekend. Unaffected directly by the storm, many recalled their plans to spend time on home repairs, with family, or watching the news coverage of the largest disaster in U.S. history. All remember getting called by supervisors or representatives from the governor's office informing them that Colorado had agreed to accept as many as 1,000 evacuees by airplane from the Houston Astrodome or New Orleans Superdome.

Evacuees were likely to be African American, and they were likely to be greeted by more White people than they were accustomed to seeing. Colorado is much Whiter than New Orleans. Those who were flown to faraway places like Denver were much more likely to be African American and poor than those who evacuated closer to home.[26] Katrina affected different parts of New Orleans differently: damaged areas were more likely to be poor, with homes occupied by renters, with households below the poverty line, and with more people reported as unemployed.[27] However, New Orleans had long had a high percentage of homeowners who were African American, and in the largely destroyed Lower Ninth Ward, most residents were homeowners.[28] Before Katrina, the New Orleans metropolitan area (which includes Orleans parish and six additional parishes) was 36 percent Black; the city of New Orleans alone was about 67 percent Black.[29] In 2005, 4.1 percent of the Colorado population was African American, while 10.6 percent of Denver's population was African American.[30] We do not know the racial composition of those who ended up in Denver after having fled New Orleans; people who worked at the reception center guessed that over 95 percent of the evacuees housed at Lowry were African American.

Hurricane Katrina evacuees came to Colorado at a time when homelessness was already on the urban political agenda. Denver was the first city in the country to complete a ten-year plan to end homelessness, of 200 that had committed to designing one. The plan is based on a "housing first" strategy, following Philadelphia's successful effort to get the chronically homeless off the streets.[31] Although not yet connected to this plan, the Black pastor of a local multiracial, nondenominational Protestant church had gone to the governor's office before Hurricane Katrina hit to request that a dormitory at Lowry be donated to his church; they would use it to house homeless people. From that base, he envisioned, the church could provide services, including faith-based rehabilitation, tutoring for children and adults, and employment workshops. It was an ambitious proposal from a newcomer to homeless service provision and the governor said no. The dormitory was scheduled for demolition.

Shortly after, when Colorado Governor Bill Owens agreed to accept evacuees, his office commissioned the use of that very building. He then asked that same pastor if his congregation could help over the weekend to prepare it for occupancy. Members of that church and others arrived; as church members and pastors phoned people they knew at least slightly, the network of volunteers grew. Because worship is somewhat racially segregated in the United States, reliance upon informal networks made it more likely that churches with substantial African American membership and leadership would be called in immediately. Along with contractors hired by the state, these volunteers worked around the clock all weekend preparing the dormitory for arrivals.[32] From the pastor's point of view, this work would not only help Katrina evacuees, a job important in its own right, but it would also build toward the homelessness project he wanted his church to do. Once established, he could, perhaps, demonstrate to the governor's office that they ought to keep the building open to serve the homeless after the Katrina evacuees were gone. Katrina evacuees and the local homeless were now much the same: homeless. Surely doing a good job with the former would be a way to learn how to do a good job with the latter.

Through this work, the churches could demonstrate their ability to care for their community, a duty that belonged to the community, and that one pastor believed had inappropriately been given to governments. Explaining how this view infused the Coalition's work, another pastor explained how charity connected to their spirituality:

> When we do this, it's like putting skin on Jesus. It's what Jesus would touch and feel, it's not just theory, it's not just philosophy, it's not even just theology. . . Well, okay, this is Jesus with skin, because I'm getting ready to take you to the grocery store, I'm getting ready to take you to the doctor, I'm getting ready to help you pay your rent, buy you clothes, put food on your table, so this is a Jesus you can see. To me, I'm just so happy that our church life, that's where I was in ministry with our congregation; we had an experience a few years ago where I challenged our congregation that there should be no needs inside of our fellowship, because if there's somebody here that has what somebody else needs, and if we can change our mindset on that, it will be profitable for the entire fellowship. So that's where my feeling was just a couple years before this event, so when I found myself in this position, it just naturally fit with the ministry of my feeling. Our theme for ministry is that we care about people. So when I stood up in the pulpit and I told our congregation what I was involved in, after a while, I told them, I said, this just is not—now that I look at it, it doesn't surprise me that God would put me in this position, because I said our church cares about people. So now here's your chance to prove it. Here's your chance; so let's see where the rubber meets the road.

Several of the pastors who were quick to get involved in serving the evacuees drew on their congregation's carework to make sense of this calling. The pastors viewed the needs of Katrina evacuees to be an extension of their work in their congregations. The Katrina evacuees provided an opportunity to serve God, but providing care for them was not necessarily different from providing care for the local poor, or for a congregation. Racial solidarity provided the context for continuity of care.

This sentiment was reflected in the comments by another Black pastor, who in thinking through his motivation to participate and how his church became involved, identified how the work with the evacuees was connected to working with the local poor who are often African American:

> The whole idea was that we were really looking at working with people who are in need and those who are homeless. Single mothers that are out there trying to raise children that are part of what we call this hotel/motel central. Since the church is only located about four blocks away from Colfax [a long commercial street, notorious for street prostitution and drug dealing, with many inexpensive hotels and motels], we work a lot with those hotels and stuff all along the whole drive of Colfax. Whenever you get up there, you'll see that there are just so many women and kids, mothers that are out there, and it's men, too, who have lost their jobs or have minimum wage jobs and the only thing they can afford are those hotels every day.

In identifying his church's experience with local urban poverty and the similar problems evacuees faced, he argued that his church was well equipped to provide service for Katrina evacuees.

It was never certain when the planes with the evacuees would arrive; volunteers and state workers waited. In all, the state welcomed about 400 evacuees in two planeloads into the dorm on the former Lowry Air Force Base. When the first planeload of people arrived, churches as well as volunteers from Colorado Victims Assistance (COVA), a local organization with dozens of volunteers trained in crisis counseling and assistance to those in trauma, were available to greet them. Having been invited by state officials, COVA volunteers were quickly included in the formal operation. Many of the evacuees who arrived at Lowry had spent much of the preceding week in standing water or in a sports stadium, which had not been designed to serve as a shelter after a disaster. The toilets had overflowed and no one could bathe. When the buses carrying evacuees from the airplanes arrived at Lowry and the doors opened, the smell of human misery was palpable.[33] One volunteer, a White woman, recalled,

> When the doors opened from the bus, all I can think to describe it would be to go open the door to a room that was really hot, like a furnace room, and you get that blast of heat. There was a gush of human stench. Just the odor of human stench, that it just took your breath away because it was so rancid. And yet, I thought the integrity of the people who were volunteering, [they] never said a word about it. Nobody ever, from my experience, made anyone feel that they were less then dignified or less than received with open arms and welcomed.

She described welcoming the evacuees as sacred work. She also noted that, despite the stench, no volunteer flinched at the miserable condition in which people arrived. Volunteers saw people's condition as outside their control, so that dignity and respect required offering prayer and assistance. One Black male pastor explained,

> I'll tell you, the people that we saw come off those busses will just tear your heart out. People were still wet, their clothes were still wet from when they were in the water. One. . . fell off once she got off the bus, and we prayed for her . . . What happened was she was just so dehydrated and so, I think some other things in terms of diabetes that they didn't know she had.

Another White female pastor made vivid the sorrows of people who have fled their home:

> There was a guy in line and he was holding a picture maybe 2–3 feet tall [and] very narrow. I had said, "Tell me about this picture." He had painted it and it had taken him years. And he talked about the fact that he had first stayed in an upper apartment and then was going apartment to apartment trying to stay dry and away from things. And when he had got to the point that there was standing water, all that he saved was this picture and he just held it above the water. That is the only belonging that he saved and it was the most cherished thing for this man.

The losses that people suffered are made vivid in the description of the one meaningful object someone had been able to carry. Despite the difficulties in trying to carry and keep the painting safely out of the water, it came to represent one man's life. A volunteer could bear witness to that meaning.

Representatives of the sixty or so Black churches who had shown up at Lowry, many of whom had spent the weekend scrubbing toilets, yearned to do more for the evacuees. Some felt called to the work because of their own connections to the city and its people: through family in New Orleans or having themselves come from there. For example, one African American woman who continued work as a volunteer with evacuees one year later explained her motivation: "You see, it's a real personal thing." After detailing which of her relatives lived on Lake Pontchartrain and which had lived on St. Anne's Street or in the Ninth Ward, she considered how they have done. "It's been rough for the seniors . . . [My senior relatives] are lucky they have children they can go live with. But how many families have children that you can go live with? So when it first came up that New Orleans had this disaster and they were flying people out . . . to Colorado, to Denver, I said okay, let me go in the garage and see what I can find."

She could see those who evacuated to Colorado as like her family, just less lucky, having fewer family connections on which they could rely. Like her, some of the long-term church volunteers had family in New Orleans, or had lived there themselves, providing a greater sense of shared community and calling to the work. Others felt called to the work because they shared religion with evacuees. For most, though, it was simply that the evacuees were African American like themselves.

For White people, service to evacuees at Lowry provided insight into daily racism in Louisiana.[34] For example, one White volunteer recalled her shock when an evacuee stepped off of the sidewalk to make room for her; another was struck by an older Black man's attempts to reassure her that she would be safe working with him. The man, who had managed a parking garage in New Orleans, reassured her, "The White man has been good to me. My bosses would trust me carrying $100–$200 cash." She explained, the experience was "almost like a reversal of time," bringing her back to the 1970s when she had lived in the rural South. She then summed up the experience of race for White volunteers at Lowry: "Many of the Caucasian people that I encountered were baffled. It wasn't in their thought process." However, those who were baffled soon worked with those who were not to agree that evacuees needed to see people "like them," which meant race provided a connection when region and class might not.

As a lead disaster relief organization, the American Red Cross was called to the scene immediately. The state first asked it to hand out "comfort kits," which contain basic necessities, such as toiletries, people often need after fleeing their homes. The Red Cross's modal volunteer is White, older, and middle class. Several African American pastors recalled that before Katrina came to Colorado, they had not known either the Red Cross or the Salvation Army, and they would not have advocated that their parishioners volunteer with them. Their experience with Katrina changed that.

Shortly after the dorm opened, the state asked the local Red Cross chapter to manage it. Although the Red Cross specializes in sheltering victims of disaster, this shelter was well outside its ordinary operations; Red Cross provides cots in school gyms, not private rooms in dormitories. As one Red Cross worker emphasized, "We don't run hotels and do not have a towel service." Nonetheless, Red Cross agreed to manage the shelter, which was quickly interpreted by many to mean it was running the whole operation. From identification to security, to food services, the Red Cross was imagined to be responsible for it all and to blame for any confusion. The security imposed was a problem to the volunteers who had been at Lowry for a couple of days but were not part of the NVOAD charities such as Red Cross or Salvation Army.

The emergency managers knew that they needed to establish security. Colfax, a long street that receives ongoing attention from the police and residents for its drug dealing and prostitution, was only a few blocks north. The media were crowding in; news coverage then brought in more volunteers, many of whom had no agency affiliation and no specific tasks to perform. Volunteers require supervision and specific tasks; volunteers at Lowry didn't immediately have either, in part thanks to the political sensitivity of the evacuation. Local residents invited evacuees into their homes. All of this cost evacuees their privacy and created potential risks to all. Thus, emergency management put up security fences and guards, checking the credentials of those who were on-site. Volunteers who were not part of an NVOAD organization lost access, and that meant the church volunteers.

Emergency managers running the operation emphasized that the residents of the dorm were free U.S. citizens, allowed to come and go as they pleased, but some people needed to be kept out and volunteers needed to think about whom they invited into their homes. Nonetheless, the security fences were open to multiple interpretations. They did indeed prevent the press from pursuing evacuees, and from allowing unknown outsiders to wander through. At the same time, they could be perceived as locking residents in; although no administrators heard complaints, some of the evacuees did say they felt imprisoned. Memories in New Orleans are long, since families stayed settled there and shared collective stories. African Americans who lost their homes in the Great Mississippi Flood of 1927 were indeed imprisoned on top of the levees for months. Even those without personal connection to the experience might have known of the cruelty to African Americans of the response to that disaster: John Barry's *Rising Tide,* a history of the 1927 flood, was the "One Book One New Orleans" selection for 2005, making it possible for the themes to have been discussed around town.[35] For the well-intentioned volunteers denied access to the dorm and its residents, many of whom were African American and had also felt called to care for their own, the walls looked exclusionary, not protective.

Managers of the dorm also faced a threat of public demonstrations by Black activists. They threatened to picket the site at Lowry to expose what they saw as racist treatment of the evacuees as prisoners. One Black pastor suggested that the emergency management staff could keep those protestors out and quiet if he could tell them that the churches were part of decision-making at Lowry.

It was not just that integration would buy off protest; emergency managers saw race as significant to service. A White male government official who codirected the initial response explained the importance of providing Black volunteers by inviting us to think through the problem of race from the inverse of what happened: "If you put people on a plane from [a town that is] 99.9 percent White and ship them to New Orleans, where they are greeted by 500 people who are all Black, you will find they are pretty uncomfortable, and you can understand why." This logic informed their decision to include pastors in decision-making and changed the decision that had taken access to

Lowry from their volunteers. At the same time, emergency managers needed to deal with fewer people than all the church volunteers who had been at Lowry; what emerged was the organization of representatives from different churches into the Coalition of Faith; emergency managers worked with the leaders who had seemed to be most committed to doing what needed to be done. The Coalition was integrated into incident command.[36]

Not only did state and local officials have good reasons for integrating representatives of Black churches, so did Red Cross. First, disaster victims sometimes want counseling or assistance from people who know community resources from the perspective of a racialized minority. Second, Red Cross depends on financial contributions. Since American culture recognizes the virtues of diversity in principle, as Peter Schuck argues, Red Cross needs to assure donors it recognizes diversity. Further, Red Cross has faced bad press, both in its use of funds after the terrorist attacks of September 11, 2001, and in its ability to work with people who are not White.[37] Challenges from local churches provided an opportunity for Red Cross and the state to include the Coalition. Each organization had its own reasons to attend to race and exclusion: for the state, political perception; for the Red Cross, its dependence on donations; and for emergency services,s to meet the needs of evacuees.

Reflecting back months later, one African American woman understood that the changes at Lowry reflected efforts to address race:

> The Salvation Army or the Red Cross came in, and they just kinda took over things, as "We're running the show" and they wouldn't let anybody in. And the pastors got together and said, "How the heck can you think you can get away with something like this? You have 99 percent African Americans out here and you're gonna tell us you're running something when you're in our community? No way." So they went to the table with the Red Cross and they formed a partnership with the CEO. They've become good friends.

She saw exclusion as the Red Cross's responsibility, since many saw Red Cross as running everything. The church members were able to go "to the table" with the various players because each—the governor's office, Red Cross, and emergency managers—had reasons to perceive race as important.

From one African American pastor's perspective, displacement required connection by race. He imagined an ordinary disaster as a fire, a more common disaster in Colorado, rather than the hurricanes that hit the Gulf Coast. Reflecting on his experience working with mainstream disaster response agencies, he recalled:

> There was already a template, a standard template with which to do for follow up services or what they call long-term recovery. We were in those meetings,

we met with FEMA [Federal Emergency Management Agency] representatives and Red Cross separately and shared our input and had concerns that the standard template was not gonna fully address the needs of these residents, because they had been totally displaced from their origin. And that's way different—you know, normally, long-term recoveries for a neighborhood where there's a fire, stay over here, even for thirty days; we're fixing your house, now you're going back, not just to your home, but you're back in your same environment, same neighborhood, you didn't lose your job, your kids going to the same school, all that stuff. None of those things were true.

Because they were displaced, evacuees' whole lives changed, and they would require long-term assistance that he envisioned church volunteers would address. The "standard template" would not work in a dorm where long-term displacement was the problem, which made it necessary to "throw the rule book out the window," as another disaster manager put it.

In addition to participating in decisions at Lowry, Coalition members, who according to one Red Cross staff member, were "out there talking to them a lot," passed up complaints from residents, including their frustrations. Taking these concerns to heart, Red Cross also brought in someone to provide training on diversity for volunteers. Addressing diversity meant recognizing how race intertwined with culture, age, and class. As others have argued, voluntary incorporation of diversity seldom means focusing on legally protected status such as race,[38] which becomes one concern among many. For example, charity workers saw southern culture as distinct, requiring more respect and formality than people in the rest of the country might expect. One Red Cross supervisor explained,

> I went out there one day and I saw an elderly African American gentleman come to the desk . . . [one volunteer] was sitting . . . with his feet up on the desk, reading or doing whatever he was doing. The client came up and he said, "Oh, how can I help you?" And he was very polite, but he sat there and held the conversation from the chair with his feet up on the desk. And when he walked away I said, "Hey, you heard some of the feedback that we're getting from the clients?" And he said, "Yeah, I think that's really unfair, 'cause we really like these people and we're being so nice and we're developing relationships with them and, I mean I feel like we're friends and that really hurt my feelings." And I said, "Well, let me tell you what this gentleman may have perceived. You know, my father's elderly, and if I don't walk up to him and look him in the eye, he views that as disrespectful." . . . So we talked about how getting up from the chair and walking up from the desk and making eye contact.

Other service providers also adapted their behavior based on their interpretation of race and culture. The Salvation Army changed the food it served, food that was available all day every day, and was universally praised as delicious by volunteers, evacuees, and state workers. One state worker noted that her teenage daughter asked that she bring some home to her. One cook was from New Orleans, and he made food spicier. A belief in the value of diversity, taken to mean culture and race, could not change the loss of home but did allow service providers to rethink their courtesies and improve service delivery.

The shelter at Lowry closed six weeks after the first evacuees arrived. By then, thousands more evacuees had come to Colorado, and both government agencies and charitable organizations worked with them. The transition out of the shelter and into more stable housing was unique here. State housing officials found available rental units and subcontracted with Catholic Charities to administer the rental program FEMA established. The state also contracted with a Coalition member, a White woman who had also volunteered at Lowry, to assist evacuees with housing and to run a hotline for new arrivals. Coalition members teamed with mental health service providers and Red Cross staff to check daily on shelter residents who did not want to leave the dorm, whether because they were suffering from post-traumatic stress, or because they were comfortable, or both. The Coalition's volunteers' approach was to "love them out the door," according to the closing date set by the state.

Despite having initially promised as much as eighteen months of housing assistance, in December 2005, FEMA began to announce its intentions to cut off rental assistance. One Coalition minister worried about how to announce the policy to evacuees. The Coalition of Faith had never been in charge of delivering housing, but he saw the Coalition's credibility on the line. Communicating policy change is difficult, and Coalition ministers took on that job at events for evacuees. FEMA did not end housing in December, announcing each month an additional month's reprieve. By April 2006, with the future of FEMA funding for housing still uncertain, one Black Coalition minister believed it was just as well for church volunteers to scale back their work and to allow professional charities to accept more responsibility. He saw the risks of trying to keep the Coalition's volunteers central, particularly as the numbers were falling away with time. He considered FEMA's pending cut-off: "It's going to get very ugly." He could not see any benefit to having evacuees associate churches with the loss of federally provided housing. Although FEMA would authorize further housing assistance on a case-by-case basis, he knew the stories of many of the evacuees who came through Lowry, and he did not believe they would be eligible.

VOLUNTARISM AND RACE WORK

As a result of their work at Lowry, three of the pastors who formed the Coalition of Faith received a commendation from the governor in his state of the state speech.[39] The three also received the Community Hero Award from the local Red Cross chapter at its annual awards and fundraising breakfast in March 2006. One pastor noted that he could envision the Coalition becoming part of the Colorado Voluntary Organizations in Aid of Disaster, which provides training for volunteers for disaster response. He came to recognize that the Coalition needed to be integrated into response structures to be quickly included in future disasters. Survivors could then see "people like them," and could have someone with whom to pray. Therefore, the work at Lowry inspired African American ministers to reconsider the organizations with which they worked and to advocate that those organizations include African American churches.

The disaster relief community has noted that Katrina added to the post–September 11 focus on disaster preparedness, which considers only potential large-scale or exotic disasters. However, the disaster most likely to occur in urban Denver is an apartment or single-family home fire, and African American pastors would like their congregants to be on the scene. Both the clergy's and the Red Cross's interest in inclusion represent a broader conversation concerning the usefulness of cultural connections in the professionalized charities.

Governor Owens, a social conservative Republican, recognized the importance of African American community leadership in his state of the state speech. Recognition is important, but it does not require changing spending priorities, nor does it require capacity building in community organizations. Finding ways to reach across racial differences in public policy has been part of the politics of race in the United States in recent years; recognizing community leadership without having to provide new resources to support that leadership is one way of doing that.

Bolstered by the success and recognition that they had received for their work, those who organized the Colorado Coalition of Faith continued to serve. Following a disaster, a local long-term recovery committee is formed. As the NVOAD training manual emphasizes, it is "YOUR disaster and YOUR community's recovery."[40] Local agencies are to take the lead. In Colorado, the Coalition of Faith became one of the leaders of the local long-term recovery committee. A Black female pastor who was part of the Coalition became the co-president of the local long-term recovery committee. In her mind this work answered her prayers as she had been looking for a new church and ministry, having grown discontent with the exclusion of women she had found in the traditional Black churches.[41] She, like many others, had earned her credibility by having worked long hours to help settle people in when Lowry first opened.

Another African American female pastor staffed the local hotline, which was meant to provide referrals for services after Lowry closed. However, she saw it as ministry, with race being a crucial part. She explained:

> I'm talking to them African American to African American. And the other thing, I'm talking to them human being to human being. And then [there's] the spiritual component. I can talk to them on that level . . . I have one guy, just love him to death, he's gay and I think he may have AIDS, but I can talk to him. And I prayed with him one day. I said when's the last time you—when was the last time you've been to church . . . That night I prayed with him . . . he was really suffering, and I delivered him food and stuff from the warehouse, and some boxes they were holding for him.

For her, prayer was part of being African American and part of being human; in turn, praying with someone in need was akin to providing the food that he needed. In efforts to assist the evacuees through their long transition to a new community and to support them in their struggles to deal with their loss, church volunteers and workers could provide something distinctive. She did not argue that the Coalition could be responsible for all the services people would need, particularly the housing assistance that was so important to many. Rather, she saw a role for spiritual and personal connection through race and religion that the Coalition could meet. For some of the religious volunteers, the secular state would not meet or acknowledge the spiritual needs people had; providing for those needs was both necessary and distinctive to religious volunteers.

The aspiration to provide prayer and housing continued well after Katrina struck. The Coalition could not use the dormitory for its homelessness project; the state would demolish it. However, the Coalition continued to raise money to help evacuees; by learning how to get grants, the Coalition increased its capacity, though not enough to participate in the largest granting opportunity that became available late in 2006. Katrina resulted in an unprecedented grant of $66 million for long-term casework, administered through the United Methodist Committee on Relief. Only organizations that were the professionalized charities that have done casework in the past, including, for example, Catholic Charities, were eligible for these grants.[42] Although there was some "grassroots" money available, the Coalition was not well-positioned to know about it and apply for it. The Coalition also remained committed to helping those in need in Denver, both by providing congregation-based help to individuals and by asking the state and local governments for a building to institutionalize its homelessness project. The money it raised through grants was substantial for a new community organization, but was not enough to solve the housing problems or difficulties evacuees had with jobs and transportation in a new community. As Dawson argues, access to public policy is difficult for African American communities. In addition, the emphasis on community self-help contributes to reluctance to engage the local state's own programs; while many of the churches participate in homelessness initiatives on the part of the city of Denver, some of the pastors expressed deep skepticism.

CONCLUSION

As many have noted, disasters bring out new organizations, dedicated to new tasks. Disasters, like other political events, are also opportunities to present policies that people have long wanted as solutions, as the disaster newly exposes old problems. For the Coalition of Faith, demonstrating capacity to care for evacuees in dire need could demonstrate the capacity to deal with the long-term homeless in Denver. Working with evacuees could allow one to demonstrate publicly what God's love meant in practice. It could also provide an opportunity to build a ministry when the usual channels had been closed. Voluntary organizations incorporated African American ministers who had not been part of disaster relief, working across boundaries that have proven difficult to bridge. The "spiraling outward" that Lichterman discusses may have happened across voluntary organizations in Colorado. Organizations in the disaster community emphasized that the next time they had to work together they would understand much better how to do so because they now knew each other. However, "putting skin on Jesus" is difficult to accomplish without the resources required to provide housing, drug rehabilitation, decent schooling, and better wages for jobs, all necessary when addressing homelessness, for evacuees and others. Hurricane Katrina, alongside a broad, diffuse national commitment to diversity and embarrassment at the national debacle, opened space for a Black-led voluntary organization to become integrated into state emergency response. However, that integration may not mean access to policy for longer-term projects or commitment of larger public resources.

NOTES

1. This research was supported by NSF SGER #0555117 and by Public Good and PINS Summer Research Associateship grants from the University of Denver. We are grateful to the community members in Denver who have given us their time and reflections.

2. Thomas E. Drabek and David A. McEntire, "Emergent Phenomena and the Sociology of Disaster: Lessons, Trends and Opportunities from the Research Literature," *Disaster Prevention and Management* 12, no. 2 (2003).

3. Alice Fothergill, Enrique G.M. Maestas, and JoAnne DeRouen Darlington, "Race, Ethnicity and Disasters in the United States: A Review of the Literature," *Disasters* 23, no. 2 (1999).

4. For discussion, see e.g., Douglas Brinkley, *The Great Deluge: Hurricane Katrina, New Orleans, and the Mississippi Gulf Coast* (New York: William Morrow, 2006), Michael E. Dyson, *Come Hell or High Water: Hurricane Katrina and the Color of Disaster* (New York: Perseus Books Group, 2006).

5. For a summary and description of the contempt with which many saw the government response, see Brinkley, *The Great Deluge*.

6. George W. Bush, *Address to the Nation,* September 15, 2005, available at http://www.nytimes.com/2005/09/16/national/nationalspecial/16bush-text.html?ex= 1153886400&en=f52aea02357c0688&ei=5070.

7. David Bositis, *Black Churches and the Faith-Based Initiative: Findings from a Survey* (Washington, D.C.: Joint Center for Political and Economic Studies, 2006).

8. W.E.B. DuBois, "The Talented Tenth," in *The Negro Problem* (New York: James Pott and Company, 1903); David Levering Lewis, *W.E.B. Dubois: Biography of a Race* (New York: Henry Holt, 1993).

9. DuBois, "The Talented Tenth."

10. See e.g., Patricia Hill Collins, *Black Feminist Thought: Knowledge, Consciousness, and the Politics of Empowerment* (New York: Routledge, 1991).

11. Karen Sacks, *Caring by the Hour: Women, Work, and Organizing at Duke Medical Center* (Urbana: University of Illinois Press, 1988).

12. Paula Giddings, *When and Where I Enter: The Impact of Black Women on Race and Sex in America* (New York: Bantam Books, 1984).

13. Katrina Bell McDonald, "Black Activist Mothering: A Historical Intersection of Race, Gender and Class," *Gender and Society* 11, no. 6 (1997).

14. Keith Lawrence, "Reconsidering Community Building: Philanthropy through a Structural Racism Lens," *Souls* 4, no. 1 (2002). Conversations concerning what communities can and should do are ongoing; see Tavis Smiley, ed., *The Covenant with Black America* (Chicago: Third World Press, 2006); Juan Williams, *Enough: The Phony Leaders, Dead-End Movements and Cultural of Failure That Are Undermining Black America—and What We Can Do About It* (New York: Crown Publishers, 2006).

15. Michael C. Dawson, "After the Deluge: Publics and Publicity in Katrina's Wake," *DuBois Review* 3, no. 1 (2006).

16. Adolph Reed, "The Black Urban Regime: Structural Origins and Constraints," *Comparative Urban and Community Research* 1 (1988).

17. Peter Schuck, *Diversity in America: Avoiding Government* (Cambridge, MA: Belknap Press of Harvard University Press, 2003).

18. Lauren B. Edelman, Sally Riggs Fuller, and Iona Mara-Drita, "Diversity and the Managerialization of Law," *American Journal of Sociology* 106 (2001); Schuck, *Diversity in America*.

19. Paul Lichterman, *Elusive Togetherness* (Princeton, NJ: Princeton University Press, 2005).

20. Robert Wuthnow, *Saving America? Faith-Based Services and the Future of Civil Society* (Princeton, NJ: Princeton University Press, 2004).

21. Wuthnow, *Saving America?*

22. Drabek and McEntire, "Emergent Phenomena and the Sociology of Disaster."

23. *Executive Order Declaring a State Disaster Emergency.* (Colorado Executive Order D00905).

24. *Executive Order Directing State Agencies to Repair Temporary Housing for Evacuees Displaced by Hurricane Katrina.* (Colorado Executive Order D01005).

25. FEMA, *President Approves Emergency Declaration for Colorado,* available at http://www.fema.gov/news/newsrelease.fema?id=18626.

26. William Frey and Audrey Singer, "Katrina and Rita Impacts on Gulf Coast Populations: First Census Findings," in *The Brookings Institution Metropolitan Policy Program* (Washington, DC: Brookings Institution, 2006).

27. John Logan, *The Impact of Katrina: Race and Class in Storm-Damaged Neighborhoods,* 2006, available at http://www.s4.brown.edu/Katrina/index.html.

28. Logan, *The Impact of Katrina.*

29. Frey and Singer, "Katrina and Rita Impacts on Gulf Coast Populations."

30. U.S. Census Bureau, "Denver County," (United States Census Bureau, 2006); U.S. Census Bureau.

31. See Denver Commission to End Homelessness, 2005. For the cities that are designing ten-year plans and an overview, see the Interagency Council on Homelessness, http://www.ich.gov/.

32. For a newspaper account, see e.g., John Aguiliar, "Safe at Last, but Anxiety Lingers at Lowry," *Rocky Mountain News,* September 5, 2005.

33. Many, of the evacuees and service providers we interviewed have described miserable conditions in the stadiums. For a written account, see Brinkley, *The Great Deluge.*

34. This point is particularly revealing given that White and Black people see racism very differently. For most White people, it is not a problem. For most Black people, it is. That remained true post-Katrina. Dawson, "After the Deluge"; Cedric Herring, "Hurricane Katrina and the Racial Gulf: A Du Boisian Analysis of Victims' Experiences," *DuBois Review* 3, no. 1 (2006).

35. See John Barry, *Rising Tide: The Great Mississippi Flood of 1927 and How It Changed America* (New York: Simon and Schuster, 1998); Brinkley, *The Great Deluge.*

36. Incident command is the command-and-control system for managing disasters, first instituted in fires, and mandated by the federal government. Those who criticize it argue that flexibility is crucial to managing uncertain events such as disasters, and that what works for fires may not work for everything else. See e.g., Richard A. Buck, Joseph E. Trainor, and B.E. Aguirre, "A Critical Evaluation of the Incident Command System and Nims" (Unpublished manuscript, in possession of authors, 2006).

37. Fothergill, Maestas, and Darlington, "Race, Ethnicity and Disasters in the United States."

38. Edelman, Fuller, and Mara-Drita, "Diversity and the Managerialization of Law."

39. Bill Owens, *State of the State Address: January 12, 2006* (State of Colorado, 2006), available at http://www.colorado.gov/governor/stateofthestate06.html.

40. NVOAD, *Long Term Recovery Manual* (National Voluntary Organizations Active in Disaster, 2004), available at http://www.nvoad.org.

41. Cheryl Townsend Gilkes, "'Together and in Harness': Women's Traditions in the Sanctified Church," in *African American Religious Thought*, ed. Cornel West and Eddie S. Glaude (Louisville, KY: Westminster John Knox Press, 2003); Evelyn Brooks Higginbotham, "Black Church: A Gender Perspective," in *African American Religious Thought*, ed. Cornel West and Eddie S. Glaude (Louisville, KY: Westminster John Knox Press, 2003).

42. See http://www.katrinaaidtoday.org/about.cfm.

Part Three

CITIZENSHIP, POLITICS, AND GOVERNMENT PRIORITIES

Chapter Eight

Stipulations

A Typology of Citizenship in the United States After Katrina

Allison M. Cotton

Perhaps the founding fathers of our nation were unable to foresee the various types of citizenship that would eventually comprise the American organization of states, and it is with great regret that we allow the disappointment to settle. Hurricane Katrina and the subsequent watershed of disaster can be used as an example of how citizens are defined and categorized in the United States based on the skill of the various people to face their obligations to the nation as well as the requirements we place on the nation to respond to citizens' needs. There are an inordinate number of responsibilities wrapped up in the word that we use to describe people who belong to this nation and an even larger group of rights that are at stake when such people draw on the protection of the government to which they belong. People sometimes drain the resources that they have come to recognize as entitlements even though the result resembles nothing more than a document signed by men that holds those rights and undergirds them with power in times of need.

Citizenry can be likened in form and fashion to the rights accorded people who deserve to inhabit a certain space and time. Like Katrina, that time and space can be disrupted by catastrophes that are unusual in daily life, but that, in one way or another, determine the course of the lifetime that is yet to come. Citizenry is, thus, determined by the existence of normalcy in one's life that is, in turn, defined by the goals of the system within which it resides. There are citizens who obtain normalcy with their lifestyles just as there are citizens who obtain normalcy with their appearance. Normalcy, then, is defined by one's competence in obtaining an inner and/or outer appearance of conformity. That is not to say that deviance is absent, but rather obscured by the appearance of normalcy that citizenship requires.

Robert Merton's typology of deviance can be used to explain why some people are able to assemble their lives in a state of perceived normalcy better than some others and how benefits are bestowed upon those who are able to do so (see Table 8.1). His is a typology that allows readers to categorize various types of adaptation according to their relative agreement with society's accepted goals such as money, power, and prestige, with society's accepted means of obtaining those goals such as employment, rank, and status:

> The conceptual scheme to be outlined is designed to provide a coherent, systematic approach to the study of sociocultural sources of deviate behavior. Our primary aim lies in discovering how some social structures exert a definite pressure upon certain persons in the society to engage in nonconformist rather than conformist conduct . . . Among the elements of social and cultural structure, two are important for our purposes. These are analytically separable although they merge imperceptibly in concrete situations. The first consists of culturally defined goals, purposes, and interests . . . these goals are more or less integrated and involve varying degrees of prestige and sentiment . . . The second phase of the social structure defines, regulates, and controls the acceptable modes of achieving these goals. Every social group invariably couples its scale of desired ends with moral or institutional regulation of permissible and required procedures for attaining these ends.[1]

Merton goes on to explain the various types of "strain" or "anomie" that citizens endure in trying to obtain society's goals, upon which much societal pressure is placed, by using society's accepted means, upon which virtually no societal emphasis is placed:

> In societies such as our own, then, the pressure of prestige-bearing success tends to eliminate the effective social constraint over means employed to this end. "The-ends-justifies-the-means" doctrine becomes a guiding tenet for action when the cultural structure unduly exalts the end and the social organization unduly limits possible recourse to approved means.[2]

The result, according to Merton, is a society with an unusually high level of crime, poverty, and mental illness: "The consequences of such structural inconsistency are psychopathological personality, and/or antisocial conduct, and/or revolutionary activities."[3]

Table 8.1. Merton's Typology of Adaptation

Adaptation	Cultural Goals	Institutionalized Means
Conformity	+	+
Innovation	+	−
Ritualism	−	+
Retreatism	−	−
Rebellion	+/−	+/−

Each adaptation, then, represents a "logically possible, alternative mode of adjustment or adaptation by individuals" to the societal condition of anomie:

> The first, "conformity," is the most common response: one simply accepts the state of affairs and continues to strive for success within the restricted conventional means available. The second type of adaptation, "innovation," is the most common deviant response: one maintains commitment to success goals but takes advantage of illegitimate means to attain them. Most crime and delinquency, especially income-producing offenses, would fit into this adaptive mode. Another deviant mode, "rebellion," rejects the system altogether, both means and ends and replaces it with a new one, such as a violent overthrow of the system. Yet another, "retreatism," refers to an escapist response: one becomes a societal dropout, giving up on both the goals and the effort to achieve them. Merton placed alcoholics, drug addicts, vagrants, and the severely mentally ill in this mode. Finally, there is "ritualism," in which one gives up the struggle to get ahead and concentrates on retaining what little has been gained by adhering rigidly and zealously to the norms.[4]

The current view applies that structure to the more basic need of belonging that forces people to first agree with the goal of belonging and then to pursue approved means for obtaining that measure of belonging. Once the person has obtained the requisite amount of belonging, that person is afforded the chance to partake of the government's protection and assistance.

We must be careful not to assume that citizenship per se requires anything less than birthright (that would be in direct contradiction to what the Constitution has said it requires), but rather to theorize about citizenship based on the actions of government agencies and their treatment of qualified people. Again, Hurricane Katrina offers ample opportunity for one to surmise the relationship between citizenship and protection based on witness accounts, news stories, and other propaganda readily available during the time of the disaster. This in no way assumes that the relationship is real, but rather that the relationship has meaning that can be gleaned from the events leading up to and following the storm.

CITIZENS OF THE STORM

In numerous accounts of Hurricane Katrina, it has been said that some people knew that the storm would hit. The levees that were placed at the base of some of the water camps in New Orleans foretold a state of readiness for the local governments who also knew that the effects of such a storm could be devastating. Without going further into who knew and when, it is apparent that someone knew that the New Orleans levees could break and that if the levees broke, there was a possibility that many people could die. The storm hit. And although numerous storms before had struck the relatively small, but hugely populated city, there was a new kind of concern for the amount of water that finally destroyed the inhabited area:

> New Orleans'[s] levees failed during Hurricane Katrina because federal engineers for decades did not anticipate the potential height of storm waters and underestimated the strength required to hold them back, the Army Corps of Engineers concluded Thursday.
> "That is a very sobering thing for us," said Lt. Gen. Carl Strock, the corps chief. "This is the first instance of a failure of a corps design of any significance."
> A well-designed levee system might not have held back the high waves and storm surge that swamped nearly 80 percent of New Orleans and vast areas nearby, but it would have minimized damage and allowed a swifter recovery, the corps said in a 6,000-page report.[5]

That concern was realized by weather forecasters leading up to the days of the worst of the storm when warnings went out to the people in the town which asked them to leave their homes immediately for lands further north where the water was less likely to rise to the level of immersion that it did in New Orleans. Some citizens left, but others did not. Why?

> The images that haunt me these days are of the people left behind. Nola King, who lost her home in Bay St. Louis, Miss. Ola Wilson, who is slowly rebuilding hers in Gulfport. Ernest Ratliff, who is trying to make a living at his New Orleans service station amid the crushed cars and debris spit out by Hurricane Katrina. And I can still hear the heavenly balm offered by Pastor Patrinell Wright and the Total Experience Gospel Choir. I traveled with the choir last week as it visited the Gulf region to perform and do some relief work.
> We were shocked and humbled by what we witnessed. But as one day rolled into the next, those feelings turned to embarrassment and anger. A year has

passed, and still, one of America's most distinctive—and divided—regions has been left battered and defiled, seemingly forgotten. While the rebuilding has started in some areas, many towns still have rubble in the streets, homes uninhabitable and businesses that are now just memories. I even saw roaming packs of dogs.

Worse, so many of the people who love this place had no choice but to leave it. Some 250,000 of the million Gulf Coast residents that fled Katrina will not return, according to a new study by Earth Policy Institute, a Washington, D.C., nonprofit environmental-research organization. For the poor who stayed, their struggle is daily and indefinite. The $2,000 checks people received from the Federal Emergency Management Agency were used—or sometimes squandered—for immediate needs, like food and hotels. And that money, doled out in the days after the storm, was spent long ago. The tens of thousands of FEMA trailers and mobile homes are shelter, but only through the end of the year. And then what?

"How can this government be so generous away from home," Wright fumed, "and sit on its own citizens?" It's unfair to blame FEMA for everything. The truth is the Gulf states were crippled by poverty, unemployment and dysfunction long before Katrina hit. So when she arrived—400 miles wide, packing a storm surge twenty-seven feet high—any stability that existed was blown apart and swept out to sea.[6]

There is some evidence to suggest that the citizens who stayed in New Orleans did so because they were unable to leave. New Orleans, although a popular vacation city, falls in the lower half of economic strata in the United States, meaning that there are a large number of poor citizens living in that city compared to the population of documented poor people in other cities in the United States. In general, poverty means that a person or family lacks minimal resources to live in a normal state of being within the definition of what it means to be a U.S. citizen. The poverty line in the United States, for example, is calculated based on the minimum amount of calories that a body needs to consume in a twenty-four-hour period without starving to death, with some consideration in the calculation for the minimum level of shelter required to protect a body from environmental elements, and the minimum level of clothing needed to protect a body from the same. In the United States, that minimum cost of supplies is calculated at $9,393 per year for an individual.[7] Hence, poverty is defined as anyone who makes less than $9,393 per year. In 2003, Louisiana's poverty rate was around 18 percent, the second highest rate in the nation, and the highest in the South, while approximately 25 percent of Orleans Parish residents endured life below the poverty line before the storm hit.[8] For that reason, it can be assumed that less than one quarter of the citizens of the city of New Orleans owned a car or had the means necessary to buy transportation out of the city for themselves and/or their family members. Unfortunately, the transportation offered to some citizens was declined:

It had been just two days since Hurricane Katrina smashed into the Gulf Coast, but the American Red Cross said donations for relief had already reached $21 million by Wednesday, with more than half of the money coming from individual donors. Many Americans gave more than money. Rescue workers and volunteers from around the country were in or were en route to Louisiana and Mississippi to help with relief efforts by midweek. Are we all obliged ethically to help when disasters like Katrina strike? And to what extent? NEWSWEEK's Jennifer Barrett spoke with Bruce Weinstein, author of "Life Principles: Feeling Good by Doing Good" (Emmis) and the syndicated column Ask the Ethics Guy, about the government's ethical responsibility to hurricane survivors . . . and what Americans can—and should—do to help. Excerpts . . .

[NEWSWEEK:] The mayor ordered residents of New Orleans to evacuate, yet some chose to stay behind—and many of them had to be rescued. Should the government pay for the rescues or should the residents be charged for ignoring the order to evacuate?

[Bruce Weinstein:] There's a practical problem with answering that satisfactorily. You have to understand why they stayed. It might not be whether they wanted to defy area officials. For some, it was a matter of where to go. Some didn't have a car or access to a vehicle. And what if they were sick or had obligations to others? I'm sure that the mayor understood, as a practical consideration, that getting everyone to evacuate wouldn't be possible.

What's the ethical obligation to those that stayed behind?

Because of the difficulty of knowing who stayed because they thumbed their nose at authority, and who stayed because they couldn't get out, we need to have a condition-blind policy for giving assistance. Perhaps if we could know, we could rank order for assistance. But we don't.

Ethically, what must the government provide in a situation like this?

It should provide food, clothing, shelter and emergency medical assistance, and get people back to where they were before the catastrophe—well, at least, to a livable condition. That's where our tax dollars go.[9]

Once the storm hit, the government was obliged to assist the citizens of New Orleans based on the assumption that government plays an important role in helping the citizenry of its territory. It is the principle that first caused our government to be established: the principle of principalities—citizens organized to protect the interests of members from infringement by other people on the people belonging to that organization. People who were thought to be undeserving of those protections, for example, were banned from the organization or executed having forfeited their rights to the protections by infringing upon the rights of the members by word and/or deed. Such banned citizens were labeled as outcasts, criminals, miscreants, or otherwise deviant species. It can be said, in the modern day, that outcasts now take on a different form; rather than just the misdeeds of stealing or robbing or assaulting other citizens, they simply offend our senses because they fail to obtain the appearance and/or qualifications of citizenship.

I propose here, then, that citizenship in the United States requires a minimum level of self-sufficiency as well as a steadfast belief in the American Credo which presupposes honor. It is not enough to simply be able to take care of yourself in the United States. A citizen is also required to believe in the same ideals of other citizens. If citizenship requires Christianity, then you must at least believe in the appropriateness of Christianity to guide the lives of people. If citizenship requires education, then you must at least believe in the idea of education as being a route to some kind of success. If citizenship requires hard work, then you must at least believe in the idea that hard work promotes stability that in turn promotes a successful organization of people. If citizenship requires obedience, then you must at least believe in the idea that obedience insures loyalty that in turn provides predictability in behavior, which then supports the control over citizens that any governmental structure must use to maintain its sovereignty. These are some of the ideals that citizenship requires members to apply in their daily lives because they augment or otherwise buttress the concept of self-sufficiency upon which our nation stands.

But there are different kinds of citizenship. Each kind, in symbiotic fashion, brings with it a certain level of assistance from the government. Government, then, is only required to provide the level of assistance that has been earned by the citizen in need of assistance. Full citizenship, of course, is awarded full assistance, while semi-citizenship requires somewhat of a lesser response. It is my contention that the various types of citizenship are directly related to the forms of assistance that were provided during and after Hurricane Katrina. Table 8.2 represents a chart of the various types of citizenship: believers, deviants, achievers, functionals, and victims, along with their relative degree of entitlement to protection. Further, the diagram illustrates whether governmental protection is provided in times of need.

TABLE 8.2. A Typology of Citizenship in the United States

Types of Citizenship	Requirements	Entitled to Protection	Protection Provided
Achievers	+	+	+
Functionals	+	+/_	+/_
Deviants	_	+/_	+/_
Believers	_	_	+
Victims	+/_	+/_	+/_

Achievers

Achievers are people who have met the requirements of citizenship and who are fully entitled to the government's protection and assistance because they have earned the right to enjoy the resources of the establishment to which they conform. These are people who not only believe in the American way, but also exemplify what it means to be an American citizen, even reaching a status above what the ordinary citizen may be capable of reaching. People like Bill Gates, Oprah Winfrey, and Lance Armstrong have beaten the odds in every regard by inventing new ways of viewing poverty, disease, and victimization, among other obstacles. Instead of allowing or even viewing such obstacles as problems, they have redefined these issues as victories or strategies or learning tools so that other Americans are empowered to follow suit. These are the Americans that are touted as success stories above all those who have struggled to maintain self-sufficiency at a low level despite their same encounter with poverty, disease, and victimization. The United States requires citizens to maintain unwavering faith in the possibility of success over the more realistic goal of obtaining mediocrity. Protection and assistance are almost always awarded to achievers:

> Evacuees who escaped Hurricane Katrina's flooding on their own are faring better almost a year later than the thousands rescued and dumped in cities saturated with evacuees, according to a report released Monday. The study, conducted by seven law firms enlisted by the Appleseed Foundation, a nonprofit social advocacy group founded by Ralph Nader, also found nonprofit and faith-based groups and local and state governments acted more quickly and efficiently than the federal government.
>
> Gulf Coast evacuees in Birmingham, Alabama, and Atlanta, Georgia, generally are doing better than those in Houston and San Antonio in Texas, the study found. Birmingham and Atlanta had fewer evacuees, and many of them had the money and connections to flee the storm on their own. Houston had more evacuees, mostly people who couldn't get out of New Orleans and had to be rescued after the storm hit. The city received a lot of New Orleans'[s] poor who did not have the resources to evacuate on their own, and many arrived with little more than the clothes they were wearing. Many were also physically or mentally ill.[10]

Functionals

Functionals are people who have met the requirements of citizenship in terms of self-sufficiency, but who may or may not qualify for governmental assistance or protection due to the fact that they are unable to obtain it. Extremely poor people, mentally or physically disabled people, and incompetent people fall into this category, not only because they may not be aware of the various entitlements and protections afforded to citizens but also because they may not fully understand their role in obtaining the protections such as filling out an application for assistance or taking an exam to establish need, and so forth. Many people in the United States still believe in the government's role of educating its citizens and of bringing help to the people who need it. Again, citizenship requires self-sufficiency which assumes some level of knowledge and applicability that some people are wholly incapable of meeting. Protection and assistance are only sometimes afforded to people who are dysfunctional:

> Another deadline is quickly approaching for those who fled the aftermath of Hurricane Katrina. Housing benefits from FEMA are set to run out at the end of the month. That's bad news for some of those least able to rebound from the wrath of the storm. Freddie Smooth for example. He lives at the Big Bass Resort. While it would seem to imply a languid place with few cares. Not so. Behind his window is a story. Many of them about Katrina. "I lose uh three granddaughters and a daughter," said Smooth, a Katrina evacuee. Smooth lives with loss and uncertainty. There's a pile of FEMA paperwork. The agency he said seems to want him to go back. "Ain't nothin' ready," claims Smooth. He isn't sure where he will end up. "Endless uncertainty," Jenny Calvird said "is worse than the storm." Legally blind, Calvird pours [*sic*] over every correspondence but still can't say whether her benefits will be extended. "I don't know where I'm going to live from one day to the next," said Calvird. The manager here has become their voice. "They are my battle and that is, that is, I'm sorry. But I love them and I can't let this happen to them. I can't face God some day and say I threw out a ninety-seven-year-old woman on the street because I wasn't able to beat the bureaucracy," said Marilyn Tyler. In all more than 100 of the senior Katrina evacuees are still here. Tyler worries about whether fully a third of them will still be eligible. And now, after almost a year they have just begun to call this home. "I'm just standing and staying and praying that I don't have to give up this home," said Calvird. FEMA tells 11 News that next week it will have teams in Houston.[11]

Deviants

Deviants are people who have failed or otherwise thwarted the requirements of citizenship such as honor and self-sufficiency, by engaging in unusual manners of self-sufficiency such as crime or religion. Crime, for example, can be used to obtain money for life's expenses, but it is a frowned-upon lifestyle because it goes against the ideals of honesty and integrity in citizenship. Religious sects or cults also fit into this category because although some claim to be against the ideals of citizenship or frown upon the goals associated with citizenship such as money, power, and prestige, they seek independence from traditional modes of thought and organization. Independence is a deeply cherished quality in the United States, but only if it is manifested in an honorable context. Clearly, it is okay to be a member of an independent group that upholds the ideals of the Constitution, but independent groups that take issue with aspects of the Constitution are deemed harmful to the welfare of society and summarily put down. Besides, deviance requires labeling—if no one knows that you are dishonest, then no one reacts to you as though you are dishonest. There are deviants among the citizenry who have not been labeled as such. Those citizens do not fit into this category. Protection and assistance is only sometimes afforded to deviant citizens:

> As Hurricane Katrina began pounding New Orleans, the sheriff's department abandoned hundreds of inmates imprisoned in the city's jail, Human Rights Watch said today. Inmates in Templeman III, one of several buildings in the Orleans Parish Prison compound, reported that as of Monday, August 29, there were no correctional officers in the building, which held more than 600 inmates. These inmates, including some who were locked in ground-floor cells, were not evacuated until Thursday, September 1, four days after flood waters in the jail had reached chest-level. "Of all the nightmares during Hurricane Katrina, this must be one of the worst," said Corinne Carey, researcher from Human Rights Watch. "Prisoners were abandoned in their cells without food or water for days as floodwaters rose toward the ceiling." Human Rights Watch called on the U.S. Department of Justice to conduct an investigation into the conduct of the Orleans Sheriff's Department, which runs the jail, and to establish the fate of the prisoners who had been locked in the jail. The Louisiana Department of Public Safety and Corrections, which oversaw the evacuation, and the Orleans Sheriff's Department should account for the 517 inmates who are missing from the list of people evacuated from the jail.[12]

Believers

Believers are people who have failed to meet the requirements of citizenship and who are not entitled to protection, but they receive governmental protection because they believe in the ideals of the nation. These are people who may not be able to take care of themselves financially, but they display a positive attitude toward their ability to someday pull themselves out of their financial predicament, for example. They do not complain. They do not ask for handouts. They do not expect other citizens to help them, due to their steadfast belief in the concept of individualism, and they are eternally grateful for the opportunities to succeed that are afforded by the ideals of a free society:

> Katrina showed that plenty of people in New Orleans are quite capable of taking care of themselves. But it also showed that there were many others who for a variety of reasons—too poor to own a car, too sick to leave a hospital—needed the help of the community. "This hurricane was instructive on every level," says William Galston, professor of civic engagement in the department of government and politics at the University of Maryland, College Park. "We learned, as if we needed to, that individual character matters. Some members of the New Orleans police force who had lost everything walked away. While that is understandable, others who had suffered equally stayed to perform their duty. We have also seen countless examples of ways in which extended families and neighborhoods and communities make a difference," he says, noting that nearly 80 percent of the people born in Louisiana stay there for their entire lives. "That creates a social network that is flexible enough and emotionally connected enough to reach out to victims of a catastrophe and do a lot of good. But not least of all, one of the functions of events such as 9/11 or Katrina is to remind us why we have government, why we need it, and how important it is that that government be adequately funded, well organized and competent." That has rarely been the message delivered by recent successful politicians during the last generation as the pendulum has swung away from the community toward the individual. In his 2000 book, *Bowling Alone*, Robert Putnam of Harvard University's school of government chronicled the demise of what could be termed America's public space, pointing to the decline in memberships in the institutions—like bowling leagues—that once brought people together. The politicians who have emphasized the individual are partly the cause of this, but their success is also the result of the forces that urged the country in this direction. "Everything has pushed people in the direction" of acting as individuals, not as a community, Crenson says.[13]

Victims

Victims are people who, through no fault of their own, may or may not have met the requirements of citizenship and for that reason, may or may not be entitled to the protection and assistance of government. In hindsight, it depends upon whether the people in power view their situation as deserving or undeserving. There are various kinds of victims in today's modern world. To be sure, people suffer from disease, poverty, disfigurement, criminal victimization, natural disasters, and immorality, among others, but whether the government intervenes on behalf of those suffering under these conditions is somewhat of a judgment call on the part of those empowered to do so. What makes the intervention of government different in the case of a hurricane than in the case of severe poverty? In other words, why did the situation in New

Orleans become headline news when the hurricane hit rather than when more than 3,200 citizens were homeless in New Orleans during the same year? What makes the disfigurement of a teenage surfer girl in Florida more worthy of public support than the triumph of love and family over traditional values on sex and marriage between a teacher and a student? Victims are only sometimes afforded the protection and assistance of government depending on whether the public blames them for the situation or not:

> We arrived Sept. 16, where the Red Cross had set up a Disaster Relief Service Center in a rodeo arena with bleachers, a snack bar and an air-conditioned hall. This particular center aimed to channel relief funds to 4,000 households. People needing aid were told to wait in line along a highway where local police would hand out 500 tickets per day for three-day periods. The tickets granted entry to the relief center. Long lines of cars formed hours before the handout even began. But getting a ticket was only the beginning. Once in the rodeo arena, people waited up to eight hours, much of it in broiling heat, for the paperwork to be processed. At the end, those who made the cut were entitled to debit cards loaded with $360 per person, up to a maximum of $1,565 for five people. The cards activated after forty-eight hours, and could be used to buy anything except alcohol, tobacco and guns. . . .
>
> Then there were those who never got into the relief system—plenty. In a local laundromat, I met a woman from New Orleans who had moved into a family home in Tylertown that had been vacant for ten years. She enrolled her two sons in school and began commuting to a job in Metarie, La.—a three hour commute each day. Another woman had moved in with her sister. Before evacuating, she had been living in Chalmette, La., an area absolutely flattened by the storm. She had lost everything. What most disturbed her was the loss of her job, which she'd held for over ten years. She said that both she and her mother had tried unsuccessfully for two weeks to get into our service center. Someone who truly needed help never got the chance to visit the Red Cross.[14]

CONCLUSION

Citizenship in the United States, then, requires self-sufficiency and honor that fits into the way that other citizens view (or want to view) their country. As a nation that believes in freedom and democracy it is only fitting that freedom be allocated by virtue of responsible stewardship—it assumes that people can be trusted to live among themselves without disrupting the rights of others to live as they please. Similarly, democracy requires that citizens govern themselves which, in turn, assumes that citizens are capable of making decisions for the welfare of everybody. As with any assumptions, they can often be wrong, but in the United States, these are touted as the most important of principles that led to and continue to guide our existence. In the same way and, perhaps, fortuitously, our nation suffers from an appalling lack of regard for circumstances or conditions that are thrust upon people through no fault of their own. It is easy to remember the images of people running, boating, riding, and walking away from New Orleans as the water swept their lives away, but it is much harder to determine who deserved help during the tragedy and who did not. According to the citizenship typology outlined previously, some people in the United States deserve to be rescued from the mud of their lives while others simply deserve to wade in it. That is an unflattering picture to paint of the lives of thousands of Americans who neither caused the hurricane nor wished for it to happen, but that is a much more advantageous view of the horrible consequences brought on by Hurricane Katrina than the view from the conscience of those who had the power to help or to prevent the level of devastation that occurred, but did not:

> "I think it is possible that one of the lessons we come away from Katrina with is not just that we need government after all, but that, gosh, if we are all in this together, then we should think about what our obligations are to one another," Putnam [of Harvard University's school of government] says. "What does it mean to say that those folks sitting in the Superdome are our fellow citizens?" Crenson [chair of the political science department at Johns Hopkins University] says that it takes leadership to make that happen. "People are ready to be good citizens, they just aren't asked anymore," he says.[15]

NOTES

1. Robert K. Merton, "Social Structure and Anomie" in *Criminological Theory: Past to Present Essential Readings,* eds. Francis T. Cullen and Robert Agnew (Los Angeles: Roxbury, [1938] 2003), 179.

2. Merton, "Social Structure and Anomie," 184.

3. Merton, "Social Structure and Anomie," 183.

4. Ronald L. Akers and Christine S. Sellers, *Criminological Theories: Introduction, Evaluation, and Application* (Los Angeles: Roxbury, 2004), 165–66.

5. Alan Levin, "Corps: Levees' Design Caused Deadly Failure," *USA Today,* June 1, 2006, <http://www.usatoday.com/news/nation/2006-06-01-levees_x.htm>.

6. Nicole Brodeur, "One Year Later Katrina Survivors Are Still Hurting," *The Seattle Times,* August 16, 2006, <http://seattletimes.nwsource.com/html/localnews/2003202052_brodeur16m.html>.

7. U.S. Census Bureau, Current Population Survey 2004 Annual Social and Economic Supplement.

8. U.S. Census Bureau, Orleans Parish, State and County Quick Facts, 2003.

9. Jennifer Barrett, "Helpful Obligations: The Ethics Guy Explains How and Why Americans Ought to Aid Those Affected by Hurricane Katrina and Why Looting is

Sometimes Ethically Permissible," *Newsweek*, September 1, 2005, <http://www.msnbc.msn.com/id/9160887/site/newsweek/>.

10. Stacy Plaisance, "Katrina's Poorest Evacuees Fare Worst, Study Finds," *The Boston Globe,* August 15, 2006, <http://www.boston.com/news/nation/articles/2006/08/15/katrinas_poorest_evacuees_fare_worst_study_finds/>.

11. Nancy Holland, "Older Katrina Survivors Wonder if Window of Uncertainty Will Slam Down on Them," *KHOU News Channel 11 Houston,* July 21, 2006, <http://www.khou.com/news/local/stories/khou060721_jj_katrinaelderly.cf0cc67.html>.

12. Corinne Carey, "New Orleans: Prisoners Abandoned to Flood Waters," *Human Rights Watch,* September 22, 2005, <http://www.hrw.org/english/docs/2005/09/22/usdom11773.htm>.

13. Michael Hill, "Katrina Shows It Takes a Community," *Baltimore Sun,* September 11, 2005, <http://www.baltimoresun.com/news/opinion/oped/bal-pe.social11sep11,1,679769.story?coll=bal-oped-headlines&ctrack=1&cset=true>.

14. Dan Cole, "What I Saw in Tylertown," *Newsweek,* October 17, 2005, <http://www.msnbc.msn.com/id/9729481/site/newsweek/>.

15. Hill, "Katrina Shows It Takes a Community."

Chapter Nine

Protect or Neglect?

Social Structure, Decision Making, and the Risk of Living in African American Places in New Orleans

Rachael A. Woldoff

Brian J. Gerber

Not long after the scope of the Hurricane Katrina disaster became apparent, a steady stream of misplaced blame began to flow into interpretations of the disaster, particularly in terms of the events that transpired in Louisiana. Criticism took the form of finding fault with the victims of the hurricane, often blaming New Orleans's residents for failing to be prepared, refusing to evacuate, or "choosing" not to evacuate in a timely fashion.[1] While it is fair to say that there is a widespread public perception that Katrina had a disproportionately heavy impact on the African American residents of New Orleans, a key element of the public discourse over *assignment of responsibility* for the Katrina disaster was the issue of race. Soon, a public debate erupted over the role of race, with one side arguing for a "colorblind" explanation of the debacle and the other side suggesting that racial bias mattered for Katrina's victims.

The Pew Research Center surveyed U.S. citizens in Katrina's aftermath and reported two interesting findings. First, related to racial inequality in general, half of those polled disagreed with the statement that the Katrina disaster demonstrates that racial inequality remains a major problem in the United States. Second, related to governmental blame, 68 percent disagreed that the government's response would have been faster if most of the victims had been White.[2] Yet within those aggregates there was important variation: the survey reported that African Americans had a far greater tendency to view Katrina through the lens of racial disparity than did White respondents.

This chapter uses these public opinion findings as a springboard for discussing the roles of local racial inequality and racialized governmental decision making in the Katrina disaster. In doing so, we consider two sociological explanations of inequality of place with regard to Hurricane Katrina: an ecological perspective and a political economy perspective. The ecological perspective suggests that place-related factors affect people's life outcomes in a patterned fashion. Thus, while individual life outcomes often vary by race, they are also determined by group-level competition for space in the larger urban system. This perspective focuses more on spatial patterns in general and deemphasizes the role of governmental action. In contrast, the political economy perspective asserts that various governmental actors and economic elites make conscious policy decisions that directly affect the level of place-related hazards vulnerability that various social groups face. The political economy perspective on urban issues is a more critical perspective on common patterns of inequality, especially as they related to place.

We begin by clarifying the ways in which the ecological and political economy perspectives are linked to New Orleans's demography and infrastructure/disaster management policies. Then, we organize the rest of the chapter around two issues fundamental to the public debate over the New Orleans situation after Katrina. *First, was the devastation that resulted from Hurricane Katrina really a class issue and not a race issue?* That is, is there evidence that race played a role in determining which groups were disproportionately hurt by Hurricane Katrina? We answer this question drawing insights from both ecological and political economy viewpoints. *Second, who, if anyone, should actually be held responsible for the ineffectual response to the flooding caused by the hurricane?* In other words, was the ineffectual response a result of specific individuals' incompetence at the federal, state, and local levels, or did larger policy decisions produce an increase in the probability of harm for particularly vulnerable persons? Given that the second question refers to policy more than ecological factors, in addressing this question, we primarily utilize a political economy approach. By addressing these two questions, we outline the ways in which the structure of residential life in New Orleans and the decisions of governmental actors intersected to exacerbate the adverse effects of Hurricane Katrina on New Orleans's most vulnerable residents.

TWO VIEWS OF RACE, CLASS, AND PLACE

Social inequality is systematically tied to place and the case of Hurricane Katrina is no exception. The outcomes of this deadly hurricane exemplify an important aspect of research on the intersections of race, class, and place: the idea of a *place hierarchy*.[3] The concept of place hierarchy involves two important facts: (1) some neighborhoods are better places to live than others; (2) place stratification is not random, but patterned. Individuals and families are better off when they live in "good" communities with quality housing; safe health conditions; reputable schools; dependable and responsive services; low rates of crime, disorder, and violence; good economic opportunities; and nourishing environments for raising children.[4] Typically, good communities require a solid infrastructure with reliable services, located a safe distance from low-lying areas near bodies of water. However, only some people live in such pro-tected environments where they can live and flourish. The media coverage of Hurricane Katrina showed the world how real place inequalities actually are— even in the United States. However, just as important, it also broadcasted that place differences in the United States are *racialized*. Based on this logic, the debates about racial inequality and blame suggest a trenchant question for the Katrina disaster: which aspects of the disaster were related to the ecology of New Orleans and which were related to government decisions?

The Ecological Perspective and Natural Processes

Robert Park's discussion of the ecological importance of cities noted that "so-cial relations are so frequently and so inevitably correlated with spatial rela-tions."[5] This was ever so apparent on Wednesday, August 31, 2005, when more than 10,000 people were marooned at the Louisiana Superdome,[6] and people began to ask themselves why so many of these evacuees were poor and African American. According to Park's human ecology perspective, the answer has a great deal to do with class and place. Living environments are stratified in a hierarchical fashion, such that cities can be seen as "mosaics of risk and protection."[7] Some places provide us with safety, while others im-peril us, leaving us vulnerable and exposed to danger. Regardless of whether the risk to the residential environment is crime, pollution, or natural disaster, the ecological perspective asserts that some places are worse than others. This approach goes further to argue that certain *populations* are more likely to live in high-quality areas than others. Thus, the community acts as a conduit for the transmission of amenities and resources to citizens. Unfortunately, in-vestments in the lives of residents are not evenly distributed across places.

The classical ecologists were interested in community as a context for peo-ple's lives and while they helped draft policies that would benefit disadvan-taged populations (e.g., juveniles in inner cities), the role of policy for urban residents was not a major focus of their theory and research. In their field work in Chicago, they employed biological metaphors in their view of cities as natural environments with limited and finite resources.[8] Treating the city as a natural laboratory, they suggested that like plants and animals, human beings *compete* for scarce urban resources, such as quality schools and desirable housing locations. In this struggle to gain access to good residential neighborhoods, groups with economic means are the winners and disadvantaged groups are relegated to the slums and ghettos. Opportunity structure and discrimination were not part of the ecologists' conversation, because the outcome of urban struggles was seen as part of a natural order, causing some to characterize the ecologists' view of cities as Darwinian.[9] Thus, to ecologists, the city operates with in a free market and the poor are "naturally" forced to live in the worst areas because of the competitive sorting process for valuable urban space. This point of view is quite consistent with the American ideology of individualism that coheres around the notion that one's effort and ability can help one to overcome historical injustices and limiting family background characteristics.[10] Hence, disadvantaged groups, whatever race/ethnicity they are, live where they do because more advantaged people emerged as winners in the competitions for desirable land or housing locations. In short, traditional ecological treatments of residential inequality focus on the idea of an orderly and natural competition for space and the resulting segregation of groups into different neighborhoods.

While still very influential, many urban scholars have critiqued human ecology for its deterministic view of urban processes.[11] Among other things, critics point out that human communities differ from plant ecosystems because they are governed by local, regional, national, and international entities. This leads to the more contemporary and critical perspective that the *decisions* and *actions* of institutional actors lead to inequality and contribute to the social problems that plague certain communities.

The Political Economy Perspective and Human Design

To supplement the relatively deterministic view of inequality in urban processes and outcomes that forms the core of human ecology, political economists emphasize institutional factors and the role of human intervention in the lives of urban residents. Political economists are part of the school of "new urban sociology"[12] that highlights the role of human decision making, institutional actors and policy-making, and the acknowledgment of cultural influences on community and urban structures.[13] This is in stark contrast to the more ecological view that suggests that cities look the way they do (e.g., segregated) because they are inherently efficient ecosystems. Like ecology, the political economy perspective suggests that communities have uneven and unequal levels of resources. However, political economists go further to argue that place inequality is caused by key decision makers who choose to invest in some communities, but not others. In that way, the spatial distribution of race and class in a community cannot be identified as a necessary outcome.

Like human ecology, political economy also argues that the wealthy are more likely to live in better places in cities, but political economists claim that the reason for this is not rooted in simple efficiency. Instead, they cite the relationships between government and owners of capital, such that city-suburban differences and increases in community inequality stem from liaisons between corporations and governments who cooperate to control local planning, business, and labor.[14] In other words, federal, state, and metropolitan governments impose planning policies and decisions on communities using legislation and subsidies that affect the distribution and quality of housing, schools, and amenities for the poor (e.g., housing construction policies, privatization of government services, housing loan policies, urban renewal, public housing programs, empowerment and enterprise zones, property tax abatements for private businesses, pro-capitalist planning for "good business environments," highway planning, and automobile policies). Those who disproportionately benefit from such extra-market arrangements (mostly wealthier individuals who help influence these key policy decisions) are more likely to live in the safer, more affluent areas. In this view, places are political and human constructs rather than the product of passive, remote, efficient market forces. In addition, with an emphasis on key decision makers, political economists examine the *intersection* of race and class, such that African Americans' class positions are inextricably linked to their historical treatment by institutional actors across generations.[15]

To better understand the racial character of Hurricane Katrina, we place this contemporary urban event in the context of these two perspectives of urban processes. Doing so helps to identify the factors and processes that collided to provide the setting for the disaster that left so many New Orleans residents stranded, homeless, in despair, and in some cases, dead.

Katrina Issue 1: Racial Inequality and Residential Vulnerability

"New Orleans is not about race. It's about class."[16]
Bill O'Reilly, September 6, 2005, "The O'Reilly Factor"
(average audience of 2,274,000 in the first quarter of 2006)

"This isn't a race issue, it's a class issue."
Jon Bon Jovi, September 21, 2005, "The Oprah Winfrey Show"
(average audience of 9,306,000 for week of 10/31/05–11/06/05)

The fact of inequality is the heart of sociology and is a key concern of other social sciences. The essence of inequality research is captured in Gerhard Lenski's question, "Who gets what and why?"[17] Applying Lenski's question to the events of Katrina prompts a critical question in its own right: When the levees failed, why were so many poor and African American residents struggling with thirst, hunger, and hygiene in the New Orleans Convention Center and Louisiana Superdome?

In the aftermath of Katrina, many public forums, talk shows, news outlets, blogs, and private discussions across the United States shared a common refrain about the "who" question: "Katrina is not about race. It's about class." Like the trial of O.J. Simpson, Hurricane Katrina left the American people polarized about race issues. In our individualistic society, it is no wonder that even with the media spotlight on the hurricane victims, most Americans believe that African Americans and others who struggle with social mobility only have themselves to blame.[18]

At first, a class-based explanation seems obvious; indeed it appears to be partially supported by the images in the television coverage of Hurricane Katrina that showed that the evacuees who possessed the fewest resources suffered the most. Interestingly, the class-based view is consistent with the ecological view and certainly has some merit. Places are the products of land markets and people of lower means are more likely to live in the least valuable areas—economically depressed areas, low-lying areas, and communities with the least protection from various natural and technological dangers.[19] Hence, the poor were the most adversely affected by the hurricane because they live in worse places and have fewer resources to survive. Indeed, there is overwhelming evidence that the poor are disproportionately exposed to hazards in their residential neighborhoods (e.g., environmental pollution, crime, vacant and low-quality housing). Oddly, the class-based ecological view may have comforted many Americans because people were able to view the poor as a unified, colorless group. However, when taking a closer look at Katrina, the race-neutral element of the class-based argument is weakened.

Disproportionate Poverty and Segregation

Poverty has a color. Even with the gains made since the Civil Rights movement, African Americans are disproportionately poor.[20] On average, African Americans have lower educational attainment, have worse jobs, earn less money, and have less wealth than Whites.[21] According to the U.S. Census Bureau, in 2000, 28 percent of the New Orleans population was poor, but of those, 84 percent were African American. When African Americans are disproportionately poor, this suggests that race *does* matter for life outcomes.

Yet, ecologists would argue that places are naturally and efficiently sorted to geographically separate the poor from the rich and African Americans from Whites. Ecologists emphasize technological and transportation changes and natural cycles of population turnover when they describe racial housing patterns. Thus, it is not surprising that they tend to think that the suburbanization of Whites was triggered by automobile technology and class-based purchasing power.[22] According to the ecologists, housing markets are natural and guided by an "invisible hand," to use Adam Smith's famous metaphor,[23] which appears to efficiently regulate the land market. When a neighborhood changes from mixed income to poor or from racially integrated to African American, ecologists describe the process in terms of invasion, dominance, and succession. In this invasion-succession model, when a group with lower status begins to integrate or "invade" a nearby neighborhood, long-time higher status residents try to stop it, but eventually the new group becomes numerically "dominant" and the higher status group abandons the old neighborhood, making succession final.

Even though aspects of these models are flawed, they are consistent with a popular, class-based explanation for Katrina. According to this view, the amount of storm damage suffered by African Americans is the result of living in neighborhoods that they can afford, which have worse housing stock. Thus, Whites and African Americans of similar class background face similar obstacles.

Indeed, many researchers attempt to empirically "explain away" the race effects that they may find in their research. For instance, by comparing poor Whites to poor African Americans, they try to control for class and look for similarities between groups. Indeed, for many outcomes, differences between groups narrow quite a bit after accounting for class, but many times they do not disappear. Thus, race still has an effect, over and above class, when looking at many outcomes related to life chances, such as educational success, family formation, and criminal justice system contact.[24]

Yet, this racial disparity in social class would not necessarily translate into a deprived living environment without a very race-based American phenomenon: segregation. In other words, just because African Americans are overrepresented among the poor does not mean they must live in *racially* segregated environments or extremely poor neighborhoods. How can we understand this? We want to believe that the increase in the size of the African American middle class, stricter enforcement of fair housing laws, and decreases in White prejudice mean that neighborhoods in U.S. cities and suburbs are integrated. However, although housing discrimination has been illegal since 1968, segregation remains a fact in our society.

Segregation matters for Hurricane Katrina because in 2000, New Orleans was one of the ten most segregated metropolitan areas in the United States and was one of five metropolitan areas to show the least amount of decline in segregation between 1980 and 2000.[25] This means that on average, African

Americans in New Orleans live in neighborhoods with very few Whites in them and Whites live in neighborhoods with very few African Americans.

But why does segregation matter for Katrina victims? Is it inherently bad to live with one's own group? Residential segregation contributed to Katrina because it geographically concentrates poor people, and African Americans are disproportionately poor.[26] U.S. poverty is concentrated in urban areas, and segregation confines deprivation to a subset of socially isolated areas rather than scattering poor people across a range of neighborhoods.[27] For instance, in 2003, the U.S. poverty rate was 12.3 percent, but the urban poverty rate was 17.5 percent and the suburban poverty rate was only 9.1 percent.[28]

New Orleans typifies the situation of segregation concentrating poverty. New Orleans residents are more likely to be in poverty (27.9 percent were poor in 1999) and are far less likely to be homeowners (46.5 percent are homeowners compared to 68.3 percent of the United States). However, for African Americans, these class-related problems are worsened by segregation. Research shows that in the absence of segregation, poverty has a smaller impact on the neighborhood environments that African Americans experience.[29] Segregation increases the chances that African Americans live in neighborhoods with high levels of community stressors. Under integrated conditions, poor African American families are scattered more evenly throughout the area, and this decreases the concentration of poverty.

Ecological analysis shows us that even with the same poverty level, if New Orleans had been more racially integrated, the evacuation might have been more successful. Consider the fact that in New Orleans, transportation was a problem for many evacuees. Census data reveal that in the United States, African Americans are more likely to live without access to a car than White Americans (33.4 percent of poor African Americans do not have car access versus 12.1 percent for poor Whites), but in the city of New Orleans, 52.4 percent of poor African Americans lacked car access versus just 17.4 percent of poor Whites.[30] This raises the possibility that if poor neighborhoods had been racially integrated, the average African American resident in a poor community would have had a better chance to escape the hurricane, because one of his or her White, car-owning neighbors may have been able to help. Related to this, segregation also exacerbates racial differences in social ties, which can help a person to survive in an emergency. Research shows that residents of extreme poverty areas have fewer social ties and their existing ties tend to be with other people who are coping with a low socioeconomic status.[31] Thus, for African Americans, living in a segregated area reduces contact with individuals who are better off than they are.

Ecologists would point out that there are also population-related reasons that New Orleans is segregated. For instance, the United States is 12.3 percent African American,[32] but Louisiana is 32.5 percent African American.[33] This means that African Americans are geographically concentrated in the state. New Orleans, itself, is 67.3 percent African American,[34] so the city further concentrates African Americans. Some make the argument that African Americans favor segregated spatial patterns and that residential segregation is the result of choice, but this flies in the face of social science research. The research on race and residential preferences shows that the average African American does not want to live in a neighborhood that is segregated.[35] However, Whites often flee neighborhoods with nontrivial representations of African Americans. The *process* of White flight is often minimized in discussions of predominantly African American cities like New Orleans, but in 1950, only one third of the New Orleans population was African American.[36] The increase between 1950 and 2000 was not caused by an influx of African American population because between 1965 and 2000, New Orleans was one of the ten metropolitan areas with the greatest loss of African American population.[37]

Despite an invasion-succession pattern, political economists would argue that these population changes tend to be "helped along," if not intentionally designed, by governmental policies, many of which benefit wealthy capitalists in the community. According to this view, class-based spatial processes related to competition are not the sole causes of human misery because such processes are aided by human actors who make decisions and policies. Segregation patterns are caused, in large part, by historic federal housing policies and practices, some of which persist in various forms today. For instance, over time and into the present, governments and banking institutions have systematically excluded groups from certain communities and channeled them into different areas using a variety of means (e.g., the Federal Housing Authority's racially restrictive covenants, blockbusting, redlining, steering, restrictive zoning and land use policies, and discriminatory practices in providing mortgages and loans and renting properties[38]). Thus, in New Orleans, as elsewhere, when Whites moved away, most African Americans could not follow them into their new communities.

In New Orleans in particular, historical policies related to slavery contributed to African American residential patterns. The race-based nature of the residential life in New Orleans is actually a metaphor for the lasting legacy of relationships between White power and government policy. While New Orleans is a city that has long had a high proportion of African Americans, African Americans were not always concentrated into poverty. Before 1890, New Orleans was more spatially integrated along racial lines than was true when the winds and flooding of Katrina hit. Slaves and former slaves once lived in "backyard" slave quarters, but state-sponsored Jim Crow laws created segregated neighborhoods.[39] Also, slavery and Jim Crow prevented African Americans from accumulating wealth over time,[40] a factor that determines where one lives.[41] Thus, race-based policies like slavery and Jim Crow have left a legacy of spatial segregation that was later cemented by White flight into the suburbs. Such policies remind us that race and class cannot always be separated.

Given these socioeconomic and residential disparities, how are African Americans to improve their life outcomes? Many argue that education is the key, but again race matters here as residential segregation bleeds into the schools. School quality is closely linked to local residential quality and property taxes, so New Orleans's schools are troubled. Sixty-five percent of New Orleans's public schools did not meet state standards in 2004, compared to 11 percent of schools in the state as a whole.[42] Again, race matters, as New Orleans had one of the nation's largest central city school districts in 2000, but also had the largest African American enrollment in the country among such schools—92.7 percent.[43] Test scores and segregated student bodies are not the only problems. The school district in New Orleans was $25 million in debt as of 2005.[44]

In the end, ecology's class-based view and political economy's race-based view each have insights to offer; class-based problems are real, but they are racialized and caused by historical factors related to policy decisions. Ecologists show us that society is structured in a patterned fashion and that demographic forces are at work. Yet, political economists demonstrate that people make decisions that exacerbate such patterns. In New Orleans, these population forces and decisions culminated so that Hurricane Katrina most harmed those people at the bottom of the American racial hierarchy. While the relationship between class and race overlaps, racial inequality remains a significant factor in its own right and the Pew survey shows that many African Americans know this.

Katrina Issue 2: Assigning Responsibilty: Policy Decisions and Governmental Actions Affecting The Katrina Disaster Event

"George Bush doesn't care about Black people . . . America is set up to help the poor and the Black people as slow as possible."
Kanye West, September 2, 2005, A Concert for Hurricane Relief
(audience of 7,400,000)

Like Kanye West, many African Americans believe that the government response to Katrina was affected by race. As mentioned earlier, the Pew Research Center asked, "Would decision makers have acted more quickly if most of the evacuees had been White?"[45] Americans strongly disagreed on this matter based on their race, with African Americans and Whites holding widely divergent views. Some argue that there is no way to know the answer to this question, but the survey attempts to explore a controversial aspect of the Katrina disaster—the racialized aspects of governmental response.

In addressing our first public issue over Katrina, we argued that the ecological and political economy explanations of race and class can be applied when examining the results of the disaster. In addressing this second issue, we assert that here too segregation plays a role in decision making for disaster events like Katrina. Broadly speaking, governments at all levels in the United States do not necessarily prioritize the needs of particularly vulnerable populations in terms of disaster management, and to the extent that African Americans are geographically concentrated in high-risk locations, this results in greater exposure to the adverse effects of a disaster event. In other words, hip hop artist Kanye West's comment captures a real, but somewhat indirect, causal chain of ecological vulnerability and policy indifference based on race and class. African Americans and poor people are systematically more vulnerable to a range of natural and technological hazards, but they lack effective redress through public policy choices.[46] In the United States, social status enables a group to effectively reduce vulnerability, but when communities are poor or African American or both, they are not typically a high priority for many elected officials.

As posited by political economists, elected officials and other actors in the policy-making milieu make conscious choices about the ways in which classes of individuals are represented in the policy process.[47] To be sure, the ecological patterns of race and residential location at issue in New Orleans were in place before George W. Bush was elected. But the specific race and class makeup of New Orleans does have a relevance to representation generally, which is in turn relevant to the events of Katrina. The basic policy agenda of the Bush administration, as it took office, did not include a proactive stance on ameliorating the general hazards vulnerability (e.g., it had no serious program of attempting to reduce environmental hazards). Such a policy agenda is relevant to Katrina because it captures the political reality that those who might benefit most from such a proactive policy stance were not part of the electoral coalition that supported Bush.[48] In other words, the policy needs of citizens like African Americans in New Orleans (highly vulnerable to a wide range of natural, technological, and other manmade hazards) were not reflected as a policy priority for the administration because those citizens were of limited electoral utility. The critical issue from a political economy perspective is whether decisions made by the Bush administration exacerbated the vulnerability of New Orleans by their policy agenda generally and their disaster management policy approach specifically.

How exactly can we parse responsibility for the Katrina debacle? A 2006 poll found support for the sentiment that the victims of the hurricane *chose* to stay in their homes and neighborhoods and thus, they have nobody to blame but themselves.[49] However, political economists are wary of such individualist explanations and argue that the local, state, and federal governmental administrations handle disaster management in ways that generate differentiated benefits. For instance, in regions where flooding is a high probability hazard, cities and neighborhoods vary in the quality of their infrastructure with some communities having better drainage systems, functioning flood walls, and larger budgets for levee construction. As Wisner, Blaikie, Cannon, and Davis note, "Disasters are a complex mix of natural hazards and human action."[50]

The latter part of that formulation, "human action," is manifest in decisions made by government. Public policy choices are relevant to the discussion of the Katrina disaster because they have a direct effect on the relative vulnerability of groups to a natural (e.g., volcano, hurricane, tornado, earthquake) or technological hazard (e.g., chemical, explosive, nuclear). Vulnerability may be defined as "the characteristics of a person or group and their situation that influence their capacity to anticipate, cope with, resist and recover from the impact of a natural hazard (an extreme natural event or process)."[51] A review of the record shows that sociodemographic characteristics are directly related to hazard vulnerability in the expected direction—poor, less educated, non-White communities are more hazard-vulnerable.[52] A variety of studies have shown that race and class are linked to hazard exposure.[53] The issue is, then, whether policy choices either attenuate or exacerbate such vulnerabilities.

We proceed with an examination of the Bush administration and the response to Katrina on two levels: (1) the broader policy context with which the administration approached disaster issues generally, which amounted to a deemphasis on federal natural disaster preparedness and mitigation efforts, and (2) the more discrete domain of how the administration specifically responded to the events of Hurricane Katrina. We begin by tackling the former to show, in the vein of the political economy approach, the way governmental policies and decisions affect various groups within a society.

MINIMIZATION OF FEDERAL NATURAL DISASTER POLICY INITIATIVES

Many have criticized President George W. Bush, Department of Homeland Security Secretary Michael Chertoff, and Federal Emergency Management Agency (FEMA) Director Michael Brown for their lack of leadership and managerial competence, but several policy-making decisions bear great relevance to the inadequate federal response to Katrina. Recognizing the presidential role in federal disaster management and wishing to improve the efficiency of the emergency management system, former President Jimmy Carter created FEMA as a stand-alone executive agency.[54] Later, President Bill Clinton elevated the position of FEMA director (held by James Lee Witt) to cabinet-level status in recognition of the significance of both the presidential role in disaster management and the importance of an effective federal response to presidential power. President Clinton is reported to have told cabinet members to give Director Witt "anything he wants,"[55] a clear demonstration of FEMA's standing in the Clinton administration. The prominence afforded to FEMA under Clinton abruptly evaporated with the incoming Bush administration—a policy shift that became even more pronounced when, following the events of the terrorist attacks on September 11, 2001, FEMA was rolled into the new Department of Homeland Security (DHS). This series of conscious policy choices downgraded the status of FEMA, especially regarding the disaster preparedness efforts that became well-established under Witt.

Academics, journalists, and homeland security specialists expressed concern about the decision to de-prioritize FEMA and disaster preparedness and warned of the potentially adverse consequences for the nation's ability to deal with a catastrophic disaster event.[56] In fact, early assessments of the Katrina response suggest that clouding FEMA's mission focus in this way hampered its effectiveness in dealing with a natural disaster such as Katrina.[57] As noted previously, hazard vulnerability is not randomly distributed in the population. Consequently, the choice to minimize the federal government's scope of involvement in natural disaster planning and preparedness reduces the ability of all levels of government to respond to catastrophic disasters—as was evidenced in the Katrina situation. Yet the reduced federal presence in disaster management can have less of a negative effect when state and local governments have either the willingness or capacity to fill the policy leadership void that is left. Unfortunately, the historical track record of effective disaster management across state and local governments is extremely uneven.[58] Further, a recent assessment by DHS of state and large-city homeland security preparedness—including the area of mass evacuation—yielded a portrait of a country quite unprepared for catastrophic disasters.[59] The net result is when the policy and administrative system surrounding disaster is less efficacious, those who are most vulnerable are the most likely to absorb disproportionate adverse effects from government decisions.

To understand the Bush decision to downgrade FEMA's role within the broader policy-making context of disaster management in the United States, it is critical to look at competing conceptions of how the federal government should function. Since the advent of FEMA where the federal government's role in managing disaster events was expanded significantly, we can observe two distinct and competing views of governance. Among other things, both

Presidents Carter and Clinton pursued more effective and efficient public management practices as major initiatives in their presidency. These reform efforts indicate an optimistic view of the capacity of the federal government to effect positive policy change and help explain Carter's interest in creating FEMA in the first place, as well as Clinton's reinvention of it some fifteen years later. This policy approach can be described as proactive, as contrasted with a more passive approach to federal policy initiatives.[60]

This second, passive, approach, holds a much more pessimistic view of federal authority and has been the stance adopted by the three Republican presidents since the creation of FEMA, but Ronald Reagan and George W. Bush, especially. For instance, George W. Bush's efforts at civil service reforms have not been designed to improve federal administrative capacity, but to limit the policy influence and standing of public employees by increasing the amount of federal work that is outsourced.[61] In that light, it is not surprising that the Bush administration was interested in promoting more outsourcing of various program functions at FEMA and disinterested in enhancing existing natural disaster preparedness programs—efforts that may have had at least some indirect effects on the Katrina response.[62]

Just as there are two broadly coherent but competing views of governance between the Democratic and Republican presidents, there is a similarly distinct view of what the federal government's primary role in disaster management policy specifically should be. The active and passive approaches can be applied directly to disaster management policy and encompass the issue of where primary policy-making and administrative responsibilities should lie. Today's disaster management system in the United States grew out of the civil defense preparedness system developed in the 1950s and 1960s. Thus, the passive governance approach for the federal government's core mission on natural or technological disasters is closely linked to the original civil defense perspective. The logic of the Civil Defense Act of 1950 was that the responsibility for civil defense in the event of an attack from an external enemy (with a nuclear attack from the Soviet Union being the paradigmatic threat) would be vested in state and local government. The federal government would take on the more limited role of mobilization in the event of a major attack. In its historic origins, the civil defense perspective conceives of the federal government as a limited partner for catastrophic events with respect to state and local responsibilities.[63]

The Reagan administration adopted the position that the mission and scope of federal actions on disaster events should be limited in scope—with the exception that particular attention should be paid to how the federal government would respond to a military attack and how the federal government could promote state and local preparedness for such an event. This passive governance approach has resurfaced in the George W. Bush administration. The Bush approach to FEMA has been to deemphasize or alter key activities initiated during the Clinton administration. With the transition of FEMA into the DHS, the agency has moved away from a focus on promoting preparedness and mitigation in the area of natural and technological hazards. FEMA's preparedness functions have been largely eliminated under DHS Secretaries Tom Ridge and Chertoff and shifted to other areas of DHS.

In essence, the Bush administration, post–September 11, has returned to the civil defense model where the federal government's lead disaster management agency is geared toward dealing with an external attack threat, with a catastrophic terrorist event replacing the Soviet nuclear attack threat. In other words, building its antiterrorism capabilities has occurred at the expense of promoting preparedness on natural disasters, as evidenced by a dramatic shift in the substantive focus of FEMA preparedness grants to antiterrorism efforts.[64] This has enormous implications for government response to major natural disaster events. A shift in focus at the federal government's lead disaster management agency means that there is a much greater likelihood that response in catastrophic disaster situations will be less effective.

The consequence of the Bush administration's approach to disaster management policy generally cannot be construed as a function of racial bias in a narrow sense. Clearly, it fits within a larger ideological conception of passive governance. However, such an acknowledgment is far from saying that race does not matter to Katrina and Bush administration policy choices over disaster management. Instead, in this case, the relationship between race and policy is *indirect*. As discussed previously, race and class play an enormously important role in determining vulnerability to various hazards, including a natural disaster like a major hurricane. The policy choice to deemphasize federal natural disaster preparedness initiatives is tantamount to increasing the probability that highly vulnerable populations will be at greater risk of suffering adverse effects in disaster situations, as was the case in New Orleans.

To be clear, the Bush administration's view that the federal government should not be involved in mitigating disaster risk is not incidental to a post–September 11th concern for terrorism. It fits a larger ideological conception of a negative view of federal policy authority and responsibility (passive governance). In fact, the view of the administration on the federal role could be summed up by Joe Allbaugh, Bush's first FEMA director. Early in his tenure, Allbaugh referred to federal disaster aid as an "oversized entitlement program" and charged that faith-based organizations were a more appropriate vehicle than the federal government for disaster victims needing assistance.[65]

The political economy approach argues that politics and government matter for a locale and that political and economic actors set rules and create policies that are aligned with their interests and goals. The preceding discussion shows how these governance approaches, whether passive or active, define policy choices that in turn affect community outcomes. To elaborate the ways in which political elites' conscious choices manifested themselves in the case of Katrina, the following section discusses the Bush administration's management of the events following the storm. The leadership failure of political elites is as central as the more space-based ecological aspects of racial and class inequality for understanding the destruction that accompanied Hurricane Katrina.

Leadership Void: The Bush Administration Response to Katrina

The previous section explained how an intentional minimization of federal natural disaster policy responsibility created a context where the response to Katrina was much less effective than it might have been—to the detriment of the most vulnerable populations. It also points us toward an examination of the immediate governmental response at the federal level: how exactly did the Bush administration manage the Katrina disaster as it unfolded? There are good reasons to focus our attention on President Bush. While disaster management policy making and implementation in the United States encompasses a vast array of local, state, federal, non-profit, and key private stakeholders, presidents also affect disaster policy and management in three critical ways. First, while the disaster management system in the United States is enormously complex and decentralized, atop it sits the federal government with FEMA, as a part of DHS, functioning as the lead agency. At first, disaster response is a local and then a state responsibility, but when a disaster of sufficient magnitude occurs, the federal government provides coordination and material resources that local and state governments are often unable to manage or produce themselves. The president is ultimately responsible for the federal government's ability to guide and direct the intergovernmental disaster management system. Second, as an elaboration of the first point, it is important to note that FEMA is best understood as a presidential agency.[66] As such, presidents have direct influence over specific activities of the lead federal agency in all phases of disaster management. Third, while critical resources flow to state and local governments from presidential decisions, most obviously in the instance of a declaration of disaster, presidents can have a much broader impact on the disaster management system by initiating policies and programs that shape actions by key federal agencies. But more important, presidents shape incentives for preparedness and mitigation planning, and response and recovery coordination, throughout the entire intergovernmental system.

It is extremely difficult to characterize George W. Bush's management of the Katrina response as anything but a failure. As Katrina struck, President Bush was on vacation, as was Vice President Dick Cheney. Emblematic of the delayed response to Katrina, and indicative of a chief executive wholly out of touch with the situation in the Gulf, a Bush political counselor, Dan Bartlett, produced a DVD with news footage for the president to watch on Air Force One before his first post-Katrina visit, so he would understand the magnitude of the devastation.[67] For a week, while people baked in the Gulf Coast sun in places like the I-10 cloverleaf or suffocated in the unbearable stench and humidity inside shelters like the New Orleans Superdome and Convention Center with little food or water, little federal presence on the ground could be detected. A *Newsweek* writer succinctly summed up the national mood about the federal response three weeks after Katrina:

> How this could be—how the president of the United States could have even less "situational awareness," as they say in the military, than the average U.S. citizen about the worst natural disaster in a century—is one of the more perplexing and troubling chapters in a story that, despite moments of heroism and acts of great generosity, ranks as a national disgrace.[68]

A proactive federal response to the impending Katrina disaster was in order. A reactive federal response to disasters, known as a "pull" system, in which the federal government waits for states to make specific requests about what they need before the federal government acts, is the norm. However, a "push" system whereby the federal government does not wait for state government requests for assistance and pre-places resources before the crisis commences is not unprecedented.[69] Bush, Chertoff, and Brown had ample warning that Katrina would be catastrophic. Max Mayfield, director of the National Hurricane Center, bluntly warned the White House and the relevant state and local leaders about the impending doom they faced.[70] The National Weather Service office in Slidell, Louisiana, similarly warned that levees in New Orleans would be overtopped, airborne debris would be widespread, windows would be blown out, and power and water shortages would "make human suffering incredible by modern standards."[71]

Had the White House heeded the warnings of the National Hurricane Center and the National Weather Service and initiated a push system while Katrina was still in the Gulf of Mexico—as it did a few weeks later before Hurricane Rita hit—the federal response would have been exponentially faster. Fully two days passed until DHS Secretary Chertoff declared Katrina an Incident of National Significance thus setting the wheels of the federal government, through the National Response Plan (NRP), slowly into motion. Chertoff, however, never activated the Catastrophic Incident Annex (CIA) portion of the NRP which would have quickly shifted the federal response mode from a reactive pull response to a proactive push response.[72] The irony remains that the NRP-CIA was written specifically for an incident such as Katrina, yet was never activated.

In fact, DHS had only just recently completed both the NRP and the National Incident Management System blueprints for how the federal government should lead an intergovernmental response to catastrophic disasters. Katrina was a first major test of the NRP, but the implementation of that planning effort failed miserably.

That brief summary of the federal response to Katrina brings us back to this section's original question about how to assign responsibility for debacle that led to such misery in New Orleans. Clearly, as a general approach to disaster management, the Bush administration demonstrated a conscious preference for limited federal action to help prepare for and mitigate the adverse consequences of disaster events by not supporting Clinton-era policy initiatives in those areas. Such a stance predated the September 11 attacks, and the shift to a civil defense approach to disasters helped cement it. We have not argued that these are race-conscious decisions per se, but given the overwhelming evidence that poor and minority communities are disproportionately harmed by such events, they are policy decisions of indifference.

Why then would the Bush administration take such a stance? Part of the answer lies with the administration's ideological approach to federal governance, as we explained previously. But we can also think of it in terms of political representation: poor, nonwhite communities are simply of little electoral relevance to the Bush administration and, as a consequence, the administration's policy efforts reflect that political reality. In this regard, it is useful to contrast George W. Bush to his immediate predecessor, Bill Clinton. Shortly after Katrina, Clinton told CNN's Larry King that one of the important lessons he learned as governor of Arkansas, and why he appointed James Lee Witt at FEMA and gave that agency such prominence, was that the poor people of his state were particularly hard hit whenever a natural disaster occurred. It is reasonable to infer that because constituencies like African Americans mattered to Clinton's political fortunes, the policy efforts of his administration were reflective of such a representation relationship. When Kanye West charged that Bush "doesn't care about Black people" and that the United States was ineffective in meeting the needs of its poor and minority citizens, he was not wrong in the sense that the governing approach, specific policy choices, and electoral logic of the Bush administration all combined to produce a highly ineffective federal response to Hurricane Katrina.

CONCLUSION

While the Katrina disaster affected, and continues to affect, residents across the socioeconomic and racial hierarchies, the debate over whether race mattered to the observed consequences of Katrina has been a key element of discourse on the disaster. Shortly after New Orleans flooded, dislocating and stranding so many, President Bush was forced to address the issue. In an attempt to defuse critics who accused his administration of being indifferent to race and class issues, Bush claimed that "the storm didn't discriminate and neither will the recovery."[74] Indeed, administration officials and supporters asserted that it was absurd to suggest the administration would *intentionally* move slowly in their disaster response.[75] However, this rhetorical tack is disingenuous; no one would claim that a hurricane could possess a discriminatory intent and relatively few people believe that the Bush administration intentionally crafted a slow, ineffective, response to the disaster.

Instead, the actual crux of the racial bias argument (which was avoided by administration officials) is that poor, non-White communities tend to face significant vulnerabilities across a range of hazards, some of which have their roots in historical public policy decisions. From such a perspective, the consequences of the Katrina disaster cannot be separated from the ecological processes related to inequality and past *intentional* government acts of discrimination and negligence that have helped to disadvantage the African American community. Given this context, the root of the racial bias argument is that New Orleans was a place with a great deal of racial and class stratification, but the Bush administration demonstrably neglected to mitigate the effects of natural and technological hazards that are known to produce disproportionately adverse results for members of racial/ethnic minority groups. Specifically, the Bush administration's opposition to proactive federal disaster preparedness and mitigation efforts, together with administrative incompetence, helped produce the terrible toll on the residents of New Orleans, especially its poorest African American residents. Thus, part of the racial critique of President Bush's handling of the disaster stems from his administration's approach to policy, an approach that was tantamount to indifference to the plight of poor minorities in the midst of natural or technological hazards.

To simplify or dismiss the issue of race, as the Bush administration attempted to do, obscures the complexity of racial/ethnic stratification systems. The tendency to simplify racial matters is widespread. For instance, many U.S. citizens publicly disapprove of face-to-face racism in the form of prejudice and stereotypes, but are reluctant to acknowledge the institutional, structural, less obvious, and more entrenched ways that race continues to play in people's lives.[76]

This simplistic perspective on race is troubling, especially when it comes to residential neighborhood conditions, which determine many aspects of our well-being. It is hard for people in White suburban neighborhoods to imagine the living situations of African Americans and it is common for them to believe that institutionalized residential inequality is a thing of the past. However, the media images of Katrina that overwhelmed us in August and September of 2005 showed that institutionalized racism continues to hit people where they live. In many ways, the Katrina disaster exposed and exemplified the very hidden and stratified nature of U.S. residential life in all of its unfavorable manifestations.

For African Americans and poor Whites, being in the wrong place at the wrong time when Hurricane Katrina flooded New Orleans was a function of the spatial structure of poverty and segregation in the United States. One of the central lessons of Katrina is that racialized place and class dynamics mattered before, during, and after the storm. Yet, as we show in this chapter, it is the combination of racialized spatial processes, as well as governmental actors' disaster management policy choices, that caused particularly adverse impacts on the region's most vulnerable citizens. The dynamic interplay of ecological factors and decision making are part of a continuous urban struggle for resources and can be seen in how Hurricane Katrina affected vulnerable individuals. Katrina serves as a metaphor for the intertwined nature of government decisions and the perilous life circumstances of many African Americans and the poor.

NOTES

1. For instance, this theme of "personal responsibility" was the subject on Fox News for two hosts of two financial programs. One host, Neil Cavuto, argued that "no one though seems to be considering that individuals need to accept some personal responsibility—from preparing for a natural disaster to preparing for retirement." Another host, Dave Ramsey, said that "when you spend everything you make, you end up standing on top of your house. That's what it amounts to. So you've got to think better than that" (see http://www.foxnews.com/story/0,2933,183951,00.html).

2. A 2005 Pew survey showed that 68 percent of Americans believed that government response would have been the same if most victims had been white and 50 percent disagreed that the disaster shows that racial inequality is still a major problem (see Pew Research Center, "Two-in-Three Critical of Bush's Relief Efforts: Huge Racial Divide over Katrina and Its Consequences," September 8, 2005, <http://people-press.org/reports/display.php3?ReportID=255>; "Katrina Has Only Modest Impact on Basic Public Values in Spite of Political Fallout," September 22,

2005, <http://people-press.org/commentary/display.php3?AnalysisID=117>.). However, according to a 2005 Pew report based on their survey, "Blacks and whites draw very different lessons from the tragedy. Seven-in-ten blacks (71 percent) say the disaster shows that racial inequality remains a major problem in the country; a majority of whites (56 percent) say this was not a particularly important lesson of the disaster." This sentiment was echoed widely in the media. For instance, in September 2005, Fox News's Bill O'Reilly said it (see http://www.foxnews.com/story/0,2933,168552,00.html). Also, in September 2005, on Oprah Winfrey's show, Jon Bon Jovi said of Katrina, "This isn't a race issue, it's a class issue and it's American people that we have to help."

3. John R. Logan and Harvey L. Molotch, *Urban Fortunes* (Berkeley: University of California Press, 1987).

4. Jeanne Brooks-Gunn, Greg J. Duncan, Pamela Kato Klebanov, and Naomi Sealand, "Do Neighborhoods Influence Child and Adolescent Development?" *American Journal of Sociology* 99 (1993): 353–95; Douglas S. Massey, "The Age of Extremes: Concentrated Affluence and Poverty in the 21st Century," *Demography* 33 (1996): 395–412; Robert J. Sampson and Jeffrey D. Morenoff, "Public Health and Safety in Context: Lessons from Community-Level Theory on Social Capital," in *Promoting Health: Intervention Strategies from Social and Behavioral Research,* eds. Brian Smedley and Leonard Syme (Washington, DC: National Academy Press, 2001), 366–89; William J. Wilson, *The Truly Disadvantaged: The Inner City, the Underclass, and Public Policy* (Chicago: University of Chicago Press, 1987).

5. Robert E. Park, "The Urban Community as a Spatial Pattern and a Moral Order," in *Robert E. Park, on Social Control and Collective Behavior: Selected Papers,* ed. Ralph H. Turner (Chicago: University of Chicago Press, 1967), 68.

6. Scott, 2005.

7. Kevin Fitzpatrick and Mark LaGory, *Unhealthy Places: The Ecology of Risk in the Urban Landscape* (London: Routledge, 2000), 107.

8. Robert E. Park, Ernest W. Burgess, and Roderick D. McKenzie, *The City* (Chicago: University of Chicago Press, 1925).

9. Logan and Molotch, *Urban Fortunes.*

10. James R. Kluegel and Eliot R. Smith, *Beliefs about Inequality: Americans' Views of What Is and What Ought to Be* (New York: Aldine de Gruyter, 1986).

11. For a discussion see Barrett A. Lee, "Urban Sociology," in *The Future of Sociology,* eds. Edgar F. Borgatta and Karen S. Cook (Beverly Hills, CA: Sage Publishing, 1988), 200–23; and David Smith, "The New Urban Sociology Meets the Old: Rereading Some Classical Human Ecology," *Urban Affairs Review* 30 (1995): 432–57.

12. Mark Gottdiener and Ray Hutchinson, *The New Urban Sociology*, 3rd ed. (Boulder, CO: Westview Press, 2006).

13. Lee, "Urban Sociology."

14. For an example see Timothy Jon Curry, Kent Schwirian, and Rachael A. Woldoff, *High Stakes: Big Times Sports and Downtown Redevelopment* (Columbus: The Ohio State University Press, 2004).

15. Melvin L. Oliver and Thomas M. Shapiro, *Black Wealth/White Wealth: A New Perspective on Racial Inequality* (New York: Routledge, 1995).

16. See Note 2. The following is a quote from an entry on a blog called the "Huffington Post" (cofounded and edited by Arianna Huffington). It is about the disaster and represents the sentiment described above, "This is not about race, this was a natural disaster, and I am so tired of race hustlers like you not taking responsiblity for yourself, your actions, and your communities. This was a double pronged natural disaster (hurricane + flood). You would have to live on Mars to not know a category 5 hurricane was bearing down on New Orleans. Where the hell is people's common sense. If they didn't have it before they just learned a very hard lesson. It is so easy to monday morning quarterback this thing and say that because of race, they were left behind. It looks to me, and to most Americans that I have talked to, that they made a conscious choice" <http://www.huffingtonpost.com/randall-robinson/new-orleans_ b_6643.html?p=4#comments>.

17. Gerhard Lenski, *Power and Privilege* (New York: McGraw-Hill, 1966).

18. Pew Research Center, "Katrina Has Only Modest Impact on Basic Public Values in Spite of Political Fallout," September 22, 2005, <http://people-press.org/commentary/ display.php3?AnalysisID=117>.

19. Karen Sawislak, *Smoldering City: Chicagoans and the Great Fire, 1871–1874* (Chicago: University of Chicago Press, 1996).

20. Latino subgroups and some Asian subgroups are also disproportionately poor, but African Americans are the focus of this chapter.

21. Dalton Conley, *Being Black, Living in the Red: Race, Wealth, and Social Policy in America* (Berkeley: University of California Press, 1999); Peter Fronczek and Patricia Johnson, "Occupations: 2000" (Washington, DC: U.S. Census Bureau, 2003); Eric Grodsky and Devah Pager, "The Structure of Disadvantage: Individual and Occupational Determinants of the Black-White Wage Gap," *American Sociological Review* 66 (2001): 542–67; Nicole Stoops, "Educational Attainment in the United States, 2003," U.S. Census Bureau, June 2004, <http://www.census.gov/prod/2004pubs/p20-550.pdf>.

22. Smith, "The New Urban Sociology Meets the Old."

23. Adam Smith, *An Inquiry into the Nature and Causes of the Wealth of Nations* (New York: Modern Library, 1937).

24. See for instance Stephen Demuth and Darrell Steffensmeier, "Ethnicity Effects on Sentence Outcomes in Large Urban Courts: Comparisons among White, Black, and Hispanic Defendants," *Social Science Quarterly* 85 (2004): 994–1011; Grace Kao and Jennifer Thompson, "Race and Ethnic Stratification in Educational Achievement and Attainment," *Annual Review of Sociology* 29 (2003): 417–42; William T. Trent, "Why the Gap between Black and White Performance in School? A Report on the Effects of Race on Student Achievement in the St. Louis Public Schools," *The Journal of Negro Education* 66 (1997): 320–29; Maureen R. Waller and Sara S. McLanahan, "'His' and 'Her' Marriage Expectations: Determinants and Consequences," *Journal of Marriage and Family* 67 (2005): 53–67.

25. John Iceland, Daniel H. Weinberg, and Erika Steinmetz, "Racial and Ethnic Residential Segregation in the United States: 1980–2000" (Washington, DC: U.S. Census Bureau, 2002).

26. Douglas S. Massey, "American Apartheid: Segregation and the Making of the Underclass," *The American Journal of Sociology* 96 (1990): 329–57.

27. Douglas S. Massey and Nancy A. Denton, *American Apartheid: Segregation and the Making of the Underclass* (Cambridge, MA: Harvard University Press, 1993).

28. Institute for Research on Poverty, "Who Was Poor in 2004?" <http://www.irp.wisc.edu/faqs/faq3.htm>; "Poverty: 2003 Highlights" (Washington, DC: U.S. Census Bureau, 2004).

29. Massey and Denton, *American Apartheid.*

30. Alan Berube and Steven Raphael, "Access to Cars in New Orleans," The Brookings Institution, <http://www.brookings.edu/metro/20050915_katrinacarstables.pdf>.

31. Loic J.D. Wacquant and William Julius Wilson, "The Cost of Racial and Class Exclusion in the Inner City," *The Annals of the American Academy of Political and Social Science* 501 (1989): 8–25.

32. Jesse McKinnon, "The Black Population," U.S. Census Bureau, August 2001, <http://ict.cas.psu.edu/resources/Census/PDF/C2K_Race_Black.pdf>.

33. "State and County Quick Facts: Orleans Parish, Louisiana" (Washington, DC: U.S. Census Bureau, 2000).

34. "State and County Quick Facts: Orleans Parish, Louisiana" (Washington, DC: U.S. Census Bureau, 2000).

35. Reynolds Farley, Elaine Fielding, and Maria Krysan, "The Residential Preferences of Blacks and Whites: A Four Metropolis Analysis," *Housing Policy Debate* 8 (1997): 763–800; Reynolds Farley and Maria Krysan, "The Residential Preferences of Blacks: Do They Explain Persistent Segregation?" *Social Forces* 80 (2002): 937–80.

36. Ronette King, "Shifting Landscape: African-Americans Have a History of Entrepreneurship in New Orleans Dating Back to Before the Civil War," *The Times-Picayne,* March 26, 2001, <http://www.nola.com/unequalopportunity/index.ssf?/t-p/frontpage/79550842.html>.

37. Amy Symens Smith, Bashir Ahmed, and Larry Sink, "An Analysis of State and County Population Changes by Characteristics: 1990–1999" (U.S. Census Bureau, Working Paper Series No. 45, 2000).

38. For a review see John Yinger, *Closed Doors, Opportunities Lost: The Continuing Costs of Housing Discrimination* (New York: Russell Sage, 1995); "Housing Discrimination is Still Worth Worrying About," *Housing Policy Debate* 9 (1998): 893–927.

39. Daphne Spain, "Race Relations and Residential Segregation in New Orleans: Two Centuries of Paradox," *Annals of the American Academy of Political and Social Science* 441 (1979): 82–96.

40. Spain, "Race Relations and Residential Segregation in New Orleans."

41. Rachael A. Woldoff, "Living Where the Neighbors Are Invested: Wealth and Racial/Ethnic Differences in Individuals' Neighborhood Homeownership Rate," in *Wealth Accumulation and Communities of Color in the United States Current Issues,* eds. Jessica Gordon Nembhard and Ngina Chiteji (Ann Arbor: University of Michigan Press, 2006), 267–93.

42. Brian Thevenot and Steve Ritea,"90 Schools in Metro Area Failing," *Times-Picayune*, August 4, 2005, <http://www.nola.com/education/t-p/index.ssf?/base/news-2/112314078132590.xml>.

43. Erica Frankenberg, Chungmei Lee, and Gary Orfield, "A Multiracial Society with Segregated Schools: Are We Losing the Dream?" (The Civil Rights Project, Harvard University, 2003).

44. Doug Gross, "N.O. Superintendent: Groups Trying to Pick School System Apart" *Associated Press*, October 21, 2005, <http://www.wwltv.com/topstories/stories/WWL102105watson.1180584cf.html>.

45. Pew Research Center, "Two-in-Three Critical of Bush's Relief Efforts."

46. See e.g., Robert Bullard, *Dumping in Dixie: Race, Class, and Environmental Quality* (Boulder, CO: Westview Press, 1990); *Confronting Environmental Racism: Views from the Grassroots* (Boston: South End Press, 1993).

47. For a classic statement on representation, see Hanna F. Pitkin, *Representation* (New York: Atherton Press, 1969). On representation in policy and administrative processes, see Sally Coleman Selden, *The Promise of Representative Bureaucracy: Diversity and Responsiveness in a Government Agency* (Armonk, NY: M.E. Sharpe, 1997).

48. Brian J. Gerber and David B. Cohen, "Who Needs a Mandate? The Election 2000 Hullabaloo and the Bush Administration's Governing Agenda," in *The Final Arbiter: The Long Term Consequences of Bush v Gore in Law and Politics*, eds. Christopher P. Banks, David B. Cohen, and John C. Green (Albany, NY: SUNY Press, 2005).

49. The 2006 Associated Press poll question read: "There are many people in this country who choose to live in areas and homes that are known to be especially susceptible to destruction by natural disasters such as landslides, earthquakes, hurricanes, and flooding. In general, when these disasters strike these areas, do you think the government should give money to local residents to help them recover, or do you think the residents of these areas should live there solely at their own risk?" More people (49 percent) said that they live at their own risk, while fewer people thought the government should help them (47 percent). (<http://www.pollingreport.com/disasters.htm>).

50. Ben Wisner, Piers Blaikie, Terry Cannon, and Ian Davis, *At Risk: Natural Hazards, People's Vulnerability and Disasters*, 2nd ed. (London: Routledge, 2003), 5.

51. Wisner et al., *At Risk*, 11.

52. See e.g., Greg Bankoff, Georg Frerks, and Dorothea Hillhorst, *Mapping Vulnerability Disasters, Development, and People* (London: Earthscan Publications, 2003); International Federation of Red Cross and Red Crescent Societies, *World Disasters Report 1999* (Geneva: IFRC, 1999); Kathleen J. Tierney, Michael K. Lindell, and Ronald W. Perry, *Facing the Unexpected: Disaster Preparedness and Response in the United States* (Washington, DC: Joseph Henry Press, 2001); Wisner et al., *At Risk*.

53. Vicki Been, "Locally Undesirable Land Uses in Minority Neighborhoods: Disproportionate Siting or Market Dynamics?" *Yale Law Journal* 103 (1994): 1383–1422, and "Analyzing Evidence of Environmental Justice," *Journal of Land*

Use and Environmental Law 11 (1995): 1–36; Bullard, *Dumping in Dixie* and *Confronting Environmental Racism*; Commission for Racial Justice, *Toxic Wastes and Race in the United States* (New York: United Church of Christ and Public Data Access, Inc., 1987); Benjamin Goldman and Laura Fitton, *Toxic Wastes and Race Revisited* (Washington, DC: Center for Policy Alternatives, 1994); Evan J. Ringquist, "Equity and the Distribution of Environmental Risk," *Social Science Quarterly* 78 (1997): 811–29; U.S. General Accounting Office, *Siting of Hazardous Waste Landfills and Their Correlation with Racial and Economic Status of Surrounding Communities* (Washington, DC: Government Printing Office, 1983). Mohai and Bryant's (1992) review of empirical research on twenty-one types of environmental hazards found that most studies demonstrated statistically significant relationships with race and income. That conclusion was echoed in a similar review by Goldman (1993).

54. Carter issued Executive Order 12148 on July 20, 1979. Richard Sylves and William R. Cumming, "FEMA's Path to Homeland Security: 1979–2003," *Journal of Homeland Security and Emergency Management* 1, no. 2 (2004), <http://www.bepress.com/jhsem/vol1/iss2/11>.

55. Carl M. Cannon and Shane Harris, "FEMA May Work Best Standing Alone," *National Journal*, September 10, 2005, no. 37: 2725.

56. See Cannon and Harris, "FEMA May Work Best Standing Alone"; Amanda Lee Hollis, "A Tale of Two Federal Emergency Management Agencies," *The Forum* 3 (2005), <http://www.bepress.com/forum/vol3/iss3/art3>.

57. Schneider, 2005.

58. See Raymond J. Burby, ed., *Cooperating with Nature: Confronting Natural Hazards with Land-Use Planning for Sustainable Communities* (Washington, DC: Joseph Henry Press, 1998).

59. U.S. Department of Homeland Security, "Nationwide Plan Review Phase 2 Report," June 16, 2006, <http://www.dhs.gov/interweb/assetlibrary/Prep_Nationwide-PlanReview.pdf>.

60. Peter J. May, *Recovering from Catastrophes: Federal Disaster Relief Policy and Politics* (Westport, CT: Greenwood Press, 1985).

61. Jonathan Walters, "Civil Service Tsunami," *Governing* 16, no. 8 (2003): 34–40.

62. For a discussion of how DHS under the Bush Administration has de-emphasized natural disaster preparedness initiatives at the federal level, see Kathleen J. Tierney, "Recent Developments in U.S. Homeland Security Policies and Their Implications for the Management of Extreme Events" (Paper presented at the First International Conference on Urban Disaster Reduction, Kobe, Japan, January 18–20, 2005).

63. May, *Recovering from Catastrophes*.

64. See e.g., Schneider, 2005.

65. Schneider, 2005, 516.

66. Sylves and Cumming, "FEMA's Path to Homeland Security."

67. Evan Thomas, "How Bush Blew It," *Newsweek*, September 19, 2005.

68. Thomas, "How Bush Blew It."

69. Select Bipartisan Committee to Investigate the Preparation for and Response to Hurricane Katrina, "A Failure of Initiative," *United States House of Representatives* 2006, <http://katrina.house.gov/>.

70. Frances Fragos Townsend, "The Federal Response to Hurricane Katrina: Lessons Learned," *The White House,* February 2006, <http://www.whitehouse.gov/reports/katrina-lessons-learned.pdf>.

71. Townsend, "The Federal Response to Hurricane Katrina," 28.

72. Select Bipartisan Committee, "A Failure of Initiative."

73. Select Bipartisan Committee, "A Failure of Initiative."

74. CNN on September 12, 2005 (http://www.cnn.com/2005/US/09/12/katrina.impact/)

75. According to the Dallas Morning News's report on September 3, 2005, when CNN suggested this, White House spokesperson Scott McClellan said, "Such allegations are baseless and absurd . . . Our highest priority is on saving and sustaining the lives of all those who are suffering and in need of help."

76. Marylee C. Taylor, "How White Attitutes Vary with the Racial Composition of Local Populations: Numbers Count," *American Sociological Review* 63 (1998): 512–35.

Chapter Ten

Blown Away

U.S. Militarism and Hurricane Katrina

Tom Reifer[1]

Hurricane Katrina—which generated the energy equivalent of 100,000 atomic bombs as it surged through the Gulf of Mexico—touched down in a United States that for decades has been spending ever-increasing resources on debt-financed wars abroad to the great detriment of urban areas, persons of color, and environmental protection and disaster preparedness (other than terrorism) at home.[2] Moreover, the storm in the Gulf Coast states is intimately related to the wars in the Persian Gulf, from Desert Storm to the current storm of the Iraq War. This chapter argues that the linkage between overseas militarism and domestic decline and inequality is the deep structural context for the failures of the government response to Hurricane Katrina. This chapter thus explores the linkages between U.S. militarism, Hurricane Katrina, and the U.S. system of political economy and ecology, especially as it affects declining cities and their populations, increasingly composed of persons of color.

The dawn of the second millennium brought both change and continuity in terms of war and the United States. Well before the terrorist attacks of September 11, 2001, the Bush administration was pursuing an increasingly aggressive foreign and military policy. In this context, as Mary Kaldor notes:

> It can be argued that the cuts of the early 1990s are equivalent to the reductions that can be expected in the normal post-1945 U.S. military procurement cycle. . . . During the downturns, military R&D is always sustained, designing and developing the systems to be procured in the next upturn. As new systems reach the more

expensive development and procurement phases, this has always coincided with renewed preoccupations with threats of various kinds.[3]

Such a focus on new threats long antedated the terrorist actions of September 11, 2001. In fact, the attacks of that day and the real threat from Al Qaeda presented neoconservative hawks with a perfect opportunity to implement ambitious plans for high U.S. military spending and aggressive overseas policies outlined long before, including pulling out of international treaties and moving forward with plans for the militarization of space.

Recently, the Air Force has been pressing the Bush administration to formally embrace an aggressive strategy for space. Here, the Air Force is essentially following the trajectory set by the recommendations of the 2001 Rumsfeld commission which urged that the military give the president the option to deploy weapons in space, and the 2002 U.S. withdrawal from the Anti-Ballistic Missile Treaty which banned such space-based weapons. This trajectory, however, is not simply a Republican Party program, but is widely embraced by the Democratic Party and among many elite circles, including in the Clinton era. Pentagon space warfare, like the late nineteenth-, and early-twentieth century Navy or later programs of the Air Force, serves both as a form of public subsidy of private profit, through funding high-technology industry, as well as a way to build the military forces to protect increased U.S. investments, for control of worldwide resources and to manage related geopolitical alliances overseas. U.S. technology, from aerospace and electronics, to computers and telecommunications, is largely an offshoot of this Pentagon system of industrial planning, a state-corporate capitalism which serves to incubate high-technology industry until it can be privatized by being turned over to for-profit corporations. Thus, a major function of the first Gulf War in 1991 was to protect the Pentagon budget by showing the relevance of the military in the aftermath of superpower confrontation. Revealed here was the extent to which the Cold War was largely a pretense for the Northern domination of the global South and the larger U.S. war against the Third World.[4]

Many of these connections are explicitly recognized by the Pentagon. In the words of U.S. Space Command's own Vision for 2020 under President Clinton, "U.S. Space Command–dominating the space dimensions of U.S. military operations to protect U.S. interests and investments. . . . During the early portion of the 21st century . . . space forces will emerge to protect military and commercial national interests and investments in the space medium due to their increasing importance."[5] Such plans continue today:

> A new Air Force strategy, Global Strike, calls for a military space plane carrying precision-guided weapons armed with a half-ton of munitions. General

Lord told Congress last month that Global Strike would be "an incredible capability" to destroy command centers or missile bases "anywhere in the world."

Pentagon documents say the weapon, called the common aero vehicle, could strike from halfway around the world in 45 minutes. . . .

Another Air Force space program, nicknamed Rods From God, aims to hurl cylinders of tungsten, titanium or uranium from the edge of space to destroy targets on the ground, striking at speeds of about 7,200 miles an hour with the force of a small nuclear weapon.

A third program would bounce laser beams off mirrors hung from space satellites or huge high-altitude blimps, redirecting the lethal rays down to targets around the world. A fourth seeks to turn radio waves into weapons whose powers could range "from tap on the shoulder to toast," in the words of an Air Force plan.[6]

The current trajectory of neoliberal militarization at home and abroad is the refocusing of the U.S. government on the so-called "war on terror," including a substantial reorganization of the federal government, replete with a new Department of Homeland Security. Indeed, in the 36 month Comprehensive Homeland Security Exercise Schedule, covering July 2004–September 2007 of the Department of Homeland Security, only 2 of the 222 exercises dealt with hurricanes, and those only looked at what if a terrorist attack happened during such an event; for the 7 national exercises in Louisiana and Mississippi, none involved hurricanes.[7]

Yet in the aftermath of the U.S. invasion and occupation of Iraq and growing insurgency and sectarian violence there, it was the rains of Hurricane Katrina and floods that followed that exposed the deeper fault lines of race, class, and gender running right through the heart of the United States. Years of neglect of the nation's most vulnerable populations, physical infrastructure, and environment—after recurrent decades of tax cuts for the wealthy and deficit-financed militarization funded by offshore borrowing, most recently for the Iraq war—were also dramatically exposed in the failure of the government to plan for and respond to Hurricane Katrina. The disaster in the Gulf Coast of the United States was a massive one, with some 90,000 square miles now covered under a federal disaster declaration, an area roughly the size of Great Britain.

The embrace of multiple wars in the twenty-first century, against the so-called Axis of Evil, notably Iraq—as well as Al Qaeda—has been used to justify the enormous rises in U.S. military-related spending. Military spending now totals well over $500 billion annually, when one includes not only the formal military budget, but money for ongoing operations and the Department of Homeland Security, under which a host of agencies, including the Federal Emergency Management Agency (FEMA) are now housed. More recently, on February 2, 2007, the Bush administration announced a record

military budget request of some $622 billion for fiscal year 2008, including
$140 billion in war-related expenses, making it "the highest level of spending
since the height of the Korean War," according to Steven Kosiak of the Center for Strategic and Budgetary Assessments.[8]

The economic stimulus of federal spending, notably increases in the military budget, are believed by many experts to have clearly minimized the period of economic recession in the early years of the twenty-first century,
though with less of an effect than during past bouts of military Keynesianism.[9] In the second quarter of 2003, from April to June, the war with Iraq and
related U.S. military actions led to the biggest increase in military spending—
some 44.1 percent—since fall 1951, the time of the enormous leap in military
spending ushering in the Korean War boom. Military spending accounted for
a full 1.69 percent of the rise in G.D.P. in the second quarter of 2003, or some
70 percent of the total increase.[10] In the first quarter of 2004, the economy
grew 4.2 percent, with military spending again making up a significant portion of the rise, accounting for up to $17.4 billion of the G.D.P. increase of
$108.5 billion in the first quarter, after adjusting for inflation.[11]

As one commentator recently noted:

> The military is now the de facto welfare state. The armed forces and the De-
> partment of Veterans Affairs are the two largest health care providers in the
> United States. The military is also a major bankroller of higher education
> through the G.I. Bill.[12]

Nevertheless, today, as during the new Cold War (beginning in the late Carter
years), the trillions of dollars for the new militarism, financed regressively
through offshore borrowing and from the wealthy awash in tax cuts, has mort-
gaged public investment, in the words of Mike Davis, "the fiscal equivalent
of several New Deals"—for generations.[13] According to one recent estimate,
while Vietnam cost U.S. taxpayers some $600 billion (in current dollars), the
costs for the Iraq war could be over $700 billion, assuming the U.S. stays
there for ten more years; another estimate, looking at the operation in
Afghanistan and Iraq and the U.S. presence in the Middle East calculates
even higher costs:

> If United States military presence in the region lasts another five years, the total
> outlay for the war could stretch to more than $1.3 trillion, or $11,300 for every
> household in the United States [with more recent estimates indicating that, assum-
> ing U.S. troops stay in Iraq until at least 2015, the war will cost over $2 trillion].[14]

As during the late 1970s and 1980s, U.S. debt-financed militarization has
been accompanied by continuing declines in federal aid to the cities and dis-

aster protection, this at a time when millions of Whites were moving from the largest metropolitan centers to the suburbs, while millions of Latinos, Asians, and Blacks were moving into increasingly impoverished, abandoned, and decaying metropolises.[15] Metropolitan New Orleans is something of a statistical anomaly here, being the only large metropolitan region of the country where African American out-migration has occurred in each decade since 1965, according to the Brookings Institution.[16] Nevertheless, the city of New Orleans still had an overwhelmingly Black majority population, both from the natural increase of Blacks and due to the fact that between 1950 and 2000, hundreds of thousands of Whites fled New Orleans—nearly two-thirds of the total number—reacting in part to efforts to integrate the schools after the victory of *Brown versus Board of Education*.[17]

Thus New Orleans underwent a dramatic shift, from Whites being a two-thirds majority in 1950 to being outnumbered by Blacks by almost three to one in 2000, becoming one of the ten to fifteen most highly racially segregated of the fifty largest metropolitan centers in the United States; by the time Katrina hit, public schools were 93.4 percent African American. Thus, like other large cities, the overlay of race and class concentrated in space—what Douglas Massey and Nancy Denton call an *American Apartheid*—meant that federal and state cutbacks to urban areas would hit these groups the hardest, while education funding through property taxes helped ensure the decline of public schools and the restoration of what Jonathan Kozol calls "apartheid schooling," as depicted in the recent book and film, *Freedom Writers*.[18]

Estimates by Demetrios Caraley and others indicate that cutbacks of 64 percent in federal aid cost cities an average amount of $26 billion annually from 1980 to 1990 (in constant 1990 dollars); during part of this same period, from 1979 to 1985, deficit-financed military spending rose from some $150 to $300 billion annually, financed by the most regressive possible means, through tax cuts for the rich and overseas borrowing[19]:

> Spent on cities and human resources, these immense sums would have remade urban America into the Land of Oz instead of the urban wasteland it has become.
>
> The social burden of servicing this deficit may be measured by comparison to the annual combined budgets of the United States' fifty largest cities. In 1980 the interest payments on the federal debt were twice as large as the aggregate big-city budgets; today they are six times larger. Alternately, the $300 billion 1990 deficit was simply equal to the annual interest costs on a federal debt soaring toward $5 trillion.[20]

While the speculative boom of the 1990s led to fantasies of permanent economic nirvana among the well-to-do, the bursting of the bubble—except in the housing market, still waiting to pop—it was thought, would bring fiscal reality to bear among sentient beings. Not so for the Bush administration, content to continue on a relentless path of ever higher military spending and tax cuts for the wealthy, seeking what commentators called a "Gucci and guns budget," the president and Republican Congress's answer to the Johnson administration's program of Guns and Butter.[21] Yet it was on the battlefields of Indochina that the hopes of the Great Society and the War on Poverty were ultimately buried, as President Johnson presented Congress with spending request after spending request for war. Today, another round of bills for presidential war is again leading to drastic devaluations of citizenship in the United States, most especially among urban constituencies of color. Once again, the bombs, as Martin Luther King, Jr., argued in the case of Vietnam, are also exploding in the ghettoes of the United States, or you could say, in the fallen levees of the Gulf Coast, being felt both in the widespread flooding of the region as well as dramatically with massive federal cuts in health, education, human services, and disaster preparedness at home, especially to the nation's metropolitan areas.[22]

With the overlap of race, class, and gender, it becomes strikingly apparent that the burden of the United States' late twentieth- and early-twenty-first-century wars fall most heavily on Latinos, Blacks, and Asians in urban areas, particularly women of color. New Orleans had a pre-storm population of some 444,000, 67.3 percent African American. Out of a total poverty rate of roughly 28 percent (relative to roughly 13 percent in the United States as a whole), some 84 percent of those living in poverty were Black. Thirty-five percent of Blacks were in poverty in the city in 2000, compared to just 11 percent of Whites. Out of 50,000 households without cars, 35 percent were Black households compared to only 15 percent of White households, with New Orleans ranking fourth of 297 metropolitan locations in number of households lacking access to cars. Poverty among female-headed households exceeded the national average by substantial margins, reaching almost 40 percent. In essence, New Orleans revealed:

> a legacy of race and class discrimination that had literally corralled and trapped African Americans and the poor into ecologically and economically vulnerable spaces from which many were unable to escape . . . in one post-Katrina study, 55 percent of the respondents who did not evacuate said that one of the main reasons they did not was that they did not have a car or other way to leave.[23]

In the New Orleans metropolitan region, almost 15 percent of persons lived in poverty and over a quarter of the children; only seven other U.S. cities had higher incidences of poverty, with New Orleans ranking sixty-fourth in median household income among the country's seventy largest cities. Mississippi and Louisiana are the two poorest states in the United States, with the highest percentage of women living under the poverty line and with women's earnings ranking extremely low among national averages. Some 90,000 persons in the storm-affected areas of Louisiana, Mississippi, and Alabama make under $10,000 annually, with Blacks making 40 percent less than their White counterparts.[24]

As far as "acts of God" or "nature" are concerned, a growing number of scientists are coming to believe that the intensity of hurricanes are increasing due to global warming, a condition of course stemming from human induced climate change as a result of greenhouse gas emissions, not helped by the refusal of the United States (by far the largest greenhouse gas polluter, responsible for 25 percent of all such gases in the atmosphere) to join the Kyoto Protocol to the United Nations Framework Convention on Climate Change, a widely adhered-to international treaty on global warming.[25] And then of course there is the devaluing of citizenship in the U.S. urban areas, as money flowed away from these areas and instead went into lily-White suburbs and edge cities.[26]

And in New Orleans, as Louisiana State University geologist Craig Colten notes, "Money flows away from water," as wealthier citizens take the higher ground and leave the poor trapped in the face of approaching hurricanes. The results of Hurricane Katrina were part of the end result of this process of the political and social enfranchisement of White suburban citizens, in inverse proportion to the disenfranchisement of poor urban constituencies of color, replete with the federal neglect of much-needed protection against hurricanes.

These dangers were made more intense by development and ever-increasing coastal populations encroaching on and steadily eroding wetlands, a million acres of Louisiana's having disappeared; indeed, as the U.S. Geological Survey noted, an average of thirty-four square miles of south Louisiana wetlands, primarily marsh, has disappeared annually over the last fifty years, representing up to 80 percent of U.S. wetland losses during this period. In 2003, the Bush administration added to the damage, effectively killing the policy of the first Bush administration that there would be no net loss of existing wetlands. Today it is estimated that the state could lose an additional 700 more square miles, with a third of the Louisiana coastland vanishing by 2050, if such coastal erosion is not addressed with a massive wetlands and coastal restoration project; such a project is essential in serving as a buffer against hurricanes, as Katrina so dramatically revealed.[27] Yet even as wetlands disappear and coastal cities sink deeper into the sea—some of them, like New Orleans, with their large populations of color—money for tax cuts for the rich, highway projects, military spending, and wars abroad—benefits from which accrue largely to suburbs and edge cities—continues unabated.

Moreover, as Mike Davis has said, this was arguably one of the most predicted and foreseen disasters, perhaps in the history of the world. The path of damage was modeled extensively on computers before the event and surveys were taken, indicating that a sizeable portion of the poor, those without cars, the disabled, and elderly, would not be able to evacuate on their own. FEMA considered a hurricane hitting New Orleans one of the three most likely disasters to affect the United States—the others being a terrorist attack in New York and an earthquake in San Francisco—and modeled this in a five-day exercise called Hurricane Pam in July 2004, with over 250 officials from fifty state, federal, local, and volunteer agencies. Much of the destruction and loss of life was foreseen, as was the need to evacuate anywhere from hundreds of thousands to over a million people. Similarly, today evidence is accumulating that suggests with the rise in sea levels due to global warming—along with the increasing intensity of hurricanes also linked to global warming—Hurricane Katrina may be an ominous sign of what lies ahead in the future for U.S. coastal cities, not to mention coastal cities across the globe.[28]

In reality, with Hurricane Ivan, as with Hurricane Katrina, while middle- and upper-income Whites and persons of color were able to leave the city and surrounding suburbs, the largely poor Black population, as well as the rest of the poor, the disabled, and elderly—in the tens of thousands and perhaps more—were trapped. Anywhere from hundreds of thousands to over a million persons along the Gulf Coast were displaced, many of them still unable to return to their homes, even as speculators swoop in to buy up cheap property. If such trends continue, current estimates indicate that in the future, New Orleans will likely return to only half its pre-storm population.[29] All this, as emphasized above, was not only predictable, if anything, warnings were even more alarming than what actually transpired. When asked after the Hurricane Pam exercise how many people might die in such a storm, FEMA spokesman David Plassey said: "We would see casualties not seen in the United States in the last century"; John Clizbe, national vice president for disaster services at the American Red Cross, said that between 25,000 to 100,000 persons would die. The Report on Hurricane Pam estimated there would be 61,000 fatalities.[30]

Starting as early as January 2005, when then–acting FEMA director Michael Brown returned back from touring the devastation caused by the Asian tsunami in late December 2004, "New Orleans was the number one disaster we were talking about," recalled Eric L. Tolbert, then a top FEMA official. "We were obsessed with New Orleans because of the risk."[31] Nevertheless, despite such knowledge, in the wake of the storm, tens of thousands of evacuees were forced to cram into the Superdome and the Convention Center, where they were bereft of food and water for some three to four days. Reporters and others noted that local, state, and federal officials were often nowhere to be found. Even on Day 5, sufficient help had not arrived. The majority Black city, as important culturally for African Americans and the United States as Harlem, with over a fifth of the population living in poverty, was left to bear the brunt of the hurricane on its own. In the end, some 80 percent of the city was under water, and substantial portions of the rest of the Gulf Coast. Over 1,500 persons died as the city of New Orleans and substantial portions of the Gulf Coast were flooded.[32] The costs of inaction were tragic in both human suffering and loss of life. Hurricane Rita then added to the misery, leading to widespread flooding of New Orleans again in late September 2005.

In addition to these life-and-death disparities of race, class, gender, and power along the suburban-edge city urban divide, there is the stagnation or decline in U.S. household incomes as a whole, with attendant poverty and social ills. While the economy grew by 3.8 percent in 2004, median household income was flat at $44,389, while 1.1 million additional persons fell into poverty, thus increasing the ranks of the official poor to 37 million. Meanwhile another 800,000 workers lost their health insurance, bringing the total to 45.8 million, a figure that would be greatly exacerbated without the veteran's welfare state, along with Medicaid and Medicare. Yet Congress is getting ready to cut $35 billion to social programs in the coming five years, including for Medicaid, which gives the poor access to health care. At the same time, the top 20 percent of income groups increased their share of the national income to 50.1 percent of the total, though only the top 5 percent experienced income gains, while income stagnated or fell for the other 95 percent of households. Despite these trends, Congress stood ready to repeal the estate tax affecting the richest families in the United States, while simultaneously looking to make deep cuts in student loans, Medicaid, and other social programs for the poor, the working class, and middle-income groups.[33]

In fact, real wages have been stagnating for the majority since the late 1970s, following the dismantling of the Bretton Woods systems of fixed exchange rates and the related ability of governments to control capital flows in the early 1970s. This was part of a more general elite counterattack on what the elite-funded think tank, the Trilateral Commission, called the "crisis of democracy," referring to the rising activism of the 1950s and 1960s, akin to Wilson's Red Scare or McCarthyism during the Truman years. These years saw the rise of the Civil Rights, anti-war, and feminist and Black and Chicano power movements, to name but a few, part of the increased concern with the interconnected issues of peace and social justice, especially inequalities of race, class, and gender. Wilson's Red Scare, Truman's McCarthyism, and the response to the "crisis of democracy" were all part of more general attacks by the state-corporate community in response to the threat of expanding democratic activism during these periods. The Bush administration represents the culmination of this larger structural process of the mobilization of state-corporate elites against the threat of democratic activism and the possibilities for real democracy in the 1960s and beyond.[34]

Coming back to the present, the mobilization of the Iraq issue which forced a vote in Congress on the war before the 2002 mid-term Congressional elections was also a way to divert attention away from the class war at home, as evidenced in widening inequality replete with rising military spending and concomitant cuts to health, education, and human services. Once again, national security ideology proved crucial in the bitter class war not only against the Third World, but against the domestic population at home. And today, while the nation's attention and fiscal resources turned toward the war in Iraq and terrorism (to which the invasion and occupation of Iraq has contributed mightily), domestic disaster preparedness for events other than terrorism suffered, much as the new Cold War took resources and attention away from the nation's increasingly impoverished cities and decaying infrastructure.

Senior regional officials in the U.S. Army Corps of Engineers had long warned of the dangers of a hurricane on the Gulf Coast, particularly the vulnerable city of New Orleans, sitting largely below sea level and sinking, along with the levees. Congress did authorize money for the Southeast Louisiana Urban Flood Control Project or SELA, in the 1990s, aimed at shoring up the levees that protected New Orleans and the Gulf Coast states and constructing pumping stations; yet after 2003, money tapered off, with cuts proposed by the Bush administration for 2005 as well, despite the fact that some $250 million in outstanding projects were left to be done. As early as 2004, the New Orleans *Times-Picayune* began to report that "local officials and Army Corps of Engineers representatives attributed the funding cuts to the rising costs of the war in Iraq."

"Facing record deficits, the Bush administration cut costs—and cut corners—by including in its 2005 budget only about a sixth of the flood-prevention funds requested by the Louisiana congressional delegation."[35] Essentially, as costs for the Iraq war grew, money for hurricane and flood control efforts declined. Moreover, some 30 percent of the National Guard and roughly half of their equipment are in Iraq, including a sizeable number from the Gulf Coast states, from one-third of those in the Louisiana National Guard and even great numbers from Mississippi. Many of those in the National Guard have full-time jobs as firefighters, police officers, and medical personnel and so would ordinarily function as first responders during crises such as Hurricane Katrina. The Governmental Accountability Office noted in July 2005 that fully one-third of the units of the National Guard were low on essential equipment, as this had gone to units getting ready to go to Iraq in upcoming months, thereby taking them away from the Army's forces capable of dealing with homeland security and disaster relief.[36] Moreover, when the Army Corps of Engineers requested some $105 million for hurricane preparation and flood relief programs, the Bush administration shaved that money to some $40 million, though President Bush and Congress did agree on passage of a $284.2 billion "pork-filled highway bill with 6,000 pet projects, including a $231 million bridge for a small, uninhabited Alaskan island."[37]

Among those concerned with the budget cuts for SELA and New Orleans was Alfred C. Naomi, senior project manager for the Army Corps of Engineers, frustrated as an intense hurricane season was predicted at the same time as $71 million was cut from the New Orleans district budget, to prepare for exactly these type of storms: "A breach under these conditions was ultimately not surprising," Naomi said. Since 2001, the Louisiana congressional delegation had pushed for far more money for storm protection than the Bush administration has accepted. Now, Naomi said, all the quibbling over the storm budget, or even over full Category 5 protection, which would cost several billion dollars, seemed tragically absurd.

"It would take $2.5 billion to build a Category 5 protection system, and we're talking about tens of billions of losses, all those lost productivity, and so many lives and injuries and personal trauma you'll never get over," Naomi said. And most recently, the Army Corps of Engineers has warned that as many as 146 levees in the United States may fail in major floods. As to the continuing need for adequate preparations for New Orleans and the Gulf Coast against future hurricanes, while the Army Corps of Engineers is currently fixing the levees up to standards they were supposed to meet pre-Katrina, they could be protected from storm surges ten times greater than Katrina for under $10 billion; as cofounder and deputy director of the Louisiana State University Hurricane Center Ivon van Heerden stated recently: "If we had the will and one month's money from Iraq, we could do all the levees and restore the coast."[38] And as the *Wall Street Journal* noted: "Despite decades of repeated warnings about a breach of levees or failure of drainage systems that protect New Orleans from the Mississippi River and Lake Pontchartrain, local and federal officials now concede there weren't sufficient preparations for a catastrophe of this scale."[39] Mainstream news organizations in the United States and abroad openly commented that they had seen better disaster relief in the Third World. Hurricane Katrina revealed a United States with many of the same characteristics of those failed states in the Third World, with a deep democratic deficit and unwillingness to respond to the needs of its citizens, especially its most vulnerable populations.[40]

In the Gulf Coast of the United States, tens of thousands of citizens were abandoned, unable to evacuate, and left for days without food, water, protection, or medical attention by local, state, and federal officials, who seemed unaware or uncaring of their plight, with President Bush not even cutting his vacation short until days after Hurricane Katrina struck. The Pentagon, occupied in Iraq, with critical equipment and National Guard units away, was initially nowhere to be found, even though according to a 1993 Government Accounting Office Report, for disasters such as Hurricane Katrina, the "DOD is the only organization capable of providing, transporting, and distributing sufficient quantities of items needed."[41] As many observed, the pictures of the suffering, stranded, and abandoned seemed more reminiscent of Bangladesh, Haiti, or Baghdad (after the U.S. invasion) in the Third World than of the United States. In a turning of the tables, scores of countries now offered aid to the United States, including some of the poorest countries on the planet.

The U.S. federal government response was widely criticized, as were the actions of local and state officials. Singled out for criticism in particular was the head of FEMA, Michael Brown, former commissioner of the International Arabian Horse Association, with no disaster management experience but importantly, a friend of Joe M. Allbaugh, manager of Bush's 2000 presidential campaign and his first director of FEMA (who upon leaving, promptly set up a private consulting firm to advise corporations with or seeking contracts in U.S.-occupied Iraq). FEMA became a dumping ground for Bush's cronies, despite the president's rhetoric about securing the homeland.

Hurricane Katrina touched down on Monday, August 29. On September 2, Bush hailed Brown's work by saying, "Brownie, you're doing a heck of a job," even though Brown was to admit on the fourth day of the flooding of New Orleans that "the federal Government did not ever know about the convention center people until today," something also revealed in an extraordinary National Public Radio interview with homeland security director, Michael Chertoff, in which it appears he first heard of the plight of these tremendous numbers of suffering people.[42] Days after Hurricane Katrina touched down though, on August 31, Chertoff said: "We are extremely pleased with the response at every level of the Federal government."[43] Eventually the incompetence and embarrassment was too much even for the administration and at least Brown was relieved of overseeing the post-storm relief effort, a job that was then given to Admiral Thad W. Allen of the Coast Guard.[44] Soon thereafter, Brown resigned, though incredibly, Chertoff stayed on.

Still there was good news for some in the aftermath of the destruction, much as with the bungled occupation of Iraq. Many of the same players that profited from the invasion and occupation of Iraq stood to benefit immensely from reconstruction efforts after Hurricane Katrina, notably Vice President Cheney's old firm Halliburton, its subsidiary Kellog, Brown and Root, and the Shaw Group, a firm making some $3 billion annually, which announced it had gotten two contracts of up to $100 million each in early September

2005, one from FEMA and the other from the Army Corps of Engineers; in this they were helped along by the former FEMA director Allbaugh, now a highly paid consultant for private corporate firms such as these. Other firms getting lucrative work include Bechtel and the Fluor Corporation, each of them receiving contracts for $100 million. Danielle Brian, head of the Project on Government Oversight, said, "Katrina, like Iraq before it, would bring the greedy and the self-interested out of the woodwork."

"This is very painful," Brian said. "You are likely to see the equivalent of war profiteering—disaster profiteering."[45] Indeed, President Bush was quick to suspend the Davis-Bacon Act, a 1931 law which mandates prevailing wages for federally funded contracts, for the work of the reconstruction of the region, though wages in the area are already low, often under $10 an hour. When it comes to workers' wages, it seems the costs are too high; when it comes to corporate contracts, however, it appears no profits are too high. In addition, the president suspended laws requiring that federal contractors file plans for affirmative action.

The president was quick to overturn prevailing wage and affirmative action for working-class people and persons of color. Already many of the questionable practices used in the reconstruction of Iraq are now being implemented in this largest effort at reconstruction in the history of the United States—which could total several hundred billion dollars—including non-competitive contracts and cost-plus provisions that guarantee profit regardless of the amount a firm spends, with contracts going to many politically well-connected companies.[46] Somehow, when it comes to money for the nation's cities, its poor, persons of color, or disaster preparedness other than terrorism, costs must be cut, while tax cuts are given to the rich; for corporate America, its war profiteers and military-corporate vultures of disaster-reconstruction capitalism, however, it seems that money from taxpayers is no object. Subsequently it was announced that no-bid contracts would be re-bid—though the news is still out on the process—given the storm of criticism, and Bush was forced by his Republican allies to end his suspension of the Davis-Bacon Act; still, the initial moves of the president in the wake of Katrina shows the leanings of the Bush administration's "compassionate conservatism."

After decades of underinvestment in the nation's cities, Hurricane Katrina exposed many of the problems once thought solved in the United States, with widening inequality, poor jobs, and a faltering system of health, education, and human services. Yet the wars of the late twentieth and twenty-first century—from the new Cold War to the Gulf Wars—their capital intensive nature, their legions of corporate mercenary soldiers, and their financing from offshore borrowing and from tax cuts for the wealthy instead are serving to increase poverty in the global South, both at home and abroad.[47]

The task now is to seize upon this exposure of the shame of the United States revealed in its vulnerable poor, impoverished persons of color and poor Whites, to take up the clarion call of Martin Luther King, Jr., for peace and social justice once again. To begin, the United States must withdraw its troops from Iraq and use the resources gained for true democratic reconstruction at home and abroad, including in Iraq, in ways that benefit the people, not market-hungry military-corporate profiteers. As the daily death toll mounts in Iraq, increasing global insecurity, and as President Bush announces his decision to send tens of thousands of additional troops to Iraq and possibly widen and expand the war, including possibly to Iran, the time for mobilization is now.[48] In a hopeful sign, already Katrina is eroding support among the U.S. public for the Iraq War, which the majority now oppose.[49]

What is needed, as during the New Deal, when massive public works helped to lift some of the poorest of the nation's citizens out of poverty—notably second-generation immigrants on the White side of the color line and their parents, some 40 million in all—is a broad commitment to democratic reconstruction and renewal at home and abroad. Yet this time, a bolder strategy of reform would need to include persons of color, notably African Americans and the burgeoning population of Latinas and Latinos. And now is also the time to make the connections between the war at home and abroad, between the struggle for peace, civil rights, and social justice, as did Martin Luther King, Jr., before he was assassinated. The disaster of the U.S. wars in the Persian Gulf is intimately related with the disaster in the Gulf Coast of the United States. Thus the largest U.S. peace and justice coalition, United for Peace and Justice, put out a statement on the aftermath of Katrina entitled: "After Katrina, Fund Full Recovery on Gulf Coast, Not War on Iraq."[50]

The period of Reconstruction after the Civil War was a time of great hope, especially for African Americans. With the defeat of Reconstruction in the late nineteenth century, as with the turning back of the much-hoped-for second Reconstruction in the late 1960s and beyond, and with it the demise of the Civil Rights movement and the Black freedom struggle, the clock was turned back on African Americans and the struggle against poverty and for social justice in "the other America."[51] President Bush announced that the reconstruction of the Gulf Coast would be among the largest such efforts in world history. Yet Bush continues to press for making his tax cuts for the wealthiest permanent, a move that would cost some $1.5 trillion over the next decade, while Congressional Republicans revealed a host of policy initiatives, from school vouchers that would further privatize public schools to tax breaks in the Gulf Coast states, belying their expressed commitment to address the hurricane's aftermath. These facts, along with other news coming out about the planned reconstruction, including the possible suspension of environmental laws, and of Bush's chief political advisor Karl Rove's prominent place as the official in charge of plans to rebuild the region, indicate how far Bush's plan is from the vision of the New Deal. Indeed, despite the urgent need, nothing has been done to change land use patterns or restore the wetlands. With hundreds of thousands still displaced, hundreds of thousands of homes flooded and destroyed, over a hundred thousand residents of Mississippi and Louisiana still living in trailers and mobile homes provided by FEMA, and with many persons struggling with post-traumatic stress disorder, rebuilding and recovery face enormous challenges as survivors struggle to stay alive, to make it through, and to rebuild their communities. There are some 22 million tons of debris and a stark lack of housing keeping tens of thousands away, with hundreds of thousands unable to return to the homes they were living in before Katrina hit, even though speculators, as noted previously, are swooping in hoping to gain from the disaster. At the same time, an estimated 100,000 Latino workers have moved to the Gulf Coast and many of them are taking part in reconstruction efforts, often as undocumented workers earning low wages.[52] Not surprisingly, Jesse Jackson spoke of a "hurricane for the poor and a windfall for the rich."

There is, however, another path. Now, as part of the broader movement for global peace and social justice, perhaps the African American freedom struggle could be taken up once again, to renew "America's unfinished revolution" of Reconstruction, so as to benefit not only the descendants of slavery but all residents of all colors on the Gulf Coast, the United States and the rest of the world as well. Such an alternative democratic vision is one consonant with the call to action and solidarity of the World Social Forum meetings. The time for peace and social justice is now. For these are the challenges of our times.

NOTES

1. Thanks to Gar Alperovitz, Noam Chomsky, Tom Dobrzeniecki, Elaine Elliott, Judith Liu, Rafik Mohamed, and Christina Shaheen for assistance with this piece, and most especially, to Vivian Holland. I also benefited from the public forum with Mike Davis and others, "Disasters in the Aftermath of Hurricane Katrina," Activist San Diego, September 12, 2005, San Diego, California. The final content is my responsibility alone though.

2. On the power of Katrina, see Ivor van Heerden and Mike Bryan, *The Storm: What Went Wrong and Why During Hurricane Katrina—The Inside Story from One Louisiana Scientist*, (New York: Viking, 2006), 29. van Heerden and Bryan go on to note that "a temperature increase of just 1 degree Fahrenheit in the Gulf could generate the energy equivalent of *one million* atomic bombs."

3. Mary Kaldor, "Beyond Militarism, Arms Races and Arms Control," *Social Science Research Council* (2002): 6–7, http://www.ssrc.org/sept11/essays/kaldor.htm.

4. See Noam Chomsky, *Deterring Democracy* (New York: Verso, 1991). See also William S. Borden, *The Pacific Alliance: United States Foreign Economic Policy and Japanese Trade Recovery, 1947–1955* (Madison: University of Wisconsin Press, 1984).

5. U.S. Space Command, *Vision for 2020*, February 1997,http://www.gsinstitute.org/gsi/docs/vision_2020.pdf. See also Ann Markusen and Joel Yudken, *Dismantling the Cold War Economy* (New York: Basic Books, 1992); Frank Kofsky, *Harry Truman and the War Scare of 1948: A Successful Campaign to Deceive the Nation* (New York: St. Martin's Press, 1993); Kenneth Flamm, *Targeting the Computer: Government Support and International Competition* (Washington, DC: Brookings, 1987); Kenneth Flamm, *Creating the Computer: Government, Industry, and High Technology* (Washington, DC: Brookings, 1988); John L. Boies, *Buying for Armageddon: Society, Economy, and the State since the Cuban Missile Crisis* (Piscataway, NJ: Rutgers University Press, 1994); Christopher Layne and Robert S. Metzger, "Reforming Post–Cold War US Arms Sales Policy: The Crucial Link between Exports and the Defence Industrial Base," *The Journal of Strategic Studies* 18, no. 4 (December 1995), 1–32; Strategic Command, Strat-Com, *Essentials of Post-Cold War Deterrence*, 1995, http://nautilus.org/archives/nuk estrat/USA/Advisory/essentials95.PDF.

6. Tim Weiner, "Air Force Seeks Approval for Space Weapons Programs," *The New York Times*, May 18, 2005, http://www.commondreams.org/headlines 05/0518-02.htm. In another recent development, the Pentagon is working on its own more advanced Internet, the Global Information Grid, that aims to give "a God's-eye-view" of future battlefields; estimated to costs hundreds of billions of dollars, a new consortium formed in September 2004 to work on the project "includes an A-list of military contractors and technology power-houses: Boeing; Cisco Systems; Factiva, a joint venture of Dow Jones and Reuters; General Dynamics; Hewlett-Packard; Honeywell; I.B.M.; Lockheed Martin; Microsoft; Northrup Grumman; Oracle; Raytheon; and Sun Microsystems" (Tim Weiner, "Pentagon Envisioning a Costly Internet for War," November 13, 2004, pp. A1, B2). See also Leslie Wayne, *New York Times,* "An Officer and a Gentleman: In Corporate Jobs, Old Generals Find a Hero's Welcome," *The New York Times*, June 19, 2005, Section 3, p. 1, 11.

7. William Arkin, "Early Warning: Natural Disasters Perfunctory Concerns," *Washington Post*, September 15, 2005, http://blogs.washingtonpost.com/earlywarning/ 2005/09/exercising_to_d.html. See the Comprehensive Homeland Security Exercise Schedule, July 15, 2004, http://media.washingtonpost.com/wpsrv/nation/national security/earlywarning/HLSExerciseScheduleJul2004.pdf.

8. James Dao, "Bush Sees Big Rise in Military Budget for Next 5 Years; Up to $451 Billion By '07; Proposed Buildup Would Rival Reagan's—Sharp Increase in Money for Supplies," *The New York Times,* February 2, 2002, pp. A1, A9. Kosiak is quoted in David S. Cloud, "Record $622 Billion Budget Requested for the Pentagon," *The New York Times,* February 3, 2007, p. A11.

9. Louis Uchitelle, "Sharp Rise in Federal Spending May Have Helped Ease Recession," *The New York Times*, March 23, 2002, pp. A1, B4. John D. McKinnon and Anne Marie Squeo, "Shaky Economic Times Limit Bang of New Defense Spending," *Wall Street Journal*, April 15, 2003, pp. A1, 12.

10. Bureau of Economic Analysis, "Gross Domestic Product: Second Quarter 2003 (Advance)," http://www.bea.gov/beahome.html; Louis Uchitelle, "Faster 2nd-Quarter Growth Fuels Optimism," *The New York Times*, August 1, 2003, pp. C1, 10; Jon E. Hilsenrath, "GDP Data Spark Hopes Recovery Is Strengthening: Economy Grew at 2.4 Percent Pace in the Second Quarter: Military Spending Surges," *Wall Street Journal*, August 1, 2003, pp. A1, 6.

11. Paraphrasing Louis Uchitelle, "U.S. Economy Grows 4.2 percent; War Spending Provides Push," *The New York Times*, April 30, 2004, pp. C1, 3; Bureau of Economic Analysis, "Gross Domestic Product: First Quarter 2004 (Advance)," http://www.bea.gov/bea/newsrel/gdpnewsrelease.htm.

12. Dalton Conley, "Turning the Tax Tables to Help the Poor," *The New York Times*, November 15, 2004, p. A23.

13. Mike Davis, *Dead Cities: And Other Tales* (New York: The New Press, 2002), 259. On the new Cold War, see Noam Chomsky, *Towards a New Cold War: Essays on the Current Crisis and How We Got There* (New York: Pantheon, 1982).

14. Linda Bilmes, "The Trillion-Dollar War," *The New York Times*, August 20, 2005, p. A27; Phyllis Bennis and Eric Leaver and the IPS Iraq Task Force, *The Iraq Quagmire: The Mounting Costs of the Iraq War and the Case for Bringing the Troops Home*, A Study by the Institute for Policy Studies and Foreign Policy in Focus, August 31, 2005, p. i., http://www.ips-dc.org/iraq/quagmire/IraqQuagmire.pdf. See Linda Bilmes and Joseph Stiglitz, "The Economic Costs of the Iraq War: An Appraisal Three Years After the Beginning of the Conflict," NBER Working Paper Series 12054, 2006, http://www.nber.org/papers/w12054.

15. Davis, *Dead Cities*, 253.

16. See Brookings Institution Metropolitan Policy Program: Katrina: Issues and Aftermath, http://www.brookings.edu/metro/katrina.htm. The other large city in which Black out-migration occurred in every decade since 1965 is Pittsburgh (see William H. Frey, *The New Great Migration: Black Americans Return to the South, 1965–2000*, May 2004, especially pp. 5, 13, http://www.brookings.edu/metro/publications/20040524_frey.htm).

17. Pierce F. Lewis, *New Orleans: The Making of an Urban Landscape* (Charlottesville: University of Virginia Press, 2003), 125–37. On the resegregation of public schools and the return to apartheid schooling some 50 years after *Brown versus Board of Education*, see Richard Kluger, *Simple Justice: The History of Brown v. Board of Education and Black America's Struggle for Equality* (New York: Vintage, 2004), and Gary Orfield and Chungmei Lei, "*Brown* at 50: King's Dream or *Plessy's* Nightmare," January 2004, The Civil Rights Project, Harvard University,http://www.civilrightsproject.harvard.edu/research/reseg04/brown50.pdf. See also Jonathan Kozol's *The Shame of the Nation: The Restoration of Apartheid Schooling in America* (New York: Crown Publishers, 2005). See also Peter Irons, *Jim Crow's Children: The*

Broken Promise of the Brown Decision (New York: Viking, 2002). In 1950, the population of New Orleans was roughly 570,000.

18. Pierce F. Lewis, *New Orleans: The Making of an Urban Landscape*), 127. On White flight, see Jason DeParle, "What Happens to a Race Deferred," *New York Times*, September 4, 2005, Section 4, 1, 4, http://www.gnocdc.org/tertiary/white.html. Douglas S. Massey and Nancy A. Denton, *American Apartheid: Segregation & the Making of the Underclass*, (Cambridge, MA: Harvard University Press, 1993). For a visual representation and statistics on this system of residential segregation and related elevation levels, showing how upper-income Whites occupy the high ground, giving them more protection against the floods, while many Blacks live in lower lying areas, see The Greater New Orleans Community Data Center, http://www.gnocdc.org/. See also U.S. Census Bureau, *Racial & Ethnic Residential Segregation in the United States: 1980–2000*, August 2002, http://www.census.gov/prod/2002 pubs/censr-3.pdf. On racial segregation in New Orleans relative to the nation's top fifty metropolitan areas, see Chester Hartman and Gregory D. Squires, "Pre-Katrina, Post-Katrina," in *There is No Such Thing as a Natural Disaster: Race, Class, and Hurricane Katrina*, Chester Hartman and Gregory D. Squires eds. (New York: Routledge, 2006), 3. See also Michael Casserly, "Double Jeopardy: Public Education in New Orleans Before and After the Storm," in Hartman and Squires eds., *There is No Such Thing as a Natural Disaster*, 200–201. School funding by property taxes combined with state and federal budget cuts ensures that poorer African American residents living in hyper-segregated communities have less money available for public schools than their White counterparts.

19. Demetrios Caraley, "Washington Abandons the City," *Political Science Quarterly* 107, no. 1 (1992), 8–11, cited in Davis, *Dead Cities*, 247. See also Demetrios Caraley, "Dismantling the Federal Safety Net: Fictions Versus Realities," *Political Science Quarterly,* 111, no 2 (1995), 225–58.

20. Davis, *Dead Cities,* 259, 253, 239–73.

21. It should be noted, though, that the freezing of domestic spending goes back to President Carter and the Democratic Congress of 1978 during the period of the mobilization of the have coalition against the have-nots, part of the rise of the broader New Right culminating in Reaganism. "1978 was the first year of Reaganomics. A Congress two-thirds controlled by Democrats endorsed the legislative agenda of the Business Roundtable by freezing social spending, deregulating the transport and phone industries, and supporting Carter's move towards higher interest rates" (Davis, *Prisoners of the American Dream* [New York: Verso, 1986], 137). Welding together Reagan's New Right coalition was military Keynesianism and the financial over-accumulation its regressive financing allowed for. The vast expansion of money capital was fueled here by the doubling of the military budget, deregulation and tax cuts, and the regressive financing of the U.S. deficit, especially from the issuance and rollover of some $13.5 trillion in marketable securities by the federal government from 1981 to 1990, ushering in the hegemony of Wall Street, the global capital markets, hedge funds, the International Monetary Fund and World Bank, and the related Washington Consensus, the effects of which were soon seen in recurrent financial crises, from Asia to Latin America. See Roy Smith, *Comeback: The Restoration of*

American Banking Power in the New World Economy (Cambridge, MA: Harvard Business School Press, 1993), 87. See also Jagdish Bhagwati, "The Capital Myth: The Difference between Trade in Widgets and Dollars," *Foreign Affairs* (May/June 1998), 7–12. See also Gordon De Brouwer, *Hedge Funds in Emerging Markets* (New York: Cambridge University Press, 2001). See also Financial Stability Forum Working Group on Highly Leveraged Institutions, Washington, D.C., March 2000, http://www.fsforum.org. See also E. Ray Canterbery, *Wall Street Capitalism: The Theory of the Bondholding Class* (Singapore: World Scientific Publications, 2000). See also Robin Broad, *Unequal Alliance: The World Bank, the International Monetary Fund & the Philippines* (Berkeley: University of California Press, 1988). See also Robert Wade and Frank Veneroso, "The Asian Crisis: The High Debt Model Versus the Wall Street-Treasury-IMF Complex," *New Left Review* no. 228 (March/April 1998), 3–24, and Robert Wade and Frank Veneroso, "The Gathering World Slump and the Battle over Capital Controls," *New Left Review*, no. 231 (September/October 1998), 13–42.

22. Frances Fox Piven, *The War at Home: The Domestic Consequences of Bush's Militarism* (New York: New Press, 2004).

23. The quote is from Manuel Pastor, Robert D. Bullard, James K. Boyce, Alice Fothergill, Rachel Morello-French and Beverly Wright, *In the Wake of the Storm: Environment, Disaster, and Race After Katrina* (New York: Russell Sage Foundation, 2006), 32–33. Davis, *Dead Cities*, 239–73. See also Thomas Alex Tizon, "Images of Evacuees Spark a Racial Debate," *Los Angeles Times*, September 3, 2005, A11; DeParle, "What Happens to a Race Deferred"; Peter Applebome, Christopher Drew, Jere Longman, and Andrew C. Revkin, "A Delicate Balance Is Undone in a Flash, and a Battered City Waits," *The New York Times,* September 4, 2005, A19, 22–23, from which comes the citation that an estimated 50,000 households in New Orleans did not have access to cars. The census of 2000 indicated the African American population was 67.3 percent. A recent *Wall Street Journal* piece, "New Architecture: As Gulf Prepares to Rebuild, Tensions Mount over Control," Jackie Calmes, Ann Carns, and Jeff D. Opdyke, September 15, 2005, A1, 10, estimates the population as "more than 75 percent African American." On car access, see Alan Berube and Steven Raphael, "Access to Cars in New Orleans," http://www.brookings.edu/metro/20050915_katrinacarstables.pdf; originally cited in Michael Eric Dyson, *Come Hell or High Water: Hurricane Katrina and the Color of Disaster* (New York: Perseus Books Group, 2006).

The break in the levees represented what van Heerden and Bryan (2006, 261) call a "catastrophic structural failure" and clearly represents the failure of both of Army Corps of Engineers and the federal government to provide adequate protection for even modest storms. See also John Barry, "After the Deluge, Some Questions," *The New York Times*, October 13, 2005, http://fireside.designcommunity.com/topic-6831.html. See also John Barry, *The Rising Tide: The Great Mississippi Flood of 1927 and How It Changed America* (New York: Simon & Schuster, 1998).

On poverty among women, see Avis A. Jones-Deweever and Heidi Hartmann, "Abandoned Before the Storms: The Glaring Disaster of Gender, Race, and Class Disparities in the Gulf," in Chester Hartman and Gregory D. Squires, eds., *There Is No Such Thing as a Natural Disaster* (New York: Routledge, 2006), 88.

24. Jackie Calmes, Ann Carns, and Jeff D. Opdyke, "New Architecture: As Gulf Prepares to Rebuild, Tensions Mount Over Control," *Wall Street Journal*, September 15, 2005, A1, 10; Dyson, *Come Hell or High Water*, 5; Jones-Deweever and Hartmann, "Abandoned Before the Storms," in Hartman and Squires, eds., *There Is No Such Thing as a Natural Disaster*, 89, 91–93.

25. Nicholas D. Kristof, "The Storm Next Time," *New York Times*, September 11, 2005, A15. See also Kerry Emanuel, "Increasing Destructiveness of Tropical Cyclones Over the Past 30 Years," *Nature*, 436/4 (2005): 686–88, ftp://texmex.mit.edu/pub/emanuel/PAPERS/NATURE03906.pdf; Kerry Emanuel, *Divine Wind: A History & Science of Hurricanes* (New York: Oxford University Press, 2005); Roger A. Pielke, Jr., Christopher Landsea, Max Mayfield, Jim Laver, and Richard Pasch, "Hurricanes and Global Warming," *Bulletin of the American Meteorological Society* 86 (November 2005): 1571–75, http://ams.allenpress.com/archive/1520-0477/86/11/pdf/i1520-0477-86-11-1571.pdf; Stefan Rahmstorf, Michael Mann, Rasmus Benestad, Gavin Schmidt, and William Connolley, "Hurricanes & Global Warming—Is There a Connection?" Realclimate.org, September 2, 2005, http://www.realclimate.org/index.php/archives/2005/09/hurricanes-and-global-warming/; Richard A. Anthes, Robert W. Corell, Greg Holland & James W. Hurrell, Michael C. MacCracker, and Kevin E. Trenberth, "Hurricanes and Global Warming: Potential Linkages & Consequences," *Bulletin of the American Meteorological Society,* 87, 5 (2006): 623–28, http://ams.allenpress.com/archive/1520-0477/87/5/pdf/i1520-0477-87-5-623.pdf; Pielke et al., "Reply to "Hurricanes & Global Warming—Potential Linkages & Consequences," 628–31, http://ams.alle press.com/archive/1520-0477/87/5/pdf/i1520-0477-87-5-628.pdf; Richard A. Kerr, "Is Katrina a Harbinger of Even More Powerful Hurricanes?" *Science* 16 (2005): 1807 http://www.ce.cmu.edu/~gdrg/readings/2005/10/19/Kerr_Katrina_Harbinger.pdf; Matthew C. Nisbet and Chris Mooney, "The Next Big Storm: Can Scientists & Journalists Work Together to Improve Coverage of the Hurricane-Global Warming Controversy," August 3, 2006, http://www.csicop.org/scienceandmedia/hurricanes/; Chris Mooney, *Storm World: Hurricanes, Politics, and the Battle over Global Warming* (Harcourt, forthcoming 2007).

Many scientists also believe that the frequency of hurricanes is increasing, as part of alternating cyclical upswings and downswings that occur roughly every thirty years or more, with the current increase part of the beginning of a new perhaps multi-decade long cycle. See also Mike Davis, "Melting Away," *The Nation*, October 7, 2005, http://www.thenation.com/doc/20051024/davis; See also J.T. Overpeck et al., "Arctic Systems on Trajectory to New, Seasonally Ice-Free State," *EOS, Transactions, American Geophysical Union* 86, 24 (August 23, 2005): 309–16, http://paos.colorado.edu/~dcn/reprints/Overpeck_etal_EOS2005.pdf.

On the political economy and ecology of so-called natural disasters, see Mike Davis, *Ecology of Fear: Los Angeles and the Imagination of Disaster* (New York: Metropolitan Books, 1998). See also Ted Steinberg, *Acts of God: The Unnatural History of Natural Disaster in America* (New York: Oxford University Press, 2003). See also Mike Tidwell, *The Ravaging Tide: Strange Weather, Future Katrinas, and the Coming Death of America's Coastal Cities* (New York: Free Press, 2006); John McQuaid and Mark Schleifstein, *Path of Destruction: The Devastation of New Orleans*

& the Coming Age of Superstorms (New York: Little Brown & Co., 2006); Al Gore, *An Inconvenient Truth* (Rodale Books, 2006).

The Kyoto Protocol was signed by some 141 countries, including all of Europe and all the developed nations except the Unites States and Australia. This is part of a larger pattern of the United States refusing to sign, pulling out of, or otherwise violating international treaties, including those it is a signatory to.

26. On the complexities of this process, see Peter Dreier, John Mollenkopf, and Todd Swanstrom, *Place Matters: Metropolitics for the Twenty-first Century*, 2nd Edition, Revised (Manhattan: University Press of Kansas, 2004).

27. See also Walter Gillis, Better Hearn Morrow, and Hugh Gladwin, eds., *Hurricane Andrew: Ethnicity, Gender, and the Sociology of Disaster* (New York: Routledge, 1997).

From the 1950s to the present, engineers have destroyed some 8,000 miles (13,000 kilometers) of the canals "through the marsh for petroleum exploration and ship traffic. These new ditches sliced the wetlands into a giant jigsaw puzzle, increasing erosion and allowing lethal doses of salt water to infiltrate brackish and freshwater marshes." According to Bob Morton, with the U.S. Geological Survey, the loss of the wetlands occurred most rapidly during the peak oil- and gas-producing times of the 1970s and early 1980s, leading him to conclude "that the removal of millions of barrels of oil and trillions of cubic feet of natural gas, and tens of millions of barrels of saline formation water lying with the petroleum deposits caused a drop in subsurface pressure—a theory known as regional depressurization." That led nearby underground faults to slip and the land above them to slump. "When I stick a straw in a soda and suck on it, everything goes down," Morton explains. "That's very simplified, but you get the idea" (*National Geographic*, "Gone with the Water," Joel K. Bourne, October 2004, http://www3.nationalgeographic.com/ngm/0410/feature5/). See also Christopher Hallowell, *Holding Back the Sea: The Struggle for America's Natural Legacy on the Gulf Coast* (New York: Harper Collins, 2001). See also the important study by the H. Heinz III Center for Science, Economics and the Environment, *Human Links to Coastal Disasters*, 2002 http://www.heinzctr.org/NEW_WEB/PDF/Full_report_human_links.pdf, and their related publications which can be accessed via their website at http://www.heinzctr.org/index.htm. See also the important article by John Tibbetts, "Louisiana's Wetlands: A Lesson in Nature Appreciation," *Environmental Health Perspective* 114, no. 1 (2006): A40–43, http://www.pubmedcentral.nih.gov/articlerender.fcgi?artid=1332684. See also Tidwell, *The Ravaging Tide*, 3–4, 65, who notes that "a rise of just two feet in sea level will, according to the EPA, eliminate up to 43 percent of all U.S. coastal wetlands"; as Tidwell makes clear, citing scores of scientific studies, global warming is widely expected to cause sea levels to rise by three feet in the coming decades. On President Bush's 2003 overturning of the first Bush administration policy on the wetlands, see Sandra Postel, "Nature's Squeeze-Man's Response: Distinctions Between Natural and Not-So-Natural Disasters," *Christian Science Monitor*, September 7, 2005, http://www.csmonitor.com/2005/0907/p09s01-coop.html; originally cited in Noam Chomsky, *Failed States*. For a brilliant documentary on Katrina, see Spike Lee's "When the Levees Broke," 2006.

28. Mike Davis, Public Forum, "Disasters in the Aftermath of Hurricane Katrina," Activist San Diego, September 12, 2005, San Diego, California. Mike Davis, "Poor, Black and Left Behind: Before Killer Katrina, There Was Ivan the Terrible," *LA Weekly News*, September 8, 2005, http://www.laweekly.com/ink/05/42/after-davis.php, is an eloquent indictment of the failure of both Democrats and Republicans to evacuate the Black poor in the face of Hurricane Ivan, a prophetic enough piece, in light of our recent experience with Hurricane Katrina. In short, Hurricane Katrina was eminently predictable, and the consequences predicted by experts, despite the lack of action, a fact often revealed in the aftermath of catastrophes.

There was no shortage of documentaries and popular and scientific articles predicting the disaster. See the video, "New Orleans & the Delta: Disappearing Delta Overview" and "The Mighty Mississippi," Public Broadcasting System, n.d., http://www.pbs.org/now/science/neworleans.html. A *Scientific American* article in October 2001 by Mark Fischetti had this to say: "New Orleans is a disaster waiting to happen . . . The low-lying Mississippi Delta, which buffers the city from the gulf, is also rapidly disappearing. . . . Each loss gives a storm surge a clearer path to wash over the delta and pour into the bowl, trapping one million people inside and another million in surrounding communities. Extensive evacuation would be impossible because the surging water would cut off the few escape routes. Scientists at Louisiana State University, who have modeled hundreds of possible storm tracks on advanced computers, predict that more than 100,000 people could die. . . . A direct hit is inevitable." The article went on to describe the entirely feasible engineering effort required to save the city from certain disaster; http://www.sciam.com/article.cfm?articleID=00060286-CB58-1315-8B5883414B7F0000; see also Mark Fischetti, "They Saw it Coming," *New York Times*, September 2, 2005, A23; Thomas Ehrlich Reifer, "Review of Mike Davis, *Dead Cities: And Other Tales*," *City and Community* 2 (2003): 369–70; Craig E. Colten, "How to Rebuild New Orleans: Restore the Marsh," *New York Times*, September 10, 2005, A27; Colten, *An Unnatural Metropolis: Wresting New Orleans from Nature* (Baton Rouge: Louisiana State University Press, 2004); Colten, *Transforming New Orleans and Its Environs: Centuries of Change* (Pittsburgh: University of Pittsburgh Press, 2001); Colten, National Public Radio, "Race, Poverty & Katrina," September 2, 2005, http://www.npr.org/templates/story/story.php?storyId=4829446; Ari Kelman, *A River and Its City: The Nature of Landscape in New Orleans* (Berkeley: University of California Press, 2003); Richard Campanella, *Time and Place in New Orleans: Past Geographies in the Present Day* (Gretna, LA: Pelican Publishing Company, 2002). On the suburban locational bias in military spending, see John H. Mollenkopf, *The Contested City* (Princeton, NJ: Princeton University Press, 1983); see also Davis, *Dead Cities*, "Who Killed L.A.? A Political Autopsy," 239–74. On Katrina as a warning sign for America's coastal cities, see Tidwell, *Ravaging Tide*. See also National Assessment Synthesis Team, U.S. Global Change Research Program, *Climate Change Impacts on the United States*, 2001, http://www.usgcrp.gov/usgcrp/Library/nationalassessment/foundation.htm.

For more on the crucial issue of the wetlands, see Ivor van Heerden, *The Storm*, especially chapter 8, "The Wetlands," 153–86.

29. A Special Report by Gulf Coast Reconstruction Watch, A Project of the Institute for Southern Studies/Southern Exposure, *One Year After Katrina: The State of New Orleans and the Gulf Coast*, 2006, 5, http://www.reconstructionwatch.org/images/One_Year_After.pdf; David Streitfeld, "Speculators Rushing in as the Water Recedes: Would-be Home Buyers Are Betting New Orleans Will Be a Boomtown. And Many of the City's Poorest Residents Could End up Being Forced Out," *Los Angeles Times*, September 15, 2005, A1, 19; Adam Nossiter, "New Orleans of Future May Stay Half its Old Size," *New York Times*, January 21, 2007, A1, 20.

30. On the Hurricane Pam exercise, see the website of http://www.globalsecurity.org/security/ops/hurricane-pam.htm, and the related links there, from which the information in this paragraph comes. See also the Report on Hurricane Pam, entitled: *Southeast Louisiana Catastrophic Hurricane Functional Plan*, Draft, August 6, 2004, IEM/TECO4-00, Innovative Emergency Management, http://msnbcmedia.msn.com/i/msnbc/Components/Interactives/News/US/Katrina/docs/Southeast_Louisiana_Catastrophic_Hurricane_Functional_Plan.pdf, prepared for Sharon Blades, under FEMA BPA HSFEHQ-04-A-0288, Task Order 001. The estimate of fatalities is on p. 7. Another report, 448 pages, not yet released to the public, called "Southeast Louisiana Catastrophic Hurricane Plan," also recognized that significant numbers of residents in New Orleans would be unable to evacuate. See Robert Block, "U.S. Had Plan for Crisis Like Katrina," *Wall Street Journal*, September 19, 2005, A3–4. See also FEMA's Southeastern Louisiana Catastrophic Hurricane Plan, http://www.kucinich.us/phpBB2/viewtopic.php?p=16789&.

31. Scott Shane and Eric Lipton, "Storm Overwhelmed Government's Preparations," *New York Times*, September 2, 2005, A1, 14. For an important work on the question of risk, see Ronald J. Daniels, Donald F. Kettl, and Howard Kunreuther, eds., *On Risk and Disaster: Lessons from Hurricane Katrina* (Philadelphia: University of Pennsylvania Press, 2006).

32. Death statistics comes from *One Year After Katrina*, 5.

33. This paragraph is drawn from "Life in the Bottom 80 Percent," Editorial, *New York Times*, September 1, 2005, A22. The figures on spending cuts, including to Medicaid, comes from David E. Sanger and Edmund L. Andrews, "Bush Rules out Raising Taxes for Gulf Relief," *The New York Times*, September 17, 2005, A1, 10.

34. See Noam Chomsky, *Turning the Tide*, especially chapter 5 (New York: Black Rose Books, 1987), 221–53. See also Noam Chomsky, *Powers and Prospects*, especially chapter 5 (Boston, South End Press, 1996), 94–131. See Robert K. Murray, *Red Scare: A Study in National Hysteria, 1919–1920* (Minneapolis: University of Minnesota, 1955); Richard M. Freeland, *The Truman Doctrine and the Origins of McCarthyism: Foreign Policy, Domestic Politics, and Internal Security, 1946–1948* (New York: New York University Press, [1970] 1985); Elizabeth A. Fones-Wolf, *Selling Free Enterprise: The Business Assault on Labor and Liberalism, 1945–1960* (Urbana: University of Illinois Press, 1994); Alex Carey, *Taking the Risk out of Democracy*, (Sydney: University of New South Wales, 1995); Judith Stephan-Norris and Maurice Zeitlin, *Left out: Reds & America's Industrial Unions* (New York: Cambridge University Press, 2003). On the dismantling of the Bretton Woods system of fixed exchange rates, the related end of capital controls and some of the consequences of these

changes, see John Eatwell, "The Global Money Trap: Can Clinton Master the Markets?" *The American Prospect,* 12 (1993): 118–26; John Eatwell and Lance Taylor, *Global Finance at Risk* (New York: New Press, 2000). See also Giovanni Arrighi, *The Long Twentieth Century: Money, Power and the Origins of Our Times* (New York: Verso, 1994).

35. Rosa Brooks, "American Caesar," *Los Angeles Times,* September 3, 2005, B15.

36. Greg Jaffe, "Katrina Will Shape Military Debate: Army Has Resisted Proposal for Guard Disaster Units: Short of People, Equipment," *Wall Street Journal,* September 12, 2005, A5; Government Accountability Office, *An Integrated Plan Is Needed to Address Army Reserve Personnel & Equipment Shortages,* July 2005, http://www.gao.gov/new.items/d05660.pdf.

37. Maureen Dowd, "United States of Shame," *New York Times,* September 2, 2005, A29; "The Man-Made Disaster," Editorial, *The New York Times,* September 2, 2005, A22. On earlier spending for freeways, see Davis, *Dead Cities,* 261. The money for the bridge was such an embarrassment it was later taken away, only to be put in the Alaska general fund.

38. Andrew C. Revkin and Christopher Drew, "Intricate Flood Protection Long a Focus of Dispute," *New York Times,* September 1, 2005, A14; Will Bunch, "Did New Orleans Catastrophe Have to Happen? 'Times-Picayune' Had Repeatedly Raised Federal Spending Issues,'" *Editor and Publisher,* August 31, 2005, http://www.mediainfo.com/eandp/news/article_display.jsp?vnu_content_id=1001051313. Others estimate the costs as much higher, but again, this is a question of fiscal priorities. Action before Hurricane Katrina would undoubtedly have saved minimally tens of billions of dollars and countless lives. The quote from Ivor van Heerden is from Mark Hosenball, "It's Cheaper to Go Dutch," *Newsweek,* September 4, 2006, 36. See also Peter Eisler, "146 U.S. Levees May Fail in Flood: Bad Maintenance Heightens Danger," *USA TODAY,* January 29, 2007, http://news.aol.com/topnews/articles/_a/146-us-levees-may-fail-in-flood/20070129095709990001?ncid=NWS00010000000001.

39. Ann Carns, Chad Tehune, Kris Hudson, and Gary Fields, "Overwhelmed: As U.S. Mobilizes Aid, Katrina Exposes Flaws in Preparation: Despite Warnings, Officials Say, There Wasn't Clear Plan for a New Orleans Disaster," *Wall Street Journal,* September 1, 2005, A1, 6.

40. For an important study looking at the very different experience of Cuba, see Oxfam, *Cuba: Weathering the Storm: Lessons in Risk Reduction in Cuba,* 2004, http://www.oxfamamerica.org/newsandpublications/publications/research_reports/pdfs/cuba_hur_eng.pdf. See also the important work of Amartya Sen, on democracy, development, and militarization. For more on the Unites States as a failed state, see Noam Chomsky, *Failed States: The Abuse of Power and the Assault on Democracy* (New York: Metropolitan Books, 2006).

41. GAO, *Disaster Management: Improving the Nation's Response to Catastrophic Disasters,* July 1993, http://archive.gao.gov/t2pbat5/149631.pdf.

42. Doug Bandow, "Federal Failure in New Orleans," *CATO Institute,* September 8, 2005, http://www.cato.org/pub_display.php?pub_id=4638. For the NPR interview with Chertoff, see http://www.npr.org/templates/story/story.php?storyId=4828771. On Brown, see Richard W. Stevenson and Anne E. Kornblut, "Director of FEMA

Stripped of Role as Relief Leader: Decision Comes After Lawmakers Put Pressure on President," *The New York Times*, September 10, 2005, A 1, 11.

43. MSNBC Reports, "Katrina: What Went Wrong?" September 17, 2005. The dates for the quotes come from this program. PBS Frontline Documentary, *The Storm*, November 22, 2005.

44. Stevenson and Kornblut, "Director of FEMA Stripped of Role as Relief Leader."

45. This paragraph is drawn from the John M. Broder, "In Storm's Ruins, a Rush to Rebuild and Reopen for Business: Contractors, and Lobbyists, Line Up," *The New York Times*, September 10, 2005, A1, 14. On Brown and Root and the military-corporate complex, see Joseph A. Pratt and Christopher Castaneda, *Builders: Herman and George R. Brown* (College Station: Texas A & M University Press, 1998). See also Naomi Klein, "The Rise of Disaster Capitalism," *The Nation*, April 14, 2005, http://www.thenation.com/doc/20050502/klein.

There is also the question of what will happen to the evacuees. Some are already pushing for the right of return to New Orleans for the evacuees, with guarantees of housing and jobs. The president's mother, Barbara Bush, had a different, more hopeful view, perhaps influenced by her husband's notion of the thousand points of light: "What I'm hearing, which is sort of scary, is they all want to stay in Texas. . . . Everyone is so overwhelmed by the hospitality. . . . And so many of the people in the arena here, you know, were underprivileged anyway, so this is working very well for them" (September 5, 2005, American Public Media, National Public Radio http://marketplace.publicradio.org/shows/2005/09/05/PM200509051.html). Then there is the political angle of some who appeared to delight in the fleeing of Blacks: Representative Richard Baker, a "ten-term Republican from Baton Rouge," was overheard as saying, "We finally cleaned up public housing in New Orleans. We couldn't do it, but God did" (Charles Bibington, "Some GOP Legislators Hit Jarring Notes in Addressing Katrina," *Washington Post*, September 10, 2005, http://www.washingtonpost.com/wp-dyn/content/article/2005/09/09/AR2005090901930_pf.html). Perhaps these views help explain the seeming callous disregard many feel the president and some federal, local, and state authorities appeared to show for those left stranded.

46. Jason DeParle, "Liberal Hopes Ebb in Post-Storm Poverty Debate: An Ideological Clash over How to Help America's Poor," *New York Times*, October 11, 2005, A1, 18; Yochi J. Dreazen, "No-Bid Contracts Win Katrina Work: White House Uses Practices Criticized in Iraq Rebuilding for Hurricane-Related Jobs," *Wall Street Journal*, September 12, 2005, A3, 5.

47. Davis, *Dead Cities*, especially Chapter 13. See also David Gonzalez, "From Margins of Society to Center of the Tragedy," *The New York Times*, September 2, 2005, A1, 19. Peter W. Singer, *Corporate Warriors: The Rise of the Privatized Military Industry* (Ithaca: Cornell University Press, 2003). Peter Gowan, *The Global Gamble: Washington's Faustian Bid for World Dominance* (New York: Verso, 1999). Peter Gowan, "The New American Century?" *The Spokesman*, 76 (2002): 5–22.

48. See the homepage of United for Peace and Justice, http://www.unitedfor peace.org: George McGovern and William R. Polk, *Out of Iraq: A Practical Plan for Withdrawal Now* (New York: Simon & Schuster, 2006). See also Thomas Ehrlich Reifer, "Changing U.S. Policy Towards Iraq: A Strategy Proposal and Scenario for

Congressional Hearings" (unpublished paper, 2007). See also Paul M. Lubeck and Thomas Ehrlich Reifer, "The Politics of Global Islam: U.S. Hegemony, Globalization, & Islamist Social Movements," in Thomas Ehrlich Reifer, ed., *Globalization, Hegemony and Power: Antisystemic Movements and the Global System* (Boulder, CO: Paradigm Publishers, 2004), 162–80; Robert Pape, *Dying to Win: The Strategic Logic of Suicide Terrorism* (New York: Random House, 2006). The aftermath of Katrina saw not a few racially inspired diatribes linking the so-called war on terror with the war on urban poor communities of color; one letter to the editor had this to say: "While I wish the survivors all the best in the days to come, I will never bring myself to visit this region once it rebuilds, because at the foundation of these communities are thugs and hoodlums no better than the agents of terror we are combating in other regions of the world." (*San Diego Union Tribune*, September 3, 2005, B9).

49. John Harwood, "Katrina Erodes Support in U.S. for Iraq War: Bush's Ratings as Crisis Manager Declines in Poll as Pessimism about the Economy Grows," *Wall Street Journal*, September 15, 2005, A4. A radio program on January 27, 2007, featured one mother of an Iraq war veteran, Tina, whose son had done two tours in Iraq and who was being called back for a third. Tina and her son went from Kansas to Washington, D.C., for the massive January 27, 2007, protests against the Iraq war, part of demonstrations nationwide; she stated that it was when she saw Katrina hit and all those people left suffering at a time when so many National Guard troops were in Iraq that she realized she had to speak out against the war. She also said she was heartened by all the military service persons and military families at the protests, and felt they were doing their patriotic duty by speaking out. Signs such as "Make Levees, Not War," were prominent at the nationwide demonstrations, which organizers estimate to have included hundreds of thousands of people.

50. http://www.unitedforpeace.org/article.php?id=3094.

51. W.E.B. Du Bois, *Black Reconstruction in America: An Essay Toward a History of the Part Which Black Folk Played in the Attempt to Reconstruct Democracy in America, 1860–1880* (New York: Atheneum, [1935] 1969); Eric Foner, *Reconstruction: America's Unfinished Revolution: 1863–1877* (New York: Harper & Row, 1988). See also Mike Davis, *Prisoners of the American Dream: Politics and Economy in the History of the US Working Class*, (New York: Verso, 1986).

52. David E. Sanger and Edmund L. Andrews, "Bush Rules out Raising Taxes for Gulf Relief," *The New York Times*, September 17, 2005, A1, 10; Center on Policy and Budget Priorities, "Katrina and the Federal Budget," http://www.cbpp.org/katrina slideshow.pdf; Paul Krugman, "Not the New Deal," *The New York Times*, September 16, 2005, A27. See also Frank Rich, "Message: I Care About Black People," *The New York Times*, September 18, 2005, A12. For a series of rich perspectives on these subjects, see the Social Science Research Council's website, "Understanding Katrina: Perspectives from the Social Sciences," http://understandingkatrina.ssrc.org/. See also Robert W. Kates, Craig Colten, Shirley Laksa, and Stephen Leatherman, "Reconstruction of New Orleans following Hurricane Katrina: A Research Perspective," *Proceedings of the National Academy of Sciences* 103 (2006): 14653–660; The Greater New Orleans Community Data Center in collaboration with the Brookings Institution, "The Katrina Index: Tracking Recovery of New Orleans and the Metro

Area," January 17, 2007, http://www.gnocdc.org/KI/KatrinaIndex.pdf, updated monthly; National Urban League Policy Institute, "Katrina: One Year Later: A Policy and Research Report on the National Urban League's Katrina Bill of Rights," 2006, http://nul.org/PressReleases/2006/KatrinaLeg percent20PolicyReport.pdf; *One Year After Katrina*, 15, 27; Pastor et al., *In the Wake of the Storm*, 29. See also Christopher Cooper, "In Katrina's Wake: Where Is the Money? Congress Authorized Billions to Rebuild, But Only Half Has Been Spent," *Wall Street Journal*, January 27, 2007, A1, 10; Environmental Defense, Coalition to Restore Coastal Louisiana, National Wildlife Federation, Gulf Restoration Foundation, Lake Ponchartrain Basin Foundation, *One Year After Katrina: Louisiana Still a Sitting Duck; A Report Card and Roadmap on Wetlands Restoration*, August 28, 2006; http://www.environmentaldefense.org/documents/5416_KatrinaReportCard.pdf.

Chapter Eleven

Spectacular Privatizations

Perceptions and Lessons from Privatization of Warfare and the Privatization of Disaster

Ganesh K. Trichur[1]

The spectacle of Hurricane Katrina in New Orleans—the pictures of terrible misery heaped upon African American poor through governmental negligence and inaction after a clearly anticipated natural disaster[2]—and the equally spectacular destruction of Iraq—through a mix of U.S. occupation, unrelenting insurgency, and furious civil war—appears to represent what Emmanuel Todd calls "the spectacle of self-destroying systems."[3] The logic of this spectacle unfolds through intertwined forms of accumulation through privatization and destructive creation of new asymmetrical spatial relations in the Persian Gulf and the Mexican Gulf. On the one hand these two forms of "accumulation by dispossession"[4] emerge out of the growing privatization of war-making in Iraq and through privatization of disaster-relief after Hurricane Katrina's landfall in August 2005. On the other hand, in response to such brazen privatization newly emerging race, class, and community solidarities within hurricane-devastated areas represent spectacles of resistance to the fetishization of disaster in the U.S. Gulf Coast and "the Big Easy."[5] As Polanyi may have argued, the social movements organized by various community groups of color supported by nationwide communities of resistance to the ruthless speed and scale of destructive re-creation of impacted areas in the New Orleans region represent movements for the "self-protection of society."[6] Perhaps, as Manning Marable foresaw, a "Third Reconstruction" that fulfills "the lost promises and broken dreams of the first and second social protest movements"[7] may emerge out of the devastating deluge to forge durable, alternative, long-term collective projects and overcome the crisis of African American consciousness in the 1980s and 1990s. In November 2005, the first civil rights protest following Hurricane Katrina took place as thousands rallied at the New Orleans Convention Center before marching across the Mississippi Bridge from New Orleans to Gretna, Louisiana—to commemorate the day after Katrina when police from Jefferson Parish and other governmental agencies prevented desperate hurricane victims from crossing the bridge. Perhaps the anemic antiwar movement and the vibrant new immigrant movement will combine with African American communities to re-create a New Left project against the consumptive decadence of the society of the spectacle.[8]

I argue that neoliberal states and the financial expansion of the 1970s and 1980s following the end of the material expansion of the post-1945 period[9] provide the theoretical and historical framework within which to locate the pursuit of profits through war-making by privatized military forces (PMFs) in the Persian Gulf, and through the post-Katrina supply of privatized welfare by many of the same PMFs in the Mexican Gulf.[10] I maintain that the effects of extreme events like Hurricane Katrina and the prospects of a Third Reconstruction closely relate to the constraints and opportunities offered by the growing crisis of the global neoliberal project. I elaborate in the first section below, on some "elective affinities" between Baghdad and New Orleans. In the second section I bring together some perceptions of the United States in the aftermath of Katrina. In the final section I suggest some lessons and lines of action for a progressive Left.

PRIVATIZATION OF WAR
AND THE PRIVATIZATION OF DISASTER

Strong affinities connect the politico-military disasters in the Persian Gulf and the socio-ecological disasters in the Gulf of Mexico. Both disasters represent profoundly disturbing crises in planning: in both the Gulfs, no attempt to plan for the aftermath—of the Iraqi invasion, and of the effects of Katrina—was ever undertaken. If there was substantial knowledge available, none of it was utilized. In the case of occupied Baghdad, what amazes is the lack of any attempt to obtain adequate knowledge of the occupied terrain, of the differences between Sunni, Shia, and Kurdish interests. What also amazes is the inability to adequately internalize military lessons of the defeat in Vietnam—the limits in short of U.S. occupation reliant on lethal capital-intensive warfare. As a result more and more observers refer to Iraq as a "quagmire," the mess created by U.S. intervention, and the even bigger mess perhaps if the United States were to find possible exits. In the case of the Gulf of Mexico what is equally amazing is the complete lack of any attempt to incorporate planning for an extreme event like Katrina. Despite the abundant variety of precedents available—for instance the immediate experience of Hurricane Ivan in September 2004, the 1993 floods, and Hurricane Betsy in 1965, Hurricane Andrew in 1992, among other hurricanes of the 1990s—no adequate preparations were made for anticipating the effects of an apparently unprecedented hurricane season. The lack of any planning for the aftermath of war and the aftermath of Katrina made the two places exemplary instances of widespread "looting" following the breakdown of the physical and social networks in the two regions. The inability (or unwillingness) to deploy occupying U.S. troops to stem a wave of looting destroyed the administrative, security, and even cultural infrastructure of Baghdad. In New Orleans, for days, desperate individuals abandoned and, in need of food and supplies, roamed the city uncontested as buildings began to burn.

Emmanuel Todd observes that "predation" is the common principle at work between "the gang of black unemployed who loot a supermarket and the group of oligarchs who try to organize the 'heist' of the century of Iraq's hydrocarbon reserves."[11] There are however deeper and more substantive points of similarity between the two Gulfs. At work is rising and unsustainable "external" costs of protection in the war on Iraq, and rising and unsustainable "internal" costs of protection in the class and race wars waged on the domestic poor. It is through the neoliberal state apparatus that the privatization of warfare and welfare appear intertwined with escalating costs of supplying external and internal protection. "External" and "internal" are really two sides of the same phenomenon, in the sense that a militarized state apparatus works on two fronts, abroad, and at home. Increasingly, this is a *privatized* military state apparatus—which emerged out of an era of military downsizing after the end of the Cold War—which knows only how to respond with overwhelming force to any problem it encounters. As part of a more general phenomenon of system-wide privatization, the market for PMFs boomed in the 1990s in an era of military downsizing (the U.S. military is one third smaller than what it was at the end of the 1991 Gulf war). Driven by changes in the military market for armed laborers the U.S. military signed more than 3,000 contracts with PMFs following the end of the Cold War. In Iraq, there are more private military contractors on the ground than there are British troops. In 2004 some 15,000 to 20,000 private military personnel handled logistics and maintenance, trained the local Iraqi army, and even fought pitched battles, so much so that Iraq has become "the biggest marketplace in the short history of the privatized military industry."[12] However, the quality and efficacy of this newly privatized military force—abroad and at home—raises disturbing questions. As multinational soldiers sometimes representing more than thirty different nationalities fighting—and dying—in the Middle East, and as an international coalition of high-cost armed laborers hired by the United States, this privatized military force represents less a "coalition of the willing" and more a "coalition of the billing." In 2004 at least ten cents out of every reconstruction dollar in Iraq was spent for security (up from seven cents in fall 2003), and these security costs are expected to increase to twenty cents for every reconstruction dollar. PMF soldiers earn two to ten times more than what their home state-military pays (a former U.S. Green Beret makes some $1,000 per day while a Gurkha soldier from Nepal earns $1,000 per month), and PMF contractors spend as much as forty cents out of every dollar on insurance for force-protection. Rising PMF casualties, as well as intelligence disconnections with the U.S. army and marines in Iraq, imply not only escalating security costs for every PMF soldier killed in action, they also suggest that the PMF boom in Iraq may be quite short-lived. Moreover, the disastrous state of infrastructural investments necessary to prop up the Iraqi economy may also indirectly undercut the PMF industry in the long-term. If "the insurance problem" illustrates the growing costs of "an ad hoc approach to doing business in the realm of war," the fact that PMFs are not formally part of the U.S. army and marines in Iraq deepens the "critical disconnect" in intelligence sharing and confusion over rights and responsibilities in the midst of combat.[13]

These limits to the privatization of warfare in Iraq were clearly exposed in June 2004—when Paul Bremer, the leader of the Coalition Provisional Authority (CPA) left Baghdad—when the CPA had already run through $20 billion dollars in Iraqi funds, mostly generated by Iraqi oil revenues and earmarked for "the benefit of the Iraqi people" (though only $300 million in U.S. funds). A bizarre turn hooked up the fortunes in the two Gulfs after Hurricane Katrina made landfall on August 29, 2005. On the one hand the Iraqi nation-building projects for which the U.S. Congress had approved a $25 billion budget came to an impasse by September 2004 due to downsizing, postponement, or abandonment of projects begun after the occupation in the context of an unrelenting insurgency. On the other hand, staggering sums earmarked for Iraqi reconstruction were shunted to private security firms assigned to guard the abandoned projects.[14] After Hurricane Katrina devastated the U.S. Gulf coast, with funds growing scarce, these same PMFs connected in various ways to the Bush administration, having profited from the plunder of Iraq through no-bid, cost-plus contracts turned to New Orleans to supply "protection" for the homeland.

Under a ten-year contract called LOGCAP which it won in 2001, the military firm Kellog, Brown and Root (KBR), a subsidiary of the energy firm

Halliburton which provided logistical support for U.S. troops in Iraq, was awarded $6.3 billion for the first two years of occupation and $4.97 billion for U.S. troop support until May 2006. After Katrina, KBR was awarded $29.8 million for rebuilding U.S. naval bases in Louisiana and Mississippi, even as it contracted with the Army Corps of Engineers (ACE) to expand immigrant detention facilities. If the Bechtel Corporation, the San Francisco–based engineering firm, was awarded $3 billion for Iraqi reconstruction contracts in the nine months after the fall of Saddam Hussein, in New Orleans Bechtel was awarded contracts for temporary housing construction. Similarly, the California-based Fluor Corporation that made a $1.1 billion deal with a London company in 2004 for construction services for water distribution and treatment systems in Iraq was awarded $1.4 billion for temporary housing construction in New Orleans. The Shaw Group Inc. which was awarded $88.7 million for Iraqi infrastructure reconstruction in early 2004 was later awarded $950 million for post-Katrina reconstruction work in New Orleans—through the mediation of Joe Allbaugh, former Federal Emergency Management Agency (FEMA) director and the director of the 2000 Bush election program—that included covering damaged homes with tarps as part of the ACE's "blue-roof program." The Shaw Group charged the government three times as much as an Alabama competitor Ystueta, and it has earned more than half a billion dollars from contracts awarded by FEMA and ACE. Another successful bidder for the plunder of Iraq was CH2M Hill, a Colorado-based company that, in a joint venture, took in a $28.5 million reconstruction contract in 2004, and teamed up with other contractors for a $12.7 million electrical power generation deal. In New Orleans CH2M Hill was awarded up to $530 million for debris removal, support for emergency operations, and setting up temporary classrooms, portable buildings, and temporary housing. In the wake of Katrina, Intelsat, a global satellite services provider that, in Iraq, had teamed up with Bechtel on a big USAID reconstruction program, agreed to new post-Katrina contracts with the Defense Department and FEMA. Similarly, days after Katrina ravaged the Gulf Coast, the Air National Guard contracted with another satellite services provider, Segovia, which had earlier served as "a key telecommunications provider for the Iraqi reconstruction efforts."[15] Perhaps the most intriguing in the list of violent entrepreneurs is Blackwater USA (BW), a PMF founded in 1997 in the Moyock swamplands of North Carolina, designed to be "the premier firearms and tactical training center in the world," as per its October 25, 2004, press release. On August 9, 2004, BW joined the International Peace Operations Association, a non-governmental association dedicated to "ensuring the highest standards of international peace and stability of operations." First employed for work in Iraq, what put BW on the map was the gruesome hanging of four of its military contractors in Falluja in March 2004. Following the failure of Iraqi reconstruction, BW works for the Department of Homeland Security in New Orleans. Jeremy Scahill notes that "Blackwater USA is the most rapidly growing and, arguably, the most successful mercenary firm in the world today." In Baghdad its $21 million contract was to guard Paul Bremer, the CPA governor in Iraq. While government documents show that Blackwater was paid $950 per day for each of its guards, some of them in New Orleans were paid $350 per day, which left the security company $600 per man per day to cover lodging, ammunition, related overhead, and profits. BW guards told Scahill that their job was to stop looters and confront criminals. According to Blackwater Press Release of November 23, 2005, the security company organized with the American Red Cross a Gulf Region Relief fundraiser and silent auction at the Sheraton Oceanfront hotel where Paul Bremer was keynote speaker. Gary Jackson, BW's president, noted that the company's "special relationship with Ambassador Bremer and the Red Cross" facilitated the successful fundraising event that was "about Americans helping Americans" and "all that is good about the American spirit." On September 13, 2005, BW claimed to continue working on its "humanitarian, security, and clean-up needs" for Katrina-devastated areas.[16]

Multiple instances of unabashedly outrageous fraud emerged as the U.S. government outsourced hurricane relief work to these out-of-state private corporations that had little idea of the socioeconomic terrain of hurricane-damaged spaces. As the Institute for Southern Studies points out, Hurricane Katrina uncovered "an existing system of political patronage that benefits a small number of private corporations while often worsening the suffering of the disadvantaged."[17] If the federal Gulf Opportunity Zone ("GO Zone") Act of December 2005 promised billions of dollars through subsidized financing and tax breaks for Gulf Coast citizens, the legislation at the same time enabled the three Gulf states to issue up to $15 billion of tax-free "GO Zone" bonds on behalf of private companies for rebuilding ventures only loosely connected to the devastations inflicted by Katrina and Rita.[18] If nineteen projects received the green light enabled by the $3 billion in tax breaks for Gulf Coast investors provided by the GO Zone Act, only two were directly linked to Katrina.[19] Katrina also opened the way for the advance of the gambling industry through construction of casinos in the Mississippi coastal city of Biloxi.[20] And while the government's Hurricane Katrina Fraud Task Force focuses attention on fraud by emergency assistance recipients, "instances of corporate contract and procurement fraud have been documented at fifty times that amount."[21] The Shaw Group and other politically connected corporations like Halliburton and Bechtel seized lucrative deals for clean-up and reconstruction without competition or oversight, while regional companies in desperate need of help were cut out off the bidding process.[22]

These sordid details systematically undermine the image of the United States as "protector" in the two Gulfs, and the endless insurgent resistance the United States encounters in Iraq accelerates its growing legitimacy crisis. If the United States claims to protect global democracy against rogue states in possession of weapons of mass destruction, it is nevertheless the United States that remains the site of the most concentrated accumulation of the means of organized violence. If the United States justifies its unabated accumulation (and sale[23]) of means of violence through ideological claims to defend freedom and democracy in a putatively un-free world of Islamic terrorism, and an axis of evil,[24] its militaristic unilateralism compels more and more nations to acquire weapons of mass destruction as means of protection against the protector.[25] As puny Arabs repeatedly demonstrate, the United States only fights a losing war in the Persian Gulf: all its armed efforts so far merely magnify its loss of power, prestige, and friends. It has not stamped out terrorism—and it will not—because it does not understand the difference between terrorism and state terrorism on the one hand, and the difference between national terrorism and international terrorism on the other. Its naïve conflation of two very differently realities actually produce and sustain more terrorism.[26] If the quagmire in Iraq deepens the crisis of U.S. legitimacy in the eyes of the rest of the world, the after-effects of Katrina have doubly magnified it. For after Katrina, the world came to see the United States as unable to take care of its own people (especially its poorest), let alone the task of ensuring the freedom of other people. Its differential practices toward its own citizens and its unsupportive stance toward its citizens of color sharply contradicts the universalism that it seeks to project abroad. Its equally differential approaches toward the death of U.S. soldiers (over 3,000 in January 2007) and the death of Iraqi civilians (in the hundreds of thousands according to some estimates) imply an asymmetrical valuation of human life. The portrayals by Al-Jazeera of gruesome Iraqi civilian deaths and human rights violations of prisoners in Abu Ghraib and Guantanamo are irreparable ideological defeats for the United States. The stunning collapse of the U.S. emergency infrastructure and the helplessness of the FEMA in the wake of Katrina, clearly revealed that the United States no longer has the adequate capacity for a full-scale *civilian response* to a major national disaster. Portrayals of helpless and harassed African American victims of Katrina on global news channels destroy the image of the United States as a benevolent caretaker. The two Gulf disasters thus demonstrate defeat on the terrain of the spectacle.

KATRINA'S IMPLICATIONS FOR U.S. POLITICAL ECONOMY

The current neoliberal conjuncture in short points to a bizarre turn whose long-term trajectory can only intensify tendencies toward de-democratization and disintegration in the United States. In an interview with the French publication *Le Figaro*, the historical anthropologist Emmanuel Todd argues that to manage a natural catastrophe like Katrina what is required is not sophisticated financial techniques, tax consultants, or lawyers, but "materiel, engineers, and technicians, as well as a feeling of collective solidarity." Hurricane Katrina confronted the United States with its deepest identity, with its capacities for technical and social response; measured in terms of its capacity for long-term prevention and planning, the United States failed disastrously as the world observed "the inadequacy of its technical resources, its engineers, and the military forces on the scene."[27] In fact, observers worldwide were startled to see how much the United States appeared as a "Third World" during the days and weeks and months after Katrina made its landfall. As Vinay Lal observes in the Indian periodical *Economic and Political Weekly*, the ideology of the free market that informs the political economy of Katrina is similar to the free market ideology of British colonial officials in late-nineteenth-century India who sacrificed famine relief to free-market principles. But as the "collateral damage" from Katrina began to mount, "it became imperative to take action, if only to prove that America is not another Third World nation or a banana republic. Neither Mumbai after the floods of July 2005, nor Aceh and Sri Lanka after tsunami of December 2004, witnessed street gun battles or widespread looting."[28] However, as Todd argues, we should avoid "over-racializing" the interpretation of the Katrina catastrophe by tracing everything to "the Black problem," in particular the disintegration of local society and the problem of looting. The looting of supermarkets by lower social strata in a moment of great distress without any relief in sight, repeats on an incomparably lower scale "the predation scheme that is at the heart of the American social system" today, which no longer rests on the Calvinist work ethic and taste for saving—but on "the quest for the biggest payoff for the least effort": money speedily acquired, by speculation and theft.[29]

More fundamentally, Todd makes two compelling arguments. In the first place, the effects of Hurricane Katrina in the United States demonstrated "the limits of a virtual economy that identifies the world as a vast video game." Todd points out that Katrina "lifted the veil on an American economy globally perceived as very dynamic, benefiting from a low unemployment rate, credited with a strong GDP growth rate. But what people have not wanted to see is that the dynamism of the United States is essentially a dynamism of consumption." For the United States at the heart of the world system acts as "a remarkable financial pump" sucking in world liquidity to the tune of $700 to $800 billion a year that is then used to finance the consumption of imported goods. Unlike European and Asian societies that developed by managing scarcity, the United States was constructed in abundance and does not appear to know how to manage scarcity, as revealed in its long-term tendency to accumulate trade deficits close to $700 billion. This "monstrous deficit" highlights the overriding weakness of the U.S. economic system, which is that it does not rest on a foundation of real domestic industrial capacity. "American industry has been bled dry and it is the industrial decline that above all explains the negligence of a nation confronted with a crisis." Todd notes that management of the catastrophe would have been much better in the New Deal U.S. economic system which was an industrial capitalism based on the production of goods, "in short, a world of engineers and technicians." By contrast, the neoliberal U.S. system is utterly at loose ends, bogged down in a devastated Iraq that it does not manage to reconstruct. "The simple deterioration in the technical capacities of a no-longer-productive American economy created the threat of a Nature that would do no more than take back its [natural] rights. Let's not point our fingers at the aggravation of natural conditions, but rather at the economic deterioration of a society that must confront a much more violent nature."

Second, Todd uses his anthropological research to claim that the map of infant mortality is always an exact copy of the map of the density of Black populations.[30] He argues that the latest figures published on this theme by the United States in 2002 demonstrate the beginning of an upturn in infant mortality rates for all the American "races," and in particular for African Americans. Todd's "demographic determinism" enabled him to predict, on the basis of rising infant mortality rates in the mid-1970s, the collapse of the Soviet Union. According to the 2006 U.S. Census Bureau, 37 million Americans in 2004 and 2005 (12.6 percent of the population) lived below the poverty line; the number of people without health insurance increased for the sixth straight year to reach 46.6 million in 2005; and Mississippi's median household income of $32,938 is the lowest in the nation.[31] The U.N.'s *Human Development Report 2005* shows that social inequalities within the United States are becoming as stark as inequalities between the United States and the rest of the world. As Stephen Jackson observes, a child born in one of the top 5 percent of the richest U.S. families can expect to live 25 percent longer than a boy born in the bottom 5 percent, and the U.S. infant mortality rate has been rising between 2001 and 2005, with African American children twice as likely to die before their first birthday as White children.[32] For Todd, the erosion of the U.S. industrial base, its growing deficit in high-technology goods, the desuetude and ineffectiveness of its military apparatus, and above all, the up-turn in infant mortality rates, point to "the possibility in the medium term of a real Soviet-style crisis in the United States." If the United States, in short, represents today "the spectacle of self-destroying systems,"[33] it is in large part because in the forty-first anniversary of the 1964 Civil Rights Act, "the U.S. seems to have returned to degree zero of moral concern for the majority of descendants of slavery and segregation. Whether the Black poor live or die seems to merit only haughty disinterest and indifference." Structural unem-ployment, race-based super-incarceration, police brutality, disappearing affir-mative action programs, and failing schools—in terms of these "life-and-death issues,"[34] Marable sees the United States as "not simply a capitalist state, but a *racist state*."[35] Foucault defines racism as the exercise of sover-eign power to introduce a break into the domain of life that is under its con-trol: "the break between what must live and must die." If racism developed with colonizing genocides, since the mid-nineteenth century, wars became the means of not only destroying the enemy race (as a biological threat), but also as a means of regenerating one's own race. "As more and more of our num-ber die, the race to which we belong will become all the purer"; in a "nor-malizing society," it is race or racism that becomes the precondition that makes killing acceptable. If we relate these observations to the constant tal-lies of U.S. soldiers killed in Iraq, and the relative unconcern with the deaths, maiming, and tortures of Iraqi or Afghani or Lebanese civilians in the hun-dreds of thousands, or for that matter with African American citizens left to die in the aftermath of Katrina, then it becomes possible to understand why Foucault argues that the most murderous states—like the Nazi State—are also, of necessity, the most racist, and why the most racist state is also "an ab-solutely suicidal state."[36]

CONCLUSION

There are basically two visions confronting the Gulf Region stormed by Ka-trina. One is the official federal and state vision that collaborates with priva-teers and free market fundamentalists in seeing the Gulf Region as a blank slate for pursuit of profits out of social disasters through grandiose plans for social engineering through urban renewal projects.[37] It emphasizes "security" demands of investors and corporations to facilitate flexible forms of capi-tal accumulation and to wrest control over the debate about how to rebuild the empty Blackness of New Orleans. In April 2006 Mike Davis noted that the current population of New Orleans on the west bank of the Mississippi was "about the same as that of Disney World on a normal day" with roughly

80 percent of the African Americans still in exile.[38] In the immediate after-math of Katrina, different developmental projects for the Gulf Coast were ini-tiated, each of which sought to shrink the footprint of New Orleans—making it a geographically smaller city by converting all the primarily Black neigh-borhoods into parks and green space. These projects included Mayor Ray Na-gin's Bring New Orleans Back Commission of September 30, 2005, spear-headed by Joseph Canizaro, a real-estate developer and one of the biggest fund-raisers of President Bush, the Baker Plan for urban renewal, and Gover-nor Kathleen Blanco's Louisiana Recovery Authority. Each of these plans embodied a tremendous impatience for a "new" New Orleans as distinct from what people of New Orleans consider special about their city, "the intimacy of neighborhoods."[39] These projects are similar to what Naomi Klein calls the U.S. project of "disaster capitalism" pursued since August 2004 via the cre-ation of the Office of the Coordinator for Reconstruction and Stabilization with a mandate to construct detailed "post-conflict" plans for the destructive creation of new business environments out of the ruins of civil wars and nat-ural disasters in the global South.[40] If the idea that underdevelopment and poverty in the global South are dangerous led in the 1990s to a new Western project of global governance in which development considerations merged with security considerations,[41] in the U.S. South the idea that African Ameri-can poverty, drug trafficking, and crime are dangerously related reinforces a perdurable system of incarceration. The prison system in New Orleans was in fact one of the first city functions to restart after Katrina, by incarcerating sus-pected looters in a state that has the highest rate of incarceration alongside some of the poorest people in the country. Adam Nossiter reports that in East Carroll Parish, one of the poorest counties in Louisiana, "the nation's culture of incarceration achieves a kind of ultimate synthesis with the local econ-omy" by reviving a form of the convict-lease system that began in the South around Reconstruction.[42]

An alternative vision, advanced by the Gulf Coast Reconstruction Watch, emphasizes "justice and human rights," and it requires restoration of good jobs, health care, housing, robust public educational systems, healthy trans-portation infrastructures, and an ethical relation with nature that conserves disappearing wetlands. It also requires vigilant monitoring of the long-term human-rights status and treatment of Katrina victims who are "internally dis-placed persons," forced to leave their places of habitual residence as a result of natural or human-made disasters.[43] The February/March 2006 Mardi Gras Report of the Southern Institute in Louisiana, concluded that "New Orleans faces deep, fundamental barriers to renewal," and that the people who suf-fered the most from Hurricane Katrina are the same people hurt the most by the nation's lack of commitment to rebuilding New Orleans.[44]

Katrina and its aftermath therefore raise important questions for those of us who would like to see a bold change of course so that alternative democratic and egalitarian futures emerge out of this unwholesome mess. Great crises are always moments of the possible; they make spaces for the emergence of the political new. Maureen Dowd remarks that the fact that we remained deaf for so long to the horrific misery and cries for help of the victims in New Orleans—most of them poor and Black—shook the faith of all Americans in American ideals. She says "It made us ashamed. Who are we if we can't take care of our own?"[45] I want to respond to Maureen Dowd with two remarks: first, shame, insofar is it is a revolutionary sentiment, carries strong transformative potential. Second, to take care of one's own assumes that there is still the *possibility* of belonging to or being in solidarity with, the community of the dispossessed. If it is impossible to adequately comprehend the enormity of the tragic—and Katrina was above all a tragic spectacle in an age that has lost the sense of the tragic—it is nevertheless possible and imperative to learn lessons from the experience of catastrophe.

In the first place, disastrous tragedies do not necessarily have to turn into catastrophes. If the hubris that accompanied the fantastic construction of levees in the Mississippi River Delta settled on a "levees-only policy" in the "century of engineers,"[46] the dialectic of disaster punctured that hubris in the 1927 Mississippi floods, and then repeatedly in the concentration of natural calamities in the decade of the 1990s. No taming or anticipation of natural disasters is adequate insofar as it does not take into account the networked predicaments of the laboring and disadvantaged poor and elderly, condemned to be first victims of largely anticipatable calamities. What prevents natural disasters from turning into catastrophes are planning, coordination, and imagination that give priority to people and their social networks across neighborhoods over the soulless and endless pursuit of profits and power.

A second and related lesson pertains to the need for ethical and ecological commitment to wetlands and coastlines embedded in larger principles of social protection against the frenzy of coastal development projects. If the sixty years spanning 1946–2006 has seen a surge in coastal development that has put more than half the U.S. population within fifty miles of the sea, this developmental frenzy peaked during the neoliberal decades (mid-1970s to mid-1990s), and further weakened natural defenses against hurricanes.[47] Efforts to restore Louisiana's disappearing wetlands remain piecemeal. Over the past century, Louisiana has lost 1.2 million acres of coastal wetlands and continues to lose thirty-five square miles per year, the fastest rate of coastal erosion in the United States. Louisiana's massive levee structures are difficult to engineer on ever-shifting coastal lands, and the levee system remains vulnerable despite $800 million spent by the ACE to rebuild damaged levees. The

350-mile system of levees and floodwalls in the New Orleans area is unready to face a milder-than-expected hurricane season, and flood threats are heightened by the city's troubled system of drainage pumps.[48] What is needed is an ecological vision that takes into account both coastal vulnerabilities to hurricane impacts in the face of long-term coastal erosion, and the means to protect poorer communities who suffer the most from the impact of natural disasters. To plan for disasters is to acknowledge that natural disasters impact different communities differently. As economic development erodes coastlines and creates uneven regional developmental patterns across the country, it not only increases the vulnerability of coastal neighborhoods to natural disasters, but differentiates in its impact across class, race, gender, and age.

I argue that the question of "what is to be done" is really a question of how to support and engage with the multiple communities of displaced evacuees and returnees in the Gulf coast, how to make them central in all future decision making. There is considerable evidence that what is unfolding in the U.S. Gulf Coast are various movements for social "self-protection" against livelihood threats from the disruption of social networks of connectedness after Katrina's landfall and after the rampant marketization of disaster. Grassroots organizations like ACORN, Peoples Hurricane Relief Fund, the NAACP, and Industrial Areas Foundation, organized and mobilized diaspora voters across the United States for the 2006 mayoral runoff between Nagin and Mitch Landrieu. The People's Hurricane Relief Fund and Oversight Committee founded in September 2005—whose motto is "nothing about us without us is for us"—advocates neighborhood projects which work through decentralized participatory planning and budgeting modeled on the experience of Kerala in India. Many faith-based movements effectively network with neighborhood communities—like the community of Christian churches and Buddhist temples that in combination with the Coordination Relief and Development Center lies at the heart of hurricane-damaged East Biloxi in Mississippi.[49] The Vietnamese community residents in the Versailles neighborhood at Village de l'Est combined with the Roman Catholic Church to advance the Citizens for a Strong New Orleans East early in 2006 to successfully challenge the Chef Menteur storm-debris landfill.[50] The communities of poor African Americans in the Lower Ninth Ward Neighborhood Network and Association convenes voices under one umbrella for protection against developers, and the largely working class Holy Cross Neighborhood Association (formed in 1981 with 100 families pre-Katrina to preserve neighborhood architecture) recombines to rebuild the Lower Ninth Ward by supplying social services (alongside planning for rebuilding the Lower Ninth Ward) to returnees. In early January 2006, the Grassroots Legal Network of the People's Hurricane Relief Fund launched an emergency demonstration that blocked a demolition project in the Lower Ninth Ward. In doing so it also combined with plaintiff homeowners, ACORN, Hope Cause, Common Ground Collective, Lower Ninth Ward Neighborhood Council, New Life Intracoastal CDC, and volunteers from the Student Hurricane Network.[51] The Treme Neighborhood group challenged the Iberville housing development project in and around downtown Treme while the Women's Health and Justice Initiative in Treme works as a center for social justice providing health care access for low-income and uninsured women of color, who along with the elderly were by far the most vulnerable after Katrina's landfall.[52] With the school system in New Orleans privatized through strong federal support for the new charter schools as against traditional schools, community-based organizations like Rethink and Community United to Reform Education are monitoring school performance based on quality of education. Safe Streets/Strong Communities is a grassroots coalition of organizations seeking to transform New Orleans's corrupt and indigent defense board into a strong body of criminal justice reform advocates.

In these class struggles against accumulation by dispossession, neighborhoods and communities in the Gulf Coast are learning how to struggle together against the new development projects of the city, state, and federal elite. Other communities across the United States—like the Coalition for Affordable Housing and the Interfaith Hurricane Task Force of Durham County, North Carolina, where 6,500 evacuees have dispersed after Katrina—are working to combine with the Gulf communities to meet resettlement needs of evacuees, and to help rebuild damaged social infrastructures of support. As Naomi Klein reminds us, the billions of dollars that the U.S. Congress and private charities raise for disaster relief, do not belong to the relief agencies or the government. It belongs to those extended families and social networks constituting the communities of the poor, grotesquely displaced by this largely preventable tragedy. The agencies entrusted with the money should be accountable to them.[53] The Common Ground center in Houma is the first to be entirely run by local residents, but they also need money and volunteers.[54] These are some concrete means of empowering them, of giving them back their city, and in the process we may also participate in the reversal of the long-term process of de-democratization that has been the hallmark of the United States since the onset of neo-liberal financial globalization in the course of the 1980s.

Steve Sherman, an activist in North Carolina, points out that like Community Labor United, similar coalitions of labor unions, church groups, nonprofits, and other activist organizations have been forming all over the United States. He suggests that the imminent battle over the future of New Orleans presents both unprecedented challenges and opportunities for these two groupings—community-labor organizations rooted in communities of color and the predominantly White peace groups—to come together and shape public debate in the United States. If the first group combines effectively the politics of class, environmentalism, and race without necessarily prioritizing any single oppression as the most important one, national coordination among them remains relatively weak even though they are well positioned to make pragmatic decisions about local situations. What is striking is that despite common grounds for coalition building, there is a substantial gulf between these grassroots coalitions of people of color and the largely White progressive peace movements, so that these two movements remain largely on separate tracks. The struggle for the future of New Orleans in that sense does create a space for realigning these two tracks of the American left.

If the struggle for the future of New Orleans creates spaces for realigning these two tracks of the U.S. Left, a third track that appears relatively unsupported in Left politics is the immigrant workers' movement that surfaced powerfully in May 2006 when millions marched in a mass demonstrations for immigrant rights all over the country, and millions boycotted buying and selling anything. Those affected most by the storm have in fact been the working classes, although the New Orleans labor force is one-third smaller today than what it was in 2005, and nearly one out of four evacuees is jobless. On the other hand, there are over 100,000 Latino construction workers in the Gulf Coast (many of whom are undocumented) lured into the Gulf Coast on false promises by business contractors after Hurricane Katrina. Some 28 percent of these workers reported difficulties in getting paid by contractors. What is remarkable is that the Mississippi Immigrant Rights Alliance (MIRA) recovered more than $700,000 worth of unpaid wages from Gulf Coast contractors. It needs to sustain its organizational momentum, for while the large influx of Latinos creates tensions with White and African American workers in the region,[55] the grounds for longer-term coalitions should not be ruled out. As Brian Kwoba[56] argues, the demonstrations, walk-outs, boycotts, marches, work-stoppages, and protests of several weeks in April and May 2006 not only inspire resistance to reactionary government legislation, they may also signal the birth of a new Left in the face of a lackluster antiwar movement despite the continued marginalization of Arabs, Muslims, and Palestinians; the stultifying silence from liberal feminist organizations after South Dakota's abortion ban; and the absence of a national movement around justice for Katrina's survivors. If these failings of the Left are unfortunate, the new predominantly working-class immigrant rights movement can rejuvenate the Left by providing an even wider basis for struggle by expanding the resistance to Jim Crow–level segregation and racism (against migrant workers), rejecting imperialist wars whose victims are predominantly working class, and reversing the attacks on reproductive rights of predominantly poor and working-class women, particularly

Latinas. This wider base must relate to the African American struggle for justice on the basis of unity against racism and resistance to the militarization of the prison-industrial complex. If "the race to incarcerate began in the 1970s at a time when states faced comparably dire financial straits," this carceral expansion has sustained itself by becoming leaner and meaner. "One of the most mean-spirited budget moves has been reducing the amount and quality of food served to people in prison." As Mary Gottschalk argues, the expansion of the carceral complex is first and foremost a problem of human rights violations and activists need to present the carceral state as an unprecedented civil rights issue,[57] especially in the Gulf Coast states which have some of the highest incarceration rates in the country.

I want to conclude by pointing out at least one other track that needs alignment with the movements discussed previously. On this track are the movements situated against the effects of the financial expansion of the late twentieth century that after Seattle 1999 converged to become a "movement of movements" in their struggles against different forms of privatization of the global commons. As Paul Ortiz notes, "New Orleans is ever more firmly joined with Chiapas, South Africa, Havana, South Korea, and other locations as sites of struggle over the future of humanity,"[58] and perhaps New Orleans should be the site of the next World Social Forum.

NOTES

1. This is a draft version of a paper presented on Monday September 19, 2005, at the St. Lawrence University Faculty Forum on the similarities between the processes at work in the "two Gulfs." A modified version was presented at the Global Studies Association conference in May 2006. This version was developed during a sabbatical in fall 2006 supported by St. Lawrence University.

2. Mike Davis, "Poor, Black and Left Behind: Before Killer Katrina, There Was Ivan the Terrible," *LA Weekly News*, September 8, 2005, http://www.laweekly.com/ink/05/42/after-davis.php. Davis examined the aftermath of 2004 Hurricane Ivan in New Orleans in terms that bear striking similarity with the predicament of poor African American evacuees in the aftermath of the 2005 Hurricane Katrina. In 2004, he writes, affluent Whites "fled the Big Easy in their SUVs, while the old and car-less—mainly Black—were left behind in their below-sea-level shotgun shacks and aging tenements to face the watery wrath."

3. Emmanuel Todd, "The Specter of a Soviet-style Crisis," *Le Figaro*, September 12, 2005, http://www.truthout.org/docs_2005/091205H.shtml.

4. David Harvey uses this concept, borrowed from Gillian Hart. Harvey's use of "accumulation by dispossession" highlights the ways in which contemporary neo-liberalism deploys privatization or the enclosure of the global commons as a means of overcoming the persistent crisis of over-accumulation since the 1970s. However, accumulation

by dispossession is a historically recurring feature of world capitalism, elaborated in Giovanni Arrighi's theoretical and historical investigation of "financial expansions" (which are also necessarily, moments of "accumulation by dispossession") over the *longue durée* (over 700 years) of world capitalist accumulation. See David Harvey, *The New Imperialism* (Oxford: Oxford University Press, 2003), which follows the world historical and theoretical synthesis of Giovanni Arrighi's *The Long Twentieth Century: Money, Power and the Origins of Our Times* (New York: Verso 1994).

5. As Mike Davis points out, New Orleans's "complex history and social geography have been reduced to a cartoon of a vast slum inhabited by an alternately criminal or helpless underclass, whose salvation is the kindness of strangers in other, whiter cities" ("Who is Killing New Orleans?" *The Nation*, April 10, 2006: 14).

6. See Karl Polanyi, *The Great Transformation* (Boston: Beacon Press, 1957), for an elaboration of mechanisms of "self-protecting society" against the "self-regulating markets" unleashed by the late-eighteenth-century Industrial Revolution.

7. Manning Marable, *Race, Reform, and Rebellion: The Second Reconstruction in Black America, 1945–1990* (Jackson: University Press of Mississippi, 1991), 229–30. After the defeat of the slaveholding South in the North-South Civil War and the creation of a "united" nation, Black Reconstruction projects from the late 1860s promoted some improvements in the lives of newly emancipated African Americans. However, most Blacks continued to face "near slavery" without the chains. From the late 1860s to the 1880s, "most blacks were severely hampered from economic advancement because of recurring depressions in New Orleans' economy, as well as pervasive racial discrimination." White reaction to Black Reconstruction triumphed in the "Compromise of 1877" with the Union government which in effect betrayed Black struggles for democracy by allowing Klan terrorism to restore the power of slaveholding oligarchies across the South. See Kristen Lavelle and Joe Feagin, "Hurricane Katrina: The Race and Class Debate," *Monthly Review*, 58, no. 3 (July/August 2006): 55–56. Endemic unemployment, few and weak labor unions, resurgent White supremacist projects, and coerced transformation of free Blacks into sharecroppers in the Yazoo-Mississippi Delta of cotton plantations, ensured not only continuation of slavery by other means, but also the terrible vulnerability of Blacks to persistent floods in the Mississippi River valley. If Black labor constructed the levees in the lower Mississippi river delta and labored on the cotton plantations of the Deep South, they were also the most vulnerable to the regular floods, like the great 1927 flood, that deluged the lives of the laboring poor. See John Barry, *Rising Tide: The Great Mississippi Flood of 1927 and How It Changed America* (New York: Simon and Schuster, 1998).

8. If the first Black Reconstruction project (1865–1877) of the nineteenth century was stultified during the high period of classical liberalism, imperialism, industrial depression, and financial expansion of the 1870s, the failure of the second Reconstruction (1970–2000) is similarly grounded in the late-twentieth-century period of neoliberalism and financialization.

9. Giovanni Arrighi, *The Long Twentieth Century*.

10. The neoliberal turn since the 1970s appears to mark a spatial disjuncture between the capitalist logic of power (the pursuit of wealth as an end in itself) and the

territorial logic of power (represented by war-making and territorial expansion as an end in itself). If the material expansion during the first half of the twentieth century was spearheaded by a combination of U.S.-led governmental and transnational business enterprises that represented the dialectical intertwining of capitalist and territorial logics of power, the neoliberal switch to financial expansion in the 1980s represents a spatial disjuncture between the territorial logic—represented by the proxy wars of the 1980s and the "open wars" of the 1990s, followed by U.S. unilateralism (the new imperialism) at the turn of the millennium—and the capitalist logic—represented by the rise of East Asia as the epicenter of world liquidity. See for instance Arrighi, *The Long Twentieth Century*. Neoliberalism is the name for the newly dominating tendencies emerging out of the crisis of over-accumulated capital relative to the exhaustion of the U.S.-led global New Deal developmental path. These tendencies are mirrored in the accumulating indebtedness of the U.S. state and economy, the U.S.-sponsored global withdrawal of developmental states from welfare-oriented roles, and the worldwide privatization of national spaces through highly mobile finance and speculative capital in a more general context of enclosure of the global commons.

11. Todd, "The Specter of a Soviet-style Crisis."

12. The U.S. State Department's "Iraq Travel Website" lists twenty firms that offer the three crucial functions performed by PMFs: military support, military training and advice, and tactical military roles. As Singer notes, the website does not mention Blackwater USA (BW) with its 15,000 private personnel; BW has at least 30–50 soldiers killed in action, including the military contractors hung on a bridge in Fallujah by the Iraqi resistance. Global Risks has 1,000 employees in Iraq including 500 Nepali Gurkhas and 500 Fijian soldiers. The names in the website include Armor Group, Baghdad Fire and Security, Control Risks Group, Custer Battles, Diligence Middle East, Erinys Iraq Ltd., etc. See Peter Singer, "Warriors for Hire in Iraq," April 15, 2004, http://www.brookings.edu/views/articles/fellows/singer20040415.htm.

13. Peter Singer, "Outsourcing the War," April 16, 2004, http://www.brookings.edu/views/articles/fellows/singer20040416.htm.

14. Rorry Carroll and Julian Borger, "Iraq Rebuilding Under Threat as U.S. Runs out of Money," *Guardian,* September 9, 2005, http://www.guardian.co.uk/international/story/0,,1566019,00.html. I am indebted to the work of Tom Engelhardt and Nick Turse, "Corporations of the Whirlwind," Tomdispatch.com, September 12, 2005, available at http://www.tomdispatch.com/index.mhtml?pid=21843, one of the earliest and most incisive sources on the connections between Baghdad and New Orleans.

15. Gulf Coast Reconstruction Watch (GCRW), *One Year After Katrina: The State of New Orleans and the Gulf Coast* (Institute for Southern Studies/Southern Exposure, August 2006: 34–38), http://www.reconstructionwatch.org/images/One_Year_After/pdf.

16. Blackwater USA, "Press Releases," http://www.blackwaterusa.com/press/, October 2004–November 2005; Alan Maas, "A Mercenary Army: Jeremy Scahill on Blackwater in New Orleans," *Counterpunch,* June 2, 2006, http://www.counterpunch.org/maass06022006.html.

17. See GCRW, 33.

18. The GO Zone program is modeled after the Liberty Zone program created to help New York city rebound after the 9/11 attacks, though the Government Accountability Office (GAO) concluded in 2004 that its benefits to New Yorkers were unclear and unknown.

19. In Alabama, proposals by new firms do not have to show any link with hurricane recovery. In Louisiana, the Shaw Group was among the first to get the green light for a new office building and office garage. In Mississippi, less than 50 percent of the 90 projects granted preliminary approval by the Mississippi Business Finance Corporation are in the three counties raked hardest by Katrina. See GCRW, 39–40.

20. Harrah's Entertainment is investing $1 billion in a casino-cum-hotel complex in Biloxi, and Donald Trump's Entertainment Resorts Inc. is committing huge investments to casinos in Hancock County along Interstate 10 in Mississippi. See GCRW, 40.

21. A review of government testimonies and documents by Gulf Coast Reconstruction Watch estimates corporate fraud from Hurricane Katrina contracts to the tune of at least $136.7 million, while government investigators point out that $428.7 million worth of contracts were plagued by problems of improper oversight and misappropriations. See GCRW, 33–35.

22. On September 18 FEMA awarded $5.2 million to Lighthouse Disaster Relief (owned by pastor Gary Heldreth) for setting up a base camp to house and feed in the predominantly White St. Bernard Parish for 1,000 emergency workers (first responders)—with disastrous results. A recent GAO study estimates improper or fraudulent payments related to Hurricane Katrina and Rita to the tune of $1.4 billion. See GCRW, 40.

23. The United States dominates global weapons sales signing deals worth $12.4 billion in 2004, or 33.5 percent of all contracts worldwide. The U.S. share of arms contracts with Southern nation-states was worth $6.9 billion or 31.6 percent of all such deals in 2004. See Thom Shanker, "Weapons Sales Worldwide Rise to Highest Level Since 2000," *New York Times,* August 30, 2005.

24. If the rest of the world no longer readily accepts the U.S. claim to represent and protect global freedom, free markets, and democracy, it is due in part to the spectacular (if irregular) antiwar movement launched on February 2003. It is also an outcome of the long-term dependence of the United States on the productive capacities of its protectorates in Europe (Germany in particular) and East Asia, as well as an increasingly autonomous and democratizing global South. The transformation of the United States into an empire of consumption is a development closely related to the development of oligarchic tendencies in the United States, itself an outcome of the financial expansion of the 1980s. To protect its empire of consumption, the United States increasingly resorts to various forms of theatrical micro-militarism. However, the extent and reach of U.S. power through its network of worldwide military bases disguises its real vulnerabilities.

25. North Korea's nuclear capabilities today clearly limit U.S. capacities to unilaterally police the rest of the world, and the Iranian intransigence to yield to pressures to abandon nuclear projects highlights again these limits to U.S. power, as does the Pyrrhic victory of Hezbollah against Israeli attacks on Lebanese civilians during mid-July 2006.

26. For the distinction between national and international terrorism, see Michael Mann, *Incoherent Empire* (New York: Verso, 2003).

27. Todd, "The Specter of a Soviet-style Crisis."

28. Vinay Lal, "New Orleans:The Big Easy and the Big Shame," *Economic and Political Weekly* (September 17, 2005): 4099–4100.

29. Todd, "The Specter of a Soviet-style Crisis."

30. Todd was one of the very few social scientists to predict the collapse of the Soviet system on the basis of increases in its rates of infant mortality during 1970–1974. In *After the Empire: The Breakdown of the American Order* published in 2003, Todd predicted an inevitable decline of the U.S. system based as it is on military expansionism. In that work Todd anticipates a 15–20 percent decline in living standards in the U.S. in the medium-term.

31. Associated Press, "U.S. Poverty Rate Remains Unchanged," *New York Times,* August 30, 2006.

32. Stephen Jackson, "Un/natural Disasters, Here and There," *Social Science Research Council*, 2005, http://understandingkatrina.ssrc.org/Jackson/pf/.

33. Todd, "The Specter of a Soviet-style Crisis."

34. Mike Davis, "Poor, Black and Left Behind: Before Killer Katrina, There Was Ivan the Terrible," *LA Weekly News*, September 8, 2005, http://www.laweekly.com/ink/05/42/after-davis.php.

35. Manning Marable, *How Capitalism Underdeveloped Black America* (Boston: South End Press), 107–108.

36. Michel Foucault, *Society Must Be Defended* (New York, Picador, 2003) 254–60.

37. This is despite President Bush's promise on the evening of September 15, 2005, in a dark and silent French Quarter in New Orleans: "We will do what it takes, we will stay as long as it takes, to help citizens rebuild their communities and their lives." Cited in Dan Baum, "The Lost Year: Behind the Failure to Rebuild," *The New Yorker,* August 21, 2006, 47–48.

38. Mike Davis, "Who Is Killing New Orleans?" *The Nation,* April 10, 2006, 11.

39. By early October business owners were hiring cheap Mexican and Hispanic labor outside of New Orleans to gut houses and clear fallen trees from the streets. On October 4th the AFL-CIO and the NAACP denounced business owners who were hiring non-union workers from out of state. Seven weeks after the storm, the Louisiana Congressman, Richard Baker, introduced a bill to finance reconstruction throughout the state (the "eighty-billion-dollar buyout" in local mythology). If the Baker Plan "made New Orleans the greatest urban-revival opportunity in recent American history," the planners were up against "New Orleanians' uncommon fondness for the old one." Governor Kathleen Blanco created a commission of her own called the Louisiana Recovery Authority spearheaded by Donald Bollinger, a believer in "Katrina-as-opportunity," and who believed that Nagin's commission should deal with the city's blighted neighborhoods by engineering them off the map. He supported a radical plan that would sprinkle the poor throughout the middle class, in the hope that they would absorb a work ethic. See Dan Baum, "The Lost Year: Behind the Failure to Rebuild," *The New Yorker*, August 21, 2006, 50–52.

40. The mandate is to change "the very social fabric of a nation" through rapid-response teams made up of private companies, nongovernmental organizations, and members of think-tanks, so that "democratic and market-oriented" states emerge out of mass societal transformation. See Naomi Klein, "The Rise of Disaster Capitalism," *The Nation,* April 14, 2005, http://www.thenation.com/doc/20050502/klein.

41. See Mark Duffield, *Global Governance and the New Wars: The Merging of Development and Security* (London: Zed Books, 2001).

42. East Carroll Parish is a forlorn jurisdiction of 8,700 people along the Mississippi River in remote northeastern Louisiana; it has one of the highest incarceration rates in the state, and it is the poorest parish in the state. Prisoners provide unpaid labor in the production-line room of pepper-sauce plants, fix houses, clear undergrowth from roadsides, and pick up trash. See Nossiter's article in *The New York Times,* July 2006.

43. On July 17, 2006, Reverend Lois Dejean of the Gert Town Revival Initiative in a testimony delivered to the United Nations Committee on Human Rights charged the U.S. government with negligence and discrimination in its response to Hurricane Katrina. See GCRW, 83–87.

44. As William Quigley notes in the Mardi Gras Report, "There is not a sign outside of New Orleans saying, 'If you are poor, sick, elderly, disabled, a child or Afro-American, you cannot return.' But there might as well be." See GCRW, 4.

45. Maureen Dowd, "The United States of Shame," *The New York Times,* September 3, 2005.

46. John Barry, *Rising Tide: the Great Mississippi Flood of 1927 and How it Changed America* (New York: Simon and Schuster, 1998), 27, 90–92.

47. Andrew Ward, "In Harm's Way: How America's Rush to the Coast Is Driving up the Cost of Hurricanes," *Financial Times,* June 5, 2006, 13.

48. Plans to close the thirty-six-foot deep waterway called the Mississippi River Gulf Outlet (MRGO)—the seventy-six mile shipping shortcut from New Orleans's inner harbor to the Gulf that boosted Katrina's storm surge by two feet into the city—are only just underway. The ACE constructed MRGO in 1965 to allow ships to avoid the twists and turns of the Mississippi and to accommodate deep-draft vessels that could not fit through the Industrial Canal's locks. Since wetlands help to reduce storm surge, absorb wave energy, and lessen the effects of daily wave action, it makes Louisiana vulnerable. Human activity converts wetlands into open water, and high levees worsen wetland losses by preventing the Mississippi from overflowing its banks and depositing fresh sediments. Canals dug in the wetlands—often connected to offshore oil and gas operations—erode marshes and provide a conduit for sea water that kills vegetation needed to stabilize the land. At the current rate of loss of coastal wetlands, an additional 800,000 acres will disappear by 2040. Even before Katrina it was estimated that it would take $14 billion and thirty years to repair Louisiana's wetlands and barrier islands. But the funds for the implementation of this project have not yet been appropriated. Inadequate governmental coordination of flood control programs and levee systems leaves the Gulf region at risk of another disaster. See GCRW, 75–80.

49. See GCRW, 6; 13. The church-based and mobile clinics of the Latino Health Outreach Project in New Orleans serve as both a community-organizing tool (sometimes against harassment by police and immigration officials) and a provider of health

care services for the thousands of Latino immigrant workers drawn to reconstruction work in the region as day laborers. See GCRW, 60.

50. As a construction and demolition (C&D) site, Chef Menteur was not required to have a protective liner. Neighborhood and environmental advocates point out that the Louisiana Department of Environment Quality expanded the definition of "C&D Debris" to include hazardous materials (like chemically treated wood) that contaminates ground and surface water supplies for New Orleans East. Many of the 1,000 Vietnamese Americans in the Village de l'Est use an adjacent canal to irrigate vegetable gardens. Louisiana Environmental Action Network and the Sierra Club filed suit against the state in August claiming regulators lacked authority to permit the wastes going into C&D landfills. Chef Menteur and Old Gentilly in New Orleans East and Industrial Pipe in Plaquemines Parish were the facilities cited in the suit. Although the struggle is not over, Chef Menteur has been closed down. See GCRW, 51.

51. The movement won a class settlement (*Kirk vs. City of New Orleans*)—brought by Advancement Project, Loyola Law Clinic, and Tracie Washington that stopped Mayor Nagin's bulldozers from destroying some 2,500 heavily damaged homes as part of the "Bring Back New Orleans" (December 2005) plan for redevelopment of New Orleans. See GCRW, 16–17.

52. GCRW, 11.

53. Naomi Klein, "Let the People Rebuild New Orleans," *The Nation,* September 8, 2005, http://www.thenation.com/doc/20050926/klein.

54. See GCRW, 7.

55. Latino immigrants were recruited by contractors across the country on the promise of fair pay, free rent, and steady jobs, and assembled in places like "Tent City" in New Orleans city park, but it turned out that these workers had to pay $300 as rent for living in tents which they had to purchase, they got no electricity, and they had to pay $5 for cold showers.

56. Brian Kwoba, "Immigrant Rights: Birth of a New Left?," *Z-Net,* May 14, 2006, http://www.zmag.org/content/showarticle.cfm?ItemID=10261.

57. Marie Gottschalk, *The Prison and the Gallows: The Politics of Mass Incarceration in America* (New York: Cambridge University Press, 2006), 241–48.

58. Paul Ortiz, "The New Battle for New Orleans," in *Hurricane Katrina: Response and Responsibilities*, ed. John Brown Childs (Santa Cruz, California, 2005), 3.

Chapter Twelve

Running Faster Next Time

Blacks and Homeland Security

Everette B. Penn

> You simply get chills every time you see these poor individuals . . . so many of these people . . . are so poor and they are so Black, and this is going to raise lots of questions for people who are watching this story unfold.
>
> —Wolf Blitzer[1]

Arguably there have been few events since the Civil Rights Movement that have galvanized the Black population of the United States more than Hurricane Katrina, specifically the horrific sights of the residents of New Orleans in late August and early September of 2005. The events surrounding Hurricane Katrina and the subsequent breakage of the levee system around the city of New Orleans exposed the vulnerability of the U.S. homeland security system and how these shortcomings directly affected Blacks in the country. Hurricane Katrina awoke the Department of Homeland Security to see beyond the tragedy of September 11, 2001, and terrorism to evolve into an all-hazards department moving to be better prepared for all natural and manmade disasters.

This chapter presents an overview of lessons learned from the federal response to Hurricane Katrina,[2] and issues, controversies, and future threats to the homeland as related to the Black population in the United States. The thesis of the chapter is that homeland security is first a *local* responsibility and Blacks in the United States should take personal responsibility for their own preparedness and safety.

THE STORM AND ITS AFTERMATH

On Tuesday, August 23, 2005, Tropical Depression Twelve formed off the coast of the Bahamas. Wednesday, the storm strengthened and was given the name Katrina, as the eleventh-named storm for the 2005 hurricane season. By Friday, August 26, the storm passed over southern Florida and preparations began for hurricane-type winds and destruction in Alabama, Louisiana, and Mississippi. The next day, as the storm moved west, people in Katrina's projected path were told to evacuate. Sunday, August 28, saw the storm develop into a Category IV (winds 131–155 mph) and briefly a Category V (winds greater than 155 mph). The National Hurricane Center advised that the levees in New Orleans could be overtopped by Lake Ponchartrain. Speaking about New Orleans, the warning stated: "Most of the area will be uninhabitable for weeks . . . perhaps longer . . . Water shortages will make human suffering incredible by modern standards."[3]

By the afternoon of the 28th, 1.2 million persons had been evacuated from Louisiana and Mississippi. This consisted of about 92 percent of the persons in the predicted path. Still, tens of thousands of the most vulnerable people remained in areas most threatened by the approaching hurricane.[4] At 6:10 A.M. CDT, Monday, August 29, in Plaquemines Parish (just east of New Orleans), Hurricane Katrina hit landfall as a powerful Category III Storm. A storm surge of twenty-seven feet was created in Louisiana and Mississippi causing six to twelve miles of inland flooding. In New Orleans high-rise buildings suffered blown-out windows and the Louisiana Superdome (where over ten thousand people had found shelter) had whole sections of its roof blown off.[5] New Orleans Mayor Ray Nagin reported the city was without primary and secondary power sources as well as sewerage, draining, communication, and power services.[6] The surge of water then caused the overtopping and breaching of the massive 350-mile levee system in several locations. "It was these overtoppings and breaches of the levee system that led to the catastrophic flooding of New Orleans."[7]

The aftermath of Hurricane Katrina and the breach of the levee system was the most destructive natural disaster in U.S. history. The official death and damage report from the federal government report on Hurricane Katrina is:

- 1,330 people dead
- 96 billion dollars in damage
- 1.1 million people over the age of sixteen evacuated
- 770,000 people displaced
- 300,000 homes destroyed

- 118 million cubic yards of debris
- 6 oil spills resulting in 7.4 million gallons of oil released into the Gulf of Mexico.

As hundreds of hours of media time were dedicated to Hurricane Katrina, a question developed: Why did people stay in New Orleans knowing a hurricane was approaching? Research examining the evacuation question is perplexing in its findings. One year before Hurricane Katrina, in 2004, research was conducted on the subject of evacuation behavior in light of an approaching hurricane. Using 400 New Orleans residents, findings indicated race and income were not the most significant variables determining who would and would not evacuate; rather, storm-specific facts and who delivered the message (with Blacks giving more trust to information coming from Black leaders) were found to have the greatest affect on evacuating.[8] Research with Black Houstonians revealed that most thought disaster-related messages were "too confusing." In the same research, 55 percent believed the government uses disasters as an excuse to remove poor and minority people from neighborhoods for future redeveloping of areas for the wealthy.[9] Other research indicates because Blacks may have large extended families the choice to leave is difficult and perhaps logistically impossible due to the lack of transportation and persons in ill health who are not easily mobile.[10] For those who did evacuate, cities such as Atlanta, Baton Rouge, Dallas, and Houston became their new home.

The city of Houston (350 miles west of New Orleans) received over 200,000 displaced New Orleans residents.[11] It was soon publicized throughout the Houston media that these "guests" from New Orleans were predominately poor Blacks involved in crime. The outpouring of support and hospitality soon turned to hostility and racial jokes as Houstonians also became aware of an increase in crime that correlated with the arrival of the displaced New Orleans residents. Houston radio programs labeled the guests as "FEMA Rats," and it was not unusual to hear statements such as "Killers: I hear they kill like 10, 15 people a night," "Go home niggers," and "Go home and drown in some Katrina water."[12] Research on the subject has concluded that some crime did increase in Houston but a combination of many variables were involved, including increase in population, reduced police force, annual spike in crime during the months of November and December, and a steady increase in crime which started before the arrival of any New Orleans residents.[13]

Almost immediately the disaster of Hurricane Katrina took on a racial tone. Perhaps it was the images of despondent African Americans in and around the Louisiana Superdome and New Orleans Convention Center. Perhaps it was

Blitzer's "too Black" statement, or rapper Kanye West's criticism of the President Bush administration during the *Concert for Hurricane Relief* telethon stating: "I hate the way they portray us in the media. You see a Black family, it says 'They're looting.' You see a white family, it says, 'They are looking for food.' . . . George Bush doesn't care about black people."[14] The aftermath of Hurricane Katrina continue to resonate with racial tones as the story of the Danziger Bridge shooting unfolds. The event that occurred on September 4, 2005, involved several African Americans being gunned downed by mostly White New Orleans police officers responding to a call of "two officers down." Seven officers rushed to the scene. Police stated upon arrival on the scene four people were shooting at them from the base of the bridge. Officers returned fire. When the shooting stopped two Blacks were killed (including a mentally retarded man shot in the back), two were maimed, and another two were injured.[15] First-degree murder charges—a potential death penalty offense—are currently pending against four of the officers involved.[16] Additionally, the lack of any mention of the Gulf Region in President Bush's 2007 *State of the Union Address,* while $110.6 billion in federal aid has been provided to the region[17] as compared to $400 billion spent on the Iraq War (with estimates as high as $2 trillion for the final cost of the U.S. involvement in Iraq),[18] provides constant consternation about Hurricane Katrina. The above examples and many others have turned the response or lack of a response from government agencies into an indictment of the U.S. federal government, leaving Blacks marginalized as they were unprepared as well as unprotected to overcome the devastation of the breakage of the levee system in New Orleans.

The Federal Response to Hurricane Katrina: Lessons Learned listed 125 specific recommendations from its four-month review. These recommendations stemmed from seventeen Hurricane Katrina Critical Challenges including:

1. National Preparedness;
2. Integrated Use of Military Capabilities;
3. Communications;
4. Logistics and Evacuations;
5. Search and Rescue;
6. Public Safety and Security;
7. Public Health and Medical Support;
8. Human Services;
9. Mass Care and Housing;
10. Public Communications;
11. Critical Infrastructure and Impact Assessment;

12. Environmental Hazards and Debris Removal;
13. Foreign Assistance;
14. Non-Governmental Aid;
15. Training, Exercises, and Lessons Learned;
16. Homeland Security Professional Development and Education; and
17. Citizens and Community Preparedness.

A detailed discussion about each of the seventeen areas is beyond the scope of this chapter but several conclusions can be made about the challenges and lessons learned including:

- There was insufficient planning and coordination at the local, state, and federal levels;
- There was a lack of basic operability and inoperability of communications;
- There were absences of plans, procedures, and policies to maintain order and civility;
- There was a need for improved coordination between business, non-governmental organizations, citizen groups, and government agencies responsible for the emergency response; and
- There was a lack of plans, procedures, and policies to coordinate the best use of foreign aid and support.

In conclusion, the report makes clear "the response to Hurricane Katrina fell short of the seamless, coordinated effort that had been envisioned by President Bush when he ordered the creation of a National Response Plan in February 2003."[19]

HOMELAND SECURITY

The National Response Plan (NRP) is the foundational document for homeland security in the United States. It provides a "playbook" of what should happen, coordination efforts, and resource and communication management guiding incidents of national significance, including terrorism, major disasters, and other emergencies. By definition it provides a comprehensive, national, all-hazards approach to domestic-incident management. Working through the National Incident Management System (NIMS) the NRP provides the structure for command, communication, coordination, and control of an incident on a field, regional, and national level through all points of an incident including prevention, preparedness, response, and recovery.[20] The fluid document is constantly evolving as the newest changes were published in May of 2006.[21]

Securing the U.S. homeland is a complexity of agencies, laws, policies, procedures, practices, and, most important, people. Although the term has become a part of the U.S. vocabulary since the events of September 11, 2001, in reality the defense of the U.S. homeland has its roots long before the tragic events in New York City, Washington, D.C., andwestern Pennsylvania.

The Department of Homeland Security (DHS) was created out of the Homeland Security Act of 2002. DHS has the following primary missions:

• To prevent terrorists acts within the United States;
• To reduce the vulnerability of the United States to terrorism at home;
• To minimize the damage and assist in the recovery from terrorists attacks that occur;
• To act as the focal point regarding natural and human-caused crises and emergency planning.[22]

The DHS engulfed twenty-two federal agencies to perform four major directorates, including Border and Transportation Security, Emergency Preparedness and Response, Science and Technology, and Information Analysis and Infrastructure Protection. DHS employs over 180,000 persons, making it one of the largest federal departments of the U.S. government.[23]

Stemming from the terrorist acts of September 11, 2001, the complexity of interagency cooperation emerged as the primary task to thwart terrorist acts of the future. In fact, three of the four mission directives that created the DHS address terrorism. It is the last directive which states the DHS will act as the "focal point" for other crises. When comparing natural disasters to terrorism in the United States the total human and financial loss of natural disasters far exceeds terrorist acts as found in Table 12.1. The estimated loss of lives from September 11, 2001, was 2,900 as compared to 1,330 from Hurricane Katrina. When property loss is compared, Hurricane Katrina dwarfs September 11, with a 96-billion-dollar loss verses 19 billion dollars for September 11. What also should be observed from the table is that the loss of human lives has gone down significantly for natural disasters, yet the property losses have greatly increased. Additionally, natural disasters of hurricanes, floods, and earthquakes occur more frequently than terrorist acts in the United States.

Since terrorism has the attention of the American public it is of interest to understand why it occurs and its early history in the United States. Many definitions exist for the term but its foundation is in differences of ideology between peoples. The cliché "One man's terrorist is another man's freedom fighter" adds clarity to the term as a small and committed group opposes the

Table 12.1. Selected U.S. Disasters Causing the Most Death and Damage to Property 1900–2005

Disaster	Year	Property Loss 2005 Dollars	Estimated Deaths
Galveston Hurricane	1900	1 billion	8,000
San Francisco Earthquake and Fire	1906	5 billion	5,000
Atlantic-Gulf Hurricane	1919	Less than 1 billion	500
Mississippi Floods	1927	3 billion	200
Hurricane San Felipe and Okeechobee Flood	1928	Less than 1 billion	2,800
Hurricane Camille	1969	6 billion	340
Hurricane Hugo	1989	11 billion	100
Hurricane Andrew	1992	33 billion	70
September 11, 2001, Terrorist Attacks	2001	19 billion	2,900
Hurricanes Charley, Frances, Ivan, and Jeanne	2004	46 billion	200
Hurricane Katrina	2005	96 billion	1,330

Data Source: Frances Townsend, *The Federal Response to Hurricane Katrina: Lessons Learned* (Washington, D.C.: White House, 2006), http://www.whitehouse.gov/reports/katrina-lessons-learned.pdf.

dominance of a more powerful group through guerrilla warfare, media influence, and fear.[24]

When studying the first incidences of terrorism in the newly formed United States, issues of class, race, and economics dominate the clash of peoples. The very principles for which the Americas were settled led to terrorist acts against Native American people. American Exceptionalism and Manifest Destiny fostered a spirit in White Americans to expand from the Atlantic seaboard to the Pacific Ocean. This belief resulted in the displacement of Native American tribes through the use of beatings, indiscriminate slaughter, torture, and intimidation.[25]

After the Civil War, the emancipation of African slaves in the United States, along with the Fourteenth Amendment, which granted citizenship to the former slaves, sprung the creation of arguably the most horrific domestic terrorist organization in the United States, the Ku Klux Klan. From the mid-1800s to today, the Ku Klux Klan has used tactics such as lynchings, bombings, burning of homes, violence, brutality, racism, and cross burning to terrorize opposed groups, primarily African Americans. "The Klan operated at night and was known as the Invisible Empire. Members would inflict vengeance on black citizens by breaking into their houses at night, dragging them from their beds, torturing them, burning their homes and stealing their possessions."[26] As recently as 2003 the U.S. Supreme Court ruled that cross burning with the "intent to intimidate" was unconstitutional because of its history of conveying a message of hate, fear, and intimidation to African Americans.[27]

Thus, a history of terrorist acts on United States soil is not unique to Americans, as further examples include the "Red Scare" in the early 1900s, hate crimes, and other acts against peoples and groups. With such a history Black Americans should be ever vigilant in being prepared for domestic as well as international terrorist acts. "Running faster next time" involves coordination at all levels of the government, but specifically at the local level with individual readiness to respond and evade death and large-scale destruction in response to a human-made or natural emergency event.

RUNNING FASTER NEXT TIME

An ABC News Poll conducted the first week of September 2005 indicated 75 percent of Americans blamed the unpreparedness of the state of Louisiana as well as New Orleans for the poor response to Hurricane Katrina. This compared with 67 percent of the respondents blaming the federal government and 44 percent blaming President Bush's leadership.[28] The findings of this report echo the intent and directives of the DHS that homeland security is a local responsibility. States and local governments assume the first and foremost line of defense for homeland security threats.[29] With this premise, all Americans, specifically the poor, need to be actively involved in their community as well as maintain a preparedness for their families in order to survive the next homeland security emergency.

In order to aid citizens' preparedness the DHS has devised the Color-Coded Threat Level System. The purpose is to alert citizens and ready government agencies at the federal, state, and local levels. The levels rise from Green being the lowest risk of a threat through Blue, Yellow, Orange, and Red, with Red noting a severe risk of a threat is highly possible.[30] Raising the threat level has economic, physical, and psychological effects because people respond to fear, not risk.[31] Since its inception in March of 2002, the system has gone to Red only once during August 10–13, 2006, due to a plot to down U.S. bound flights over the Atlantic Ocean leaving the United Kingdom.[32]

The damage caused by Hurricane Katrina alone was and continues to be a reminder about the awesome power of *natural* threats to the United States. But future threats will be just as ominous. Three likely disaster scenarios from the DHS include the explosion of a nuclear device, pandemic influenza, and a major earthquake. Estimates include deaths ranging from 1,500 to over 10,000 for each of these scenarios. Damage in 2005 dollars is predicted to be over 87 billion dollars.[33] One of the worst-case scenarios is the outbreak of a pandemic influenza. Using historical data from the three previous outbreaks in the twentieth century it is estimated a modern pandemic outbreak could lead to 200,000 to 2 million deaths in the United States alone.[34] These and other likely scenarios are most often predicted to occur in highly urban areas of the country, specifically large cities such as New York, Los Angeles, Chicago, Washington, D.C., Philadelphia, and Houston. In common with these high-risk cities is a large population of Black citizens. Thus, the likelihood of large numbers of Blacks being involved in the next homeland security event is high, and lends support for African Americans being vigilant in their preparedness at the local and individual levels.

"Running faster" from the next homeland security event is two-fold. First, local involvement by Blacks at the city and county level is essential. Second, individual preparedness for family members and one's own personal safety are necessary. In his 2002 *State of the Union Address,* President Bush called for every American to commit at least two years (4,000 hours) of service over the rest of his or her lifetime. This call gave life to the USA Freedom Corps, which has a homeland security focus: response in cases of crisis, rebuilding communities, and extending American compassion throughout the world.[35]

Broad in scope, the request responds to the need for Americans to be actively involved in defending the homeland of the United States in their own communities. First responders, such as police officers, firefighters, and public works employees are essential, but history has shown when a homeland security disaster takes place it is not a law enforcement officer, emergency medical technician, firefighter, or public works employee who is the first person on the scene; rather it is the U.S. citizen who sees the event unfold, calls for help, runs to save others, and provides information to emergency personnel. Thus, it is imperative that Black Americans are well informed as well as trained about protecting from and responding to emergencies in their own communities.

The two primary disaster volunteer organizations found throughout the United States are the Citizens Corps and the Community Emergency Response Team. Citizens Corps stems from the need to capture the human capital of the U.S. citizen. Around the country this grassroots organization encourages citizens to play an active role in homeland security. Its website lists 2,135 local Citizen Corps Councils serving 73 percent of the U.S. population. Its goal is to engage citizens in the prevention of, protection from, response to, and recovery from all potential hazards and threats.[36] A program under the Citizens Corps is the Community Emergency Response Team (CERT). Developed out of the California earthquake catastrophes in the mid-1980s, the concept came from the need to have trained civilians prepared to assist first responders. Through the Federal Emergency Management Agency (FEMA), the Emergency Management Institute, and the National Fire Academy, CERT training is available so citizens can be a ready force in their own communities.[37]

The Corporation for National and Community Service has a variety of additional opportunities for people of all ages to get involved and serve their community. For example, Senior Corps allows persons fifty-five and older to volunteer in their own community through a variety of programs. As the population of the United States grows older from 31.2 million in 1990 over the age of fifty-five to a projected 70 million in 2030, the link between the skills of seniors and defending the homeland will be strong.[38] These senior Americans, many whom have lived through World Wars, a Cold War, social conflict, and economic hardship, possess a myriad of skills and experience that can aid local governments and community organizations in achieving their homeland security goals.[39]

Finally, the Bush administration has also pushed the use of faith-based organizations as a means to respond to the needs of local communities. These faith-based organizations do not lose or modify their religious identity when receiving federal funds but may not use the funds for religious activity, and must conduct programming in areas separate from where religious activities are conducted.[40] The involvement of Blacks in churches and community organizations, as well as in local governments, is imperative. This community involvement strengthens social bonds, community affiliation, and identification. It allows the community to be an active agent in its own destiny rather than individuals without plans or protection for their own personal safety and quality of life.

An example of community organizing in New Orleans, which has had a direct result in producing a better life for New Orleans residents before and after Hurricane Katrina, is the Association of Community Organizations for Reform Now (ACORN). This international organization consisting of more than 350,000 members has become a voice for Katrina survivors by leading a rally in Washington, D.C., preventing the city of New Orleans from taking land through eminent domain in flood-damaged communities, gutting almost 2,000 homes to preserve them for later rebuilding, and working to create the "People's Plan" for the rebuilding of New Orleans's Ninth Ward. This plan will restore the community and enable former residents and business owners to return to New Orleans.[41]

Finally, family and individual preparedness depends on receiving information and responding to it effectively. On the *Ready.gov* website, plans and ideas are available on how to prepare self, business, and family for a disaster. The site stresses three forms of action: get a kit, make a plan, and be informed. Under "Get a Kit" is a list of items recommended to be included in a basic emergency supply kit. "Make a Plan" informs readers how important it is to be able to contact and gather family members who may be located at work, school, or daycare in time of an emergency. Helpful hints are provided in reference to maintaining communication and how information will be disseminated from government agencies. Finally, "Be Informed" provides a website listing of eighteen possible threats, ranging from biological threats to winter storms. Each threat provides information about what it is, the danger, and how to stay safe during the emergency. A final suggestion is that Americans commit a weekend to update phone numbers and emergency plans, and buy supplies so that each family can be best prepared for an emergency.

CONCLUSION

Sadly, it is inevitable that the United States will face another natural or human-made disaster. Floods, tornados, hurricanes, storms, earthquakes, and terrorism are common threats to the U.S. homeland. The question becomes: How well prepared are citizens to prevent, respond to, and recover from horrific events? Today's threats are too eminent to presume the federal government can and will be able to respond. History has provided support that the poor and Blacks face public policies, institutional arrangements, and domestic terrorism at greater numbers than other people of the United States.

As billions of dollars are available for governmental, civic, business, and community organizations in the name of homeland security, involvement has financial as well as personal safety implications. For Blacks to "run faster" next time, an activism must arise which learns from Hurricane Katrina and uses the same call to action as others have in the past: "Never Again!"

NOTES

1. Wolf Blitzer, "The Situation Room," September 1, 2005, http://transcripts.cnn.com/ Transcripts/0509/01/sitroom.02.html.

2. Frances Fragos Townsend, "The Federal Response to Hurricane Katrina: Lessons Learned," *The White House,* February 2006, www.whitehouse.gov/reports/katrina-lessons-learned.pdf. The 217-page document was prepared by Townsend, the assistant to the president for Homeland Security and Counterterrorism. The document was prepared in response to President Bush's September 15, 2005, request for a "comprehensive review of the Federal response to Hurricane Katrina so that the country could be better prepared for any challenge of nature or act of evil men."

3. U.S Department of Commerce, National Oceanic and Atmospheric Administration, National Weather Service, New Orleans/Baton Rouge Forecast Office, Slidell, LA, "Urgent Weather Message," August 28, 2005.

4. Townsend, "The Federal Response to Hurricane Katrina," 29.

5. Townsend, "The Federal Response to Hurricane Katrina," 34.

6. Ray Nagin, "Testimony Before a Hearing on Hurricane Katrina: Preparedness and Response by the State of Louisiana on December 14, 2005," House Select Committee to Investigate the Preparations for and Response to Hurricane Katrina, 109th Congress, 1st session, 3.

7. Townsend, "The Federal Response to Hurricane Katrina," 34. It is significant to note that the federal government report states the overtopping and breaches of the levee system led to the catastrophic flooding of New Orleans.

8. Randolph Burnside, "Leaving the Big Easy: An Examination of the Hurricane Evacuation Behavior of New Orleans Residents Before Hurricane Katrina," *Journal of Public Management and Social Policy* 12, no. 1 (2006): 49–61.

9. Franklin Jones, Carroll Robinson, Walter McCoy, Marva Johnson, Sean Herlihy, and Karen Callaghan, *The 2006 Houston Survey of African Americans* (Houston: Texas Southern University).

10. Burnside, "Leaving the Big Easy."

11. *Houston Chronicle,* "Katrina's Legacy: Hurricanes Routinely Reshape Coastlines, but This One Racially Altered the Gulf Coast Populations as Well," June 12, 2006, B6.

12. Trymaine Lee, "Evacuee Packed Houston Sees Jump in Crime," *Times-Picayune,* January 2, 2006, Metro Section, 1.

13. Everette B. Penn and Jaya Davis, "Hurricane Katrina: Crime and Race Issues in a Pre-Post Houston" (Unpublished manuscript, 2006).

14. Lisa DeMoraes, "Kanye West's Torrent of Criticism, Live on NBC," *Washington Post,* September 3, 2005.

15. John Burnett, "What Happened on New Orleans' Danziger Bridge?" *National Public Radio.*

16. Laura Maggi, "Danziger Officers Await DA's Decision: Jordan Could Seek Death Penalty for Four," *Times-Picayune,* January 20, 2007.

17. Department of Homeland Security, "Hurricane Katrina: What Government is Doing," www.dhs.gov/katrina.

18. The Iraq Study Group, James H. Baker, III, and Lee H. Hamilton, *The Iraq Study Group Report: The Way Forward—A New Approach* (New York: Vintage Books, 2006).

19. Townsend, "The Federal Response to Hurricane Katrina," 3.

20. Department of Homeland Security. *National Response Plan,* (Washington, D.C.: Department of Homeland Security, December 2004).

21. Department of Homeland Security, *National Response Plan.*

22. Homeland Security Act of 2002, Pub. Law 107–296, 116 Stat. 2135 (2002).

23. Department of Homeland Security, "History," www.dhs.gov.

24. James A. Fagin, *When Terrorism Strikes Home: Defending the United States* (Boston: Pearson/Allyn & Bacon, 2006).

25. Fagin, *When Terrorism Strikes Home.*

26. Fagin, *When Terrorism Strikes Home,* 35.

27. *Virginia v. Black,* 538 U.S., 343 (2003).

28. Gary Langer, "Poll: Bush Not Taking Brunt of Katrina Criticism," *ABC News,* September 12, 2005.

29. Townsend, "The Federal Response to Hurricane Katrina."

30. Department of Homeland Security, *National Response Plan.*

31. Gary S. Becker and Y. Rubinstein, "Fear and the Response to Terrorism: An Economic Analysis" (Paper presented at the first annual Threat Anticipation Workshop: Social Science Methods and Models, University of Chicago, April 7–9, 2005).

32. Department of Homeland Security, "Homeland Security Advisory System," www.dhs.gov.

33. Townsend, "The Federal Response to Hurricane Katrina."

34. Homeland Security Council. *National Strategy for Pandemic Influenza: Implementation Plan* (U.S. Government Printing Office: Washington, D.C., May 2006).

35. State of the Union 2002, *Online News Hour,* January 29, 2002.

36. The website www.citizencorps.gov even allows the user to input their own zip code to find the closest Citizen Corps Council in their area.

37. Community Emergency Response Team, "About CERT," www.citizencorps.gov/cert.

38. Michael J. Grabowski and Everette B. Penn, "The Blue and Gray: Partnerships of Police and Seniors in the Age of Homeland Security," *Journal of Homeland Security* (October 2003), at http://www.homelandsecurity.org/newjournal/articles/grabowski.html.

39. Grabowski and Penn, "The Blue and Gray."

40. Executive Order 13279, December 12, 2002.

41. ACORN, "Message from ACORN's National President," www.ACORN.org.

Conclusion
Hillary Potter

A significant number of independent groups of scholars took on the task of conceptualizing and researching the many implications of Hurricane Katrina from the first warning of the storm[1] through the present day. None of this book's contributors had intentionally set out to "chase storms" in order to carry out their research interests. To be sure, the scholars in this book are not hazards or disasters researchers, in the strict sense of the classification. The common thread among those who have presented their work here is their concentration on the relevance of race and ethnicity in social life and social processes. As evidenced throughout the preceding selections, race/ethnic relations and identity are alive in the United States, but are certainly not well. *Racing the Storm* demonstrates that racialized stereotypes continue to be a major factor in U.S. social, cultural, and political settings. Whether it was Katrina survivors, groups summoned to assist with the aftermath, or the nation of spectators, deleterious stereotypes prevailed about people of color (in particular, about African Americans), and affected the way in which others responded to a natural disaster, which, by many people's observations, resulted in unnatural consequences. The outcome of Katrina has found many—whether scholars, lay people, entertainers, or government officials—appalled by a course of events that seemed to go against how "we," as U.S. citizens, are expected to aid people in need. Arguably, however (and as purported throughout this volume), the racial make-up of many of those who were victims to Katrina caused a good portion of the U.S. populace to redefine the treatment to be afforded to certain individuals. It was this that brought the authors in this book into the fold of "disasters research." Not because of the disaster, per se, but because of what Katrina told us about the state of racial/ethnic identity politics and social interaction.

What are the lessons to be learned from the storm about disaster rescue and relief, specifically? Even though we are *not* disasters researchers, since Katrina did *begin* as a natural disaster, it is important to offer something to the interdisciplinary field of disasters research that necessarily considers concerns of disparity and discrimination. Indeed, previous research has already found that (1) people of color with fewer economic resources reside in homes that are not "disaster proof," (2) disaster warning information is sometimes dispersed in a racially disparate way, (3) emergency relief workers have exhibited insensitivity to the needs of people of color that fall outside of those considered "mainstream" needs, (4) poor people of color experience difficulty in recovering from the disaster due to their already disadvantaged status, and (5) there esists downward mobility of and deficient government assistance to poor people of color during the reconstruction, who have typically had to relocate away from the disaster-stricken area because of the immense damage to their already inadequate homes.[2] Out of the works presented in this volume, several recommendations can be made (in support of what we already know from extant research) that coalesce issues of race, ethnicity, and culture with responses to natural disasters:

- *Work toward improving the living conditions of lower income people, many of whom are people of color, in areas and housing structures that will suffer more damage from disasters*. People of color are disproportionately living in neighborhoods and homes that possess inadequate and hazardous materials (both physical and chemical), leaving them vulnerable to greater environmental harms. This concern extends beyond issues of class and further verifies the strong effect of race, because many cities and towns across the United States remain segregated. Segregation of poor Blacks into environmentally ill neighborhoods only serves to exacerbate their living circumstances and the extent to which they will suffer from natural disasters.
- *Establish reasonable and reliable escape access to disadvantaged individuals living in disaster-prone areas*. Continuing from the previous point, one of the many hardships of residing in environmentally unjust neighborhoods in disaster-prone regions is that the ability to flee from an impending hazard is diminished. Better strategy must be implemented that takes into account the different ways in which individuals and groups learn of and re-

spond to disasters from which they must take shelter. Many responses may be based in group and cultural variations in beliefs around such things as the true harm of an anticipated natural disaster or having to leave possessions behind in the wake of a disaster.

- *Utilize diverse groups of helping individuals in disaster relief efforts.* Volunteer and paid relief workers need to more closely match those who are being assisted. One of the best ways to do this is to seek out groups that are already in the helping business, such as religious congregations. Greater efforts should be made on a regular basis to encourage people from underrepresented groups to become volunteers in organizations previously established to assist with disaster relief. Further, government bureaucracy must better address how these community groups are being introduced into the relief efforts and the roles they will play. These concerns are particularly important in dealing with issues of the racial heterogeneity of the United States.

- *Implement and require ongoing diversity training (that has been proven to be effective) for disaster relief organizations and workers.* Training with individuals who are officially acknowledged and authorized as disaster relief workers in organizations such as the Red Cross and Americorps must be more effectively trained to employ efforts that are racially and culturally sensitive and relevant. Disasters, whether natural or human-made, will continue to affect individuals of varied identities and life experiences and, many times, in different ways.

- *Ensure nonbiased treatment in temporary sheltering.* Based on the use of existing racialized stereotypes, evacuees of color may suffer from prison-like environments when being "given" assistance. Even if such actions are *not* based on stereotyping, the perception is that the prison-like atmosphere is racially motivated. Disparate treatment of the individuals living and working in the shelter and the use of heavy, visible weaponry aid in making a disaster relief shelter a form of imprisonment instead of a safe haven.

- *Supply shelter provisions that are more amenable to the population being served.* While the "comforts of home," such as food, religious practices, reading materials, and music which the clientele is accustomed to, may seem trivial when compared to assuring disaster survivors are safe, are healthy, and will have financial resources and somewhere to live after residing in the temporary shelter, it is important that these staples are provided. Supplying such provisions may ease the trauma and life transitions survivors are experiencing. Relying on the default of U.S. culture—that is, a culture where the experiences and preferences of White middle- and upper-class groups are treated as the norm—denies the recognition of the multitude of rich cultures that the country now possesses.

- *Empower marginalized individuals by promoting self-reliance in the absence of assistance.* With the assistance of people of color in better economical and influential positions, preparing for the next disaster should involve those who will be greatly affected and who are without the material and networking resources to escape the impending ravage. Existing voluntary organizations can assist in assuring that those most in need are trained in disaster preparedness. Community activism around this and other socially relevant matters for the community allows for protection that public institutions are unable to or may not readily provide.
- *Provide more inclusive and better assistance to poor people of color in the reconstruction of a disaster-affected area.* Many times, individuals displaced from their home as a result of a natural disaster have intentions of returning "home." However, the ability of poor people and poor people of color to go home is not as readily available as it is to those who were not as socially disadvantaged prior to the hazard. Often, such circumstances occur due to the bureaucratic obstacles of securing government funding for assistance in this endeavor and the lack of a physical home to return to due to the poor quality of the structure prior to the disaster, which has since been blown, swept, or washed away.

Although these recommendations have been seen as obvious solutions to many who have commented on the outcome of Katrina, they are stated here as based on the academic and systematic approach taken by the contributors to this volume. More importantly, such propositions must continue to be expressed until we are assured that the foreboding desolation that resulted from Katrina does not occur again in what is considered the richest and most powerful nation in the world.

While doing what we can as individuals and a society to aid in the continuing recovery of Katrina survivors, we can also use Katrina as an instrument for examining the status and significance of race and ethnicity in the United States. This scrutiny takes us beyond environmental (in)justice and leads to the broader and greater implications of what was exhibited by way of Hurricane Katrina, that is, the "bigger picture" of the circumstances under which we live. Accordingly, what have we learned from Hurricane Katrina about race relations in the United States? On the whole, we have learned that we are not a colorblind nation where racial discrimination no longer exists, everyone is treated on equal grounding, and anyone who works hard enough can "pull themselves up by their own bootstraps" and live the "American dream." On the contrary, the chapters in this book have provided evidence that the U.S. society is laden with racialized stratification, colorblind racism, covert racism, racialized perceptions of crime, racialized perceptions of immigration, and racialized government and civic priorities.

NOTES

1. Scholars beginning their research at this stage were generally scholars whose research agendas already had them engaged in hazards research.

2. For an overview of racial/ethnic disparities addressed in natural disasters research, see Alice Fothergill, Enrique G.M. Maestas, and JoAnne DeRouen Darlington, "Race, Ethnicity and Disasters in the United States: A Review of the Literature," *Disasters* 23, no. 2 (1999): 156–73; Anthony A. Peguero, "Latino Disaster Vulnerability: The Dissemination of Hurricane Mitigation Information Among Florida's Homeowners," *Hispanic Journal of Behavioral Sciences* 28, no. 1 (February 2006): 5–22; Kathleen Tierney, "Foreshadowing Katrina: Recent Sociological Contributions to Vulnerability Science," *Contemporary Sociology* 35, no. 3 (May 2006): 207–12. See also Walter Gillis Peacock, Better Hearn Morrow, and Hugh Gladwin, *Hurricane Andrew: Ethnicity, Gender, and the Sociology of Disasters* (New York: Routledge, 1997).

Appendix 1.1

Scale Details and Reliabilities for Participants' Reactions to the Katrina Aftermath

DISSATISFACTION JUDGMENTS

Dissatisfaction with Federal Government's Response Timing (α = .73)

1. The federal government's response to the hurricane and its aftermath should have been faster. (reverse coded)
2. In my opinion, the President did all he could to get relief efforts going quickly. (reverse coded)
3. In my opinion, the FEMA director did all he could to get relief efforts going quickly. (reverse coded)

Dissatisfaction with Local Governments' Response Timing (α = .89)

1. In my opinion, the Governor of Louisiana did all she could to get relief efforts going quickly. (reverse coded)
2. In my opinion, the Mayor of New Orleans did all he could to get relief efforts going quickly. (reverse coded)

Dissatisfaction with Government's Overall Response ($\alpha = .79$)

1. The way New Orleans local government officials handled the hurricane and its aftermath was appropriate. (reverse coded)
2. The way Louisiana state government officials handled the hurricane and its aftermath was appropriate. (reverse coded)
3. The way US Federal Government officials handled the hurricane and its aftermath was appropriate. (reverse coded)

LIABILITY JUDGMENTS

Liability Assigned to Federal Government Relative to New Orleans Residents

1. Please indicate the percentage of costs of rebuilding the city of New Orleans you believe should be paid by the US Federal government.
2. Please indicate the percentage of costs of rebuilding the city of New Orleans you believe should be paid by New Orleans residents.

Percentage of Liability Assigned to Local Government ($\alpha = .92$)

1. Please indicate the percentage of costs of rebuilding the city of New Orleans you believe should be paid by the Louisiana state government.
2. Please indicate the percentage of costs of rebuilding the city of New Orleans you believe should be paid by the City of New Orleans local government.

CONFIDENCE JUDGMENTS

Confidence in Authorities' Ability to Respond to Future Disasters ($\alpha = .83$)

1. The federal government's response to the hurricane and its aftermath has made me more confident in its ability to respond to natural disasters.
2. The federal government's response to the hurricane and its aftermath has made me more confident in its ability to respond to terrorist attacks.
3. I am confident that our military personnel will be able to provide the necessary relief during future natural disasters.
4. I am confident that our local civilian police personnel will be able to provide the necessary relief during future natural disasters.

5. I am confident that our homeland security personnel will be able to provide the necessary relief during future natural disasters.

GROUP IDENTIFICATION MEASURES

Identification with Government Officials (α = .74)

1. I identify with federal government officials.
2. My feelings about federal government officials are mostly positive.
3. I do not consider federal government officials to be important. (reverse coded)
4. Federal government officials are not trustworthy. (reverse coded)
5. I identify with Louisiana state government officials.
6. My feelings about the Louisiana state government officials are mostly positive.
7. I do not consider Louisiana state government officials to be important. (reverse coded)
8. Louisiana state government officials are not trustworthy. (reverse coded)
9. I identify with New Orleans local government officials.
10. My feelings about the New Orleans local government officials are mostly positive.
11. I do not consider New Orleans local government officials to be important. (reverse coded)
12. New Orleans local government officials are not trustworthy. (reverse coded)

Identification with Katrina Victims (α = .39)

1. I identify with Hurricane Katrina victims.
2. My feelings about the Hurricane Katrina victims are mostly positive.
3. I do not consider Hurricane Katrina victims to be important. (reverse coded)
4. Hurricane Katrina victims are not trustworthy. (reverse coded)

EXPOSURE TO MEDIA COVERAGE MEASURE

On average, how many hours per day did you spend engaged in each of the following activities during the unfolding of the Hurricane Katrina disaster: (a) watching televised news coverage of the hurricane and its aftermath;

(b) listening to radio coverage of the hurricane and its aftermath; and (c) reading print media coverage (e.g., internet, newspaper, magazine) of the hurricane and its aftermath.

MEMORY MEASURES

Recollections of Percentages of Black and Poor Pre-Katrina Evacuees ($\alpha = .92$)

1. What percentage of Black New Orleans residents evacuated before Hurricane Katrina made landfall?
2. What percentage of poor New Orleans residents evacuated before Hurricane Katrina made landfall?

Recollections of Percentages of White, Wealthy, and Middle-Class Pre-Katrina Evacuees ($\alpha = .84$)

1. What percentage of White New Orleans residents evacuated before Hurricane Katrina made landfall?
2. What percentage of wealthy New Orleans residents evacuated before Hurricane Katrina made landfall?
3. What percentage of middle-class New Orleans residents evacuated before Hurricane Katrina made landfall?

Recollections of the Timing of the Mandatory Evacuation Order

1. How many days before Katrina made landfall in New Orleans was the mandatory evacuation order issued to its residents?

Recollections of the Arrival of Federal Assistance

1. How many days after Hurricane Katrina made landfall did federal agencies take to respond to the New Orleans crisis?

FAULT ATTRIBUTION MEASURES

Fault Attributions About Federal Government

1. The federal government deliberately responded to the hurricane and its aftermath in the manner that it did.

Fault Attributions about Post-Katrina Evacuees

1. New Orleans residents who did not evacuate before Hurricane Katrina made landfall stayed behind because they chose to.

CAUSAL ATTRIBUTION MEASURES

Positive Dispositional Attributions about Katrina Victims ($\alpha = .86$)

1. New Orleans residents who did not evacuate before Hurricane Katrina made landfall stayed behind because they were optimistic.
2. New Orleans residents who did not evacuate before Hurricane Katrina made landfall stayed behind because they were brave.
3. New Orleans residents who did not evacuate before Hurricane Katrina made landfall stayed behind because they were proud.
4. New Orleans residents who did not evacuate before Hurricane Katrina made landfall stayed behind because they were resilient.

Negative Dispositional Attributions about Katrina Victims ($\alpha = .76$)

1. New Orleans residents who did not evacuate before Hurricane Katrina made landfall stayed behind because they were lazy.
2. New Orleans residents who did not evacuate before Hurricane Katrina made landfall stayed behind because they were uneducated.
3. New Orleans residents who did not evacuate before Hurricane Katrina made landfall stayed behind because they were opportunists.
4. New Orleans residents who did not evacuate before Hurricane Katrina made landfall stayed behind because they wanted to be first in line to receive free aid.

Positive Situational Attributions about Katrina Victims ($\alpha = .63$)

1. New Orleans residents who did not evacuate before Hurricane Katrina made landfall stayed behind because they were infirm (i.e., sick, elderly).
2. New Orleans residents who did not evacuate before Hurricane Katrina made landfall stayed behind because they did not have transportation.
3. New Orleans residents who did not evacuate before Hurricane Katrina made landfall stayed behind because they had no place to relocate to.
4. New Orleans residents who did not evacuate before Hurricane Katrina made landfall stayed behind because they did not believe that the hurricane was going to hit their communities.

Negative Situational Attributions about Katrina Victims (α = .59)

1. New Orleans residents who did not evacuate before Hurricane Katrina made landfall stayed behind because they believed their property would be seized by the government.
2. New Orleans residents who did not evacuate before Hurricane Katrina made landfall stayed behind because they felt that going to emergency shelters was inconvenient.

Negative Dispositional Attributions about Federal Government Officials (α = .84)

1. The federal government's ineffective response to the hurricane and its aftermath was related to the racial make-up of the victims.
2. The federal government's ineffective response to the hurricane and its aftermath was related to the socioeconomic status of the victims.
3. The federal government did not respond sooner to the hurricane and its aftermath because government officials were insensitive to the impact on victims.

Attributions that Federal Response Failures were due to the Disaster's Unprecedented Nature (α = .74)

1. The federal government's ability to respond quickly and effectively to the hurricane and its aftermath was hindered by the unprecedented magnitude of the natural disaster.
2. The federal government's ability to respond quickly and effectively to the hurricane and its aftermath was hindered by the absence of good predictions about its path and size.
3. The federal government did not respond sooner to the hurricane and its aftermath because the government was cautious.
4. The federal government did not respond sooner to the hurricane and its aftermath because the government was overwhelmed.
5. The federal government's ineffective response to the hurricane and its aftermath was because government officials were not convinced that the hurricane was going to hit New Orleans.

Attributions that Federal Response Failures were due to Homeland Security Challenges (α = .73)

1. The federal government's capacity to respond to the hurricane and its aftermath was limited by the war in Iraq.

2. The federal government's ability to respond quickly and effectively to the hurricane and its aftermath was due to the lack of available resources.
3. The federal government's ability to respond quickly and effectively to the hurricane and its aftermath was hindered by the need to focus on securing the homeland from terrorism.

RESPONSIBILITY ATTRIBUTION MEASURES

Responsibility Assigned to Federal Government Relative to New Orleans Residents

1. Please indicate the percentage of responsibility for the negative outcomes that occurred following Hurricane Katrina that you would assign to the US Federal Government.
2. Please indicate the percentage of responsibility for the negative outcomes that occurred following Hurricane Katrina that you would assign to New Orleans residents.

Percentage of Responsibility Assigned to Local Government ($\alpha = .95$)

1. Please indicate the percentage of responsibility for the negative outcomes that occurred following Hurricane Katrina that you would assign to Louisiana state government.
2. Please indicate the percentage of responsibility for the negative outcomes that occurred following Hurricane Katrina that you would assign to the City of New Orleans local government.

Appendix 1.2

Appendix 1.2. Descriptive Statistics and Scale Endpoints for Participants' Reactions to the Katrina Aftermath

Measures	Scale	Mean (SE)	Number of Respondents
Dissatisfaction Judgments			
Dissatisfaction with federal government's response timing	1–6	5.38 (0.06)	236
Dissatisfaction with local government's response timing	1–6	2.70 (0.06)	237
Dissatisfaction with government's overall response	1–6	4.91 (0.07)	236
Liability Judgments			
Liability assigned to federal government relative to New Orleans residents	0–1	0.80 (0.01)	216
Liability assigned to local government	0–100%	23.70 (0.02)	218
Confidence Judgments			
Confidence in authorities' ability to respond to future disasters	1–6	2.23 (0.06)	235
Group Identification Measures			
Identification with government officials	1–6	3.04 (0.05)	219
Identification with Katrina victims	1–6	4.74 (0.05)	235
Exposure to Media Coverage Measure			
Exposure to media coverage	0–24 hours	5.51 (0.38)	234
Memory Measures			
Recollections of percentages of Black and poor pre–Katrina evacuees	0–100%	15.16 (0.75)	179
Recollections of percentages of White, middle–class, and wealthy pre–Katrina evacuees	0–100%	70.88 (1.38)	176

		Mean (SD)	N
Recollections of the timing of the mandatory evacuation order	# days prior to landfall	3.96 (0.83)	184
Recollections of the arrival of federal assistance	# days after landfall	7.06 (0.59)	193
Fault Attribution Measures			
Fault attributions about federal government	1–6	3.86 (0.10)	232
Fault attributions about post–Katrina evacuees	1–6	3.31 (0.10)	234
Causal Attribution Measures			
Negative dispositional attributions about post–Katrina evacuees	1–6	1.96 (0.06)	236
Positive dispositional attributions about post–Katrina evacuees	1–6	2.88 (0.08)	234
Negative situational attributions about post–Katrina evacuees	1–6	3.06 (0.08)	237
Positive situational attributions about post–Katrina evacuees	1–6	4.64 (0.06)	236
Negative dispositional attributions about federal government officials	1–6	4.63 (0.08)	235
Attributions that federal response failures were due to the disaster's unprecedented nature	1–6	2.49 (0.06)	232
Attributions that federal response failures were due to homeland security challenges	1–6	2.84 (0.09)	236
Responsibility Attribution Measures			
Responsibility assigned to the federal government relative to New Orleans residents	0–1	0.75 (0.01)	228
Responsibility assigned to local government	0–100%	28.94 (0.02)	228

Bibliography

Adams-Fuller, Terri M., Angela P. Cole, Billie L. Saddler, and Tarra Jackson. "A Critical Analysis of the Impact of the Homeland Security Advisory System on Local Law Enforcement and the Public." *Criminal Justice Studies* (In press, 2007).

Adorno, Theodor W. "On Jazz." In *Essays on Music,* edited by Richard Leppert, 470–95. Berkeley: University of California Press, [1936] 2002.

Aguiliar, John. "Safe at Last, but Anxiety Lingers at Lowry." *Rocky Mountain News,* September 5, 2005.

Akers, Ronald L., and Christine S. Sellers. *Criminological Theories: Introduction, Evaluation, and Application.* Los Angeles: Roxbury, 2004.

Allport, Gordon. *The Nature of Prejudice.* Oxford, England: Addison-Wesley, 1954.

Amrhein, Saundra. "In Big Easy Cleanup, 'Us' vs. 'Them.'" *St. Petersburg Times,* October 23, 2005.

Anthes, Richard A., Robert W. Corell, Greg Holland, James W. Hurrell, Michael C. MacCracker, and Kevin E. Trenberth, "Hurricanes & Global Warming: Potential Linkages and Consequences." *Bulletin of the American Meteorological Society* 87 (2006): 623–28. http://ams.allenpress.com/archive/1520-0477/87/5/pdf/i1520-0477-87-5-623.pdf.

Applebome, Peter, Christopher Drew, Jere Longman, and Andrew C. Revkin. "A Delicate Balance Is Undone in a Flash, and a Battered City Waits." *The New York Times,* September 4, 2005.

"Apres Vous, M. Toussaint." *Daily Yomiuri,* Japan, June 3, 2006. http://www.elvis-costello.com/news/2006/06/apres_vous_m_toussaint.html.

Arkin, William. "Early Warning: Natural Disasters Perfunctory Concerns." *Washington Post*, September 15, 2005.

Arrighi, Giovanni. *The Long Twentieth Century: Money, Power and the Origins of Our Times*. New York: Verso, 1994.

Associated Press. "Illegal Migrants in—Katrina's Wake." *Australian*, September 10, 2005.

——. "Illegals Go Their Own Way." *Herald Sun*, September 10, 2005.

——. "Immigrants Do New Orleans' Dirty Work: City Leaders Think Jobs Should Go to Locals Hurt by Katrina." *CNN*, October 7, 2005.

Astarita, Glenn. "Post-Katrina Jazz in New Orleans." January 8, 2006. http://www.all aboutjazz.com/php/article.php?id=20250.

Austerlitz, Paul. *Kente Cloth to Jazz: A Matrix of Sound*. Middleton, CT: Wesleyan University Press, 2005.

Bandow, Doug. "Federal Failure in New Orleans." *CATO Institute*, September 8, 2005. http://www.cato.org/pub_display.php?pub_id=4638.

Bankoff, Greg, Georg Frerks, and Dorothea Hillhorst. *Mapping Vulnerability Disasters, Development, and People*. London: Earthscan Publications, 2003.

Barrett, Jennifer. "Helpful Obligations: 'The Ethics Guy' Explains How and Why Americans Ought to Aid Those Affected by Hurricane Katrina and Why Looting Is Sometimes Ethically Permissible." *Newsweek*, September 1, 2005. http://www.msnbc.msn.com/id/9160887/site/newsweek/.

Barry, John M. *Rising Tide: The Great Mississippi Flood of 1927 and How It Changed America*. New York: Simon & Schuster, 1998.

——. "After the Deluge, Some Questions." *The New York Times*, October 13, 2005. http://fireside.designcommunity.com/topic-6831.html.

Bartol, Curt R., and Anne. M. Bartol. *Psychology and the Law: Theory, Research, and Application*. Belmont, CA: Thompson, 2004.

Baudrillard, Jean. *Jean Baudrillard, Selected Writings*, Mark Poster, ed., Stanford: Stanford University Press, 1988.

Baum, Bruce. *The Rise and Fall of the Caucasian Race: A Political History of Racial Identity*. New York: New York University Press, 2006.

Baum, Dan. "The Lost Year: Behind the Failure to Rebuild." *The New Yorker*, August 21, 2006: 44–59.

——. "Deluged: When Katrina Hit, Where Were the Police?" *The New Yorker*, January 9, 2006.

Becker, Gary S., and Y. Rubinstein. "Fear and the Response to Terrorism: An Economic Analysis." Paper presented at the first annual Threat Anticipation Workshop: Social Science Methods and Models, University of Chicago, April 7–9, 2005.

Becker, Howard S. "Jazz Places." Paper given at the Albright-Knox Art Gallery, March 21, 2002. http://buffaloreport.com/020401beckerjazzplaces.html.

Been, Vicki. "Locally Undesirable Land Uses in Minority Neighborhoods: Disproportionate Siting or Market Dynamics?" *Yale Law Journal* 103 (1994): 1383–1422.

——. "Analyzing Evidence of Environmental Justice." *Journal of Land Use and Environmental Law* 11 (1995): 1–36.

Belsie, Laurent, and Kris Axtman. "Post-Katrina, New Orleans Coming Back More Hispanic." *Christian Science Monitor,* June 12, 2006.

Bennis, Phyllis, Eric Leaver, and the IPS Iraq Task Force. *The Iraq Quagmire: The Mounting Costs of the Iraq War and the Case for Bringing the Troops Home*, A Study by the Institute for Policy Studies and Foreign Policy in Focus. August 31, 2005. http://www.ips-dc.org/iraq/quagmire/IraqQuagmire.pdf.

Berger, Randall R., and Jeremy Hein. "Immigrants, Culture, and American Courts: A Typology of Legal Strategies and Issues in Cases Involving Vietnamese and Hmong Litigants." *Criminal Justice Review* 26 (2001): 38–61.

Berry, John W., Ype H. Poortinga, Marshall H. Segall, and Pierre R. Dasen. *Cross-Cultural Psychology: Research and Applications,* 1st ed. Toronto: Cambridge University Press, 1992.

Berube, Alan, and Steven Raphael. "Access to Cars in New Orleans." The Brookings Institution. http://www.brookings.edu/metro/20050915_katrinacarstables.pdf.

Bhagwati, Jagdish. "The Capital Myth: The Difference Between Trade in Widgets & Dollars." *Foreign Affairs*, May/June 1998: 7–12.

Bibington, Charles. "Some GOP Legislators Hit Jarring Notes in Addressing Katrina." *Washington Post*, September 10, 2005. http://www.washingtonpost.com/wp-dyn/content/article/2005/09/09/AR2005090901930_pf.html.

Bilmes, Linda. "The Trillion-Dollar War." *The New York Times*, August 20, 2000.

Bilmes, Linda, and Joseph Stiglitz. "The Economic Costs of the Iraq War: An Appraisal Three Years After the Beginning of the Conflict." National Bureau of Economic Research Working Paper Series 12054 (2006).http://www.nber.org/papers/w12054.

Block, Robert. "U.S. had Plan for Crisis like Katrina." *Wall Street Journal*, September 19, 2005.

Bogle, Donald. *Prime Time Blues: African Americans on Network Television.* New York: Farrar, Straus, and Giroux, 2001.

Boies, John L. *Buying for Armageddon: Society, Economy, and the State since the Cuban Missile Crisis*. Piscataway, NJ: Rutgers University Press, 1994.

Bonilla-Silva, Eduardo. *Racism Without Racists: Color-Blind Racism and the Persistence of Racial Inequality in the United States.* Lanham, MD: Rowman & Littlefield, 2003.

Borden, William S. *The Pacific Alliance: United States Foreign Economic Policy and Japanese Trade Recovery, 1947–1955.* Madison, WI: University of Wisconsin Press, 1984.

Bositis, David. *Black Churches and the Faith-Based Initiative: Findings from a Survey.* Washington, DC: Joint Center for Political and Economic Studies, 2006.

Bourne, Joel K., Jr. "Gone with the Water." *National Geographic*, October 2004. http://www3.nationalgeographic.com/ngm/0410/feature5/.

Brewington, Kelly. "New Orleans Rebuilds as Tensions Rise: Influx of Latino Workers Has Local Businesses and Contractors Feeling Left Out." *Baltimore Sun Reporter,* October 14, 2005.

Brinkley, Douglas. *The Great Deluge: Hurricane Katrina, New Orleans, and the Mississippi Gulf Coast.* New York: William Morrow/Harper Collins, 2006.

Broad, Robin. *Unequal Alliance: The World Bank, the International Monetary Fund and the Philippines*. Berkeley: University of California Press, 1988.

Broder, John M. "In Storm's Ruins, a Rush to Rebuild and Reopen for Business: Contractors, and Lobbyists, Line Up." *The New York Times*, September 10, 2005.

Brodeur, Nicole. "One Year Later Katrina Survivors Are Still Hurting." *The Seattle Times,* August 16, 2006. http://seattletimes.nwsource.com/html/localnews/2003202052_brodeur16m.html.

Brookings Institution. "New Orleans After the Storm: Lessons from the Past, a Plan for the Future." The Brookings Institution Metropolitan Policy Program, 2005. http://www.brookings.edu/metro/pubs/20051012_NewOrleans.pdf.

———. "The Katrina Index: Tracking Recovery of New Orleans & the Metro Area." January 17, 2007. http://www.gnocdc.org/KI/KatrinaIndex.pdf.

Brooks, Richard R.W,. and Haekyung Jeon-Slaughter. "Race, Income and Perceptions of the United States Court System." *Behavioral Sciences and the Law* 19 (2001): 249–264.

Brooks, Rosa. "American Caesar." *Los Angeles Times*, September 3, 2005.

Brooks-Gunn, Jeanne, Greg J. Duncan, Pamela Kato Klebanov, and Naomi Sealand. "Do Neighborhoods Influence Child and Adolescent Development?" *American Journal of Sociology* 99 (1993): 353–95.

Brown, Linda Reed. "Katrina Recovery Efforts: New Needs Emerge Among Hispanic Workers." *Church World Service Newsroom,* June 15, 2006. http://www.churchworldservice.org/news/archives/2006/06/491.html.

Buck, Richard A., Joseph E. Trainor, and B.E. Aguirre. "A Critical Evaluation of the Incident Command System and Nims." Unpublished manuscript, 2006.

Bullard, Robert. *Dumping in Dixie: Race, Class, and Environmental Quality*. Boulder, CO: Westview Press, 1990.

———., ed. *Confronting Environmental Racism: Views from the Grassroots*. Boston: South End Press, 1993.

Bunch, Will. "Did New Orleans Catastrophe Have to Happen? 'Times-Picayune' had Repeatedly Raised Federal Spending Issues." *Editor and Publisher*, August 31, 2005.

Burby, Raymond J., ed. *Cooperating with Nature: Confronting Natural Hazards with Land-Use Planning for Sustainable Communities*. Washington, DC: Joseph Henry Press, 1998.

Burnside, Randolph. "Leaving the Big Easy: An Examination of the Hurricane Evacuation Behavior of New Orleans Residents Before Hurricane Katrina." *Journal of Public Management and Social Policy* 12, no. 1 (2006): 49–61.

Bush, George W. *Address to the Nation,* September 15, 2005. http://www.nytimes.com/2005/09/16/national/nationalspecial/16bush-text.html?ex=1153886400&en=f52aea02357c0688&ei=5070.

Calmes, Jackie, Ann Carns, and Jeff D. Opdyke. "New Architecture: As Gulf Prepares to Rebuild, Tensions Mount Over Control." *Wall Street Journal,* September 15, 2005.

Campanella, Richard. *Time and Place in New Orleans: Past Geographies in the Present Day*. Gretna, LA: Pelican Publishing Company, 2002.

Campbell, Edna F. "New Orleans in Early Days." *Geographical Review* 10, no. 1 (1920): 31–36.

———. "New Orleans at the Time of the Louisiana Purchase," *Geographical Review* 11, no. 3 (July 1921): 414–25.

Campbell, Monica. "Post-Katrina Easing of Labor Laws Stirs Debate," *Christian Science Monitor*, October 4, 2005: 1.

Campbell, Richard, Christopher R. Martin, and Bettina Fabos. *Media and Culture: An Introduction to Mass Communication*. Boston: Bedford/St. Martin's, 2005.

Campo-Flores, Arian. "A New Spice in the Gumbo: Will Latino Day Laborers Locating in New Orleans Change its Complexion?" *Newsweek,* December 5, 2005.

Cannon, Carl M., and Shane Harris. 2005. "FEMA May Work Best Standing Alone." *National Journal*. September 10, 2005, no. 37: 2725.

Canterbery, E. Ray. *Wall Street Capitalism: The Theory of the Bondholding Class*. Singapore: World Scientific Publications, 2000.

Caraley, Demetrios. "Washington Abandons the City." *Political Science Quarterly* 107 (1992): 8–11.

———. "Dismantling the Federal Safety Net: Fictions Versus Realities." *Political Science Quarterly* 111 (1995): 225–58.

Carey, Alex. *Taking the Risk out of Democracy*. Sydney: University of New South Wales, 1995.

Carey, Corinne. "New Orleans: Prisoners Abandoned to Flood Waters." *Human Rights Watch,* September 22, 2005. http://www.hrw.org/english/docs/2005/09/22/usdom11773.htm.

Carey, James. *Communication as Culture*. Boston: Unwin Hyman, 1975.

Carns, Ann, Chad Tehune, Kris Hudson, and Gary Fields. "Overwhelmed: As U.S. Mobilizes Aid, Katrina Exposes Flaws in Preparation: Despite Warnings, Officials Say, There Wasn't Clear Plan for a New Orleans Disaster." *Wall Street Journal,* September 1, 2005.

Carter, David, L. "Hispanic Interaction with the Criminal Justice System in Texas: Experiences, Attitudes, and Perceptions." *Journal of Criminal Justice* 11 (1983): 213–27.

———. "Hispanic Perception of Police Performance: An Empirical Assessment." *Journal of Criminal Justice* 13 (1985): 487–500.

Carr, David. "More Horrible than Truth: News Reports." *The New York Times*, September 19, 2005.

Carroll, Rorry, and Julian Borger. "Iraq Rebuilding under Threat as US Runs out of Money." *The Guardian*, September 9, 2005. Available at http://www.guardian.co.uk/Iraq/Story/0,2763,1566176,00.html.

Casserly, Michael. "Double Jeopardy: Public Education in New Orleans Before and After the Storm." In *There Is No Such Thing as a Natural Disaster: Race, Class, and Hurricane Katrina*, edited by C. Hartman and G.D. Squires, 197–214. New York: Routledge.

Castillo, Eduardo. "Latin America Searches for Missing in Katrina's Aftermath." *Associated Press,* September 3, 2005.

Castillo, Juan. "Mexico Estimates 145,000 Displaced by Katrina: Official Says Deportation Fears Keeping Victims in Shadows." *Austin American-Statesman,* September 7, 2005.

CBS News. "Race an Issue in Katrina Response." September 3, 2005.

——. "Rapper Blasts Bush over Katrina: Kanye West Says Bush 'Doesn't Care About Black People' on Telethon." September 3, 2005.

——. "Blacks Rally around Katrina Cause: Hurricane Inspires Record Outpouring of Aid in Black America." September 9, 2005.

Cevallos, Diego. "Latin American Storm Victims Adrift." *Interpress Service News Agency,* September 21, 2005.

Chavez, Leo R. *Covering Immigration: Popular Images and the Politics of the Nation.* Berkeley: University of California Press, 2001.

Chomsky, Noam. *Towards a New Cold War: Essays on the Current Crisis and How We Got There.* New York: Pantheon, 1982.

——. *Turning the Tide.* New York: Black Rose Books, 1987.

——. *Deterring Democracy.* New York: Verso, 1991.

——. *Powers and Prospects.* Boston: South End Press, 1996.

——. *Failed States: The Abuse of Power and the Assault on Democracy.* New York: Metropolitan Books, 2006.

Chow, Henry. P.H. "The Chinese Community Leaders' Perceptions of the Criminal Justice System." *Canadian Journal of Criminology* 38 (1996): 477–84.

Cloud, David S. "Record $622 Billion Budget Requested for the Pentagon." *The New York Times,* February 3, 2007.

CNN.com. "Lt. Gen. Honore a 'John Wayne Dude.'" September 3, 2005. http://www.cnn.com/2005/US/09/02honore.profile/index.html.

CNN Larry King Live. "Interview with Ray Nagin." September 14, 2005. http://edition.cnn.com/TRANSCRIPTS/0509/14/lkl.01.html.

Cockrell, Eddie. "New Orleans Music in Exile." *Variety,* April 3, 2006. http://www.variety.com/review/VE1117930122?categoryid=1023&cs=1 (September 1, 2006).

Cole, Angela P,. and Ewart A.C. Thomas. "Group Differences in Fairness Perceptions and Decision Making in Voting Rights Cases." *Law and Human Behavior* 30 (2006): 543–60.

Cole, Dan. "What I Saw in Tylertown." *Newsweek,* October 17, 2005. http://www.msnbc.msn.com/id/9729481/site/newsweek/.

Collins, Patricia Hill. *Black Feminist Thought: Knowledge, Consciousness, and the Politics of Empowerment.* New York: Routledge, 1991.

Colten, Craig E. "How to Rebuild New Orleans: Restore the Marsh." *The New York Times,* September 10, 2005.

—— *An Unnatural Metropolis: Wresting New Orleans from Nature.* Baton Rouge: Louisiana State University Press, 2004.

——., ed. *Transforming New Orleans and Its Environs: Centuries of Change.* Pittsburgh: University of Pittsburgh Press, 2001.

——. "Race, Poverty & Katrina." *National Public Radio,* September 2, 2005. http://www.npr.org/templates/story/story.php?storyId=4829446.

Commission for Racial Justice. *Toxic Wastes and Race in the United States.* New York: United Church of Christ and Public Data Access, Inc., 1987.

Conley, Dalton. *Being Black, Living in the Red: Race, Wealth, and Social Policy in America*. Berkeley, CA: University of California Press, 1999.

——. "Turning the Tax Tables to Help the Poor." *The New York Times*, November 15, 2004.

Cooper, Christopher. "In Katrina's Wake: Where Is the Money? Congress Authorized Billions to Rebuild, But Only Half Has Been Spent." *Wall Street Journal*, January 27, 2007.

Cordescu, Andrew. *New Orleans, Mon Amour: Twenty Years of Writings from the City*. Chapel Hill: Algonquin Books, 2006.

Cullen, Francis T., Liquin Cao, James Frank, Robert H. Langworthy, Sandra L. Browning, Renee Kopache, and Thomas J. Stevenson. "'Stop or I'll Shoot:' Racial Differences in Support for Police Use of Deadly Force." *American Behavioral Scientist*, 39 (1996): 449–60.

Curry, Timothy Jon, Kent Schwirian, and Rachael A. Woldoff. *High Stakes: Big Times Sports and Downtown Redevelopment*. Columbus: The Ohio State University Press, 2004.

Cutler, Brian L., and Donna M. Hughes. "Judging Jury Service: Results of the North Carolina Administrative Office of the Courts Juror Survey." *Behavioral Sciences and the Law* 19 (2001): 305–20.

Daniel, Pete. *Deep'n As It Come: The 1927 Mississippi Flood*. New York: Oxford University Press, 1977.

Daniels, Ronald J., Donald F. Kettl, and Howard Kunreuther, eds. *On Risk and Disaster: Lessons from Hurricane Katrina*. Philadelphia: University of Pennsylvania Press, 2006.

Dao, James. "Bush Sees Big Rise in Military Budget for Next 5 Years." *The New York Times*, February 2, 2002.

Davis, John A. "Justification for No Obligation: Views of African American Males toward Crime and the Criminal Law." *Issues in Criminology* 9 (1974): 69–75.

Davis, Mike. *Prisoners of the American Dream: Politics and Economy in the History of the US Working Class*. New York: Verso, 1986.

——. *Ecology of Fear: Los Angeles and the Imagination of Disaster*. New York: Metropolitan Books, 1998.

——. *Dead Cities: And Other Tales*. New York: The New Press, 2002.

——. "Poor, Black and Left Behind: Before Killer Katrina, There Was Ivan the Terrible." *LA Weekly News*, September 8, 2005.http://www.laweekly.com/ink/05/42/after-davis.php.

——. "Melting Away." *The Nation*, October 7, 2005. http://www.thenation.com/doc/20051024/davis.

——. "Who Is Killing New Orleans?" *The Nation*, April 10, 2006, 11–20.

Dawson, Michael C. "After the Deluge: Publics and Publicity in Katrina's Wake." *DuBois Review* 3 (2006): 239–49.

DeBose, Brian. "HUD Chief Foresees a 'Whiter' Big Easy." *Washington Times*, September 30, 2005.

DeBrouwer, Gordon. *Hedge Funds in Emerging Markets*. New York: Cambridge University Press, 2001.

De la Garza, Rodolfo O., and Louis DeSipio. "A Satisfied Clientele Seeking More Diverse Services: Latinos and the Courts." *Behavioral Sciences and the Law* 19 (2001): 237–48.

DeMoraes, Lisa. "Kanye West's Torrent of Criticism, Live on NBC." *Washington Post*, September 3, 2005.

Demuth, Stephen, and Darrell Steffensmeier. "Ethnicity Effects on Sentence Outcomes in Large Urban Courts: Comparisons among White, Black, and Hispanic Defendants." *Social Science Quarterly* 85 (2004): 994–1011.

DeParle, Jason. "What Happens to a Race Deferred." *The New York Times*, September 4, 2005.

———. "Liberal Hopes Ebb in Post-Storm Poverty Debate: An Ideological Clash Over How to Help America's Poor." *The New York Times*, October 11, 2005.

Department of Homeland Security. *National Response Plan: December 2004*. Washington, DC: Department of Homeland Security.

———. "Hurricane Katrina: What Government Is Doing."http//:www.dhs.gov/katrina.

Donato, Katherine, Nicole Trujillo-Pagán, Carl L. Bankston III, and Audrey Singer. "Reconstructing New Orleans after Katrina: The Emergence of an Immigrant Labor Market." In *The Sociology of Katrina: Perspectives on a Modern Catastrophe*, edited by David Brunsma, David Overfelt, and Steve Picou. Lanham, MD: Rowman & Littlefield, *Forthcoming*.

Douglass, Frederick. "The Nation's Problem." (1889). http://teachingamericanhistory.org/library/index.asp?document=494.

Dowd, Maureen. "United States of Shame." *The New York Times*, September 3, 2005.

Drabek, Thomas E., and David A. McEntire. "Emergent Phenomena and the Sociology of Disaster: Lessons, Trends and Opportunities from the Research Literature." *Disaster Prevention and Management* 12, no. 2 (2003): 97–112.

Dreazen, Yochi J. "No-Bid Contracts Win Katrina Work: White House Uses Practices Criticized in Iraq Rebuilding for Hurricane-Related Jobs." *Wall Street Journal*, September 12, 2005.

Dreier, Peter, John Mollenkopf, and Todd Swanstrom. *Place Matters: Metropolitics for the Twenty-first Century*, 2nd ed. rev. Lawrence: University Press of Kansas, 2004.

DuBois, W.E.B. "The Talented Tenth." In *The Negro Problem*. New York: James Pott and Company, 1903.

———. *Black Reconstruction in America: An Essay toward a History of the Part Which Black Folk Played in the Attempt to Reconstruct Democracy in America, 1860–1880*. New York: Atheneum, 1935/1969.

Duffield, Mark. *Global Governance and the New Wars: The Merging of Development and Security*. London and New York: Zed Books.

Duke, Lynne. "Block that Metaphor: What We Mean When We Call New Orleans Third World." *Washington Post*, October 9, 2005.

Duke, Lynne, and Teresa Wiltz. "A Nation's Castaways; Katrina Blew in, and Tossed up Reminders of a Tattered Racial Legacy." *Washington Post*, September 5, 2005.

Dyson, Michael Eric. *Come Hell or High Water: Hurricane Katrina and the Color of Disaster*. New York: Basic Books, 2006.

———. "Denying a Racist Past Slows US Policy." *The Age*, December, 28 2002.

———. *Race Rules: Navigating the Color Line*. New York: Vintage/Random House, 1997.

Eaton, Leslie. "Study Sees Increase in Illegal Hispanic Workers in New Orleans." *The New York Times*, June 8, 2006.

Eatwell, John. "The Global Money Trap: Can Clinton Master the Markets?" *The American Prospect*, no. 12 (Winter 1993): 118–26.

Eatwell, John, and Lance Taylor. *Global Finance at Risk*. New York: The New Press, 2000.

Edelman, Lauren B., Sally Riggs Fuller, and Iona Mara-Drita. "Diversity and the Managerialization of Law." *American Journal of Sociology* 106 (2001): 1589–1600.

Eisler, Peter. "146 U.S. Levees May Fail in Flood: Bad Maintenance Heightens Danger." *USA Today*, January 29, 2007.

Emanuel, Kerry. "Increasing Destructiveness of Tropical Cyclones over the Past 30 Years." *Nature*, 436/4 (2005): 686–88. ftp://texmex.mit.edu/pub/emanuel/PAPERS/NATURE03906.pdf.

———. *Divine Wind: A History and Science of Hurricanes*. New York: Oxford University Press, 2005.

Engelhardt, Tom, and Nick Turse. "Corporations of the Whirlwind." September 12, 2005. http://www.tomdispatch.com/index.mhtml?pid=21843.

Entmann, Robert M., and Andrew Rojecki. *The Black Image in the White Mind: Media and Race in America*. Chicago: University of Chicago Press, 2000.

Environmental Defense, Coalition to Restore Coastal Louisiana, National Wildlife Federation, Gulf Restoration Foundation, Lake Ponchartrain Basin Foundation. *One Year After Katrina: Louisiana Still a Sitting Duck; a Report Card & Roadmap on Wetlands Restoration*, August 28, 2006. http://www.environmentaldefense.org/documents/5416_KatrinaReportCard.pdf.

Evans, Nicholas M. *Writing Jazz*. New York: Garland Publishing, 2000.

Everett, Donald E. "Emigres and Militiamen: Free Persons of Color in New Orleans, 1803–1815." *The Journal of Negro History* 38, no. 4 (October 1953): 377–402.

Fagin, James A. *When Terrorism Strikes Home: Defending the United States*. Boston: Pearson/Allyn & Bacon, 2006.

Farley, Reynolds, Elaine Fielding, and Maria Krysan. "The Residential Preferences of Blacks and Whites: A Four Metropolis Analysis." *Housing Policy Debate* 8 (1997): 763–800.

Farley, Reynolds, and Maria Krysan. "The Residential Preferences of Blacks: Do They Explain Persistent Segregation?" *Social Forces* 80 (2002): 937–80.

Fears, Darryl. "For Illegal Immigrants, Some Aid Is Too Risky; Fears Abound as Government Won't Promise Immunity from Deportation." *The Washington Post*, September 20, 2005.

FEMA. *President Approves Emergency Declaration for Colorado*. http://www.fema.gov/news/newsrelease.fema?id=18626 (September 5, 2005).

Fenigstein, Allan, and Charles Carver. "Self-Focusing Effects of Heartbeat Feedback." *Journal of Personality and Social Psychology* 36 (1978):1241–1250.

Filosa, Gwen. "Lower 9 Residents Differ on Desire to Return." *The Times-Picayune,* August 24, 2006.

Fine, Gary Alan, and Patrcia A. Turner. *Whispers on the Color Line: Rumor and Race in America.* Berkeley: University of California Press, 2001.

Fischetti, Mark. "They Saw It Coming." *The New York Times*, September 2, 2005.

———. "Drowning New Orleans." *Scientific American,* October 2001. http://www.sciam.com/article.cfm?articleID=00060286-CB58-1315-8B5883414B7F0000.

Fishman, Laura T. "The Black Bogeyman and White Self-Righteousness." In *Images of Color, Images of Crime: Readings*, 3rd ed., edited by Coramae Richey Mann, Marjorie S. Zatz, and Nancy Rodriguez, 197–211. Los Angeles: Roxbury Publishing Company, 2006.

Fitzpatrick, Kevin, and Mark LaGory. *Unhealthy Places: The Ecology of Risk in the Urban Landscape.* London: Routledge, 2000.

Flamm, Kenneth. *Targeting the Computer: Government Support and International Competition.* Washington, DC: Brookings, 1987.

———. *Creating the Computer: Government, Industry, and High Technology*. Washington, DC: Brookings, 1988.

Foner, Eric. *Reconstruction: America's Unfinished Revolution: 1863–1877.* New York: Harper and Row, 1988.

Fones-Wolf, Elizabeth A. *Selling Free Enterprise: The Business Assault on Labor and Liberalism, 1945–1960.* Urbana: University of Illinois Press, 1994.

Foster, Margaret. "In Sudden Demolition, New Orleans Loses Its first Historic Building Since Katrina." *OnLine Preservation,* October 13, 2005. http://www.nationaltrust.org/magazine/archives/arc_news_2005/101305.htm (September 1, 2006).

Fothergill, Alice, Enrique G.M. Maestas, and JoAnne DeRouen Darlington. "Race, Ethnicity and Disasters in the United States: A Review of the Literature." *Disasters* 23, no. 2 (1999): 156–73.

Foucault, Michel. *Society Must Be Defended.* New York: Picador, 2003.

Frankenberg, Erica, Chungmei Lee, and Gary Orfield. "A Multiracial Society with Segregated Schools: Are We Losing the Dream?" The Civil Rights Project, Harvard University, 2003.

Freeland, Richard M. *The Truman Doctrine and the Origins of McCarthyism: Foreign Policy, Domestic Politics, and Internal Security, 1946–1948*. New York: New York University Press, 1970/1985.

Frey, William H. *The New Great Migration: Black Americans Return to the South, 1965-2000*, May 2004. http://www.brookings.edu/urban/pubs/20040524_Frey.pdf.

Frey, William H., and Audrey Singer. "Katrina and Rita Impacts on Gulf Coast Populations: First Census Findings." In *The Brookings Institution Metropolitan Policy Program*, Brookings Institution, 2006.

Fronczek, Peter, and Patricia Johnson. *Occupations: 2000.* Washington, DC: U.S. Census Bureau, 2003.

Fukurai, Hiroshi, Edgar W. Butler, and Jo-Ellen Huebner-Dimitrius. "Spatial and Racial Imbalances in Voter Registration and Jury Selection." *Sociology and Social Research* 72 (1987): 33–83.

Fukurai, Hiroshi, Edgar W. Butler, and Richard Krooth R. "Where Did the Black Jurors Go? A Theoretical Synthesis of Racial Disenfranchisement in the Jury System and Jury Selection." *Journal of Black Studies* 22 (1991): 196–215.

Garcia, Venessa, and Liqun Cao. "Race and Satisfaction with Police in a Small City." *Journal of Criminal Justice* 33 (2005): 191–96.

Gautier, Ana María Ochoa. "Nueva Orleáns, La Permeable Margen Norte del Caribe." *Nueva Sociedad* 201 (January/February 2006): 61–72.

Gerber, Brian J., and David B. Cohen. "Who Needs a Mandate? The Election 2000 Hullabaloo and the Bush Administration's Governing Agenda." In *The Final Arbiter: The Long Term Consequences of Bush v Gore in Law and Politics*, edited by Christopher P. Banks, David B. Cohen, and John C. Green. Albany, NY: SUNY Press, 2005.

Giddings, Paula. *When and Where I Enter: The Impact of Black Women on Race and Sex in America*. New York: Bantam Books, 1984.

Gilkes, Cheryl Townsend. "'Together and in Harness': Women's Traditions in the Sanctified Church." In *African American Religious Thought*, edited by Cornel West and Eddie S. Glaude, 629–50. Louisville, KY: Westminster John Knox Press, 2003.

Glassner, Barry. *The Culture of Fear*. New York: Basic Books, 1999.

Gold, Scott. "Chaos in the Superdome." *Los Angeles Times*, September 1, 2005.

———. "Refugees Forced to Endure Appalling Conditions." *Irish Times*, September 2, 2005.

Goldman, Benjamin, and Laura Fitton. *Toxic Wastes and Race Revisited*. Washington, DC: Center for Policy Alternatives, 1994.

Gonzalez, David. "From Margins of Society to Center of the Tragedy." *The New York Times*, September 2, 2005.

Gonzales, Richard. "Katrina May Help Heal Old Wounds." *Buffalo News*, September 25, 2005.

Goodman, Amy. "Honduran Immigrants in New Orleans: Fleeing Hurricanes Mitch, Katrina and Now the U.S. Government." *Democracy Now!* September 13, 2005. http://www.democracynow.org/article.pl?sid=05/09/13/1354211.

———. "Workers in New Orleans Denied Pay, Proper Housing and Threatened with Deportation." *Democracy Now!* December 16, 2005. http://www.democracynow.org/article.pl?sid=05/12/16/1457237&mode=thread&tid=25.

Gore, Al. *An Inconvenient Truth*. New York: Rodale Books, 2006.

Gottdiener, Mark, and Ray Hutchinson. *The New Urban Sociology*, 3rd ed. Boulder, CO: Westview Press, 2006.

Gottschalk, Marie. *The Prison and the Gallows: The Politics of Mass Incarceration in America*. New York: Cambridge University Press, 2006.

Gowan, Peter. *The Global Gamble: Washington's Faustian Bid for World Dominance*. New York: Verso, 1999.

———. "The New American Century?" *The Spokesman* 76 (2002): 5–22.

Grabowski, Michael J., and Everette B. Penn. "The Blue and Gray: Partnerships of Police and Seniors in the Age of Homeland Security." *Journal of Homeland Security* (October 2003). http://www.homelandsecurity.org/newjournal/articles/grabowski.html.

Gray, Herman. *Watching Race: Television and the Struggle for Blackness.* Minneapolis: University of Minnesota Press, 1995.

Greenberg, Jeff, Sheldon Solomon, and Tom Pyszczynski. "Terror Management Theory of Self-Esteem and Cultural Worldviews: Empirical Assessments and Conceptual Refinements." In *Advances in Experimental Social Psychology Volume 29,* edited by Mark Zanna, 61–139. San Diego, CA.: Academic Press, 1997.

Griffin, Emory. *A First Look at Communication Theory, 2nd Edition.* Boston: McGraw-Hill College, 1994.

Grodsky, Eric, and Devah Pager. "The Structure of Disadvantage: Individual and Occupational Determinants of the Black-White Wage Gap." *American Sociological Review* 66 (2001): 542–67.

Gross, Doug. "N.O. Superintendent: Groups Trying to Pick School System Apart." *Associated Press,* October 21, 2005. http://www.wwltv.com/topstories/stories/WWL102105watson.1180584cf.html.

Gulf Coast Reconstruction Watch. *One Year after Katrina: The State of New Orleans and the Gulf Coast,* A Project of the Institute for Southern Studies/Southern Exposure, 2006. http://www.reconstructionwatch.org/images/One_Year_After.pdf.

Halim, Shaheen, and Beverly L. Stiles. "Differential Support for Police Use of Force, the Death Penalty, and Perceived Harshness of the Courts: Effects of Race, Gender, and Region." *Criminal Justice and Behavior* 28 (2001): 3–23.

Hallowell, Christopher. *Holding Back the Sea: The Struggle for America's Natural Legacy on the Gulf Coast.* New York: Harper Collins, 2001.

Harriman, Ed. "Where Has All the Money Gone?" *London Review of Books* 27, no.13 (July 7, 2005).

——. "Cronyism and Kickbacks." *London Review of Books* 28, no. 2 (January 26, 2006).

Hartman, Chester, and Gregory D. Squires, eds. *There Is No Such Thing as a Natural Disaster: Race, Class, and Hurricane Katrina.* New York: Routledge, 2006.

Harvey, David. *The New Imperialism.* Oxford and London: Oxford University Press, 2003.

Harwood, John. "Katrina Erodes Support in U.S. for Iraq War: Bush's Ratings as Crisis Manager Declines in Poll as Pessimism about the Economy Grows." *Wall Street Journal,* September 15, 2005.

Hastorf, Albert, and Hadley Cantril. "They Saw a Game: A Case Study." *Journal of Abnormal and Social Psychology* 49 (1954): 129–34.

Haygood, Wil, and Ann S. Tyson. "'Was As If All of Us Were Already Pronounced Dead'; Convention Center Left a Five-Day Legacy of Chaos and Violence." *Washington Post,* September 15, 2005.

Hebert, Christopher G. "Sentencing Outcomes of Black, Hispanic, and White Males Convicted under Federal Sentencing Guidelines." *Criminal Justice Review* 22 (1997): 133–41.

Heider, Fritz. *The Psychology of Interpersonal Relations.* New York: Wiley, 1958.

Heinz, H., III, Center for Science, Economics and the Environment. *Human Links to Coastal Disasters,* 2002. http://www.heinzctr.org/NEW_WEB/PDF/Full_report_human_links.pdf.

Henao, Luis Emilio. *The Hispanics in Louisiana*. New Orleans: Latin American Apostolate, 1982.

Herring, Cedric. "Hurricane Katrina and the Racial Gulf: A Du Boisian Analysis of Victims' Experiences." *DuBois Review* 3, no. 1 (2006): 129–44.

Higginbotham, Evelyn Brooks. "Black Church: A Gender Perspective." In *African American Religious Thought*, edited by Cornel West and Eddie S. Glaude, 187–208. Louisville, KY: Westminster John Knox Press, 2003.

Hill, Michael. "Katrina Shows It Takes a Community." *Baltimore Sun*, September 11, 2005.

Hilsenrath, Jon E. "GDP Data Spark Hopes Recovery Is Strengthening: Economy Grew at 2.4% Pace in the Second Quarter, Military Spending Surges." *Wall Street Journal*, August 1, 2003.

Hirsch, Arnold. *Making the Second Ghetto: Race and Housing in Chicago, 1940–1960*. New York: Cambridge University Press, 1983.

Hogg, Michael, and Graham Vaughan. *Social Psychology*. New York: Prentice Hall, 2002.

Holland, Nancy. "Older Katrina Survivors Wonder if Window of Uncertainty Will Slam Down on Them." *KHOU News Channel 11 Houston*, July 21, 2006. http://www.khou.com/news/local/stories/khou060721_jj_katrinaelderly.cf0cc67.html (January 20, 2007).

Hollis, Amanda Lee. "A Tale of Two Federal Emergency Management Agencies." *The Forum* 3 (2005). http://www.bepress.com/forum/vol3/iss3/art3.

hooks, bell. *Reel to Real: Race, Sex and Class at the Movies*. New York: Routledge, 1996.

Hosenball, Mark. "It's Cheaper to Go Dutch." *Newsweek*, September 4, 2006.

Houston Chronicle. "Katrina's Legacy: Hurricanes Routinely Reshape Coastlines, but This One Racially Altered the Gulf Coast Populations as Well." June 12, 2006.

Hughes, Langston. *The Langston Hughes Reader*. New York: George Braziller, 1958.

Iceland, John, Daniel H. Weinberg, and Erika Steinmetz. *Racial and Ethnic Residential Segregation in the United States: 1980–2000*. Washington, DC: U.S. Census Bureau, 2002.

Institute for Research on Poverty. *Who Was Poor in 2004?* http://www.irp.wisc.edu/faqs/faq3.htm.

International Federation of Red Cross and Red Crescent Societies. *World Disasters Report 1999*. Geneva: IFRC, 1999.

Iraq Study Group, James H. Baker III, and Lee H. Hamilton. *The Iraq Study Group Report: The Way Forward—A New Approach*. New York: Vintage Books, 2006.

Irons, Peter. *Jim Crow's Children: The Broken Promise of the Brown Decision*. New York: Viking, 2002.

Jackson, Stephen. "Un/natural Disasters, Here and There." *Social Science Research Council*, 2005. http://understandingkatrina.ssrc.org/Jackson/pf/.

Jaffe, Greg. "Katrina Will Shape Military Debate: Army Has Resisted Proposal for Guard Disaster Units: Short of People, Equipment." *Wall Street Journal*, September 12, 2005.

Jewell, K. Sue. *From Mammy to Miss America and Beyond: Cultural Images and the Shaping of US Social Policy.* New York: Routledge, 1993.

Jacobs, Mark D., and Nancy Weiss Hanrahan, eds. *The Blackwell Companion to the Sociology of Culture.* Malden, MA: Blackwell Publishing, 2005.

Jacobsen, David J. *The Affairs of Dame Rumor.* New York: Rinehart, 1948.

Johnson, Allen, Jr. "A Fruitful Relationship." *Gambit* 19 (December 1, 1998): 21–25.

Jones, Franklin, Carroll Robinson, Walter McCoy, Marva Johnson, Sean Herlihy, and Karen Callaghan. *The 2006 Houston Survey of African Americans.* Houston: Texas Southern University.

Jones-Deweever, Avis A., and Heidi Hartmann. "Abandoned before the Storms: The Glaring Disaster of Gender, Race, and Class Disparities in the Gulf." In *There Is No Such Thing As a Natural Disaster: Race, Class, and Hurricane Katrina,* edited by C. Hartman and G.D. Squires, 85–102. New York: Routledge, 2006.

Kaldor, Mary. "Beyond Militarism, Arms Races and Arms Control." *Social Science Research Council,* 2002. http://www.ssrc.org/sept11/essays/kaldor.htm.

Kao, Grace, and Jennifer Thompson. "Race and Ethnic Stratification in Educational Achievement and Attainment." *Annual Review of Sociology* 29 (2003): 417–42.

Kates, Robert W., Craig Colten, Shirley Laksa, and Stephen Leatherman. "Reconstruction of New Orleans following Hurricane Katrina: A Research Perspective." *Proceedings of the National Academy of Sciences* 103 (2006): 14653–14660.

Keil, Thomas J., and Gennaro F. Vito. "Race and the Death Penalty in Kentucky Murder Trials: 1976–1991." *American Journal of Criminal Justice* 20 (1995): 17–36.

Kelley, Harold. "The Processes of Causal Attribution." *American Psychologist* 28, no. 2 (1973): 107–28.

Kelman, Ari. *A River and Its City: The Nature of Landscape in New Orleans.* Berkeley: University of California Press, 2003.

Kerr, Richard A. "Is Katrina a Harbinger of Even More Powerful Hurricanes?" *Science* 39 (September 16, 2005): 1807. http://www.ce.cmu.edu/~gdrg/readings/2005/10/19/Kerr_Katrina_Harbinger.pdf.

King, Ronette. "Shifting Landscape: African-Americans Have a History of Entrepreneurship in New Orleans Dating Back to Before the Civil War." *The Times-Picayne* March 26, 2001. http://www.nola.com/unequalopportunity/index.ssf?/t-p/fronpage/79550842.html.

Kinney, Aaron. "'Looting' or 'Finding'?" Salon.com, September 1, 2005. http://dir.salon.com/story/news/feature/2005/09/01/photo_controversy/index.html.

Klein, Naomi. "The Rise of Disaster Capitalism." *The Nation,* April 14, 2005. http://www.thenation.com/doc/20050502/klein.

———. "Let the People Rebuild New Orleans." *The Nation.* September 8, 2005. http://www.thenation.com/doc/20050926/klein.

Klinenberg, Eric. *Heat Wave: A Social Autopsy of Disaster in Chicago.* Chicago: University of Chicago Press, 2002.

Kluegel, James R., and Eliot R. Smith. *Beliefs about Inequality: Americans' Views of What Is and What Ought to Be.* New York: Aldine de Gruyter, 1986.

Kluger, Richard. *Simple Justice: The History of Brown v. Board of Education and Black America's Struggle for Equality.* New York: Vintage, 2004.

Knopf, Terry Ann. *Rumors, Race and Riots.* New Brunswick, NJ: Transaction Publishers, 2006.

Kofsky, Frank. *Harry Truman and the War Scare of 1948: A Successful Campaign to Deceive the Nation.* New York: St. Martin's Press, 1993.

Kozol, Jonathan. *The Shame of the Nation: The Restoration of Apartheid Schooling in America.* New York: Crown Publishers, 2005.

Kristof, Nicholas D. "The Storm Next Time" *The New York Times*, September 11, 2005.

Krugman, Paul. "Not the New Deal." *The New York Times*, September 16, 2005.

Kwoba, Brian. "Immigrant Rights: Birth of a New Left?" *Z-Net*, May 14, 2006. http://www.zmag.org/content/showarticle.cfm?ItemID=10261.

Lal, Vinay. "New Orleans: The Big Easy and the Big Shame." *Economic and Political Weekly* (September 17, 2005): 4099–100.

Lavelle, Kristen, and Joe Feagin. "Hurricane Katrina: The Race and Class Debate." *Monthly Review* 58, no. 3 (July–August 2006): 52–66.

Landa, Victor. "Conned and Mistreated in Katrina's Wake." *San Antonio Express-News,* November 20, 2005.

——. "Labor, Not Border, Decides U.S. Churn." *San Antonio Express-News,* December 12, 2005.

Laurel, Lety. "Faces of Katrina." *San Antonio Express-News,* September 8, 2005.

Lawrence, Keith. "Reconsidering Community Building: Philanthropy through a Structural Racism Lens." *Souls* 4, no. 1 (2002): 45–53.

Layne, Christopher, and Robert S. Metzger. "Reforming Post–Cold War U.S. Arms Sales Policy: The Crucial Link between Exports and the Defense Industrial Base." *The Journal of Strategic Studies* 18, no. 4 (1995): 1–32.

Lee, Barrett A. "Urban Sociology." In *The Future of Sociology,* edited by Edgar F. Borgatta and Karen S. Cook, 200–23. Beverly Hills, CA: Sage Publishing, 1988.

Lee, Orville. "Race after the Cultural Turn." In *The Blackwell Companion to the Sociology of Culture,* edited by Mark D. Jacobs and Nancy Weiss Hanrahan, 234–50. Malden, MA: Blackwell Publishing, 2005.

Lee, Trymaine. "Evacuee Packed Houston Sees Jump in Crime." *Times-Picayune,* January 2, 2006.

Lenski, Gerhard. *Power and Privilege.* New York: McGraw-Hill, 1966.

Levin, Alan. "Corps: Levees' Design Caused Deadly Failure." *USA Today,* June 1, 2006. http://www.usatoday.com/news/nation/2006-06-01-levees_x.htm.

Lewis, David Levering. *W.E.B. Dubois: Biography of a Race.* New York: Henry Holt, 1993.

Lewis, Pierce F. *New Orleans: The Making of an Urban Landscape.* Charlottesville: University of Virginia Press, 2003.

Lichterman, Paul. *Elusive Togetherness.* Princeton, NJ: Princeton University Press, 2005.

Lind, E. Allen, and Tom R. Tyler. *The Social Psychology of Procedural Justice.* New York: Plenum, 1988.

Lubeck, Paul M., and Thomas Ehrlich Reifer. "The Politics of Global Islam: U.S. Hegemony, Globalization, and Islamist Social Movements." In *Globalization,*

Hegemony and Power: Antisystemic Movements and the Global System, edited by Thomas Ehrlich Reifer, 162–80. Boulder, CO: Paradigm Publishers, 2004.

Logan, John R. "The Impact of Katrina: Race and Class in Storm-Damaged Neighborhoods." Brown University Spatial Structures in the Social Sciences. http://www.s4.brown.edu/Katrina/report.pdf.

Logan, John R., and Harvey L. Molotch. *Urban Fortunes.* Berkeley: University of California Press, 1987.

Lovato, Roberto. "The Latinization of the New New Orleans." *New America Media,* October 18, 2005. http://crm.ncmonline.com/news/view_article.html? article_id=fa92e2c88a63985418da75582292b5c7.

Maas, Alan. "A Mercenary Army: Jeremy Scahill on Blackwater in New Orleans." *Counterpunch,* June 2, 2006. http://www.counterpunch.org/maass06022006. html.

MacCurdy, Raymond R. *A History and Bibliography of Spanish-Language Newspapers and Magazines in Louisiana, 1808–1949.* Albuquerque: University of New Mexico Press, 1951.

MacDonald, John M. "The Effect of Ethnicity on Juvenile Court Decision Making in Hawaii." *Youth and Society* 35 (2003): 243–63.

Maggi, Laura. "Danziger Officers Await DA's Decision: Jordan Could Seek Death Penalty for Four." *Times-Picayune,* January 20, 2007.

Mann, Michael. *Incoherent Empire.* New York: Verso, 2003.

Marable, Marable. *How Capitalism Underdeveloped Black America.* Boston: South End Press, 1983.

———. *Race, Reform, and Rebellion: The Second Reconstruction in Black America, 1945–1990.* Jackson: University Press of Mississippi, 1991.

Markusen, Ann, and Joel Yudken. *Dismantling the Cold War Economy.* New York: Basic Books, 1992.

Marquardt, Steve. "'Green Havoc': Panama Disease, Environmental Change, and Labor Process in the Central American Banana Industry." *The American Historical Review* 106, no.1 (2001): 49–80.

Marsalis, Wynton. "Marsalis on Katrina's 'Race/Class' Issue." *EUR Web* September 6, 2005. http://www.eurweb.com/printable.cfm?id=22179.

Marx, Karl, and Friedrich Engels. *The German Ideology. Including Theses on Feuerbach and Introduction to the Critique of Political Economy.* Amherst, NY: Prometheus Books, [1932] 1998.

Massey, Douglas S. "American Apartheid: Segregation and the Making of the Underclass." *The American Journal of Sociology* 96 (1990): 329–57.

———. "The Age of Extremes: Concentrated Affluence and Poverty in the 21st Century." *Demography* 33 (1996): 395–412.

Massey, Douglas S., and Nancy A. Denton. *American Apartheid: Segregation and the Making of the Underclass.* Cambridge, MA: Harvard University Press, 1993.

May, Peter J. *Recovering from Catastrophes: Federal Disaster Relief Policy and Politics.* Westport, CT: Greenwood Press, 1985.

McDonald, Katrina Bell. "Black Activist Mothering: A Historical Intersection of Race, Gender and Class." *Gender and Society* 11, no. 6 (1997): 773–95.

McGovern, George, and William R. Polk. *Out of Iraq: A Practical Plan for Withdrawal Now.* New York: Simon & Schuster, 2006.

McKinnon, Jesse. "The Black Population." U.S. Census Bureau, August 2001. http://ict.cas.psu.edu/resources/Census/PDF/C2K_Race_Black.pdf.

McKinnon, John D., and Anne Marie Squeo. "Shaky Economic Times Limit Bang of New Defense Spending." *Wall Street Journal*, April 15, 2003.

McQuaid, John, and Mark Schleifstein. *Path of Destruction: The Devastation of New Orleans and the Coming Age of Superstorms.* New York: Little Brown & Co., 2006.

Medina, Blanca Rosa Morales. "Diversity in Mainstream Suburbia: An Investigation into the Social and Economic Conditions of the Hispanic Population of Jefferson Parish, Louisiana." Master's Thesis: University of New Orleans, 1998.

Menjivar, Cecilia and Cynthia Bejarano. "Latino Immigrants' Perception of Crime and Police Authorities in the United States: A Case Study from the Phoenix Metropolitan Area." *Ethnic and Racial Studies* 27 (2004): 120–48.

Mercadel, Kevin. "Why Are New Orleans' 20 Historic Districts on the National Trust Endangered List?" National Trust for Historic Preservation. http://www.nationaltrust.org/hurricane/mercadel.html.

Merton, Robert K. "Social Structure and Anomie." In *Criminological Theory: Past to Present Essential Readings,* eds. Francis T. Cullen and Robert Agnew, 178–85. Los Angeles: Roxbury, (1938)2003.

Miller, Dale T., and Michael Ross. "Self-Serving Biases in the Attribution of Causality: Fact or Fiction?" *Psychological Bulletin* 82 (1975): 213–25.

Moberg, Mark. "Crown Colony as Banana Republic: The United Fruit Company in British Honduras, 1900–1920." *Journal of Latin American Studies* 28, no. 2 (1996): 357–81.

Mollenkopf, John H. *The Contested City.* Princeton, NJ: Princeton University Press, 1983.

Mooney, Chris. *Storm World: Hurricanes, Politics, and the Battle over Global Warming.* San Diego, CA: Harcourt, forthcoming.

MSNBC.com. "Katrina Jazz Concert Strikes Political Tone." September 19, 2005. http://www.msnbc.msn.com/id/9390988/.

Murray, Robert K. *Red Scare: A Study in National Hysteria, 1919–1920.* Minneapolis: University of Minnesota Press, 1955.

National Assessment Synthesis Team, U.S. Global Change Research Program. *Climate Change Impacts on the United States*, 2001. http://www.usgcrp.gov/usgcrp/Library/nationalassessment/foundation.htm.

National Park Service. "New Orleans Jazz Neighborhood History Map." http://www.nps.gov/jazz/Maps_neighborhoods.htm.

National Urban League Policy Institute. *Katrina: One Year Later: A Policy and Research Report on the National Urban League's Katrina Bill of Rights*, 2006. http://nul.org/PressReleases/2006/KatrinaLeg%20PolicyReport.pdf.

Navarrette, Ruben, Jr. "A City about to Change Colors." *The San Diego Union-Tribune,* October 18, 2005.

———. "The Language of Race." *San Diego Union-Tribune*, January 22, 2006.

The New York Times. "Life in the Bottom 80 Percent." September 1, 2005.

The New York Times. "The Man-Made Disaster." September 2, 2005.

Nichols, Bill. "Illegal Workers Found at La. Base." *USA TODAY,* October 24, 2005.

Nickell, Patti. "Agent for Change: Louisiana's HCC is Working to Make New Orleans the Next Big Gateway to Latin America." *Hispanic Trends* (July/August 2005): 64.

Nisbet, Matthew C., and Chris Mooney. "The Next Big Storm: Can Scientists and Journalists Work Together to Improve Coverage of the Hurricane–Global Warming Controversy." *Committee for Skeptical Inquiry*, August 3, 2006. http://www.csicop.org/scienceandmedia/hurricanes/.

Nossiter, Adam. "Outlines Emerge for a Shaken New Orleans." *The New York Times,* August 26, 2006.

——. "With Jobs to Do, Louisiana Parish Turns to Inmates." *The New York Times,* July 5, 2006.

——. "New Orleans of Future May Stay Half Its Old Size." *The New York Times*, January 21, 2007.

NVOAD. *Long Term Recovery Manual.* National Voluntary Organizations Active in Disaster, 2004. http://www.nvoad.org.

Ogletree, Charles J. *All Deliberate Speed.* New York: W.W. Norton & Company, 2004.

Oliver, Melvin L., and Thomas M. Shapiro. *Black Wealth/White Wealth: A New Perspective on Racial Inequality*. New York: Routledge, 1995.

Omi, Michael, and Howard Winant. *Racial Formation in the United States: From the 1960s to the 1990s*, 2nd ed. New York: Routledge, 1994.

Orfield, Gary, and Chungmei Lei. Brown *at 50: King's Dream or* Plessy's *Nightmare*. The Civil Rights Project, Harvard University, January 2004.http://www.civilrights project.harvard.edu/research/reseg04/brown50.pdf.

Osio, Patrick Jr. "Americans Can Fill Immigrants' Jobs." *The San Diego Union-Tribune,* September 26, 2005.

Overby, Marvin L., Robert D. Brown, and John M. Bruce. "Race, Political Empowerment, and Minority Perceptions of Judicial Fairness." *Social Science Quarterly* 86 (2005): 444-462.

Overpeck, Jonathan T., Matthew Sturm, Jennifer A. Francis, Donald K. Perovich, Mark C. Serreze, Ronald Benner, Eddy C. Carmack, F. Stuart Chapin III, S. Craig Gerlach, Lawrence C. Hamilton, Larry D. Hinzman, Marika Holland, Henry P. Huntington, Jeffrey R. Key, Andrea H. Lloyd, Glen M. MacDonald, Joe McFadden, David Noone, Terry D. Prowse, Peter Schlosser, and Charles Vörösmarty. "Arctic Systems on Trajectory to New, Seasonally Ice-Free State." *EOS, Transactions, American Geophysical Union* 86, no. 24 (August 2005): 309, 312–13. http://paos.colorado.edu/~dcn/reprints/Overpeck_etal_EOS2005.pdf.

Owens, Bill. *State of the State Address: January 12, 2006*. Colorado, 2006. http://www.colorado.gov/governor/stateofthestate06.html.

Oxfam America. *Cuba: Weathering the Storm: Lessons in Risk Reduction in Cuba*, 2004. http://www.oxfamamerica.org/newsandpublications/publications/research_reports/pdfs/cuba_hur_eng.pdf.

Pae, Peter. "Immigrants Rush to New Orleans as Contractors Fight for Workers." *Los Angeles Times,* October 10, 2005.

Page, Susan, and Maria Puente. "Poll Shows Racial Divide on Storm Response." *USA TODAY*, September 12, 2005.

Pape, Robert. *Dying to Win: The Strategic Logic of Suicide Terrorism.* New York: Random House, 2006.

Park, Robert E. "The Urban Community As a Spatial Pattern and a Moral Order." In *Robert E. Park, on Social Control and Collective Behavior: Selected Papers* edited by Ralph H. Turner, 55–68. Chicago: University of Chicago Press, 1967.

Park, Robert E., Ernest W. Burgess, and Roderick D. McKenzie. *The City.* Chicago: University of Chicago Press, 1925.

Parker, Keith D., Anne B. Onyekwuluje, and Komanduri S. Murty. "African-Americans' Attitudes toward the Local Police: A Multivariate Analysis." *Journal of Black Studies* 25 (1995): 396–409.

Pastor, Manuel, Robert D. Bullard, James K. Boyce, Alice Fothergill, Rachel Morello-French, and Beverly Wright. *In the Wake of the Storm: Environment, Disaster, and Race after Katrina* (New York: Russell Sage Foundation, 2006). http://www.russellsage.org/news/060515.528528.

Peacock, Walter Gillis, Better Hearn Morrow, and Hugh Gladwin. *Hurricane Andrew: Ethnicity, Gender, and the Sociology of Disasters.* New York: Routledge, 1997.

Peek, Charles W., Jon P. Alston, and George D. Lowe. "Comparative Evaluation of the Local Police." *The Public Opinion Quarterly* 42, no. 3 (1978): 370–79.

Peguero, Anthony A. "Latino Disaster Vulnerability: The Dissemination of Hurricane Mitigation Information among Florida's Homeowners." *Hispanic Journal of Behavioral Sciences* 28, no. 1 (February 2006): 5–22.

Penn, Everette B., and Jaya Davis. "Hurricane Katrina: Crime and Race Issues in a Pre-Post Houston." Unpublished manuscript, 2006.

Pew Research Center. "Two-in-Three Critical of Bush's Relief Efforts: Huge Racial Divide over Katrina and Its Consequences." September 8, 2005. http://people-press.org/reports/display.php3?ReportID=255.

———. "Katrina Has Only Modest Impact on Basic Public Values in Spite of Political Fallout." September 22, 2005. http://people-press.org/commentary/display.php3?AnalysisID=117.

Pickel, Mary Lou. "Immigrant Workers Rile New Orleans: Rules Shelved, Crews Labor for Meager Pay." *Atlanta Journal-Constitution*, October 19, 2005: 1A.

Pielke, Roger A., Jr., Christopher Landsea, Max Mayfield, Jim Laver, and Richard Pasch. "Hurricanes and Global Warming." *Bulletin of the American Meteorological Society* 86 (November 2005): 1571–75. http://ams.allenpress.com/archive/1520-0477/86/11/pdf/i1520-0477-86-11-1571.pdf.

———. "Hurricanes and Global Warming—Potential Linkages and Consequences," *Bulletin of the American Meteorological Society* 87 (May 2006): 628–31. http://ams.allenpress.com/archive/1520-0477/87/5/pdf/i1520-0477-87-5-628.pdf.

Pitkin, Hanna F. *Representation.* New York: Atherton Press, 1969.

Piven, Frances Fox. *The War at Home: The Domestic Consequences of Bush's Militarism.* New York: The New Press, 2004.

Plaisance, Stacy. "Katrina's Poorest Evacuees Fare Worst, Study Finds." *The Boston Globe,* August 15, 2006. http://www.boston.com/news/nation/articles/2006/08/15/katrinas_poorest_evacuees_fare_worst_study_finds/.

Pogrebin, Robin. "Lured by the Work, but Struggling to Be Paid." *The New York Times,* October 17, 2005.

Polanyi, Karl. *The Great Transformation*. Boston: Beacon Press, 1957.

Postel, Sandra. "Nature's Squeeze-Man's Response: Distinctions between Natural and Not-So-Natural Disasters." *Christian Science Monitor*, September 7, 2005. http://www.csmonitor.com/2005/0907/p09s01-coop.html.

Pratt, Joseph A., and Christopher Castaneda. *Builders: Herman and George R. Brown*. College Station: Texas A & M University Press, 1998.

Quinones, Sam. "Migrants Find a Gold Rush in New Orleans." *Los Angeles Times*, April 4, 2006.

Quirk, John. "Superintendent's Message—Hurricane Katrina." New Orleans Jazz National Historical Park, September 7, 2005. http://www.nps.gov/jazz/pphtml/newsdetail20340.html.

Rahmstorf, Stefan, Michael Mann, Rasmus Benestad, Gavin Schmidt, and William Connolley. "Hurricanes and Global Warming—Is There a Connection?" September 2, 2005. http://www.realclimate.org/index.php/archives/2005/09/hurricanes-and-global-warming/.

Reed, Adolph. "The Black Urban Regime: Structural Origins and Constraints." *Comparative Urban and Community Research* 1 (1988): 138–89.

Reifer, Thomas Ehrlich. "Review of Mike Davis, *Dead Cities: And Other Tales*." *City and Community* 2 (2003): 369–70.

———. "Changing U.S. Policy towards Iraq: A Strategy Proposal and Scenario for Congressional Hearings." Unpublished paper, 2007.

Reuters News Service. "Katrina's Aftermath: Uprooted Hispanic Immigrants Ask What to Do after Katrina. New Orleans Was Home to One of America's Largest Populations from Honduras, Mexico." *The Houston Chronicle*, September 12, 2005.

Revkin, Andrew C., and Christopher Drew. "Intricate Flood Protection Long a Focus of Dispute." *The New York Times*, September 1, 2005.

Reyes, Raul A. "Katrina's Next Expose: Immigration Woes." *USA TODAY*, October 14, 2005.

Rich, Frank. "Message: I Care about Black People." *The New York Times*, September 18, 2005.

Ringquist, Evan J. "Equity and the Distribution of Environmental Risk." *Social Science Quarterly* 78 (1997): 811–29.

Roberts, Genevieve. "Hurricane Katrina: The Suicide of a Policeman Who Could Not Endure His City's Fate." *Independent*, September 7, 2005.

Roberts, Penny Brown. "Hispanic Workers Likely to Affect N.O. Culture." May 6, 2006. http://www.2theadvocate.com/news/2758411.html?showAll=y.

Rocchio, Vincent F. *Reel Racism: Confronting Hollywood's Construction of Afro-American Culture*. Boulder, CO: Westview, 2000.

Rodriguez Owsley, Beatrice. *The Hispanic-American Entrepreneur: An Oral History of the American Dream*. New York: Twayne Publishers, 1992.

Roediger, David R. *Colored White: Transcending the Racial Past*. Berkeley: University of California Press, 2002.

Rome, Dennis M. "The Social Construction of the African American Criminal Stereotype." In *Images of Color, Images of Crime: Readings*, 3rd ed., edited by Coramae Richey Mann, Marjorie S. Zatz, and Nancy Rodriguez, 78–87. Los Angeles: Roxbury Publishing Company, 2006.

Root, Jay, and Aaron C. Davis. "Undocumented Immigrants Flock to Jobs on Gulf Coast." *Duluth News Tribune,* October 12, 2005.

Rosenblatt, Susannah, and James Rainey. "Katrina Rumors." *Los Angeles Times,* September 27, 2005.

Ross, Elmer Lamar. "Factors in Residence Patterns among Latin Americans in New Orleans: A Study in Urban Anthropological Methodology." Ph.D. diss, University of Georgia, 1973.

Ross, Lee. "The Intuitive Psychologist and His Shortcomings: Distortions in the Attribution Process." In *Advances in Experimental Social Psychology Volume 10,* edited by Leonard Berkowitz, 173–200. New York: Academic Press, 1977.

Rozemberg, Hernán. "The Changing Face of the Gulf Coast Work Force." *San Antonio Express-News,* March 19, 2006.

Russell, Gordon. "Nagin Orders First-Ever Mandatory Evacuation of New Orleans." *Times-Picayune,* August 28, 2005.

Russell, Katheryn. *The Color of Crime: Racial Hoaxes, White Fear, Black Protectionism, Police Harassment, and Other Microaggressions.* New York: New York University Press, 1998.

Sacks, Karen. *Caring by the Hour: Women, Work, and Organizing at Duke Medical Center.* Urbana, IL: University of Illinois Press, 1988.

Salmon, Jacqueline. "Counterparts Excoriate Red Cross Katrina Effort." *Washington Post,* April 5, 2006.

Sampson, Robert J., and Jeffrey D. Morenoff. "Public Health and Safety in Context: Lessons from Community-Level Theory on Social Capital." In *Promoting Health: Intervention Strategies from Social and Behavioral Research,* edited by Brian Smedley and Leonard Syme, 366–89. Washington, DC: National Academy Press, 2001.

Sanger, David E., and Edmund L. Andrews. "Bush Rules out Raising Taxes for Gulf Relief." *The New York Times,* September 17, 2005.

Sawislak, Karen. *Smoldering City: Chicagoans and the Great Fire, 1871–1874.* Chicago: University of Chicago Press, 1996.

Schuck, Peter. *Diversity in America: Avoiding Government.* Cambridge, MA: Belknap Press of Harvard University Press, 2003.

Selden, Sally Coleman. *The Promise of Representative Bureaucracy: Diversity and Responsiveness in a Government Agency.* Armonk, NY: M.E. Sharpe, 1997.

Select Bipartisan Committee to Investigate the Preparation for and Response to Hurricane Katrina. "A Failure of Initiative." US. House of Representatives, 2006. http://katrina.house.gov/.

Shane, Scott, and Eric Lipton. "Storm Overwhelmed Government's Preparations." *The New York Times,* September 2, 2005.

Shanker, Thom. "Weapons Sales Worldwide Rise to Highest Level Since 2000." *The New York Times,* August 30, 2005.

Sherif, Muzafer, O.J. Harvey, B. Jack White, William Hood, and Carolyn Sherif. *Intergroup Conflict and Cooperation: The Robbers Cave Experiment.* Norman, OK: Institute of Group Relations, 1961.

Sherman, Steven. "The American Left and the Battle for New Orleans." *Counterpunch,* September 9–11, 2005. http://www.counterpunch.org/sherman09092005.html.

Sims, Harold. *Descolonización en México: El Conflicto Entre Mexicanos y Españoles (1821–1831)*. Mexico City: Fondo de Cultura Económica, 1982.

Singer, Peter W. *Corporate Warriors: The Rise of the Privatized Military Industry.* Ithaca: Cornell University Press, 2003.

———. "Warriors for Hire in Iraq." The Brookings Institution, 2004. http://www.brookings.edu/views/articles/fellows/singer20040415.htm.

———. "Outsourcing the War." The Brookings Institution, 2004. http://www.brookings.edu/views/articles/fellows/singer20040416.htm.

Smedley, Audrey, and Brian Smedley. "Race As Biology Is Fiction, Racism As a Social Problem Is Real: Anthropological and Historical Perspectives on the Social Construction of Race." *American Psychologist* 60 (2005): 16–26.

Smiley, Tavis, ed. *The Covenant with Black America*. Chicago: Third World Press, 2006.

Smith, Adam. *An Inquiry into the Nature and Causes of the Wealth of Nations.* New York: Modern Library, 1937.

Smith, David. "The New Urban Sociology Meets the Old: Rereading Some Classical Human Ecology." *Urban Affairs Review* 30 (1995): 432–57.

Smith, Roy C. *Comeback: The Restoration of American Banking Power in the New World Economy*. Cambridge, MA: Harvard Business School Press, 1993.

Spain, Daphne. "Race Relations and Residential Segregation in New Orleans: Two Centuries of Paradox." *Annals of the American Academy of Political and Social Science* 441 (1979): 82–96.

Spell, J. R. "A New Orleans Edition of La Risa," *Hispania* 23, no. 1 (1940): 81–84.

Spera, Keith. "Planners Promise Bigger Jazzfest." WWOZ Radio, November 12, 2005. www.wwoz.org.

Stampp, Kenneth M., ed. *The Causes of the Civil War.* Englewood Cliffs, NJ: Spectrum, 1961.

Starr, B. James, Lloyd R. Sloan, and Tarl R. Kudrick. "Just Deserts: African American Judgments of Justice in Stories of Varying Cultural Relevance." *Cross-Cultural Research* 31, no. 2 (1997): 137–54.

Steinberg, Ted. *Acts of God: The Unnatural History of Natural Disaster in America.* New York: Oxford University Press, 2003.

Stephan-Norris, Judith, and Maurice Zeitlin. *Left Out: Reds and America's Industrial Unions*. New York: Cambridge University Press, 2003.

Stevenson, Richard W., and Anne E. Kornblut. "Director of FEMA Stripped of Role As Relief Leader: Decision Comes after Lawmakers Put Pressure on President." *The New York Times*, September 10, 2005.

Stoops, Nicole. "Educational Attainment in the United States, 2003." U.S. Census Bureau, June 2004. http://www.census.gov/prod/2004pubs/p20-550.pdf.

Streitfeld, David. "Speculators Rushing in as the Water Recedes: Would-be Home Buyers Are Betting New Orleans Will Be a Boomtown. And Many of the City's Poorest Residents Could End Up Being Forced Out." *Los Angeles Times*, September 15, 2005.

Suverza, Alejandro. "Buscan a Paisanos en Louisiana." *El Universal,* September 8, 2005.

Sylves, Richard, and William R. Cumming. "FEMA's Path to Homeland Security: 1979–2003." *Journal of Homeland Security and Emergency Management* 1, no. 2 (2004). http://www.bepress.com/jhsem/vol1/iss2/11.

Symens Smith, Amy, Bashir Ahmed, and Larry Sink. *An Analysis of State and County Population Changes by Characteristics: 1990–1999*. U.S. Census Bureau, Working Paper Series No. 45, 2000.

Tajfel, Henri, and John Turner. "The Social Identity Theory and Intergroup Behavior." In *Psychology of Intergroup Relations*, edited by Stephen Worchel, 7–24. Chicago: New-Hail, 1986.

Taylor, Marylee C. "How White Attitudes Vary with the Racial Composition of Local Populations: Numbers Count." *American Sociological Review* 63 (1998): 512–35.

Thevenot, Brian, and Steve Ritea. "90 Schools in Metro Area Failing." *Times-Picayune*, August 4, 2005. http://www.nola.com/education/t-p/index.ssf?/base/news-2/112314078132590.xml.

Thomas, Evan. "How Bush Blew It." *Newsweek*, September 19, 2005.

Thomas, Ewart A.C., and Mary Parpal. "Liability as a Function of Plaintiff and Defendant Fault." *Journal of Personality and Social Psychology* 53 (1987): 843–57.

Tibbetts, John. "Louisiana's Wetlands: A Lesson in Nature Appreciation." *Environmental Health Perspective* 114, no. 1 (2006). http://www.pubmedcentral.nih.gov/articlerender.fcgi?artid=1332684.

Tidwell, Mike. *The Ravaging Tide: Strange Weather, Future Katrinas, and the Coming Death of America's Coastal Cities*. New York: Free Press, 2006.

Tierney, Kathleen J. "Recent Developments in U.S. Homeland Security Policies and Their Implications for the Management of Extreme Events." Paper presented at the First International Conference on Urban Disaster Reduction, Kobe, Japan, January 18–20, 2005.

———. "Foreshadowing Katrina: Recent Sociological Contributions to Vulnerability Science." *Contemporary Sociology* 35, no. 3 (May 2006): 207–12.

Tierney, Kathleen J., Michael K. Lindell, and Ronald W. Perry. *Facing the Unexpected: Disaster Preparedness and Response in the United States*. Washington, DC: Joseph Henry Press, 2001.

Tinkler, Chris, and Daryl Passmore, "Rape Threat to Our Women." *Sun Herald News*, September 4, 2005.

Tizon, Thomas Alex. "Images of Evacuees Spark a Racial Debate." *Los Angeles Times*, September 3, 2005.

Todd, Emmanuel. *After the Empire: The Breakdown of the American Order.* New York: Columbia University Press, 2003.

———. "The Specter of a Soviet-style Crisis." *Le Figaro*, September 12, 2005. http://www.truthout.org/docs_2005/091205H.shtml.

Townsend, Frances Fragos. "The Federal Response to Hurricane Katrina: Lessons Learned." *The White House,* February 2006. http://www.whitehouse.gov/reports/katrina-lessons-learned.pdf.

Townsend, Peter. *Jazz in American Culture*. Jackson: University Press of Mississippi, 2000.

Tregle, Joseph G., Jr. "Early New Orleans Society: A Reappraisal." *The Journal of Southern History* 18, no. 1 (1952): 20–36.

Trent, William T. "Why the Gap between Black and White Performance in School? A Report on the Effects of Race on Student Achievement in the St. Louis Public Schools." *The Journal of Negro Education* 66 (1997): 320–29.

Trope, Yaacov. "Identification and Inferential Processes in Dispositional Attribution." *Psychological Review* 93 (1986): 239–57.

Turley, Alan C. "Max Weber and the Sociology of Music." *Sociological Forum* 16, no. 4 (2001): 633–53.

Tyler, Tom R. "Public Trust and Confidence in Legal Authorities: What Do Majority and Minority Group Members Want from the Law and Legal Institutions." *Behavioral Sciences and the Law* 19, no. 2 (2001): 215–35.

Uchitelle, Louis. "Sharp Rise in Federal Spending May Have Helped Ease Recession." *The New York Times*, March 23, 2002.

———. "Faster 2nd-Quarter Growth Fuels Optimism." *The New York Times*, August 1, 2003.

———. "U.S. Economy Grows 4.2%; War Spending Provides Push." *The New York Times*, April 30, 2004.

United for Peace and Justice. "After Katrina, Fund Full Recovery on Gulf Coast, Not War on Iraq." September 2, 2005. http://www.unitedforpeace.org/article.php?id=3094.

United States Space Command. *Vision for 2020*, February 1997.http://www.gsinstitute.org/gsi/docs/vision_2020.pdf.

U.S. Census Bureau. "State and County Quick Facts: Orleans Parish, Louisiana." Washington, DC: U.S. Census Bureau, 2000.

———. "Racial and Ethnic Residential Segregation in the United States: 1980–2000." Washington, DC: U.S. Census Bureau, 2002. http://www.census.gov/prod/2002 pubs/censr-3.pdf.

———. "State and County Quick Facts: Orleans Parish, Louisiana." Washington, DC: U.S. Census Bureau, 2003.

———. "Poverty: 2003 Highlights." Washington, DC: U.S. Census Bureau, 2004.

———. "Denver County." Washington, DC: U.S. Census Bureau, 2006.

———. "Quick Facts. Arapahoe County." Washington, DC: U.S. Census Bureau, 2006.

U.S. Department of Homeland Security. "Nationwide Plan Review Phase 2 Report." June 16, 2006. http://www.dhs.gov/interweb/assetlibrary/Prep_NationwidePlanReview.pdf.

U. S. General Accounting Office. *Siting of Hazardous Waste Landfills and Their Correlation with Racial and Economic Status of Surrounding Communities*. Washington, DC: Government Printing Office, 1983.

———. *Disaster Management: Improving the Nation's Response to Catastrophic Disasters*. Washington, DC: Government Printing Office, July 1993. http://archive.gao.gov/t2pbat5/149631.pdf.

U.S. Government Accountability Office. *An Integrated Plan Is Needed to Address Army Reserve Personnel and Equipment Shortages*. Washington, DC: Government Printing Office, July 2005. Available at http://www.gao.gov/new.items/d05660.pdf.

Vallone, Robert, Lee Ross, and Mark Lepper. "The Hostile Media Phenomenon: Biased Perception and Perceptions of Media Bias in Coverage of the Beirut Massacre." *Journal of Personality and Social Psychology* 49 (1985): 577–85.

Van Heerden, Ivor, and Mike Bryan. *The Storm: What Went Wrong and Why During Hurricane Katrina—The Inside Story from One Louisiana Scientist.* New York: Viking, 2006.

Varney, James. "40 Jailed in Raid on Immigrants: But Legal Groups Say City Needs Workers." *Times-Picayune,* March 18, 2006.

Wacquant, Loic J.D., and William Julius Wilson. "The Cost of Racial and Class Exclusion in the Inner City." *The Annals of the American Academy of Political and Social Science* 501 (1989): 8–25.

Wade, Robert, and Frank Veneroso. "The Asian Crisis: The High Debt Model Versus the Wall Street-Treasury-IMF Complex." *New Left Review,* no. 228 (March/April 1998): 3–24.

———. "The Gathering World Slump and the Battle over Capital Controls." *New Left Review*, no. 231 (September/October 1998): 13–42.

Waller, Maureen R., and Sara S. McLanahan. "'His' and 'Her' Marriage Expectations: Determinants and Consequences." *Journal of Marriage and Family* 67 (2005): 53–67.

Walsh, Bill. "FEMA's Dome Airlift Plan Never Got off the Ground, Concept Not Viable, National Guard Says." *Times-Picayune*, December 9, 2005.

Walters, Jonathan. "Civil Service Tsunami." *Governing* 16, no. 8 (2003): 34–40.

Ward, Andrew. "In Harm's Way: How America's Rush to the Coast is Driving up the Cost of Hurricanes." *Financial Times*, June 5, 2006.

Wayne, Leslie. "An Officer and a Gentleman: In Corporate Jobs, Old Generals Find a Hero's Welcome." *The New York Times,* June 19, 2005.

Weiner, Tim. "Pentagon Envisioning a Costly Internet for War." *The New York Times*, November 13, 2004.

———. "Air Force Seeks Approval for Space Weapons Programs." *The New York Times*, May 18, 2005.

Weitzer, Ronald, and Steven A. Tuch. "Race, Class, and Perceptions of Discrimination by the Police." *Crime and Delinquency* 45 (1999): 494–507.

———. "Race and Perceptions of Misconduct." *Social Problems* 51 (2004): 305–25.

West Bank Bureau. "68 Immigrants Rounded Up, Arrested." *Times-Picayune,* April 7, 2006.

Wilder, David. "Cognitive Factors Affecting the Success of Intergroup Contact." In *Psychology of Intergroup Relations,* edited by Stephen Worchel, 49–66. Chicago: New-Hall, 1986.

Wiley, Deane C. "Black and White Differences in the Perception of Justice." *Behavioral Sciences and the Law* 19 (2001): 649–55.

Williams, Juan. *Enough: The Phony Leaders, Dead-End Movements and Cultural of Failure That Are Undermining Black America and What We Can Do about It*. New York: Crown Publishers, 2006.

Williams, Leslie. "Thousands Hold Rally for Immigrant Rights: Hispanic Demonstrators March through CBD." *Times-Picayune,* May 2, 2006.

Williams, Lloyd. "The No Latino Left Behind Act: Last One Out of Mexico Turn-off the Lights." *New York Beacon*, April 13–19, 2006, 13(15): 8.

Wilson, George and Roger Dunham. "Race, Class, and Attitudes toward Crime Control." *Criminal Justice and Behavior* 28 (2001): 259–69.

Wilson, William J. *The Truly Disadvantaged: The Inner City, the Underclass, and Public Policy.* Chicago: University of Chicago Press, 1987.

Wisner, Ben, Piers Blaikie, Terry Cannon, and Ian Davis. *At Risk: Natural Hazards, People's Vulnerability and Disasters,* 2nd ed. London: Routledge, 2003.

Woldoff, Rachael A. "Living Where the Neighbors Are Invested: Wealth and Racial/Ethnic Differences in Individuals' Neighborhood Homeownership Rate." In *Wealth Accumulation and Communities of Color in the United States Current Issues*, edited by Jessica Gordon Nembhard and Ngina Chiteji, 267–93. Ann Arbor: University of Michigan Press, 2006.

Wortley, Scot. "Justice for All? Race and Perceptions of Bias in the Ontario Criminal Justice System: A Toronto Survey." *Canadian Journal of Criminology* 38 (1996): 439–43.

Wright, Richard. *12 Million Black Voices: A Folk History of the Negro in the United States.* New York: Viking Press, 1941.

Wrightsman, Lawrence S., Edie Greene, Michael T. Nietzel, and William H. Fortune. *Psychology and the Legal System* (Belmont, CA: Wadsworth, 2000).

Wuthnow, Robert. *Saving America? Faith-Based Services and the Future of Civil Society.* Princeton, NJ: Princeton University Press, 2004.

Yinger, John. *Closed Doors, Opportunities Lost: The Continuing Costs of Housing Discrimination.* New York: Russell Sage, 1995.

———. "Housing Discrimination Is Still Worth Worrying About." *Housing Policy Debate* 9 (1998): 893–927.

Young, Robert L. "Race, Conceptions of Crime and Justice, and Support for the Death Penalty." *Social Psychology Quarterly* 54 (1991): 67–75.

Young, Vernetta. "Demythologizing the 'Criminalblackman': The Carnival Mirror." In *The Many Colors of Crime: Inequalities of Race, Ethnicity, and Crime in America*, edited by Ruth D. Peterson, Lauren J. Krivo, and John Hagan, 54–66. New York: New York University Press, 2006.

Index

Contributors

Terri Adams-Fuller is an assistant professor of sociology at Howard University. She received her B.A. (1990) in political science and her M.A. (1996) in sociology at the University of Maryland, College Park, and her Ph.D. (2002) in sociology at Howard. Dr. Adams-Fuller's research interests are in criminology and gender relations. Her research has been published in the *Journal of Black Studies*.

Meera Adya is a visiting assistant professor at Syracuse University in the Department of Psychology. She received her B.A. (1998) in psychology at Queen's University, and her M.A. (2002) and Ph.D. (2004) in social psychology and her J.D. (2002) at the University of Nebraska, Lincoln. Her research interests are in psychology and law, individual and group decision-making, memory processes, and alternative dispute resolution.

Duke W. Austin is a doctoral student in sociology at the University of Colorado at Boulder. He received his B.A. (1998) at the University of Texas, Austin. Mr. Austin's research interests are in the stratification of race, class, and gender.

Angela P. Cole is an assistant professor at Howard University in the Department of Psychology. She earned her B.S. (1994) in psychology at Howard and her Ph.D. (1999) in cognitive psychology at Stanford University. She was a post-doctoral fellow from 1999–2001 at the University of Michigan, Ann Arbor. Dr. Cole's area of research is in social psychology, focusing on justice, decision-making, and public policy.

O. Jackson Cole is an associate professor in the Department of Psychology at Howard University and is currently serving as the executive assistant to the president at Howard. He earned his B.S. (1964) and M.S. (1966) in psychology at Howard, and his Ph.D. (1972) in personality psychology at the University of Michigan. Dr. Cole has been the principal investigator or co-principal investigator on grants in excess of four million dollars.

Allison M. Cotton is an assistant professor of criminology and criminal justice at the Metropolitan State College of Denver in Colorado. Dr. Cotton received a bachelor's degree in sociology from the University of Colorado at Boulder in 1991, a master's degree in sociology from Howard University in Washington, D.C., in 1995, and a Ph.D. in sociology from the University of Colorado at Boulder in 2002. Dr. Cotton has authored several published papers including two articles on criminal justice issues for the forthcoming series *Controversies in Criminal Justice* edited by Gregg Barak for Greenwood Press in 2008 and an essay in the *Race and Justice Scholar* called "Play the Race Card for Pete's Sake!"

Brian K. Gerber is an assistant professor in the Division of Public Administration at West Virginia University. He received his B.A. (1990) in history at the University of Wisconsin, Oshkosh, his M.A. (1993) in political science at the University of New Mexico, and his Ph.D. (2000) in political science at the State University of New York at Stony Brook. His research interests include homeland security policy implementation and bureaucratic organization and discretion. His research has appeared in journals such as the *Journal of Public Administration Research and Theory*, *Political Research Quarterly*, *Policy Studies Journal*, *State Politics and Policy Quarterly,* and *Public Finance and Management*.

Angela Glymph is a doctoral student in the Department of Psychology at Howard University. She earned her B.A. (2001) in psychology at the University of Maryland, Baltimore County, and her M.S. (2005) in psychology at Howard University. Her primary research areas include group dynamics, social justice, and decision making.

Arie Kruglanski is a professor of psychology at the University of Maryland, College Park. He received his B.A. (1966) in psychology at the University of Toronto, and his M.A. (1967) and Ph.D. (1968) in social psychology from the University of California, Los Angeles. Dr. Kruglanski has numerous publications, including articles appearing in the *Journal of Personality and Social Psychology*, *Psychological Inquiry*, *Psychological Bulletin*, and *Psychological Review*.

Michelle K. Miles is a doctoral student in media studies at the University of Colorado at Boulder. She earned her B.A. (1993) from San Diego State University and her M.A. (1995) from Northwestern University. Her current research focuses on the representations, receptions, and interpretations of interracial (specifically Black-White) interaction in the U.S. mass media.

Monica Miller is an assistant professor at the University of Nevada, Reno, in the Department of Criminal Justice and the Interdisciplinary Ph.D. Program in Social Psychology. She earned her B.A. (1998) in psychology, M.A. (2002) and Ph.D. (2004) in social psychology, and J.D. (2002) at the University of Nebraska, Lincoln. Dr. Miller's research interests are in social psychology, law, and policy, specifically in the areas of legal decision-making, family law, and legal regulation of sexual behavior. She has numerous publications in social science journals, law reviews, and encyclopedias. Her work has appeared in the *Thurgood Marshall Law Review*, *Journal of Law and Social Changes*, and *Behavioral Sciences and the Law*. She currently has a book manuscript, *Religion in Criminal Justice*, under contract at LFB Publishing.

Joshua B. Padilla is a doctoral student in the Interdisciplinary Ph.D. Program in Social Psychology at the University of Nevada, Reno. He earned an A.A. (1998) in psychology and an A.A. (1999) in sociology at Bakersfield College, and his B.A. (2002) and M.A. (2004) in psychology at California State University, Bakersfield. His primary research areas include social identity of disadvantaged groups and social psychology and the law among disadvantaged groups.

Susan C. Pearce is a visiting assistant professor of sociology at West Virginia University. She earned her B.A. (1977) in sociology at Mississippi College, her M.Div. (1980) at the Southeastern Baptist Theological Seminary, and her M.A. (1992) and Ph.D. (1997) in sociology at the New School for Social Research. Her research has been published in *General Anthropology* and *Immigration Policy in Focus*. She is the co-editor (with E. Clifford) of *Reformulations: Markets, Policy, and Identities in Central and Eastern Europe* (Warsaw, Poland: IFIS Publishers, 2000).

Everette B. Penn is an assistant professor of criminology at the University of Houston–Clear Lake. He holds a Ph.D. in criminology from Indiana University

versity of California, Riverside, where he
y department. Dr. Reifer is the co-editor
g *Globalization: Challenges and Oppor-*
Brill Academic Press), and the editor of
wer: Antisystemic Movements and the
: Paradigm Publishers). He is currently
, *Profits and Power*.

t in the Interdisciplinary Ph.D. Program
y of Nevada, Reno. She earned her B.A.
University and her M.A. (2005) in Inter-
e University of Nevada, Reno. Her re-
logy interface, including juvenile justice
ducing recidivism in violent offenders.

hair in the Department of Political Sci-
e received her B.A. (1980) in political
ornia, San Diego, and her M.A. (1983)
ence and Social Policy Program at the
Her research focuses on law and social
he book *Immigration* (Burlington, VT:
r of *Public Pensions: Gender and Civic*
nell University Press, 2003) and *Creat-*
Politics and Administrative Law in Eng-
gan Press, 1997), as well as articles in
tical Studies, *Law and Social Inquiry*,

dent in the interdisciplinary Ph.D. pro-
ersity of Nevada, Reno. She earned her
. (2004) in interdisciplinary social psy-
Reno.

fessor in global studies at St. Lawrence
l his Ph.D. (1998) in economics from
search focuses on global political econ-
ast Asian transformations. His research
Journal of World Systems Research.

rofessor at Wayne State University in
es and the Department of Sociology.

She received her B.A. (1994) in sociology at Emmanuel College and her M.A. (1997) and Ph.D. (2003) in sociology at the University of Michigan, Ann Arbor. Dr. Trujillo-Pagán's research interests are in work, health, and stratification among Latinos.

Rachael A. Woldoff is an assistant professor of sociology at West Virginia University. She earned her B.A. (1995) in sociology from Pennsylvania State University and her M.A. (1998) and Ph.D. (2003) in sociology from the Ohio State University. Dr. Woldoff's research interests focus on social status and demography of minorities, and community context, disadvantage, urban crime, and race/ethnicity. Her work has been published in *Social Forces*, *Sociological Focus*, *The American Sociologist*, and *Crime Prevention and Community Safety*. Dr. Woldoff is the co-author (with K. Schwirian and T. Curry) of *High Stakes: Big Time Sports and Downtown Redevelopment* (Columbus: The Ohio State University Press 2004) and was a contributing author in a 2006 book entitled *Wealth Accumulation and Communities of Color in the United States*.